The Waite Court

ABC-CLIO SUPREME COURT HANDBOOKS

The Burger Court, Tinsley E. Yarbrough
The Fuller Court, James W. Ely, Jr.
The Hughes Court, Michael E. Parrish
The Stone Court, Peter G. Renstrom
The Taft Court, Peter G. Renstrom
The Taney Court, Timothy S. Huebner
The Waite Court, Donald Grier Stephenson, Jr.
The Warren Court, Melvin I. Urofsky

Forthcoming:
The Chase Court, Jonathan Lurie
The Jay/Ellsworth Court, Matthew P. Harrington
The Marshall Court, Robert L. Clinton
The Rehnquist Court, Thomas R. Hensley
The Vinson Court, Michal R. Belknap
The White Court, Rebecca S. Shoemaker

Peter G. Renstrom, Series Editor

ABC-CLIO SUPREME COURT HANDBOOKS

The Waite Court

Justices, Rulings, and Legacy

Donald Grier Stephenson, Jr.

ABC-CLIO
Santa Barbara, California • Denver, Colorado • Oxford, England

Library of Congress Cataloging-in-Publication Data

The Waite Court : justices, rulings, and legacy / by Donald Grier Stephenson, Jr.
p. cm. — (ABC-CLIO Supreme Court handbooks)
Includes bibliographical references and index.
ISBN 1-57607-829-9 (hardcover : alk. paper); ISBN 1-57607-830-2 (e-book)
1. United States. Supreme Court—History—19th century. 2. Waite, Morrison R. (Morrison Remick), 1816–1888. 3. Constitutional history—United States. I. Title. II. Series.

KF8742.S742 2003
347.73'26'09034—dc22

2003020338

07 06 05 04 03 10 9 8 7 6 5 4 3 2 1

ABC-CLIO, Inc.
130 Cremona Drive, P.O. Box 1911
Santa Barbara, California 93116-1911

This book is printed on acid-free paper ♾.
Manufactured in the United States of America

In memory of my father
Donald Grier Stephenson
(1911–2002)
and
in honor of my grandson
Jackson Kincaid Coyle,
winsome young man of two

Contents

Series Foreword

There is an extensive literature on the U.S. Supreme Court, but it contains discussion familiar largely to the academic community and the legal profession. The ABC-CLIO Supreme Court series is designed to have value to the academic and legal communities also, but each volume is intended as well for the general reader who does not possess an extensive background on the Court or American constitutional law. The series is intended to effectively represent each of fourteen periods in the history of the Supreme Court with each of these fourteen eras defined by the chief justice beginning with John Jay in 1789. Each Court confronted constitutional and statutory questions that were of major importance to and influenced by the historical period. The Court's decisions were also influenced by the values of each of the individual justices sitting at the time. The issues, the historical period, the justices, and the Supreme Court's decisions in the most significant cases will be examined in the volumes of this series.

ABC-CLIO's Supreme Court series provides scholarly examinations of the Court as it functioned in different historical periods and with different justices. Each volume contains information necessary to understand each particular Court and an interpretative analysis by the author of each Court's record and legacy. In addition to representing the major decisions of each Court, institutional linkages are examined as well—the political connections among the Court, Congress, and the president. These relationships are important for several reasons. Although the Court retains some institutional autonomy, all the Court's justices are selected by a process that involves the other two branches. Many of the significant decisions of the Court involve the review of actions of Congress or the president. In addition, the Court frequently depends on the other two branches to secure compliance with its rulings.

The authors of the volumes in the ABC-CLIO series were selected with great care. Each author has worked extensively with the Court, the period, and the personalities about which he or she has written. ABC-CLIO wanted each of the volumes to examine several common themes, and each author agreed to work within certain guidelines. Each author was free, however, to develop the content of each volume, and many of the volumes advance new or distinctive conclusions about the Court under examination.

Each volume will contain four substantive chapters. The first chapter will introduce the Court and the historical period in which it served. The second chapter will examine each of the justices who sat on the particular Court. The third chapter will represent the most significant decisions rendered by the particular Court. Among other things, the impact of the historical period and the value orientations of the individual justices will be developed. A fourth and final chapter will address the impact of each particular Court on American constitutional law—its doctrinal legacy.

Each volume will contain several features designed to make the volume more valuable to those whose previous exposure to the Supreme Court and American constitutional law is limited. Each volume will have a reference section that will contain brief entries on some of the people, statutes, events, and concepts introduced in the four substantive chapters. Entries in this section are arranged alphabetically. Each volume will also contain a glossary of selected legal terms used in the text. Following each of the four chapters, a list of sources used in the chapter and suggestions for further reading will appear. Each volume will also have a comprehensive annotated bibliography. A listing of Internet sources is presented at the end of the bibliography. Finally, there will be a comprehensive subject index and a list of cases (with citation numbers) discussed in each volume. ABC-CLIO is delighted with the quality of scholarship represented in each volume and is proud to offer this series to the reading public.

Permit me to conclude with a personal note. This project has been an extraordinarily rewarding undertaking for me as series editor. Misgivings about serving in this capacity were plentiful at the outset of the project. After tending to some administrative business pertaining to the series, securing authors for each volume was the first major task. I developed a list of possible authors after reviewing previous work and obtaining valuable counsel from several recognized experts in American constitutional history. In virtually every instance, the first person on my list agreed to participate in the project. The high quality of the series was assured and enhanced as each author signed on. I could not have been more pleased. My interactions with each author have been most pleasant, and the excellence of their work will be immediately apparent to the reader. I sincerely thank each author.

Finally, a word about ABC-CLIO and its staff. ABC-CLIO was enthusiastic about the project from the beginning and has done everything necessary to make this series successful. I am very appreciative of the level of support I have received from ABC-CLIO. Alicia Merritt, senior acquisitions editor, deserves special recognition. She has held my hand throughout the project. She has facilitated making this project a reality in every conceivable way. She has encouraged me from the beginning, provided invaluable counsel, and given me latitude to operate as I wished while keeping me on track at the same time. This project would not have gotten off the ground without Alicia, and I cannot thank her enough.

—Peter G. Renstrom

Preface

The Waite Court commenced with the swearing-in of Morrison Remick Waite as the seventh chief justice on March 4, 1874. His death on March 23, 1888, concluded a fourteen-year period that was as remarkable, exciting, and consequential as any in Supreme Court history. When Waite took office, the guns of the Civil War had been silent for slightly less than a decade; no adult had escaped the costs of that holocaust. The political, economic, and social transformations set in motion by the war's outcome had only begun to be grasped in all their complexities. The last cases for which Waite wrote for his Court were decided only four days before he died. They concerned the telephone patent of Alexander Graham Bell and symbolized the dawn of a new age: voice communication in real time between individuals miles apart had become a reality. The United States was truly a nation in flux.

Thanks to the development of a national economy made possible by the railroads, to population growth, and to ratification of the three Reconstruction amendments between 1865 and 1870, the Waite Court confronted the conundrum of democratic government—majority rule versus minority rights—on a scale and in more novel contexts than any previous court. In one category was an explosion of legislation, from state and local governments especially—Congress would not become energized on the issues until the 1890s—that tried to cope with problems arising from technology, urbanization, and economic interdependency. Would the revamped Constitution, as construed by judges, constrain lawmakers as they responded to the challenges of a new day?

In another category were the unique questions that resulted from the North's victory in the Civil War and the emancipation of slaves. The Thirteenth Amendment's abolition of slavery, although important, was not considered enough. Most members of Congress between 1865 and 1875 believed that additional safeguards were needed to protect basic rights of citizenship, including the right to vote. These were enshrined in the Fourteenth and Fifteenth amendments and in statutes that sought to implement them. What was the extent of congressional power under these new amendments? What state laws did the new amendments now forbid? Both these questions spawned their own concerns. The short-lived expansion of executive power during the war had been quickly eclipsed by a postwar, Republican-controlled Congress determined to dominate, perhaps even to recast, the national government. Would the Court acquiesce in this new state of affairs or attempt to impose limits? Similarly, the Fourteenth Amendment appeared fundamentally to alter the federal balance by giving the national government, including the federal judiciary, unprecedented supervision of the states. Would the Court accept the new order that the amendments seemed to dictate? Answers to these and other questions in the Waite years have had far-reaching effects for the American people in the ensuing years.

As for the fourteen men who sat with Waite over the course of his chief justiceship, fully one-third of them have been accorded great or near-great status by scholars of the Supreme Court. Rarely has there been a period in Supreme Court history when such talent graced the bench at the same time. The tenures of these preeminent justices extended over nearly the entire fourteen years of the Waite Court. Their tenures plus those of the remaining ten justices were configured conveniently to create what amounted to three discrete Courts, each marked by relatively stable membership and a somewhat different character. Chapter 1 calls them the first (1874–1877), middle (1877–1881), and last (1881–1888) Waite Courts.

Many of Waite's colleagues had extensive pre-Court experience as judges and in nonjudicial government roles, including elective office and partisan politics. The Waite Court was thus hardly a conclave of political neophytes. Five of them, after all, helped to decide the disputed presidential election of 1876. For the first time the Court counted among its members some who had fought in the Civil War. Indeed, the last justice to join the Court before Waite's death had been an officer in the Confederate Army. Moreover, some Waite justices had colorful personalities, all were strong-willed individuals, and a few were ornery men. All had led interesting lives. Most were hardworking at a time when the Court's docket, measured by the number of decisions each term and the backlog of cases, was the busiest in history. As the presumed leader of his Court, Chief Justice Waite thus faced no small challenge.

The Waite Court significantly differentiated itself in Supreme Court history by reaffirming the power to govern. With one notable exception—its suspicion of federal civil rights laws—decisions of the Waite bench were generally characterized by judicial restraint. More so than the Chase Court that preceded it and the Fuller Court that followed, the Waite Court was inclined to defer to the policy choices of the elected branches of government.

The Supreme Court of Waite's day was organizationally and jurisdictionally truly a court in transition—moving from what might be called a "classical" to a "modern" institution. This shift from classical to modern was gradual, not sudden. It began only a few years before Waite's appointment and was practically complete by the end of the nineteenth century. This change thus contrasts in its slower pace, if not in its overall effects, with the more familiar and far more sudden transformation that the

Court underwent between 1937 and 1940. Then, the nation witnessed a judicial and constitutional revolution from what scholars usually call the "old Court" to the "new Court." It was then that Franklin Roosevelt's New Deal program to cope with the Great Depression met a Supreme Court that, for a short time, stymied many of the president's initiatives. The result was Roosevelt's bold attempt at court packing and the hasty change of mind by two justices that gave Roosevelt the five sure votes he needed so that his program could receive constitutional approval. This flip-flop was promptly followed by the Court's adoption of a new agenda for itself, one that elevated civil liberties into a preferred position in the hierarchy of constitutional values and demoted property interests that heretofore had been accorded heightened judicial protection.

The era of the classical Court was marked by (1) an exceedingly limited federal jurisdiction; (2) a structure that made the bench mainly a court of errors, not a court of legal policy; and (3) onerous circuit-riding duties as trial court judges. In contrast, the era of the modern Court that was in place by the dawn of the twentieth century has been marked by (1) a vastly expanded federal jurisdiction; (2) a marked increase in cases involving individual rights; and (3) a structure that has allowed the Court to become a court of policy for the nation. The first and second attributes arose from the outcome of the Civil War and the ratification of the Reconstruction amendments. A major step toward the third was taken with passage of the Circuit Court of Appeals Act in 1891.

Viewed alongside these developments, the Waite Court was truly part classical and part modern. Organizationally, it had far more in common with the Marshall Court (1801–1835) than with the Fuller Court (1888–1910) that succeeded it. For example, the Waite Court remained the sole court of appeal for almost all cases originating in the federal courts. This was distressing because the number of such cases had surged. In other respects, however, the Waite Court had more in common with the Fuller Court and later twentieth and twenty-first century courts than with any predecessor courts. Given the nature of the Reconstruction amendments, cases arising under them invariably involved a claim that constitutional or congressionally created rights had been violated. Among other questions, these included juror and voting rights cases that addressed the fundamental right to be counted among "We the People." Thus in the transition over which Waite presided there are the earliest signs of the development of a rights culture in which Americans would routinely look to the judiciary both to vindicate and to sustain their liberties.

To develop these and other themes and to provide essential information, the book is divided into two parts. Part One consists of four chapters. It is here that the deeds, doctrines, personalities, and times of the Waite Court unfold. The first chapter explores the legacy the Waite Court inherited from the Civil War and the Chase Court (1864–1873); the nature of the Court's business and issues that commanded the

Court's attention during Waite's chief justiceship; the politics surrounding the appointment of each of the fifteen justices of the Waite Court; and the aggregate character of the bench, including, where relevant, individual voting characteristics, blocs, and other patterned behavior. Chapter 2 is largely a collection of biographical essays that provide a close look at each of the justices of the Waite Court, in the order of their appointment. A summary of a justice's pre-Court career is followed by review of the justice's contributions to the jurisprudence of the period. Chapter 3 begins with an analysis of the Reconstruction amendments and the all-important *Slaughterhouse Cases* that the Chase Court decided only eleven months before Waite arrived. It then highlights the significant decisions of the Court between 1874 and 1888 in several areas: civil rights, the Bill of Rights, due process of law, and the commerce clause. Chapter 4 on legacy and impact returns to the theme of the Waite Court as a transition institution, examines the role of the justices in resolving the disputed presidential election of 1876, and evaluates Waite as Court leader. Finally, from a perspective of nearly twelve decades, it summons Waite and his associate justices to the bar of history to assess their successes and shortcomings.

Part Two consists of a variety of reference materials to supplement Part One. The initial section contains an alphabetical list of key people, laws, and events important to any understanding of the Waite Court. This is followed by a chronology of events beginning with the inauguration of President James Buchanan in 1857 and concluding with passage of the Circuit Court of Appeals Act in 1891. Part Two concludes with a table of all cases (with citations) that are cited in the book, a glossary of legal and political terms, and an annotated bibliography.

Throughout the book, emphasis (as indicated by italicization) within quotations is in the original, unless otherwise noted. References to specific cases within the text of the chapters follow the customary style in legal literature. Most cases are known by the identities of the opposing parties or, sometimes in subsequent references, by the identity of one of the parties, as in *Munn v. Illinois*, the *Munn* case, or simply *Munn*. When several cases raising the same question were decided together, the custom has often been to refer to them instead by the subject of the cases. Thus, a citation to *United States v. Stanley* or *United States v. Ryan* is rarely seen; rather, these two cases and several more are collectively called the *Civil Rights Cases*. For a very few cases, tradition allows both types of nomenclature, as illustrated by *Munn v. Illinois*, which was also one of the *Granger Cases*. To conform with the style used in other volumes in the Supreme Court Handbooks series, italicization highlights the full or partial names of cases within the text of the chapters, regardless of whether a case has come to be best known by its litigants or by its subject matter.

Quotations from noncase material such as books and journal articles are followed by brief author-date-page citations. Complete bibliographical data for these sources appear in the end-of-chapter references in Part One and in the annotated bibliography in Part Two. To avoid cluttering the text with too many page citations, the many mainly brief quotations from cases are identified only by the name of the case from which they were taken and the year of decision. This system seems appropriate because opinions in most Waite-era cases were generally short and because the full citation for each case appears in the Table of Cases in Part Two.

This book would not have been possible without the invitation from Peter Renstrom, general editor of ABC-CLIO's Supreme Court Handbooks series. For me, his invitation was not only an honor but a grand opportunity to return significantly to a study of the Waite Court. Some years ago, I was privileged to spend some time in the Manuscript Division of the Library of Congress perusing the Waite Papers, among other collections. That research contributed to an article I wrote for the *William and Mary Law Review* on Supreme Court leadership, with Waite as its focus. Fourteen years later, Kenneth Mott invited me to give a presentation at a Gettysburg College symposium on "The Civil War Amendments." My topic on the early application of the Fifteenth Amendment placed me squarely back into the Waite years and resulted in a paper that was published the following year in the *University of Missouri–Kansas City Law Review*. Most recently, the Waite Court's general emphasis on judicial restraint provided a useful contrast to the more activist Fuller Court and its role in the 1896 presidential election that I analyzed in a chapter of my *Campaigns and the Court* in 1999. Aside from these endeavors, Waite Court decisions have always figured prominently in the courses on American constitutional law that I teach. Cases like *Munn v. Illinois* and the *Civil Rights Cases*, to name but two, remain securely in the canon of constitutional interpretation at undergraduate or graduate levels in the disciplines of political science, history, and law. The Waite era yielded special moments in Supreme Court history. Because of the Waite bench's impact on the Constitution, because of the justices themselves, and because of the institutional transformation then underway, it remains a fascinating time.

No one completes even a modest undertaking like this one without the help of others, seen and unseen. The end-of-chapter references reflect much that I owe to prior scholarship. These works of others reveal the rich resources available to anyone exploring this period of constitutional development in the United States. Over the years, my students in courses on American government and constitutional law at Franklin and Marshall College have made it possible for me to say, on most days at least, that I enjoy going to work. They have been parties with me in a classroom dialogue on the Supreme Court's role in the American political system. We have tried to understand the implications of judicial review—the authority of a court to judge the validity of legislative, executive, and lower court actions —in a government founded on the consent of the governed. Over sixty years ago, the preeminent constitutional scholar Edward S. Corwin observed that judicial review "represents an attempt by American Democracy to cover its bet." Our history attests that Corwin, as usual, was right.

For support and counsel throughout this project, I am indebted to series editor Peter Renstrom. His helpful comments have surely made this book far better than it otherwise would have been. I also owe thanks to others who read pieces of the manuscript along the way. James F. Van Orden, in particular, gave me the benefit of his sharp mind and eye for both style and content. The numerical data appearing in tables and graphs in Chapter One would not be nearly so orderly and revealing had it not been for the assistance of Corey J. Baughman, a man of many talents, who rescued me more than once from the avalanche of decisions that the Waite Court generated in term after term. Thanks are due as well to Alicia Merritt, acquisitions editor at ABC-CLIO, who excels in knowing exactly the right combination of prompting and patience to apply or extend, and to Melanie Stafford, who guided the book through production. Nonetheless, any remaining defects or errors or other sins of omission or commission are my responsibility alone.

Finally, I am thankful for family. My father, Donald Grier Stephenson, who was a judge in Newton County, Georgia, for a quarter-century, lived long enough both to know about this project and to talk with me on the telephone about its progress from time to time. He and my mother, Katherine Mason Williams Stephenson, who died nine months before the contract for this book was signed, were loving parents who sparked my interests in politics and law when I was a youngster. Mother was a member of one of the first classes of women admitted to the University of Georgia. On a shelf in my study is the textbook, complete with her handwritten notes on the Constitution in the margin, from the survey course she took in Athens, Georgia, on U.S. government.

About a year's worth of writing on this book remained to be done at the time of my father's death. A difficult period was made much more bearable for me because of the disproportionate burden that, due to proximity, my brother Mason Williams Stephenson and his wife Linda Partee Stephenson assumed. They took primary responsibility for closing up the Stephenson homeplace that our family called "Fairfield," and in handling day-to-day matters that arose with respect to the disposition of Daddy's estate. I remain in their debt for all that they have done.

Next to my parents, I owe most to Ellen who, after more than three decades of marriage and despite my love of writing, is as loving, caring, and understanding as ever. Without her I would not be father to our two wonderful children, Todd and Claire. They, along with Mason and Linda, are a reminder that life is made more fulfilling by all that one's family can provide. No one could fairly ask for more.

Donald Grier Stephenson, Jr.
Lancaster, Pennsylvania

PART ONE

Justices, Rulings, and Legacy

1

The Waite Court and the Period

The simplicity of the ceremony contrasted with its importance. On March 4, 1874, senior Associate Justice Nathan Clifford of Maine administered the constitutional, judicial, and "ironclad" oaths to Morrison Remick Waite of Ohio as the seventh chief justice of the United States. Waite had been plucked from relative obscurity. Finding a chief justice had not been easy for President Ulysses Grant, now in his second term. Waite was apparently the president's seventh choice for the seat that had been empty since May 7, 1873, when Chief Justice Salmon Portland Chase died.

Waite took his seat in the center chair under the clock in the Capitol's Old Senate Chamber, elegant quarters the Supreme Court had occupied for only fourteen years. By custom the associate justices arranged themselves in alternating order of seniority, with Clifford occupying the chair to Waite's right. Next to Clifford were Samuel Miller of Iowa, Stephen J. Field of California, and Joseph P. Bradley of New Jersey. On Waite's left sat second-most senior Associate Justice Noah Swayne of Ohio. Next to Swayne were David Davis of Illinois, William Strong of Pennsylvania, and Ward Hunt of New York, the Court's junior justice. These were accomplished men with years of service in law and politics. Several are still regarded among the most judicially talented and intellectually gifted individuals ever to sit on the Supreme Court. "What does all this mean?" asked Waite rhetorically nine days later in a letter to his wife Amelia. "I suppose I shall realize it all bye and bye. But it seems strange now" (Stephenson 1973, 899).

During Waite's fourteen-year tenure as chief, the Court occupied a pivotal position in the life of a nation that had entered a new era. Nine years after the guns went silent at Appomattox Courthouse and Durham Station, the United States had realized a truly national economy, one bound together by a nationwide rail network for transporting people and goods. An expanded federal jurisdiction forced an unprecedented volume of cases on the justices that posed questions both novel and routine. Indeed, it was the Waite Court's travail, as it tried unsuccessfully to keep abreast of its docket, that prompted Congress in 1891 to take the first steps toward establishing the contemporary federal judicial system. The Court also encountered on a large scale the legal legacy of the Civil War, including application of three new constitutional amendments and various civil rights statutes enacted by Congress between 1866 and 1875 to protect African Americans, almost all of whom had been slaves until 1865. Other cases reflected the growing number of state and local policies to foster internal improvements and to cope with industrial expansion and urban growth. Additionally, five members of the Waite Court directly helped to resolve the disputed presidential election of 1876.

Reference above to the "Waite Court" is a reminder that chief justices lend their names to periods of Supreme Court history. People speak and write of the Marshall Court (1801–1835), the Hughes Court (1930–1941), the Burger Court (1969–1986), and so on. This does not mean the chief justice has necessarily been the dominant or a leading personality on his bench. He may be, as with John Marshall, but then again he may not, as with Fred Vinson (1945–1953). Every chief justice is primus inter pares (first among equals) by the nature of the office, but this means only that the chief justice reigns and does not necessarily rule. By the end of this volume, the reader will be in a position to decide whether Waite truly led his Court, whether the Waite Court nomenclature is little more than a chronological convenience, or whether the record falls somewhere in between.

Legacy of the Chase Court

Except for the Supreme Court's first decade after 1790, at no time have its justices written on a completely blank slate. This is so for at least three reasons. First, as it decides cases in the present, the Court looks to the past—to precedent—as authority for what the law is. Decisions by an earlier Court do not bind a later one, but they will almost always be taken into account. By the mid-nineteenth century, this mass of prior decisions had become a kind of gloss on the law itself. For instance, in cases interpreting the Constitution, the Court came to refer less to the Constitution itself, and more to what earlier cases said about the Constitution. Second, the Court's membership changes, but these changes are usually gradual. For example, all eight of the brethren whom Waite joined on March 4 had worked alongside his predecessor, and most had worked with Chase's predecessor, Roger Brooke Taney. Third, carryover justices not only may have decided cases containing issues that will face the Court in the future, but themselves are a medium through which institutional lore, traditions, procedures, and expectations are passed from one judicial generation to the next in an informal socialization process. Thus, each bench leaves a legacy for a later one.

That was certainly true for the Supreme Court under Chase. The Chase bench restored respect for, and confidence in, the judiciary in the uncertain climate of post–Civil War America. Moreover, although the Chase bench was prepared to draw on the arsenal of judicial power, a majority could also display a jurisdictional caution that persisted well into the Waite years. President Abraham Lincoln's former treasury secretary, Chase, bequeathed to Waite a changed bench in changed circumstances.

Chase was sworn in on December 15, 1864, in the closing months of the Civil War, replacing Taney, who had died October 12, 1864, after twenty-eight years of service. Chase inherited a Court whose reputation had been badly tarnished, at least from the perspective of the dominant Republican Party and many northern Democrats, too. This was chiefly because of the Court's 1857 ruling in *Dred Scott v. Sandford,* a decision greatly pleasing to southern slave owners for reasons far beyond the Court's immediate holding that Dred Scott remained a slave. Thrusting itself into the most vexing and divisive political issue of the day, the bench voted 7–2 to deny Congress and territorial legislatures authority to ban slavery in the territories. The Court furthermore proclaimed that both free and enslaved African Americans were "not intended to be included, under the words 'citizens' in the Constitution, and can therefore claim none of the rights and privileges which that instrument provides for and secures to citizens of the United States," including the right to sue in federal court. *Dred Scott* not only invalidated the founding free-soil principle of the new Republican Party that had emerged in time for the 1856 election but also placed the Court on the losing side in both the forthcoming presidential election of 1860 and the Civil War.

Before Chase's appointment, the Court seemed, in the words of Senator John Hale, a "citadel of slavery," and during the early war years the Court appeared to Republicans to be amply stocked with southern sympathizers. As explained more fully later in this chapter, Lincoln's blockade policy and the northern theory of southern secession survived a legal challenge by a single vote in the *Prize Cases* (1863). However, a prudent attitude of deference by the majority toward Lincoln did not preclude opposing moves by Taney. Sitting as circuit judge in Baltimore, the chief justice challenged the president's unilateral suspension of the writ of habeas corpus by issuing a writ to Union officers holding a suspected Maryland secessionist. On the president's instructions, army officers ignored the judicial directive (*Ex parte Merryman,* 1861). Moreover, Taney in a posture of anticipation drafted hostile opinions on constitutional questions involving other Lincoln policies, were they to come before the Court. The perceived precarious constitutionality of administration policies not only caused Republicans to lose sleep but, as discussed below, guided Lincoln's judicial appointments and drove Congress to add a tenth justice to the bench.

The fact that Lincoln and his cabinet discussed in 1864 whether they should attend Taney's funeral indicated the overall stature of the Court and Taney. Similarly, in February 1865, a bill to place a marble bust of Taney alongside Marshall's in the courtroom provoked stiff opposition in the Senate. "The name of Taney," thundered Charles Sumner of Massachusetts, "is to be hooted down the page of history. . . . He administered justice . . . wickedly, and degraded the Judiciary of the country and degraded the age. . . . Taney shall not be represented as a saint by any vote of Congress, if I can help it." Sumner and others killed the measure. No such bill passed until 1874 when busts were authorized simultaneously for both Chase and Taney. Recognition for Taney was overdue: alongside his colossal blunder in *Dred Scott* was an otherwise creative and commendable record.

Rapid changes in membership following Lincoln's inauguration immeasurably aided restoration of much of the Supreme Court's former luster. The result was practically a reconstituted bench in record time. By 1865 Lincoln justices comprised a majority of the Court. This was no longer the *Dred Scott* Court. And by the time of Chase's death, only a single prewar justice, Clifford, remained.

However, Congress was unwilling to take chances. A Lincoln-configured bench was one thing. One fashioned by the soon-to-be-impeached Andrew Johnson would be something else entirely. A Union Democrat from Tennessee who had been put on the ticket with Lincoln in 1864 and who became president upon Lincoln's assassination in 1865, Johnson had never joined the Republican ranks or gained their confidence. As noted in more detail below, Congress in 1866 accordingly reduced the number of justices from ten to seven, with the shrinkage to occur as justices departed, thus denying the new president any appointments to the High Court.

This remade and then bobtailed bench was nonetheless prepared to wield judicial power. From 1861 until 1870, the Court invalidated twenty-four state statutes or local ordinances, a number substantially higher than that of previous decades. From Chase's appointment until 1870, the Court also set aside no fewer than seven acts of Congress, compared with only one each in the Marshall and Taney courts. Still, none of the postwar rulings struck at a major piece of the Republican Reconstruction program, the major legislative undertaking of the decade. With the significant and temporary exception noted below, the Court was generally cautious with respect to the Congress and the president elsewhere. When the justices declared in *Ex parte Milligan* (1866) that civilians could not be tried by military courts in wartime if civil courts were functioning, they did so after the war was over. When congressional leaders feared the Court might use *Milligan* to invalidate rule by military commissions in the conquered South, Congress repealed part of the Court's jurisdiction at the moment the justices had the case under advisement. The Court then backed away, unanimously ruling that it no longer had authority to decide the case (*Ex parte McCardle*, 1869).

A large exception to this pattern was *Hepburn v. Griswold* (1870). The holding was not only ironic and controversial but the Court's reversal of itself a year later fueled charges of political tampering and court packing, illustrating, as Waite would later learn, that the Court is rarely far removed from politics. To help finance the Civil War, *Treasury Secretary* Chase went along with the administration's decision in 1862 to issue paper currency called greenbacks not redeemable in gold coin. The Republican-dominated Congress insisted the greenbacks be legal tender for all debts and taxes so that the greenbacks could gain acceptance. Even though the new paper dollars quickly depreciated in value, creditors were legally bound to accept them from debtors. In *Hepburn*, the Court in a dubiously reasoned opinion by *Chief Justice* Chase ruled 4–3 that the act violated the Constitution, at least with respect to debts contracted before the greenback laws' passage. Not only had the Court invalidated key fiscal policy, but the bench split along party lines. Chase, who had hungered for the Republican presidential nomination in 1856, 1860, and 1864, and who had courted both the Democratic and Republican presidential nominations in 1868 and hoped for the Democratic nomination in 1872, was joined by Democratic justices Clifford, Samuel Nelson, and Field. Dissenters were Republicans Swayne, Davis, and Miller. Debtors, who would always outnumber creditors at the polls, were furious. They now feared they would have to repay loans in the more expensive specie instead of depreciated greenbacks. With the Court's allotment reset at nine, President Grant, who had been highly critical of the decision, named Republicans Strong and Bradley to the bench. When the administration quickly steered two other cases to the Court, Strong and Bradley joined the three *Hepburn* dissenters in upholding the legal tender laws for debts contracted both before and after passage (*Legal Tender Cases*, 1871).

Salmon Chase's Court witnessed three significant textual additions to the Constitution itself. Ratified in late 1865, the Thirteenth Amendment banished slavery and involuntary servitude throughout the United States. The Fourteenth Amendment of 1868 addressed the status of former slaves. Its very first sentence interred a particularly odious part of *Dred Scott* and provided constitutional underpinning for the language of the Civil Rights Act of 1866, which declared the former slaves to be citizens. "All persons born or naturalized in the United States . . .," decreed this amendment, "are citizens of the United States and of the state wherein they reside." The rest of the first section of the Fourteenth Amendment for the first time extended federal protection to certain undefined individual rights against infringement by the states: "*No state* shall make or enforce any law which shall abridge the privileges or immunities of citizens of the United States; nor shall *any State* deprive any person of life, liberty, or property, without due process of law; nor deny to any person within its jurisdiction the equal protection of the laws" (emphasis added). In 1870 the Fifteenth Amendment, pushed especially by Republicans whose continued hold on power depended partly on black voters in both northern and southern states, barred racial discrimination at the polls. Furthermore, to protect these new federal rights, eight "removal" acts between 1866 and 1872 expanded the jurisdiction of lower federal courts, permitting various categories of cases ordinarily tried in state courts to be transferred to a U.S. circuit court under certain circumstances.

Yet, three decisions suggested a hesitancy to expand the reach of federal jurisdiction, even when Congress and/or the Constitution plainly seemed to have done so, indicating the Chase Court hardly thought itself subservient to the statutory and amending processes. Each decision was the immediate product of this legal and constitutional upheaval wrought by northern victory in the Civil War and the immediate postwar dominance of the Republican Party.

The first of the decisions reflecting hesitancy to recognize the breadth of the constitutional and statutory revolution at hand has also been called the Supreme Court's first civil rights case (Howard 1999, 4). *Blyew v. United States* (1872) turned on two provisions of the 1866 Civil Rights Act. Section 1 declared that citizens of the United States "of every race and color, shall have the same rights in every state and territory . . . to be parties and give evidence . . . and to have full and equal benefit of all laws and proceedings for the security of persons and property as is enjoyed by white citizens . . ., any law, statute, ordinance, regulation, or custom to the contrary notwithstanding." Section 3 provided for the removal or transfer from state to federal court of all cases "civil and criminal, *affecting persons* who are denied or cannot enforce [in state courts] any of the rights secured to them by the 1st section of the act" (emphasis added).

Kentucky officials charged two white men named John Blyew and George Kennard with the grisly 1868 murder of several members of the Foster family and a blind woman more than ninety years of age who lived with them. The victims were "of the African race." The only survivors and witnesses of the murder were the two Foster children, one of whom died of injuries soon after making a statement to authorities. State law, however, barred blacks from testifying against whites in criminal trials in state courts. Believing the surviving witness to be an "affected" person, authorities moved the prosecution to the federal circuit court under section 3 of the 1866 act. Blyew and Kennard were found guilty. Voting 6–2, with Chase not participating, the Supreme Court declared that the circuit court had no jurisdiction and reversed. Justice Strong read section 3 narrowly: although Congress intended the law to protect African Americans from a denial of their rights in civil and criminal cases, the act applied only to the parties to a case, in this instance Blyew, Kennard, and the United States. Those called as witnesses and the deceased victims "are no more affected by it than is every other person." The bench seemed inclined to construe federal civil rights legislation in a way that avoided a deep intrusion into the traditional affairs of the states.

The second indication of the cautious approach of the Court was a trio of decisions called the *Slaughterhouse Cases* (1873), which gave the Court its first opportunity to construe the recently ratified Fourteenth Amendment. Motivated partly by greed and partly by public health concerns, the Louisiana legislature chartered the Crescent City Live-Stock Landing and Slaughtering Company and mandated that all butchering of animals in New Orleans and vicinity be done on its premises. Other slaughtering businesses were prohibited from using their own shops and were required, for a fee, to use Crescent City's facilities. About 1,000 displaced butchers then retained former Supreme Court Justice John Archibald Campbell to press their case in the Supreme Court. An Alabaman who had resigned from the bench when his state seceded, Campbell was one of the stars of the Louisiana bar—"leave it to God and Mr. Campbell," said his admirers (Gillette 1969a, 939). The suit was ironic: Campbell, the late Confederacy's assistant secretary of war, demanded on behalf of his mainly white clients that the Fourteenth Amendment—that key symbol of Union victory and national power—displace states' rights.

Speaking for a majority of five, with Chase, Field, Bradley, and Strong in dissent, Justice Miller was entirely unreceptive to the butchers' constitutional objections. The first clause of the Fourteenth Amendment, he said, created no new rights. It merely conferred on the national government the duty of protecting rights adhering in national, but not state, citizenship. Rights adhering in national citizenship included those such as coming to the seat of government, protection on the high seas, and qualifying for government offices. By contrast, state citizenship, which predated the Constitution, encompassed the more fundamental rights of acquiring, possessing, and using property, which the butchers thought Louisiana had infringed. Thus they had no claim under the U.S. Constitution. Miller was equally cool to application of the equal protection and due process clauses. He doubted the relevance of the former except in cases involving rights of the recently freed slaves. As for standards of due process, under no interpretation he had seen could the challenged statute be deemed deficient.

The Court's narrow view of the amendment's protection against states' abuses translated into a limited view of federal judicial power. Miller refused to recognize that the Fourteenth Amendment had fundamentally changed the relationship between the national and state governments. To do otherwise, Miller correctly maintained, "would constitute this Court a perpetual censor upon all legislation of the states on the civil rights of their own citizens, with authority to nullify such as it did not approve." Even the amending process, apparently, could not alter the federal balance.

A third case pointing to a modest role for the Court in the political system and an awareness of limited judicial resources was decided in the months between the death of Chase and the swearing-in of Waite. The *Sewing Machine Companies Case* (1874) turned on the extent of the diversity jurisdiction of the federal courts—suits between citizens of different states on matters that would otherwise be tried in state courts. Authorized by the Constitution as part of the judicial power and put into effect by Congress in 1789, diversity jurisdiction was designed to provide, in disputes involving more than $500, a federal forum for out-of-state litigants who might encounter prejudice in local court. By 1874, it accounted for the bulk of cases decided by the U.S. circuit courts. The traditional rule had been that the circuit courts could accept a case only if there was no identity of citizenship between any of the parties on one side of the case and any of the parties on the other side. Although Congress in 1867 made important changes in the wording of the diversity jurisdiction statute that suggested otherwise, the Court ruled 6–2 in the *Sewing Machine Companies*

The Waite Court from 1874 to 1877: (left to right) Joseph P. Bradley, Stephen J. Field, Samuel F. Miller, Nathan Clifford, Morrison R. Waite, Noah H. Swayne, David Davis, William Strong, and Ward Hunt. (J. M. Fasset, Collection of the Supreme Court of the United States)

Case that the traditional rule still governed. The Waite Court subsequently would adhere to this more narrow reading (*Vannever v. Bryant*, 1874). A contrary decision would have shifted a substantial number of suits from state to federal court.

The Waite Court: A Collective Portrait

The bench Waite joined differed in character from the benches Chase and Taney encountered at the outset of their tenures. As depicted in Table 1.1, the associate justices in 1874 as a group were significantly less experienced in terms of length of Supreme Court service when compared to the two earlier cohort groups. This was of course a function of the relatively rapid turnover in membership during the fourteen years before Waite's appointment. Waite's associates averaged under nine years, while both the Chase and Taney associates averaged about twelve years in 1864 and 1836, respectively. Thus there was less institutional memory on hand at the beginning of the Waite Court. Although less experienced, Waite's bench was older than either the Taney or Chase benches had been in 1864 and 1836.

In terms of rate of turnover in personnel, however, the three court periods in the half century after 1836 were roughly comparable. There were fourteen associate jus-

Table 1.1
Supreme Court Experience and Age of Associate Justices at the Onsets of the Taney, Chase, and Waite Courts

Chief Justice	*Year of Appointment*	*Average Years of Supreme Court Service by Colleagues*	*Average Age of Colleagues*	*Number of Associate Justices ≤50*	*Number of Associate Justices ≤60*
Taney	1836	12.5	59.5	2	2
Chase	1864	11.8	61.8	3	5
Waite	1874	8.75	62.3	0	5

tices appointed during Taney's 28.5 years of service, three during Chase's eight and a half years, and six during Waite's fourteen. On average, therefore, one appointment occurred every two years between 1836 and 1864, one every 2.8 years between 1864 and 1873, and one every 2.3 years between 1874 and 1888, inclusive. Cumulatively the three court periods are somewhat above the historical turnover average of one new appointment every 2.1 years, following President George Washington's appointment of the initial six.

Turnover is important in part because it defines a discrete or "natural" court within a longer court period. A discrete court encompasses the years in which the membership of the Court is stable or nearly so, when the same justices are deciding cases. Thinking of the Court in this way helps in making comparisons and drawing conclusions across time.

The pattern of departures and arrivals during the Waite Court lends itself to division into three discrete courts. As shown in Table 1.2, the first Waite Court opened with Waite's swearing-in on March 4, 1874, and concluded in the spring of 1877 after David Davis's resignation in March.

The second or middle Waite Court began with the start of the next term in October 1877, and ended with the conclusion of the 1880–1881 term. As shown in Table 1.3, most of the members of the first Waite Court carried over through the middle one. However, Justice John Marshall Harlan was sworn in to take Davis's place in December 1877. Then, from December 1880 until July 1881, three members of the first Waite Court departed: Strong, Swayne, and Clifford. Arriving well before the end of the term, Justice William B. Woods filled the seat vacated by Strong.

The third or last Waite Court extended from the fall of 1881 through Waite's death in March 1888. When the Court began its term in October 1881, Stanley Matthews was in the seat that had been Swayne's, as Table 1.4 indicates. By early 1882, Horace Gray had taken Clifford's place, just days before Hunt's retirement. Hunt in turn was replaced three months later by Samuel Blatchford. From that point in the

Table 1.2 First Waite Court: March 4, 1874 (86 U.S.) through 1876–1877 Term (94 U.S.)

Justice	*Appointed By*	*Replaced*	*Judicial Oath Taken*	*Service Terminated*
Waite	Grant	Chase	3–4–1874	3–23–1888
Clifford	Buchanan	Curtis	1–21–1858	7–25–1881
Swayne	Lincoln	McLean	1–27–1862	1–24–1881
Miller	Lincoln	Daniel	7–21–1862	10–13–1890
Davis	Lincoln	Campbell	12–10–1862	3–4–1877
Field	Lincoln	(new seat)	5–20–1863	12–1–1897
Strong	Grant	Grier	3–14–1870	12–14–1880
Bradley	Grant	(new seat)	3–23–1870	1–22–1892
Hunt	Grant	Nelson	1–9–1873	1–27–1882

Table 1.3 Middle Waite Court: 1877–1878 Term (95 U.S.) through 1880–1881 Term (103 U.S.)

Justice	*Appointed By*	*Replaced*	*Judicial Oath Taken*	*Service Terminated*
Waite	Grant	Chase	3–4–1874	3–23–1888
Clifford	Buchanan	Curtis	1–21–1858	7–25–1881
Swayne	Lincoln	McLean	1–27–1862	1–24–1881
Miller	Lincoln	Daniel	7–21–1862	10–13–1890
Field	Lincoln	(new seat)	5–20–1863	12–1–1897
Strong	Grant	Grier	3–14–1870	12–14–1880
Bradley	Grant	(new seat)	3–23–1870	1–22–1892
Hunt*	Grant	Nelson	1–9–1873	1–27–1882
Harlan (I)	Hayes	Davis	12–10–1877	10–14–1911
Woods	Hayes	Strong	1–5–1881	5–14–1887

*Disabled on 12–23–1878; participated in no decisions thereafter; did not resign until 1–27–1882.

spring of 1882, the Court's membership remained stable until Woods died in May 1887. L. Q. C. Lamar filled that vacancy in the late twilight of Waite's chief justiceship.

What were the Waite Court justices like? What did they have in common? In what respects were their backgrounds different? A look at the circumstances and politics of their nominations comes later in this chapter, and examination of their lives follows in the next chapter. But some collective traits merit attention here.

The nine members of the first Waite Court were born within a thirteen-year

Table 1.4 Last Waite Court: 1881–1882 Term (104 U.S.) through March 23, 1888 (126 U.S.)

Justice	*Appointed By*	*Replaced*	*Judicial Oath Taken*	*Service Terminated*
Waite	Grant	Chase	3–4–1874	3–23–1888
Miller	Lincoln	Daniel	7–21–1862	10–13–1890
Field	Lincoln	(new seat)	5–20–1863	12–1–1897
Bradley	Grant	(new seat)	3–23–1870	1–22–1892
Hunt	Grant	Nelson	1–9–1873	1–27–1882
Harlan (I)	Hayes	Davis	12–10–1877	10–14–1911
Woods*	Hayes	Strong	1–5–1881	5–14–1887
Matthews**	Garfield	Swayne	5–17–1881	3–22–1889
Gray	Arthur	Clifford	1–9–1882	9–15–1902
Blatchford	Arthur	Hunt	4–3–1882	7–7–1893
Lamar, L.	Cleveland	Woods	1–18–1888	1–23–1893

*Became ill in the spring of 1886 and did not sit during the 1886–87 Term.
**Appointed too late to take part in decisions during 1880–81 Term.

period, from 1803 (Clifford) to 1816 (Miller, Field, and Waite). That fact is significant because it meant they entered professional life during what historians call the Jacksonian era in U.S. history. President between 1829 and 1837, Andrew Jackson in 1824 received the popular vote plurality, but not the electoral vote majority. Jackson founded the Democratic Party. His advocacy of popular sovereignty, with its suspicion of a dominant national government, including federal judicial power, profoundly influenced political thinking in the United States during the late 1820s, 1830s, and 1840s. His party won every presidential election but two between 1828 and 1856, inclusive.

Like almost all Americans in the early nineteenth century, these Waite justices were Protestant in religious upbringing and practice, with the Congregationalist, Episcopalian, Presbyterian, Quaker, and Unitarian denominations represented. All, of course, were lawyers. (Tradition, not the Constitution, requires federal judges to be trained in the law and admitted to the bar.) Seven received a college education, but only three (Davis, Strong, and Hunt) had any formal classroom instruction in the few fledgling law schools of their day. The rest followed the route almost everyone then took into the legal profession. They read law under another's tutelage, and learned by studying texts, by asking questions, by doing small tasks, and by observing everything their mentor did. Education in law schools would not become the common preparation for practice until the twentieth century. (Robert H. Jackson, who sat from 1941 until 1954, was the last person appointed to the Court who gained entrance to the bar mainly through legal apprenticeship.)

With the exception of the Kentucky-bred Miller, who was the first justice to have been born west of the Appalachian mountains, all were born in East Coast states. Most, however, took part in the westward migration and prospered in their profession elsewhere: Waite relocated from Connecticut to Ohio (and in the 1830s and 1840s, Ohio was still considered part of the western country). Swayne moved from Virginia to Ohio, Miller from Kentucky to Iowa (distinguishing himself further as the first justice appointed from a state west of the Mississippi River), Davis from Maryland to Illinois, and Field from Connecticut to California. Four remained strictly easterners: Clifford left New Hampshire for Maine. Strong forsook Connecticut for Pennsylvania, and Bradley set out to make his fortune in New Jersey instead of his birth state of New York. Only Hunt never pulled up roots, spending virtually all his pre-Court life in New York.

No one could describe the justices of the first Waite Court as political neophytes. All were politically active before their nominations to the Supreme Court, each having established a record that revealed where he stood on the important issues of the day, including the overriding issue of 1860: the survival of the Union. They were also strong party men. Of the five who began as Democrats, three became Republicans, as did all four Whigs. Moreover, all were experienced in public affairs, although ironically that experience was more legislative than judicial. While four had served in at least one county or state judgeship, six had either been elected to the state legislature or had run unsuccessfully for that or another office at the state level. Two others had been elected to the U.S. House of Representatives, and still another had lost a race for Congress. In addition, the bench included an attorney general of the United States, one county prosecutor, and a participant at an international arbitration.

The six individuals who reached the Supreme Court during the middle and last Waite Courts were likewise born during a thirteen-year period: from 1820 (Blatchford) to 1833 (Harlan). In religion all were Protestant, including two Presbyterians, one Congregationalist, and one Methodist. (Taney had been the first Roman Catholic named to the Court. The second Catholic, Edward D. White, would not be appointed until 1894, with Louis D. Brandeis following in 1916 as the first Jewish appointee.) In contrast to the earlier group of Waite justices, each had a formal college education. Four followed the standard practice of the day in reading law, including Matthews who studied under the law office tutelage of future Chief Justice Chase in Cincinnati. Two (Harlan and Gray) attended law school.

Reflecting the maturation of some of the western settlements, the new arrivals in the middle and last Waite Courts were decidedly less eastern in their origins, with just three (Gray, Blatchford, and Lamar) born east of the Appalachians. The six were also less peripatetic than the original nine. Half of them (Harlan, Gray, and Blatchford) developed professionally in the states where they were born, while a fourth (Matthews) returned to his birth state of Ohio after a two-year sojourn in Tennessee. Woods migrated south, and only Lamar moved west.

The Waite Court from 1877 to 1881: (left to right) Joseph P. Bradley, Samuel F. Miller, Morrison R. Waite, Stephen J. Field, Stanley Matthews; (back row— left to right) William B. Woods, Horace Gray, John Marshall Harlan, and Samuel Blatchford. (C. M. Bell, Collection of the Supreme Court of the United States)

Lamar was the single Democrat among the six at the time of appointment to the Supreme Court, although Matthews began his professional life in that party before becoming a Republican. Woods and Blatchford were originally Whigs, and Gray had been an outspoken Free-Soiler. Harlan also started out as a Whig, was briefly a Know-Nothing, and was a relative latecomer to Republican ranks. During the Civil War, while firmly supporting the Union, he strenuously opposed Lincoln's reelection in 1864 and, while flirting with Democrats, spoke out against the Reconstruction policies of the radical Republicans, including ratification of the Thirteenth Amendment. Then, in what was practically a road-to-Damascus conversion, he campaigned for Republican presidential nominee Ulysses Grant in 1868. Like the nine members of the first Waite bench, Harlan and the other five took party allegiance seriously even as circumstances in tumultuous times forced a shift from one party to another. Such loyalty was not unusual; independents would not comprise a sizeable bloc of the electorate until after the middle of the twentieth century.

All had been active in, or at least closely associated with, electoral politics. Harlan, Woods, Matthews, and Lamar had each held one or more elective offices (Lamar's included both the U.S. House of Representatives and the U.S. Senate), Gray had run unsuccessfully for state attorney general, and Blatchford had been private secretary to the governor of New York. Moreover, the newcomers in the middle and last courts were more experienced judicially than Waite's initial colleagues. Only Lamar had not been a judge. Harlan, Matthews, and Gray had held judgeships at the county or state level, while Woods and Blatchford had been U.S. circuit judges. Overall, the pre-Court experiences of these six followed the pattern set by the justices of the first Waite Court, with one important exception: the Court acquired its first Civil War veterans. Harlan, Woods, and Matthews each had been officers in the Union army, and Lamar had served in the army of the Confederacy.

Assembling the Waite Court

Every U.S. president, or at least his advisers, has been acutely aware of the importance of appointments to the Supreme Court. Given the Supreme Court's influence in the political system and the indeterminate nature of judicial tenures, selecting a justice is often among the most significant and far-reaching decisions any president makes. "The good that Presidents do is often interred with their Administrations," editorialized *The Nation* a half century after Waite's death. "It is their choice of Supreme Court Justices that lives after them" (Mason and Stephenson 2002, 6). Yet it is also true that nomination of Supreme Court justices never occurs in a political vacuum; a nomination can easily be fraught with controversy because of circumstances that have little or nothing to do with the professional qualifications of the nominee.

As shown in Tables 1.2, 1.3, and 1.4, the three Waite Courts consisted of a total of fifteen justices who were named to the bench by presidents Buchanan, Lincoln, Grant, Hayes, Garfield, Arthur, and Cleveland between 1858 and 1888. The presidents who selected Waite and his original eight colleagues influenced the bench well into the future: tenures of those justices averaged 19.7 years, with a median of 19 years, or the equivalent of almost five presidential terms. It should come as no surprise, then, that three members who were present at Waite's swearing-in—Miller, Field, and Bradley—were still sitting when he died. The six justices who arrived during the middle and last Waite Courts tended not to sit as long, with average and median tenures of 14.2 and 9.6 years, respectively. Even so, two of the chief justice's colleagues from the last Waite Court—Harlan and Gray—would sit into the twentieth century: Gray until 1902 and Harlan until 1911.

Nathan Clifford

The single vacancy that President James Buchanan successfully filled came about because of the resignation of Justice Benjamin Curtis, a brilliant Massachusetts lawyer who had been appointed by President Millard Fillmore in 1851. (Ironically, Buchanan himself had previously spurned at least three formal invitations to join the Court, but he had declined each time so that he could pursue his quest for the presidency.) Curtis, more than any other member of the Taney Court, deserved credit for developing a concurrent theory of the commerce power that the Court could apply with some consistency. Despite wide-ranging acclaim for his work, Curtis grumbled about the inadequacy of an associate justice's remuneration, even though Congress increased the annual salary from $4,500 to $6,000 in 1855. But it was *Dred Scott* that caused him to leave Washington in a huff in late summer of 1857. For him the Court had become an agent of political forces that he loathed, and Curtis doubted whether damage to the Court's reputation could ever be repaired.

The problem Buchanan confronted in making a selection was not only that *Dred Scott* had exacerbated sectional tensions, but that controversies over slavery in Kansas and enforcement of the Fugitive Slave Act persisted. "Buchanan will have a chance to make the Court still less acceptable to this part of the country," wrote the Bay State's Robert C. Winthrop, former speaker of the U.S. House of Representatives (Warren 1926, II, 322).

Curtis resided in the First (the New England) Circuit, as had the four justices who preceded him in that seat. Would the president follow tradition—it was not a legal requirement—and nominate from within the circuit? The link between circuits and appointments persisted because of a justice's circuit court duties. Presumably a justice chosen from the region of the country where he would sit on circuit meant he would already be familiar with legal questions unique or common to the area and would know, and be known by, its bench and bar.

The practice assured regional diversity, but not proportional balance, on the high court. For example, the Ninth Circuit, consisting of Mississippi and Alabama, counted barely 1 million inhabitants in 1860, while the more commercially complex and litigious Seventh Circuit, composed of Ohio, Indiana, Illinois, and Michigan, claimed over 6 million. The practice also reflected the slave and free state organization of the circuits. Taney was from Maryland (Fourth Circuit), James Wayne from Georgia (Sixth), John Catron from Tennessee (Eighth), Campbell from Alabama (Ninth), and Peter Daniel from Virginia (Fifth). All states in these five circuits were slave states. Aside from the First Circuit seat that Curtis had vacated, seats from free circuits were held by Robert Grier from Pennsylvania (Third), Nelson from New York (Second), and John McLean from Ohio (Seventh).

Buchanan looked at Isaac Toucy of Connecticut (one of Polk's attorneys general) and across party lines to the celebrity Whig lawyer Rufus Choate of Massachusetts. Choate himself pushed the candidacy of Claims Court chief judge John J. Gilchrist of New Hampshire. William L. Yancey of Alabama would appeal to southerners, but would draw opposition from other sections for precisely that reason.

The president agonized over the nomination for three months, before sending to the Senate the name of Nathan Clifford of Maine. In doing so, Buchanan went with a known entity. He picked someone with whom he was politically, professionally, and personally comfortable, having served as secretary of state in President Polk's cabinet at the same time Clifford had been attorney general. The nominee had been a faithful Democrat since Jackson's day. He espoused Old Hickory's brand of political egalitarianism, while being entirely sympathetic to the defense of slavery championed especially by the southern wing of the party (Abraham 1992, 114).

Clifford was compatible with Buchanan's views, but was he confirmable? For a time, Clifford's fate was in doubt, as the nomination sparked bitter debate that persisted for five weeks. Acrimony on Capitol Hill carried over into the newspapers. Clifford was both mediocre and a tool of the Democratic Party, wrote the Washington correspondent of the *New York Tribune* in December and January. The president was "determined to bring [New England] down to the level of the other Circuits and appoint Clifford" to a Court that had become "a party machine, to do the bidding of the dominant faction and to supply places to reward party hacks" (Warren 1926, II, 323).

In the congressional elections of 1856 Democrats had retained control of the Senate, but these were not ordinary times. The vote of 26–23 on January 12, 1858, was among the closest on record for a successful nomination. Clifford's razor-thin confirmation was possible only because of the absence of two of his most outspoken Senate opponents (Charles Sumner and Simon Cameron), and a last-minute change of mind by Phillip Allen of Rhode Island. Otherwise, the nomination would have failed 25–26. However, the invectives did not cease, and clouds of partisan and sectional doubt did not dissipate just because Clifford took his oath. The *New York Post* reminded its readers he owed his "appointment exclusively to his party associations, . . . without any independence or great legal ability. There is perhaps some satisfaction in the belief, which this appointment strengthens, that the weakness and evident character of the Court . . . will produce an entire remodelling of it." Since "the proper business of the northern minority on the Bench is merely to fall in with and say yes to any extravagances which the southern majority may choose to promulgate," insisted the *New York Tribune*, "Mr. Clifford is admirably fitted for the place in which he has been put" (Warren 1926, II, 323–324).

Noah H. Swayne

Buchanan might have been credited with a second successful Supreme Court nomination had he moved swiftly after Justice Peter V. Daniel died on May 31, 1860. The significance of the vacancy was apparent to all, especially in light of the appraisal already rendered by the sulfurous *New York Tribune:* "This Court, as now arranged, is scandalously sectional, grossly partial, a mockery of the Constitution, a serf of the slave power, and a disgrace to the country" (Warren 1926, II, 360). The president had no plans for a second term, much preferring a return to Wheatland, his home in Lancaster Township, Pennsylvania, to continued occupancy of the White House. Buchanan even considered leaving the vacancy for his successor to fill. Still, he had slightly more than nine months remaining in his term. To maintain their regional advantage, southerners demanded a nomination from a southern state. Others opposed a southern nomination on the same grounds. Not until February 5, 1861—barely a month before the end of his term, well after the outcome of the presidential election was known, and after senators from some southern states had resigned their positions—did Buchanan make his move, picking his secretary of state and former attorney general, Jeremiah S. Black, for Daniel's seat. Like Buchanan, Black was a Pennsylvanian, a party stalwart, and acceptable to southerners, but Senator Stephen A. Douglas (the just-defeated presidential nominee of the northern wing of the Democratic Party) disliked Black. The nomination failed by one vote, 25–26. Buchanan's delay was Black's undoing. Republican senators wanted the nomination to be Lincoln's. (Black later served as reporter for the Supreme Court between 1861 and 1864, and published two volumes of decisions.)

President Lincoln had every incentive to move more quickly than Buchanan. Besides the vacancy he inherited, two others opened in April. Justice John McLean died just as Justice Campbell resigned to join the Confederacy. The Court was now dangerously understaffed. Moreover, Lincoln could turn a nomination to strategic advantage by choosing someone who would not alienate slave-owning border states, and so halt further hemorrhaging of the Union. Foremost, Lincoln wanted to take no chances. He needed nominees who supported both the Union and his war aims.

However, the identity of Lincoln's first nominee—Noah H. Swayne of Ohio—did not become known until January 21, 1862. Practically pro forma consideration by the Senate followed rapidly, with a lopsided favorable vote of 38–1 on January 24.

In filling McLean's seat first, the president made a regional nod in the direction of Daniel's Virginia. A Virginian by birth, Swayne had owned slaves before freeing them and moving west, so he had connections with the culture of the upper South and border region. His legal career included defense of several fugitive slave cases, and so he appealed to abolitionists. He had excellent credentials among Ohio Republicans, and the Ohio delegation had given Lincoln critical third-ballot support at the party's nominating convention in 1860. A conservative on economic issues, Swayne enjoyed the support of business and financial leaders, whose confidence and cooperation were essential to the success of the war effort.

Swayne clearly had coveted McLean's seat and worked tirelessly to secure it. Leaving no possible advantage untapped, he skillfully managed his own campaign for the Court. It began on April 4, the day of McLean's death, when Swayne wrote to fellow Ohioan and cabinet member Salmon Chase, "If you deem it proper to give me your friendly support you will lay me under a lasting obligation." Swayne also enlisted the support of Ohio's two senators and its representatives and had them convey their enthusiasm to Lincoln. William Dennison, the state's governor, for whom Swayne had worked, traveled to Washington to press his friend's case. Swayne secured the help of Samuel Tilden as well. "It has occurred to me," Swayne wrote to the New York lawyer and future Democratic presidential candidate, "that the aid of Mr. B. Ogden [a railroad financier] may be very important. He will best know how to give it. . . . I think it very probable you also can make yourself felt." Tilden then arranged for an array of prominent lawyers in New York to lobby the White House on Swayne's behalf. Later, as weeks stretched into months, while Lincoln was no doubt preoccupied with everything that followed the April 12 attack on Fort Sumter, Swayne journeyed to Washington "to learn the lay of the land." "I am not sanguine as to the result," Swayne had already written Tilden (Gillette 1969b, 991). But he might as well have been. With no other apparent contenders who could approach his resourcefulness at marshaling bipartisan endorsements from people who mattered, Swayne's candidacy allowed Lincoln one of his few easy first-year decisions.

Samuel F. Miller

As the Senate confirmed Swayne, the seats vacated by Daniel in 1860 and Campbell in 1861 remained unfilled. Both had come from southern circuits, but the southern circuits now existed in name only. Of the Court's earlier members from southern states, only Justice Wayne of Georgia remained. Lincoln had explained the difficulty in his first message to Congress on December 3, 1861:

> Two of the outgoing Judges resided within the States now overrun by revolt, so that if successors were appointed in the same localities, they could not now serve upon their Circuits; and many of the most competent men there would not take the personal hazard of accepting to serve even here upon the Supreme Bench. I have been unwilling to throw all the appointments Northward, thus disabling myself from doing justice to the South on the return of peace. (Basler 1953–1955, V, 33–53)

Secession thus focused congressional attention on a long overdue chore: circuit reorganization. Wisconsin, Minnesota, Iowa, Kansas, Florida, Texas, California, and Oregon had been admitted to the Union after the last reorganization in 1837. So there were now states in circuits that were not, practically speaking, any longer part of the Union, and there were states in the Union that were not part of any circuit. Filling the Daniel and Campbell seats would therefore await completion of this task.

Of course, redrawing circuit boundaries involved much more than questions of judicial efficiency and balance. Representatives and senators eyeing one or more candidates for the Court were fully conscious of how circuit boundaries could boost or sink a prospective nominee's chances. For example, early front-runners for the positions included Interior Secretary Caleb B. Smith of Indiana, Wisconsin's Senator James Doolittle, and Illinois's Senator Orville H. Browning. If Indiana and Ohio were linked to form Justice Swayne's Seventh Circuit (as they later were), that would extinguish Smith's hopes, as happened. If Wisconsin, Illinois, and Michigan were placed in the same circuit (as happened), the expectation was that neither Doolittle nor Browning would be nominated (neither would be) because Michigan's dominance would guarantee a justice from that state (it did not).

Circuit reorganization presented both an opportunity and a challenge for Iowa attorney Samuel F. Miller, who craved a seat on the Supreme Court because he wanted "to wield public power" (Fairman 1939, 44). If Iowa were placed in a circuit with neighboring Illinois, for example, Miller's chances for a nomination would be slim indeed. If Iowa were joined with Kansas, Minnesota, and Missouri, the combination of Miller's legal reputation on the west bank of the Mississippi and the depth of local support would make him a leading contender. Thus, for Miller and his allies, the prize of a Supreme Court seat required success on two fronts: first, creating a circuit consisting of trans-Mississippi states only; and second, persuading Lincoln that Miller was the man to be appointed from that circuit. Efforts on both fronts began soon after the House in December 1861 and the Senate in January 1862 started work on circuit reorganization.

Success on the first front was due mainly to Senator James W. Grimes and Representative James F. Wilson of Iowa. Both desired Miller's nomination and worked tirelessly on behalf of a trans-Mississippi circuit. However, congressional horse trading on circuit juggling during the next six months yielded Senate and House reorganization plans that conflicted in crucial respects with respect to Miller's chances. The Senate version joined Iowa to Illinois; the House version called for a reconfigured Ninth Circuit consisting of Iowa, Kansas, Minnesota, and Missouri. (The far west states of California and Oregon would be excluded from this reorganization. Each had its own circuit judge who was not a Supreme Court justice.) As adjournment loomed with prospects of no bill acceptable to both houses, the bills went to conference committee, where Wilson was one of three House members. Even at the risk of jeopardizing reorganization entirely, he insisted on inclusion of the trans-Mississippi circuit as part of the bill reported back to both houses. With Grimes on watch in the Senate, the conference version with its Miller-friendly circuit passed both houses and received Lincoln's signature on July 15, 1862.

Meanwhile, Miller and his allies stirred up a beehive of activity to ensure that any nomination from a properly reconfigured circuit went to him. It was as if Miller was applying Confederate General Nathan Bedford Forrest's recipe for battlefield success to the politics of judicial selection: "to get there fustest with the mostest." Miller's troops overwhelmed any possible competitors. Friends and supporters inundated the White House with appeals for Miller's appointment. They included the Iowa governor, the state's U.S. senators and representatives, members of the state bar and state legislature, the justices of the Iowa Supreme Court, and the state attorney general. Missives extolled Miller's record as a lawyer and informed the president that he had left Kentucky years before because of his opposition to slavery. His devotion to the Union seemed sealed by the fact that he had used his own funds to help outfit a regiment when war began. The Iowa attorney general recommended Miller not only because he was an "earnest Patriot and conscientious Republican" but, attempting to turn a possible liability into an asset, because he "*has never held a public office*" (Silver 1998, 65, emphasis added). Later, a petition on Miller's behalf bearing the names of more than 100 members of Congress arrived on Lincoln's desk.

To these entreaties were added personal calls on the president by various dignitaries. During one visit early in the search, John Kasson, whom Lincoln had appointed assistant postmaster in Des Moines and who was later elected to Congress, discovered that Lincoln had no idea who Miller was. *Samuel* Miller's reputation as a lawyer had obviously never reached Springfield, Illinois, where Lincoln had practiced law. Lincoln supposed all the fuss was about former Iowa congressman *Daniel* Miller. (Even after Miller's nomination, the *New York Tribune* would make the same mistake.) On another occasion, Iowa's Governor Samuel Kirkwood and Senator James Harlan and several representatives called on Lincoln to convey their support with respect "to that appointment." At first, no one mentioned either Miller's name or the office he sought, and the president took advantage of that. According to one account, Lincoln "picked up his pen, and drawing a paper to him as if to make the appointment in compliance with their wishes, said to them, 'what is the office and whom do you wish to be placed in it?'" Nearly overcome with the prospects of such instant success, Senator Harlan explained. "We wish to have Mr. Miller of Iowa chosen by you to the vacancy on the Supreme Bench." Replacing the pen, the president hesitated. "[T]hat is a very important position and I will have to give it serious consideration. I had supposed you wanted me to make some one a Brigadier General for you" (Silver 1998, 66).

The president had his joke and the delegation left empty-handed, but the lobbying campaign soon had its intended effect. Lincoln sent Miller's name to the Senate on July 16, the day after he signed the reorganization bill. Miller must have had his bags packed; Chief Justice Taney administered the oath of office to him in Washington on July 21, less than a week later. Miller was not the only one who benefited by the appointment. For Governor Kirkwood, the appointment eliminated a potential political rival; indeed, he was able to succeed Harlan in the Senate, a seat that otherwise might have gone to Miller himself.

David Davis

With the new circuit system in place, Lincoln looked seriously only to Illinois to fill Campbell's seat. The leading contenders were U.S. district judge Thomas Drummond, Senator Browning, and Illinois circuit judge David Davis. Lincoln had known each for years, with his association with Davis dating to 1835. Drummond had numerous supporters, including Secretary of War Edwin Stanton, as did Browning and Davis. Drummond wrote Lincoln, asking for the nomination because he needed the higher salary (Silver 1998, 73). Browning had already written Lincoln that he desired appointment to the Supreme Court. But it was Davis who probably had the greatest claim on the new president. He had canvassed energetically for Lincoln in the unsuccessful 1858 Senate race that gave Lincoln national visibility, had skillfully engineered Lincoln's nomination at the 1860 Republican convention, had been the candidate's campaign manager, and shared Lincoln's values.

Davis was agreeable to a U. S. district court judgeship were Drummond to go to the Supreme Court, and had even confided to a friend in April 1861 that he would prefer the district court to the "Supreme Judgeship," given the arduous labors the latter entailed. Yet he was cool to Lincoln's later suggestion of a cabinet post were the nomination to go to Browning. Meanwhile Browning's political fortunes in Illinois dimmed among radical Republicans who shared their displeasure with the president. Furthermore, Browning had not been an entirely reliable vote for the administration, displaying a streak of independence that might become more pronounced on the bench. Still, with support among fellow senators, Browning remained the frontrunner. For Lincoln, the decision had become far more complicated than with Swayne or Miller. He had to weigh friendship, gratitude, and prudence. For whatever reasons, Lincoln notified Davis of his intentions on August 27, and a recess appointment was tendered on October 17, 1862. With Davis's investiture on December 10, the Court was fully staffed for the first time since May 31, 1860.

Stephen J. Field

Opportunity for Lincoln's fourth appointment to the Court was case-driven. Between February 10 and 25, 1863, the justices heard arguments in the *Prize Cases.* Involving captured ships and their cargoes, these cases challenged the legality of the Union blockade of Confederate ports. If southerners were engaged only in insurrection, the blockade would be illegal under international law. Declaring the hostilities to be war in a legal sense would legitimize the blockade but would confer recognition on the Confederacy as a nation. Other countries would then be free to recognize it as such. Additionally, the blockade had begun in April 1861 but had not been formally approved by Congress until July. What was the status of seizures in the interim? In a large sense the Republican theory of the war and the Union seemed to hang in the balance. By a one vote margin on March 10, the Court sustained both the blockade and the administration's theory of a de facto war.

Understandably, concern pervaded the administration and Congress even prior to this close call that the Court had to be made firmly safe for the Union. Not coincidentally a bill was introduced in the Senate on February 20, 1863, to provide for a new circuit consisting of California and Oregon and to add a ninth associate justice to the Supreme Court. Lincoln signed the measure into law on March 3, seven days before the decision in the *Prize Cases* was announced. At one level, the legislation was a warning to the bench that its size and jurisdiction, perhaps even its existence, lay in Congress's hands. At another level, the legislation recognized the importance of cementing the Pacific Coast states into the Union, particularly in light of the fact that 1862 had been another dismal year for northern generals on the battlefield.

If Lincoln agonized over several candidates before choosing Davis, Stephen J. Field, who was chief justice of the California Supreme Court, seemed the obvious choice for the tenth seat. "A forty-niner, not a miner" (Kens 1997, 11), Field had given up a law partnership in New York with brother David Dudley to seek further fortune on the West Coast. (Another brother, Cyrus W., bought and sold railroads and would later be responsible for laying the trans-Atlantic cable.) Stephen Field was a Democrat, but was loyal to the Union; that was an important consideration in a divided nation and in a state where Democrats from southern states comprised a vocal minority. When the transcontinental telegraph line began operation in October 1861, one of its first messages was from Chief Justice Field to President Lincoln expressing the loyalty of Californians to the Union. Moreover, Field enjoyed near unanimous endorsement from those who mattered in California politics, including its congressional delegation and governor (and aspiring railroad baron), Leland Stanford. Besides, he would bring valuable expertise to Washington. As much as anyone, Field understood the complex land title cases so prevalent in the state (Swisher 1935, 116).

Ironically, on February 23, Lincoln nominated Field to be U.S. circuit judge, a position Field declined because he considered it inferior to state chief justice. After the tenth seat materialized, Lincoln sent Field's name to the Senate again on March 6. An easy confirmation followed on March 10. Field scheduled his investiture for May 20, his father's birthday.

William Strong and Joseph P. Bradley

After Lincoln named Salmon Chase to succeed Chief Justice Taney in 1864, there were no additions to the Supreme Court until 1870. As noted, upon Justice Catron's death in 1865, Congress reduced the size of the bench to deny appointments to President Johnson, and the number of sitting justices dropped to eight when Justice Wayne died in 1867. Within barely a month of the end of Johnson's term in 1869, Congress restored the Court's roster to nine (where it has remained ever since). At the same time it authorized separate circuit judgeships for the nine circuits. Newly sworn-in President Ulysses Grant was thus handed a Supreme Court vacancy to fill. The retirement of mentally debilitated Justice Robert C. Grier soon gave him a second.

On December 14, Grant picked his capable attorney general, Ebenezer Hoar of Massachusetts, for the "new" (or restored) seat. The nomination played well in the press but not in the Senate. Carpetbag Republican senators from southern states wanted a southerner added to the bench. Hoar's support of civil service reform alienated those wedded to the spoils system, and he had opposed the impeachment of former President Johnson. That combination of positions cost him support among key members of his party. By the end of the month it was clear the nomination was in trouble.

Meanwhile, Justice Grier sent his resignation to Grant, to become effective on February 1, 1870. In *Hepburn v. Griswold* (the first round in the legal tender litigation the Court had decided but would not announce until February 7), Grier had voted on opposite sides at the same conference on the same question. A committee of the brethren then prevailed upon him to step down, a move made easier because of half-pay provisions in a new retirement law. With Grier on the way out, a majority of the House and Senate signed a petition urging Grant to name former Secretary of War Edwin Stanton, like Grier a Pennsylvanian.

Grant saw a deal in the making. If he bowed to congressional pressure and nominated Stanton, the Senate would surely feel obliged to approve Hoar. So Grant forwarded Stanton's name to the Senate on December 20, where he was quickly confirmed 46–11. Four days later, however, Stanton died, leading *The Nation* to criticize the president for acting so hastily. "[T]he immediate result . . . was the curious spectacle of a Judge dead and buried in state while his predecessor sits on the Bench and goes to the funeral" (Warren 1926, II, 508). On February 3, the Senate rejected Hoar 24–33. Poor Grant still had two nominations to make. As Chief Justice Chase was reading his opinion in *Hepburn v. Griswold*, President Grant announced the nominations of Pennsylvania jurist William Strong for Grier's seat and New Jersey attorney Joseph P. Bradley for the other.

Strong's confirmation came easily on February 18. Bradley's nomination, however, ran into rough water. Although Democrats applauded Bradley, radical Republicans thought him too conservative, and southern Republicans remained disgruntled. Moreover, two of Bradley's most important clients were the Camden and Amboy Railroad and the Delaware and Raritan Canal Company, which functioned together as the "Joint Companies." This connection presented special obstacles to confirmation because of exclusive transportation privileges the companies had acquired and Bradley, as counsel, had defended. "No man whose business is buying members of legislatures and paying cash for them is fit for the Supreme Bench," a New Jersey state senator wrote to Senator Charles Sumner (Friedman 1969, 1187). Additionally, the Pennsylvania Railroad and Simon Cameron, its chief defender in the Senate, had long resented the Camden and Amboy because of its role in denying the Pennsylvania Railroad a right of way in New Jersey. There was even a serious attempt in the Senate, later tabled by the House, to require nominees to be residents of the circuits they would serve, a stipulation that would have disqualified Bradley.

That Bradley was nominated and then confirmed with only nine negative votes on March 21 was doubtless due to an impressive array of corporate and political sponsors who helped the nominee navigate the shoals. Bradley's friend George Harding, a prominent Philadelphia lawyer, rounded up an impressive team to advance Bradley's claim on a Supreme Court seat. The list included former senator Frederick Frelinghuysen of New Jersey, Grant's Secretary of State Hamilton Fish (formerly on the board of the Joint Companies), John Stockton (who succeeded Frelinghuysen in the Senate and who had also been counsel to the Joint Companies), and Navy Secretary George Robeson.

The timing gave rise to claims that Grant had packed the bench, especially after Strong and Bradley later joined the three *Hepburn* dissenters in reversing the February 7th decision (*Legal Tender Cases*, 1871). These claims are most probably unfounded. Both men had been under consideration for some time. On Hoar's recommendation, Grant initially had preferred Strong over Stanton, and Grier had urged Grant months before to select Bradley when he retired. Secondly, even if Grant had advance knowledge of what the decision would be, nearly any Republican nominated to the Court would have supported the constitutionality of the acts. Indeed, of more than sixty state judges who had ruled in legal tender cases, every Democrat thought the laws unconstitutional, while virtually every Republican judge (including Strong) took the opposite side (Fairman 1941, 977). Given the administration's belief that the laws should be sustained, surely Strong and Bradley would not have been nominated had they been known as *opponents* of the laws, but that is a far different thing than saying they were nominated *because* they were dependable votes to sustain the legislation.

Ward Hunt

Grant's fourth successful nomination for his third Supreme Court vacancy was expeditiously handled and occasioned little difficulty. By mid-1872 speculation abounded that failing health would force Justice Samuel Nelson, a Democrat from New York, to retire. New York's Senator Roscoe Conkling, a close friend and policy confidant to the president, suggested Ward Hunt for the seat. A judge on that state's court of appeals, Hunt was a firm Republican, having had a hand in the party's creation in 1856. Nelson, however, held off retirement until after the November election, on the chance Grant might be defeated. On November 28 a reelected Grant learned of Nelson's resignation. There were the usual pleas that a southern Republican be appointed, but, with the backing of New York's business leaders and its entire congressional delegation, the president acceded to Conkling's wishes and forwarded Hunt's name to the Senate on December 3. A 53–11 confirmation vote followed on December 11.

Morrison R. Waite

Replacing Nelson took barely two weeks. In contrast, replacing Chief Justice Chase consumed eight months. Waite's nomination on January 19, 1874, and confirmation on January 21, marked the end of an appointment charade and parade. "We had 'a time' over the Chief Justiceship," Secretary of State Fish exclaimed on the day of the nomination. "It has been a hard parturition" (Magrath 1963, 19).

By most accounts, the Ohio lawyer who succeeded Chase was Grant's seventh choice for the post (explaining Waite's newly acquired nickname: "His Accidency"

[Abraham 1992, 131]). Grant had apparently never met Waite; indeed, Waite was not widely known outside Ohio and had never argued a case before the U.S. Supreme Court. He had "every requisite except repute," insisted Senator Hannibal Hamlin on January 18 in a last-ditch effort to forestall his nomination (Conkling 1889, 463). But Waite's name was surely familiar to Grant. Friends had recommended him for the chief justiceship months before. Further, he had been one of three U.S. counsel at the international arbitration over the *Alabama* claims that resulted in an award of $15.5 million for the United States, one of the few achievements of Grant's third-rate and scandal-ridden presidency. (The *Alabama* and the *Florida* were Confederate warships built in Great Britain that preyed on Union ships. The tribunal at Geneva that made the award against Great Britain had been created by the Treaty of Washington of 1871, which Hamilton Fish negotiated.)

Grant was perhaps distracted from the start by the very vocal aspirations of some sitting justices for Chase's job. Indeed, every Republican member of the Court except Davis and Hunt were active candidates. Strong had an agent working for him. Miller characterized Swayne as having "artfully beslobbered the President," while Miller himself engaged in the tactics of inundation that had worked with Lincoln (Fairman 1939, 265). Robeson pressed Bradley's name. In the interest of maintaining harmony on the bench, Grant prudently ignored all such entreaties.

Six months into the process, the president tendered an offer to his friend Senator Conkling, who dispensed federal patronage in New York. Conkling immediately declined. Grant then turned to his attorney general, George H. Williams. But the Senate, leaders of the bar, the press, and much of the public balked at this nomination because Williams seemed marginally qualified at best. After the nominee asked that his name be withdrawn from consideration, Grant decided on seventy-four-year-old Caleb Cushing, an outstanding lawyer and statesman from Massachusetts. Yet Cushing, whom nearly everyone but Grant considered too old for the job, had vacillated too often in his long career (from Whig through Tyler Whig, Democrat, Johnson Constitutionalist, and finally to Republican) and so had made more than the usual number of political enemies. Then the Washington *Chronicle*, a paper that belonged to Justice Miller's son-in-law, made public a letter Cushing had written to Confederate president Jefferson Davis in 1861 recommending a government clerk. It had turned up in a trunk of Confederate documents. Shortly before such politics compelled Grant to withdraw Cushing's name, *The Nation* spoke for liberal Republicans in observing that the president had "at last entered the small circle of eminent lawyers and then with great care has chosen the worst man in it" (Magrath 1963, 12). In quick succession, Grant tendered the position (but no formal nomination) to three others: Senator Timothy Howe of Wisconsin, Senator Oliver Morton of Indiana, and Fish, his secretary of state. Only then did the president look to the safe, sober, and confirmable attorney from Toledo.

There was relief, if not praise, for choice number seven. "The President has, with remarkable skill, avoided choosing any first-rate man," observed *The Nation.* "Mr. Waite stands in the front rank of second-rate lawyers. . . . [C]onsidering what the President might have done, and tried to do, we ought to be very thankful. . . ." Diarist and former Navy Secretary Gideon Welles was more blunt. "It is a wonder," he wrote his son, "that Grant did not pick up some old acquaintance, who was a stage driver or bartender for the place. We may be thankful that he has done so well" (Stephenson 1973, 904).

John Marshall Harlan

The first change in the composition of the Waite Court occurred with Justice Davis's election to the U.S. Senate in January 1877 and resignation from the bench on March 4. Rutherford B. Hayes of Ohio thus had a Supreme Court vacancy dropped on his doorstep on the day of his inauguration. Several contenders quickly emerged, including Judge Drummond of Illinois (again), U.S. Circuit Judge William B. Woods, and Justice Miller's brother-in-law William P. Ballinger, a Galveston, Texas, lawyer. But from the start, John Harlan of Kentucky had the inside track.

This was true for at least two reasons. First, Harlan, who was both famous and notorious and whose career generously revealed that he would rather be right than consistent, had been law partner of Benjamin Bristow, the first U.S. solicitor general and Grant's last treasury secretary. Bristow's fight against corruption within his own department made him a contender for the 1876 Republican presidential nomination, and Harlan headed the Kentucky delegation at the convention. Republican regulars and antireform elements supported New York's James Blaine. When it became apparent Bristow would lose, Harlan shifted Kentucky's votes to Hayes at a critical moment, assuring Hayes the nomination. Hayes was in Harlan's debt, although Bristow and Harlan soon had a permanent falling-out.

Second, as president in the wake of the disputed elections of 1876, Hayes named Harlan to a commission to determine the legitimate government in Louisiana. Two governors claimed lawful dominion: the carpetbag Republican administration of Stephen Packard and the Democratic administration of Confederate veteran and amputee Francis Nicholls. Federal troops shored up the former, white voters the latter. Partly on Harlan's recommendation, Hayes abandoned Packard, and withdrew the army. Harlan thus enabled Hayes to defuse a crisis in the first months of his presidency.

When Hayes sent Harlan's name to the Senate on October 16, the reasons for Harlan's nomination gave rise to the opposition against it. Republican regulars, led by Senator Conkling, were terrified by the prospects of reform and so objected to Harlan's prior efforts on behalf of Bristow's campaign. More liberal Republicans questioned the sincerity of Harlan's Republicanism. He had freed his slaves only on the eve of the Civil War and had opposed the Emancipation Proclamation and the Thirteenth Amendment before his conversion to the party. They also blamed him for the demise of the Packard regime in Louisiana. For the same reasons, Democratic senators liked him. Yet weighing favorably with Republicans was Harlan's skillful command of a Kentucky regiment that saw service in Tennessee and Alabama during the war.

When the Senate judiciary committee considered his nomination—and in those days the committee neither held hearings nor called the nominee to testify—it split evenly, but the nomination went forward mysteriously with a favorable recommendation. On November 29 the Senate handily approved Harlan on a voice vote (Yarbrough 1995, 86–114).

William B. Woods

The sixteen months between December 1880 and April 1882 witnessed a significant change in the Supreme Court's membership as the middle Waite Court became the last Waite Court. Six nominations by three presidents yielded four new justices.

Major goals of Rutherford Hayes's presidency were healing the sectional wounds among whites in the North and South and uniting the country. Therefore, in making nominations to the Supreme Court, it is not surprising that he favored moderates who had wide geographical appeal. Harlan fit that mold. So did U.S. Circuit Judge William B. Woods of Georgia, whom Hayes swiftly selected when Justice Strong retired on December 14, 1880.

Strong's premature departure was a surprise, but it was purposeful. With three colleagues suffering from various disabilities, Strong wanted to make a statement, leaving while he was still in good mental and physical health.

Justice Bradley, who had been allotted the large Fifth Circuit that stretched from Georgia to Texas, made it known that he wanted the compact and more accessible Third Circuit (Delaware, New Jersey, and Pennsylvania) that had been Strong's. Hayes in turn wanted to make the first nomination from a southern state since John Campbell's in 1853, so an open Fifth Circuit fit into his plans. It would go to a Republican of course, but a Republican who enjoyed the confidence of southern Democrats. Woods was an obvious choice and the only person seriously considered. Ohio-reared and a brigadier general in Sherman's army, he had been judge for the Fifth Circuit since 1869. By hard work and evenhandedness he had avoided being tagged as carpetbagger or interloper. With cross-regional support, this strong Union-Democrat-turned-Republican raised few concerns in the Senate, where he was confirmed 39–8 on December 21.

Stanley Matthews

President Hayes's choice of fellow Ohioan Stanley Matthews to fill the seat vacated by Justice Swayne on January 24, 1881, was both surprising and thoroughly understandable. The fact that he eventually secured a seat on the Court was nothing short of a miracle. Not only did Matthews reach the Court by way of a second-try, cliff-hanging confirmation vote, but his nomination marked the first time organized interests attempted to block a Supreme Court appointment (Maltese 1995, 36).

With barely a month remaining in his term, most thought Hayes would leave selection of Swayne's replacement to his successor, fellow Republican and president-elect James Garfield. But Hayes nominated Matthews immediately. The two had been friends in college, had served in the same regiment during the Civil War, and were related by marriage. Like Hayes, Matthews had practiced law in Cincinnati, and had campaigned for Hayes in 1876. Indeed, Hayes's presidency was partly due to Matthews's labors on his behalf as one of the Republican counsel to the congressionally authorized commission to resolve the disputed presidential election. Democrat Tilden won the popular vote, but the electoral vote remained in doubt. By convincing the commission not to inquire into the conduct of the balloting in states with contested electoral votes, the certified results that favored Hayes presumably would not be questioned. But they were questioned when Democrats, who thought the election had been stolen, stalled the electoral count. Matthews invited dissident Democrats to his Washington hotel room, and within days of the scheduled inauguration, fashioned the Compromise of 1877: in exchange for Democratic acquiescence in Hayes's election, the new president would order the withdrawal of the last of federal troops from southern states. Hayes owed Matthews a lot.

Both Hayes and Matthews were amazed at the formidable opposition that materialized almost overnight to the nomination. The problem was not Matthews's connections with Hayes or to the disputed election, but the nominee's identity with corporate power, especially the railroads. Not only had he long been a railway lawyer and served as president of the National Railway Convention, but in his three years in the U.S. Senate he had been on a retainer from railroad magnate Jay Gould. The Grange, an agricultural organization that was especially strong in the Midwest, opposed Matthews over the railroads' economic hold on farmers. As will be discussed in Chapter 3, the Court in *Munn v. Illinois* (1877) had upheld Granger laws from several states that fixed rates charged by railroads and grain warehouses. Matthews and others like him would surely put that decision in jeopardy, members of the Grange thought. More narrowly decided were the *Sinking Fund Cases* (1879), which required the Pacific railroads to pay interest on the $64 million in bonds the federal government had floated to finance construction of the transcontinental lines. As senator, Matthews had opposed the Thurman Act, challenged in the *Sinking Fund Cases.* "Shall Stanley Matthews," asked a Kentucky newspaper, "who sat in the Senate as the attorney for the Pacific railroads, wear the silk gown as their attorney on the bench of the Supreme Court?" (Maltese 1995, 41).

Matthews's fate was in the hands of the Senate judiciary committee, chaired by Democrat Allen Thurmond of Ohio. Despite a last-minute lobbying campaign by Hayes, the committee refused to report favorably on the nomination, and it died as the session ended.

At this point, there was little sign that Matthews had a future on the Supreme Court. President-elect Garfield had thus far offered no support to Matthews. Conventional wisdom suggested the new president would look elsewhere to fill Swayne's seat. The improbable happened on March 14, however, when the new president renominated Matthews. The reasons are not completely clear, although Matthews's resuscitation may have had something to do with $300,000 that Gould and another entrepreneur apparently contributed to Garfield's campaign (Magrath 1963, 246, n. 42).

Opposition formed again, although this time the terrain was altered. Thurman was no longer in the Senate and the Senate was evenly split between Democrats and Republicans. On May 9, the judiciary committee sent the nomination to the floor with a negative recommendation. However, on May 12 the full Senate approved Matthews, 24–23. "I could not understand how any one could vote against me," a chastened Matthews confided to Hayes (Maltese 1995, 43). Ironically, a Republican (George Edmunds of Vermont) led the fight against the nominee. Even more ironically, as time would show, Mississippi Democrat L. Q. C. Lamar marshaled votes for Matthews. Only nine Republicans voted for him. Among the thirteen opposed was Conkling who was locked in a patronage dispute with Garfield.

Horace Gray

Justice Clifford's mental and physical decline had been noticeable for several years, but he tenaciously held on through the Hayes administration. He had chaired the electoral commission that handed the election to Hayes, although Clifford cast his votes for Tilden. He thereafter had nothing to do with Hayes and would not recognize him as president. By 1880 Clifford was near collapse. As Justice Miller reported, "Judge Clifford reached Washington in the 8th of October. . . . I saw him within three hours after his arrival, and he did not know me or any thing, and though his tongue framed words there was no sense in them" (Atkinson 1999, 60).

By the spring of 1881, assuming Clifford's retirement was imminent, President Garfield spoke to Massachusetts senator George Hoar about the scholarly and reserved Horace Gray, who, then chief justice, had been a member of the Supreme Judicial Court of Massachusetts since 1864. (Gray was also to be Stanley Matthews's son-in-law.) Hoar forwarded to Gray the president's request for copies of some of his judicial opinions. Although Gray was eager to accept an appointment to the federal high court, he declined Garfield's request, fearing others might construe it as inappropriate eagerness on his part. There matters stood when Charles Giteau, a disappointed and probably deranged office seeker, shot the president on July 2. Clifford died on July 25. After Chester A. Arthur became president upon Garfield's death on September 19, Hoar approached Arthur on Gray's behalf about the open seat. There seems to have been no other serious candidate. Gray was preeminently qualified, had the added advantage of living in Clifford's First Circuit, and enjoyed broad support in the bar and among business leaders. Confirmation came easily on December 20, 1881, just a day after Arthur formally submitted the nomination. Gray allowed the president to look statesmanlike and helped him somewhat downplay his less savory patronage-rich past as customs collector for the port of New York and close ties with Conkling.

Samuel Blatchford

Justice Hunt's health posed a serious problem for the Waite Court. During 1877 he was absent from many sessions because of gout. Then on December 23, 1878, he suffered a stroke and took part in no decisions thereafter. Two factors probably delayed his resignation until January 27, 1882. Recall that Hunt owed his appointment to Senator Conkling. By 1879 Conkling and President Hayes had had a falling-out over patronage, and Hunt was disinclined to leave his successor in Hayes's hands. But money, or rather its absence, was the more compelling factor; Hunt had not served long enough to qualify for a pension. To assist both Hunt and the Court, former justice, now Senator, David Davis pushed through special legislation extending benefits to the ailing justice, provided he leave the bench within thirty days.

Reverting to his past links with the spoils system, the president picked Conkling for this Second Circuit seat. Although the Senate confirmed Conkling 39–12, the appointment played badly in the press. The Gray nomination drew "universal approval," declared *Harper's Weekly*, but Conkling's had been received "with universal amazement." "Legal learning, he has not," noted *The Nation* (Warren 1926, II, 624). The comment was inaccurate; still, Conkling's political career did not inspire confidence that he was suited for the Supreme Court. Having earlier turned down Grant's offer of the chief justiceship, Conkling may have done himself, the bench, and the country a favor by declining appointment again.

Arthur then tendered the seat to Senator Edmunds who had led the campaign against Matthews. When Edmunds declined, the president in mid-March 1882 reverted to statesman and selected Circuit Judge Samuel Blatchford, a Republican who was highly qualified, well regarded, and politically well connected in the Empire State. Best of all he aroused little controversy. With confirmation by voice vote on March 27, a tradition continued: since 1806 New York had been represented on the Supreme Court.

L. Q. C. Lamar

With Grover Cleveland's election in 1884, Democrats occupied the White House for the first time in a quarter century. A social, economic, and good government conservative, the new president would presumably expect those values in a Supreme Court nominee. A vacancy would also allow appointment of the first Democrat since 1863 and might occasion restoration of true sectional balance on the bench.

That opportunity did not arise until near the end of Cleveland's term, when Justice Woods died in May 1887. From the start Cleveland seemed disposed to nominate his capable interior secretary, Lucius Quintus Cincinnatus Lamar of Mississippi. Although he lacked judicial experience, Lamar was among the most politically experienced and talented post–Civil War appointees. He had practiced law in both Georgia and Mississippi and had held a professorship at the University of Mississippi. As a member of the House and Senate, he was known as "The Great Pacificator" due to untiring efforts to heal sectional wounds. But Lamar had also drafted the Mississippi Ordinance of Secession, had been special envoy of the Confederacy to Russia, and was a colonel and judge advocate with Lee at Appomattox in 1865. Thus, his appointment could be the "last step" toward national reconciliation and reunion (Meador 1986, 27), or it could reopen old war wounds.

Once word spread in Washington in early fall that the president would probably pick Lamar, opposition to the ex-Confederate solidified among Senate Republicans, who held a two-vote majority over Democrats. In mid-January 1888 the Judiciary Committee reported negatively on two grounds: Lamar lacked sufficient legal experience, and he was too old (Paul 1969, 1443–1444). The first was unfounded. The background of many capable and warmly received nominees had also been more political than legal. As for the second, Lamar at sixty-two was the same age as Hunt and Blatchford at the start of their tenures. (Charles Evans Hughes was sixty-eight when he was named chief justice in 1941, an age not equaled by any other nominee to date.) Clearly Cleveland was not going for the long ball, and from the Republican perspective, that should have been a plus. (As it happened, Republican Benjamin Harrison named Lamar's successor in early 1893.) But Republicans were still trying to squeeze partisan advantage by waving the "bloody shirt" one more time. Had they succeeding in blocking the nomination, the message would have been clear. Confederate veterans were to be forever disqualified from the Supreme Court. At the last moment, however, a handful of western Republicans broke ranks and chose honor over party, thus sealing the confirmation 32–28 on January 16. Otherwise the vote was along party lines, with no Republican north of the border states voting to confirm.

A Changing America

An earlier section outlined the major constitutional changes that occurred in the wake of the Civil War. During Waite's years as chief justice, the United States underwent major social, demographic, and economic changes as well that affected the work of the Supreme Court. Furthermore, national identity had been transformed. For the first time a chief justice assumed his post under circumstances in which the continued existence of the Union was not seriously discussed. Until 1865, the survival of the United States overshadowed nearly every political issue and had been uppermost in the minds of members of Congress, presidents, and Supreme Court justices. Of course, no one knew with certainty how the balance of power between national and state governments would evolve in the decades after 1865, but everyone acknowledged that there would be one, and only one, United States: "an indestructible Union, composed of indestructible states," as Chief Justice Chase had said.

The population of the United States more than doubled between 1850 and 1880, rising from 23 million in 1850, to 31 million in 1860, to 39 million in 1870, to 50 million in 1880. The Civil War recast the country's economic base by energizing the industrial revolution already underway. The Union army counted 1 million men under arms, and the Union navy was briefly second only to Great Britain's. A force of such unprecedented size had to be equipped and supplied. By war's end, moreover, the smaller transportation and manufacturing infrastructure in the southern states had been largely destroyed or rendered unusable. That would have to be rebuilt. Thus, manufacturing establishments, numbering 123,000 in 1850 and 140,000 in 1860, jumped to 252,000 in 1870 and to 355,000 in 1880. Accordingly, the percentage of Americans living in cities increased as well, from 15 percent in 1850 and 20 percent in 1860, to 25 percent in 1870 and 28 percent in 1880. The United States was still a nation of farms and small towns but was also fast becoming a nation of factories and cities, too. Steam power in factories and on the rails brought Americans together in the late nineteenth century just as the internal combustion engine would disperse them in the twentieth century.

Increased industrialization and the emergence of a truly national economy were greatly facilitated by expansion of railroads, especially by completion of the first transcontinental route in 1869, when the Central Pacific, building from the west, joined in the Utah Territory with the Union Pacific, building from the east. (There would be five transcontinental lines by century's end.) Railroad mileage exploded after 1850, as Table 1.5 demonstrates. Because economic growth and even community survival came to depend on easy access to a rail line, cities, counties, and states, as well as the federal government, made stock purchases and offered loans, monopolies, tax exemptions, liberal charter provisions, and land grants—all as inducements for rail construction. Railroad development in turn required the development of whole new industries to provide equipment and supplies, just as coal's displacement of wood as the primary locomotive fuel in the 1850s heightened demand for more mines and miners.

Yet more was happening than an increase in the volume of goods produced and an expanded capacity to ship them more quickly and efficiently than ever before. Technology was revolutionizing the way goods were produced and how Americans lived their lives. This phenomenon was reflected in the number of patents issued annually by the U.S. Patent Office for new inventions: 2200 such patents issued in 1850, 4400 in 1860, 12,000 in 1870, and 13,000 in 1880. Indeed, just four days before his death on March 23, 1888, Waite announced the Court's 4–3 decision in the *Telephone Cases*, which involved eight challenges in circuit courts to Alexander Graham Bell's 1876 patent for the telephone. Waite's opinion sustaining the patent and

Table 1.5 Railroad Mileage in the United States, 1850–1888

Year	*Number of Rail Miles*
1850	9,000
1860	31,000
1870	53,000
1874	72,000
1880	116,000
1888	149,000

Bradley's much shorter dissent consumed more than 500 pages in the *U.S. Reports*. Together these various statistics pointed to a level of commercial activity (and legislation to cope with problems ensuing in its wake) that was bound to become a fruitful source of litigation for the federal courts. Moreover, economic booms and busts furnished additional grist for the judicial mill.

Expanding Jurisdiction, Exploding Docket

Today, as in Waite's time, almost all cases the Supreme Court decides involve its appellate jurisdiction, meaning that the cases come to the Supreme Court from state courts and the lower federal courts. (A very small class of cases each year, comprised of suits between states, involve the Court's original jurisdiction, meaning that they are heard for the first time at the High Court level.) Under section 25 of the Judiciary Act of 1789, cases from a state's highest court qualified for Supreme Court review if: (1) the case involved a "federal question" (i.e., the case implicated the U.S. Constitution, a federal statute, or a treaty of the United States) and (2) the state court had ruled adversely to the federal claim. (In 1914, Congress extended the second qualification to include instances when the state court had upheld the federal claim.) But here some of the similarities between the judiciary of Waite's era and our own largely come to an end.

Prior to 1891, the lower federal judiciary consisted of district and circuit courts. Curiously, however, with the exceptions of circuit judges authorized during a brief period in 1802 and circuit judges later designated for California and Oregon after 1855, Congress provided no circuit judges for the nation until nine were authorized in 1869. Instead, circuit courts were staffed by a district court judge and a Supreme Court justice assigned to that circuit. Congress would not totally relieve the justices of such circuit-riding duties until 1891, when the modern system of courts of appeals with their own judges began to take shape. Yet, even after circuit judges were added in 1869, the crush of cases meant that much circuit court work was still handled by district judges.

Until the late 1860s the business of the lower federal courts consisted almost entirely of admiralty and state-law cases, the latter qualifying for a federal forum because of the parties' diversity of citizenship. With these was a much smaller number of cases involving violations of federal criminal laws. Ordinarily no appeal went to the Supreme Court in federal criminal cases unless there was a certification of division between the judges in the circuit court. Not until 1889 did Congress grant the Court jurisdiction to hear appeals even in federal capital cases. Criminal cases from state courts, a staple of the modern Court's docket, would not become commonplace until the 1960s as the Court completed the process of construing the Fourteenth Amendment to apply most of the protections of the Bill of Rights to the states.

The business of the circuit courts, and hence that of the Supreme Court, began to change markedly after the Civil War. The removal acts Congress passed meant that more cases involving matters of state, not federal law, could be heard in federal court, and they were. Additionally, just as losing litigants in section 25 cases from state courts had an appeal by right to the Supreme Court, diversity cases could be appealed by right to the Supreme Court if the amount at issue met a certain threshold. An abundance of appeals by right meant that the Supreme Court had no control over its docket. If a case fell into the Court's jurisdiction, the Court was obliged to decide it. Thus, the inflow of Supreme Court business was dictated by the volume of cases in the lower federal courts and, to a much lesser extent, the number of federal question cases in state courts. (The Court's ability today to select almost all the cases it decides originated on a small scale in 1891 and was greatly enlarged in 1925.) Moreover, as of 1875, substantial inequalities in threshold amounts persisted for all categories of federal cases, depending on the court that heard the complaint: $5,000 from the circuit courts; $3,000 in cases appealed from the Court of Claims (a special court created in 1855 to hear monetary suits against the federal government), $2,500 from the Supreme Court of the District of Columbia, $2,000 from the Supreme Court of the Washington Territory, and $1,000 from all other territorial supreme courts.

As the Chase Court had done occasionally, the Waite Court initially avoided decisions wherever possible that expanded even further their jurisdiction (and hence the volume of cases). For example, in 1867 Congress amended section 25 and omitted the clause confining Supreme Court review to state court rejection of the federal claim. Did the omission mean that, where a federal question was present, the justices were now to look into all errors in the record, state or federal? There was strong evidence that was exactly what Congress meant. In *Murdock v. City of Memphis* (1875), the Court ruled 5 to 3, with Waite not participating, that no such change had been intended. The majority was openly concerned about the alarming consequences of a contrary holding. There would be "no conceivable case so insignificant

Table 1.6 Number of Cases Pending in the U.S. Supreme Court, 1850–1890

Term	*Cases Pending*
1850	253
1860	310
1870	636
1880	1,212
1884	1,315
1886	1,396
1888	1,563
1890	1,800

in amount or unimportant in principle," fumed Justice Miller, "that a perverse and obstinate man may not bring it to this Court by the aid of a sagacious lawyer raising a Federal question in the record—a point which he may be wholly unable to support by the facts, or which he may well know will be decided against him, the moment it is stated." Two months later in the Judiciary (or Removal) Act of 1875, however, Congress all but undid *Murdock.* Under this legislation, the jurisdiction of the circuit courts was expanded to include for the first time all suits presenting federal questions. Heretofore, such matters would have been almost the exclusive province of state courts, subject only to section 25 review. The existing diversity jurisdiction was retained. Because Supreme Court review of circuit court decisions involved all legal questions, state or federal, that had been decided upon, Congress effectively thrust onto the Court much of what the justices had tried to dodge in *Murdock.* Yet the legislation contained no provisions to assist the Court in coping with the torrent of litigation that followed.

This expanded jurisdiction therefore stretched judicial resources, and the economic transformation underway only compounded the problem. The magnitude and complexity of the changes at work were reflected by the expanding girth of Judge John F. Dillon's monograph, *Removal of Causes from State Courts to Federal Courts.* The first edition appeared in 1877 with 105 pages; the third edition four years later, with 168 pages (Warren 1926, II, 685, n. 1). In 1873, there were 29,013 cases pending in the lower federal courts. By 1880, the figure had grown to 38,045. In 1890, two years after Waite's death, it was 54,194 (Frankfurter and Landis 1928, 60). What had been a thoroughly manageable caseload for the Supreme Court as late as 1860 got completely out of hand, as Table 1.6 illustrates. These data take on added significance when one remembers that the number of opinions issued by the Supreme Court grew by no more than 50 percent, fluctuating during Chief Justice Waite's thirteen complete terms from a low of 205 to a high of 311 (Table 1.7). The increase in output represented a Herculean effort, but it could not hide the fact that the Supreme Court's docket, like those of the circuit courts, became a docket in arrears.

The Business of the Waite Court

The most significant decisions of the Waite Court will be examined in Chapter 3. Some of those had a far-reaching impact. But there were more than 3,000 other decisions that occupied the justices' time and tended to define the day-to-day work of the bench. Appreciation of the Waite Court requires some awareness of these cases, most of which have long since dropped completely from sight.

In light of preceding sections, it is clear that cases the Waite Court decided mirrored cases heard throughout the United States, at least in federal courts. Keep in mind that the justices had no authority to reject a case even when it was obvious that the court below had decided it correctly. Neither could they decline the case if they thought it trivial, or if they preferred to devote their energies to novel legal issues or conflicts between lower courts on important questions of federal law. The absence of the power of discretionary review, a hallmark of the contemporary Supreme Court, was telling. This partly explains why the docket of the Supreme Court in, say, 2003 vividly contrasts with any docket of the Waite Court. Today, nearly all cases the Supreme Court decides involve public law: disputes concerning the interpretation and application of the U.S. Constitution, acts of Congress, and rules promulgated by federal administrative agencies.

In Waite's day, many cases involved private law matters. As shown in Figure 1.1, federal constitutional cases made up only a small part of each term's work. Constitutional cases never accounted for more than about 12 percent of a term's business, and more often than not hovered closer to 5 percent. Although there were important exceptions that will be examined in Chapter 3, the bulk of constitutional cases in Waite's day involved either allegations that a state or municipality had impaired the obligation of a contract in violation of Article I, section 10, or had impermissibly restrained commerce among the states in violation of Article I, section 8.

The relatively small number of constitutional cases does not mean that most cases were inconsequential. Many were highly significant, but often only for the particular litigants involved, or for a small number of similarly situated persons. Such fact-bound cases—and there were hundreds of them—had little value as precedents and did little in clarifying the law. Moreover, they were not likely to be written about in major newspapers or to excite people beyond the particular community that might be affected. Most would surely never be debated in Congress or become entangled in electoral campaigns.

Table 1.7 depicts the variety of business that came through the Waite Court's door. Except perhaps for residual Civil War claims that declined with time, a decrease

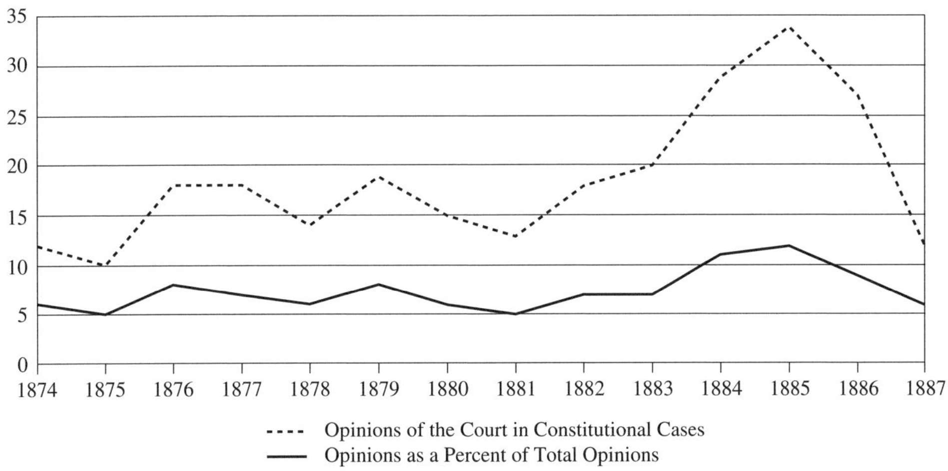

Figure 1.1 Opinions of the Court in Constitutional Cases by Term

in admiralty and maritime cases resulting from jurisdictional changes, and an increase in land and mining claims caused by western migration, the data show no pronounced trend. Jurisdictional and commercial law cases consistently outnumbered those in other categories. The Court's business reflected courtroom fights across the United States. Thus the Court was far more often a supreme court of errors, sitting mainly to correct mistakes in the courts below. In contrast to today's Court, the Waite Court was more supervisor than innovator, more engaged in dispute resolution for individual parties than in policymaking for the nation, more focused on the words of lower court judges than on the words of the Constitution.

A glance at some of this ordinary, run-of-the-mill, but interesting, litigation illustrates the variety of questions that commanded the Supreme Court's time and the substance of a justice's workday between 1874 and 1888. Each case is instructive in its own way.

A year after Waite became chief justice, *United States v. Home Insurance Company* (1875) presented one of a series of residual Civil War issues the Court would continue to face for more than a decade. Early in the conflict, the Georgia legislature issued a corporate charter to Home Insurance Company. After the collapse of the Confederacy, the company sued the United States in the Court of Claims under the Captured and Abandoned Property Act to recover the proceeds of the sale of cotton seized by federal troops at Savannah in late 1864. Relying on Lincoln's theory of secession and the Union, the government had insisted unsuccessfully in Claims Court that the company had no legal existence and so could not file suit. Secession was illegal and therefore unrecognized; thus was born the designation "Civil War," preferred by northerners, over "War Between the States," preferred by southerners. Accord-

Table 1.7 Opinions of the Court Issued during the Chief Justiceship of Morrison R. Waite, 1874–1888

Terms	*1874*	*1875*	*1876*	*1877*	*1878*	*1879*	*1880*	*1881*	*1882*	*1883*	*1884*	*1885*	*1886*	*1887***	*Totals*
Issues*															
AD	20	11	8	10	4	4	8	8	8	3	4	4	8	2	105
BK	9	8	3	5	4	1	6	9	7	9	6	7	8	1	83
CL	0	5	4	3	3	0	0	1	5	6	12	11	10	5	65
CO	81	75	97	117	61	90	62	90	76	91	82	71	105	52	1150
CW	15	10	0	11	10	5	3	2	6	4	4	3	4	2	79
EF	4	4	12	3	3	8	1	5	6	12	8	2	5	6	79
GC	5	7	1	5	10	5	5	4	6	6	8	7	8	12	89
IN	1	3	1	1	0	2	1	0	1	3	1	4	4	0	22
JR	26	40	50	31	41	53	70	59	66	66	52	79	68	49	750
LD	14	12	12	19	24	13	9	7	12	12	26	17	16	13	205
MB	2	11	9	11	22	14	28	13	17	19	12	11	14	5	188
OT	2	3	6	3	3	4	5	1	3	4	2	0	1	2	39
PP	6	4	14	13	7	11	8	9	12	9	19	24	18	9	161
PT	11	7	17	11	7	10	13	24	16	21	24	14	22	19	215
RD	0	2	0	1	0	3	1	0	3	2	2	1	0	0	15
TR	0	1	0	0	0	1	0	0	0	1	2	0	3	3	11
TX	9	11	5	26	19	18	14	10	20	11	10	23	17	15	209
Total opinions:	205	214	239	270	218	242	234	242	264	279	274	278	311	195	3465

Note: Some opinions disposed of more than one case.

*Many cases involved more than one issue; the table highlights the principal issue resolved by the Court. Data exclude memorandum cases and those affirmed by an equally divided bench.

**Through March 23, 1888, the date of Waite's death.

KEY

AD: admiralty and maritime

BL: bankruptcy

CL: civil liberties, including habeas corpus, Bill of Rights questions, and interpretation of criminal laws

CO: commercial law, including interpretation of contracts, mortgages, negligence, stock, and insurance

CW: residual issues from the Civil War, usually involving one of the two confiscation acts or the Captured and Abandoned Property Act

EF: estate, probate, and family law

GC: claims against the U.S. government involving pay, jobs, status, and pensions

IN: disputes involving Native American tribes

JR: jurisdiction and judicial procedure, especially under the several removal acts passed by Congress

LD: land and mining claims; disposition of public lands; eminent domain

MB: state and local government bonds; local government powers

OT: statutory interpretation, government operations; congressional commerce power

PP: state police power, involving dormant commerce clause, impairment of contracts, and Fourteenth Amendment

PT: patent, copyright, and trademark

RD: racial discrimination

TR: treaties

TX: national, state, and local tax laws; U.S. customs and duties ingly, actions taken by governments in the seceding states were unlawful. The Chase Court had accepted this theory in *Texas v. White* (1869), when it held that a sale of state-owned securities after 1862 in support of the war effort had been invalid. (Reconstruction itself was justified, even though the seceding states had never legally left the Union, because the rebellion had temporarily suspended those states' rights as full-fledged members of the Union.)

However, in *Texas v. White*, Chief Justice Chase had suggested in dicta (language in a court opinion not necessary for the decision in the case) that not all actions by illegal governments were unlawful. Those "necessary to peace and good order among citizens, such . . . as Acts sanctioning and protecting marriage and the domestic relations . . . [and] regulating the conveyance and transfer of property . . . must be regarded in general as valid when proceeding from an actual, though unlawful, government." Accepting Chase's dicta as the law of the land, the Waite Court had to answer the question whether the chartering of insurance companies fell within the "peace and good order" exception of legal actions by an illegal, if functioning, government. Conceding that the Georgia legislature when it incorporated Home Insurance "was not the legitimate Legislature of the State," Justice Strong acknowledged in his opinion for the Court that the body was still a legislature. To be sure, everything it did hostile to the Union was invalid, but "no good reason can be assigned why all their other enactments, not forbidden by the Constitution, should not have the force which the law generally accords to the action of public officers." Any other conclusion "would work great and unnecessary hardship upon the people of those States, without any corresponding benefit to the citizens of other States, and without any advantage to the National Government." Thus, although chartered by an invalid entity, the company was a valid entity and was entitled to sue in the Court of Claims.

Disputes over land titles and mining claims remained a staple of the Court's docket during Waite's years. Such litigation often entailed not only review of sometimes musty records to identify persons domiciled in certain places for certain periods in years gone by and of what was surveyed by whom at what time, but also interpretation of possibly applicable acts of Congress. All were present in the *Hot Springs Cases* (1876). This trio of cases, which the Court combined and decided with a single opinion, involved disputes between three claimants (two of whom claimed the same tract of land) and the U.S. government. At issue was title to the Hot Springs district in the lateral ranges of the Ouachita Mountains, about 60 miles southwest of Little Rock, Arkansas. The area had already become a retreat for those seeking the healing powers of the mineral waters that bubbled from the springs. As early as 1804, President Thomas Jefferson had commissioned a study of the springs' properties.

Disputes over Hot Springs titles had festered for half a century when Congress in 1870 took action. It created a ninety-day window of opportunity for claimants to file suit in the Court of Claims, with a right of appeal to the Supreme Court that losing parties would surely take. (Here, as with other matters, Congress was exceedingly generous in appropriating the time and energy of the federal judiciary.) That it took six years from beginning to end to resolve the *Hot Springs Cases* indicates the growing case backlog then faced by the federal courts.

One of the litigants was John C. Hale, successor to John Percifull, who seemed to have settled in the disputed area as early as 1813, predating even the formal 1818 transfer of the region from the Quapaw Indians to the United States. An 1814 land statute laid out a procedure for occupants of an area to file for a title with the federal Land Office on completion of public surveying. However, the Hot Springs district was not federally surveyed until 1838, after which Percifull's heirs filed for a title under the 1814 act. The Land Office rejected the claim because an 1832 act of Congress authorized the governor of the Arkansas Territory to lease the mineral springs in the district and reserved the land for later disposal by the government. Yet another congressional statute, this one enacted in 1843, inferentially lent support to Hale's claim. Speaking for the full bench, Justice Bradley was unimpressed. "If it was intended to repeal the Act of 1832 and to confirm Percifull's title, why was it not so expressed? A plain word or two would have done it." Even the extent of Percifull's actual occupancy in the early years seemed shrouded in doubt. "There is no clear evidence of an intent on his part, at that time (1814) or previously, to make this retired spot in the Indian country his home." The Court rejected Hale's and the remaining two claims, deciding that title belonged to the government.

Not all appeals from the Court of Claims involved interests as substantial as those pressed by Home Insurance and Hale. Months prior to the *Hot Springs Cases* decision, the Court's time and four pages in the *U.S. Reports* were absorbed by John M. Ashfield, an Interior Department employee who served as "a watchman . . . of the public grounds in Washington." He had been paid at the rate of $720 per year, but he convinced the Claims Court that Congress intended his salary to be $900 per year instead. The justices reversed the court below and instructed it to dismiss Ashfield's petition (*United States v. Ashfield*, 1876).

Apparent shenanigans, or worse, enlivened an appeal from the U.S. Circuit Court for the District of Ohio in *Hoffman v. Hancock Mutual Life Insurance Co.* (1876). Justin Thayer, general agent for the company in Cleveland, Ohio, appointed A. C. Goodwin as a subagent or broker who would receive 30 percent of the first premium paid on any life insurance policy he sold. In 1869 Goodwin gave Frederick Hoffman a receipt, which Goodwin had signed, indicating payment of $922.57 as the first annual premium on Hoffman's $8,000 endowment life policy. Payment consisted of a horse valued at $400, a sixty-day $100 note to Goodwin, a canceled debt for $53.57 that Goodwin owed to Hoffman, and a premium note of $369. Goodwin referred the policy application to Thayer but said nothing about the receipt. Soon after, Thayer received the policy from the home office and demanded payment from Hoffman. When Thayer learned about the unusual form in which the premium had been paid, he refused to hand over the policy.

After unsuccessful attempts to sell the horse, Thayer agreed to turn over the policy if Hoffman would take back the horse and pay $250. Hoffman refused and sued the company in county court to recover what he had given to Goodwin. After one court decision in the company's favor and a decision on retrial that favored Hoffman, and while the company was demanding a third trial, Hoffman died. His widow Henrietta unsuccessfully pressed a suit in federal circuit court against the company for the full value of the policy.

Throughout this episode, the company had yet to receive a premium. Yet, was Hancock Mutual bound by the actions of its agent and subagent? "[T]he act of the agent is as binding upon the principal as if it were done by the principal himself," declared Justice Swayne for the full Court in restating the premise of the law of agency. "But," he continued, "it is an elementary principle . . . that whatever an agent does can be done only in the way usual in the line of business in which he is acting. . . . Life insurance is a cash business. Its disbursements are all in money, and its receipts must necessarily be in the same medium." If Thayer had the authority to accept a horse in payment, he could have accepted other horses, and the company would eventually have found itself in the horse trading or livery business instead, all against its charter. Thus the widow had no right to proceeds of the policy because what had transpired "was a fraud as respects the Company. Hoffman should have known that neither Goodwin or Thayer had any authority to enter into such an arrangement . . . [and so] [n]o valid contract . . . could arise from such a transaction." This finding was fatal to Mrs. Hoffman's case.

Maritime disputes had been a sizeable part of federal court business from the beginning. Indeed, the importance of waterborne commerce along the East Coast in the late eighteenth century, coupled with recognition that a forum for admiralty disputes was needed apart from state tribunals, was a major reason for creation of lower federal courts in 1789. By the 1870s, due partly to flourishing shipping on rivers and the Great Lakes, the volume of such cases increased. Additionally, clashing technologies of sail versus steam on the high seas and other waterways generated litigation that required conclusions of fact different from those faced in *Hoffman*.

At some time after nine o'clock on the night of January 21, 1871, the schooner *Sarah Watson* was about 30 miles south of Cape Hatteras sailing northeastward from Wilmington to New York City. Its lights were properly hung and burning. At the same time, the steamer *Sea Gull* was cruising southward from Baltimore to Charleston. The *Sea Gull* and the *Sarah Watson* collided, causing the schooner to sink with its cargo of resin. Owners of the *Sarah Watson* wanted compensation for the loss from the owners of the *Sea Gull*.

"Experience shows that ships and vessels engaged in navigation," explained Justice Clifford as he mistook the obvious for the profound, "are liable to be exposed to collision when approaching each other from opposite directions, or on intersecting lines . . . and that reasonable precautions are indispensable . . . to avoid such disasters . . ." (*Schooner Sarah Watson v. Steamer Sea Gull*, 1875). Indeed, rules of navigation for schooners and steamers that the Court had to apply were relatively straightforward. Application, however, frequently necessitated weighing competing claims of fact. Because steamers could move more swiftly, alter course and speed more quickly, and promptly reverse direction, or come to a stop, it was the responsibility of the crew of a steamer to steer clear of an approaching schooner. The latter's duty in such situations was to stay its course, unless an emergency dictated otherwise. When the lookout on the steamer spotted the schooner on the night of January 21, the officer in charge gave the order for a sharp turn to starboard. This was the wrong command to issue. When he realized his mistake, he called for a sharp turn to port. Only at the last moment was an order given to stop the engine. This scenario would ordinarily mean that the *Sea Gull* was to blame. But had the *Sarah Watson* also behaved improperly, adding its own negligence to that of the steamer? If so, then owners of the *Sea Gull* would at most be only partly liable for the loss of the schooner and its cargo.

The answer to this question required detailed examination and assessment by Clifford and his colleagues of all trial court testimony by the ships' crewmembers in an effort to reconstruct the sequence of events in the schooners' last minutes. The justices became in effect an admiralty court of inquiry. They held that if the schooner had departed from its original course (and there were doubts about that), the shift was taken only in a desperate effort to avoid collision with the steamer. Thus the circuit court was directed "to enter a decree in favor of the libelants [owners of the *Sarah Watson*] for the whole value of the schooner, her freight and cargo."

Another major source of litigation for Waite's bench, especially after 1875, were matters of federal court jurisdiction and procedure. The outcome of numerous cases turned on whether a case could be heard in state court exclusively or removed to U.S. circuit court.

F. L. Ames and others were directors of the congressionally chartered Union Pacific Railroad. They and the Kansas Pacific Railway began legal proceedings in the U.S. circuit court in Kansas after the state had begun state court proceedings against the railroads for violating provisions of the charters of state-chartered roads that had been absorbed within the congressionally chartered railroad corporations. The questions the Supreme Court faced involved no consideration of wrongdoing or possible violations by the Union Pacific. Rather, the bench had to decide whether the controversies had arisen "under the laws of the United States," thus allowing removal under an 1875 act from the state court to the circuit court. Moreover, if the case properly fell under the provisions of the 1875 act, the question then became whether such litigation against a state could proceed only under the Supreme Court's original (as opposed to appellate) jurisdiction. The circuit court had ruled contrary to the railroads, and had affirmed the jurisdiction of the state court.

Speaking for the full Court as he did more than any other justice on jurisdictional questions, Waite explained that the 1875 statute authorizing removal seemed clear. "The language . . . is 'Any suit . . . brought in a state court . . . arising under the Constitution or laws of the United States' may be removed by either party. This is broad enough to cover such a case as this. . . ." The burden of proof lay "on those who would withdraw any case within that power from the cognizance of the circuit courts to sustain their exception 'on the spirit and true meaning of the' Act." The reference in Article III of the Constitution that the Supreme Court should have original jurisdiction in cases when a state was a party was not intended by the framers to be exclusive with the Supreme Court; rather, discretion lay with Congress "to distribute that power among the courts" (*Ames v. Kansas*, 1884).

Litigation over state and local government bonds added to the Waite Court's caseload, as it had to Chase's Court. As Table 1.7 shows, bond cases peaked in the Supreme Court between 1878 and 1883. The post–Civil War years were a time of major internal improvements. States old and new built or rebuilt infrastructure, usually financing such projects through indebtedness. As inducements to local economies, municipalities also sold bonds to buy stock in railroad companies laying new roadbed. Taxes of course would have to be collected to service the indebtedness. Bonds also were sold and resold as they were traded among investors.

Municipal bonds could become legally troublesome in different ways. For example, failure to make good on interest payments on validly issued bonds amounted to an impairment of contract in violation of the Constitution. This could occur if the railroad, whose stock a town had purchased with borrowed money, failed financially or decided not to build the line it had planned. There being no improvements at hand, disgruntled taxpayers might then put pressure on local authorities to halt payment on the bonds. Typically federal courts insisted that payments continue, even if additional taxes had to be imposed on the community. Different legal difficulties appeared when someone challenged the authority of a municipality to issue bonds in the first place. The argument would be that the local government had contravened in some way the state statute authorizing it to incur indebtedness. If the courts agreed, the bonds would be invalid, and purchasers of the bonds would be left holding worthless securities. It seemed that no one could be sure of the legal validity of such indebtedness until the Supreme Court had spoken.

This second legal problem thus required the federal courts to scrutinize and apply state law. This responsibility exacerbated relations with the states, especially because of the Taney-era case of *Swift v. Tyson* (1842). Section 34 of the landmark Judiciary Act of 1789 had decreed that "the laws of the several States, except where the Constitution, treaties or statutes of the United States shall otherwise require or provide, shall be regarded as the rules of decision in trials at common law in the courts of the United States in cases where they apply." In *Swift*, Justice Joseph Story construed "laws" to mean statutes only. Federal courts otherwise were to apply "general law" (a kind of national common law) in matters involving contracts and commercial law. On these questions, federal courts were not bound by a state court's interpretation of its own state law. *Swift* was not overruled until *Erie Railroad v. Tompkins* (1938).

Two cases from the U.S. circuit court in Kansas illustrated the degree of oversight federal courts applied. A Kansas law empowered a city council "to encourage the establishment of manufactories and such other enterprises as may tend to develop and improve such City" either by direct appropriation or through the issuance of bonds. Topeka had sold bonds payable to the King Wrought Iron Bridge Manufacturing and Iron Works Company to entice the company to open bridge shops in the city. The critical question, declared Justice Miller for everyone but Clifford, was whether the taxation to cover interest on the bonds "was for a public purpose." There was no such purpose here. "If it be said that a benefit results to the local public of a town by establishing manufactures, the same may be said of any other business or pursuit which employs capital or labor. . . . No line can be drawn . . . which would not open the coffers of the public treasury to the importunities of two thirds of the business men of the city or town" (*Savings and Loan Association v. Topeka City*, 1875).

Two years later, the validity of bonds of another Kansas municipality came before the Court. Burlington Township had issued $8,000 in bonds to aid John Stow in the construction of a steam-powered gristmill in the community. State law authorized municipalities to issue bonds "for the purpose of building bridges, . . . or to aid in the construction of railroads or water-power . . . or for other works of internal improvement." Stow's mill was steam-powered precisely because ordinary waterpower was unavailable. Was this an improvement for a public purpose or was it more like the bridge factory in the previous case? "It would require great nicety of reasoning," declared Justice Hunt for everyone but Field, "to give a definition of the expression 'internal improvement,' which should include a grist-mill run by water, and exclude one operated by steam. . . . It would be a poor consolation to the people of this Town to give them the power to going in and out of the Town upon a railroad, while they were refused the means of grinding their wheat" (*Burlington Township v. Beasley*, 1877).

The Waite Court at Work

As the preceding section suggests, the business of the Waite Court required extraordinary labor by each justice and, during times when one or more justices might be incapacitated, an increased workload for the others. For each case, the justices read briefs submitted by attorneys, and they listened to oral arguments in many of them as well. In addition, a significant amount of time was consumed by the opinions the justices crafted. Except for oral arguments and conferences, the justices typically worked alone at home; the Court's tight quarters at the Capitol contained no space for individual chambers.

Since Chief Justice Marshall's day, the Court has spoken through the medium of the opinion of the Court—a statement of the case and the law representing the views of at least a bare majority of the bench. (The opinion of the Court is also referred to as the majority opinion.) Responsibility for designating the author of an opinion falls to the chief justice, if the chief is in the majority. If the chief is in the minority, the senior associate justice in the majority makes the assignment. Although many factors may affect opinion assignment, Waite, like most chiefs, tried to distribute the burden as equitably as possible.

Figure 1.2 illustrates this pattern in the first, middle, and last Waite Courts. Waite typically assigned to himself the multitude of mainly minor jurisdictional cases to be decided. Usually these required little explanation and could be disposed of in a paragraph or two. Otherwise, departures from the normal practice usually reflected a justice's arrival late in a period (as with Woods in the middle and Lamar in the last Court) or physical and/or mental infirmities (as with Hunt early in the middle Court).

Dissents—statements objecting to the result reached by the majority—present a more complex picture. At first glance, dissents seem noticeable only because of their relative rarity. Almost all the decisions by the Waite Court appearing in printed form in the *U.S. Reports* were decided unanimously. Dissents were noted in 13 percent of the cases in the first court, 9 percent in the middle court, and 6 percent in the last. These data include many instances when no dissenting opinion was published, only a notation such as "Mr. Justice Clifford dissents." This stands in sharp contrast to the Court's work in recent decades when fewer than 40 percent of cases may be decided unanimously, and when justices rarely dissent without also explaining why.

Yet as Figure 1.3 shows, some justices were much more likely than others to dissent. Field and Clifford stand out in the first Waite Court. The same pair were prominent dissenters in the middle court, trailed closely by Bradley, Strong, and Miller. Harlan led in the last court, again with Bradley, Field, and Miller at his heels.

The data in the figures also indicate that Waite Court justices, when they dissented at all, tended to dissent not alone, but with others. The small number of dissenting votes, relative to the number of unanimous cases, makes meaningful statistical analysis risky;

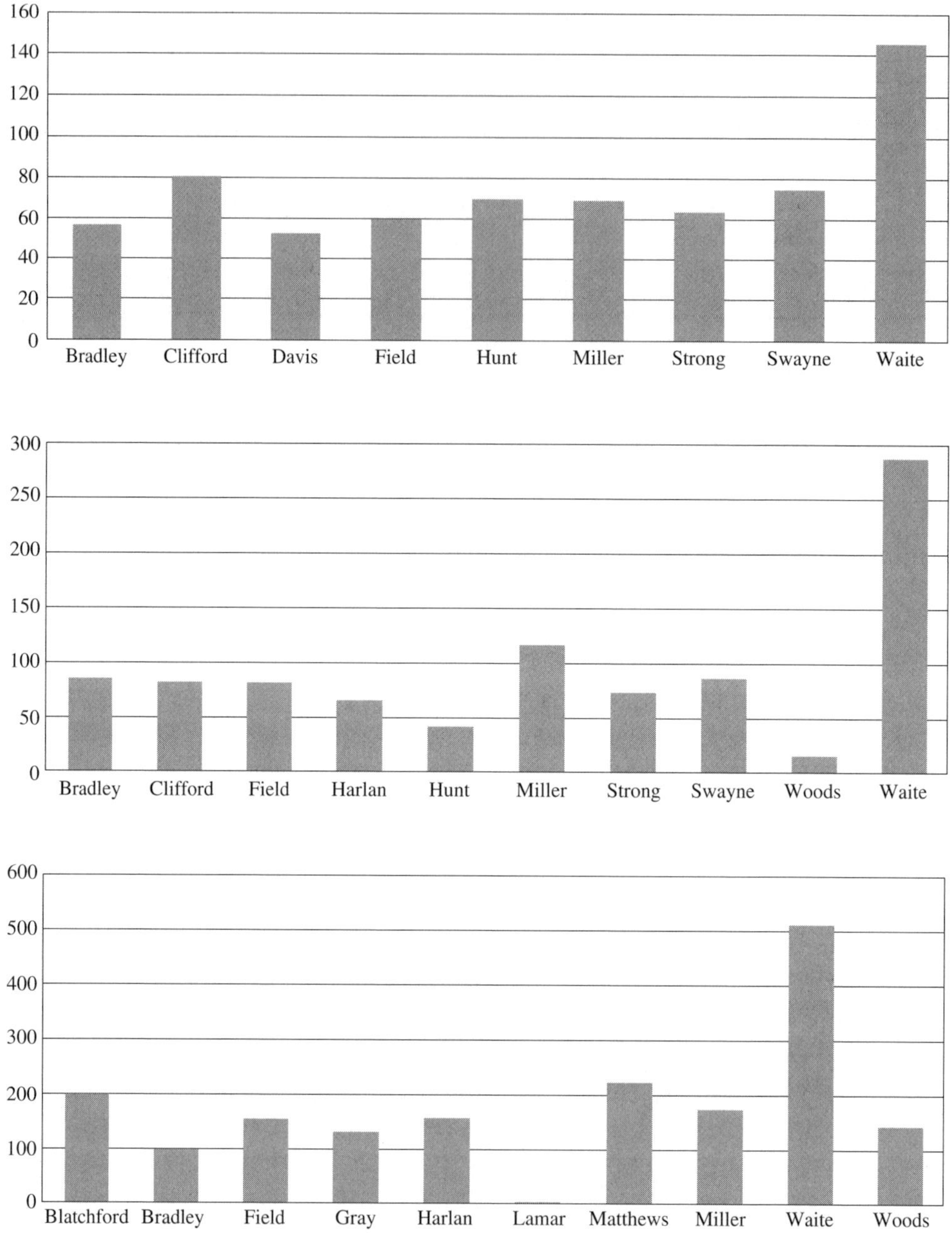

Figure 1.2 Opinions of the Court, by Justice, in the First, Middle, and Last Waite Courts

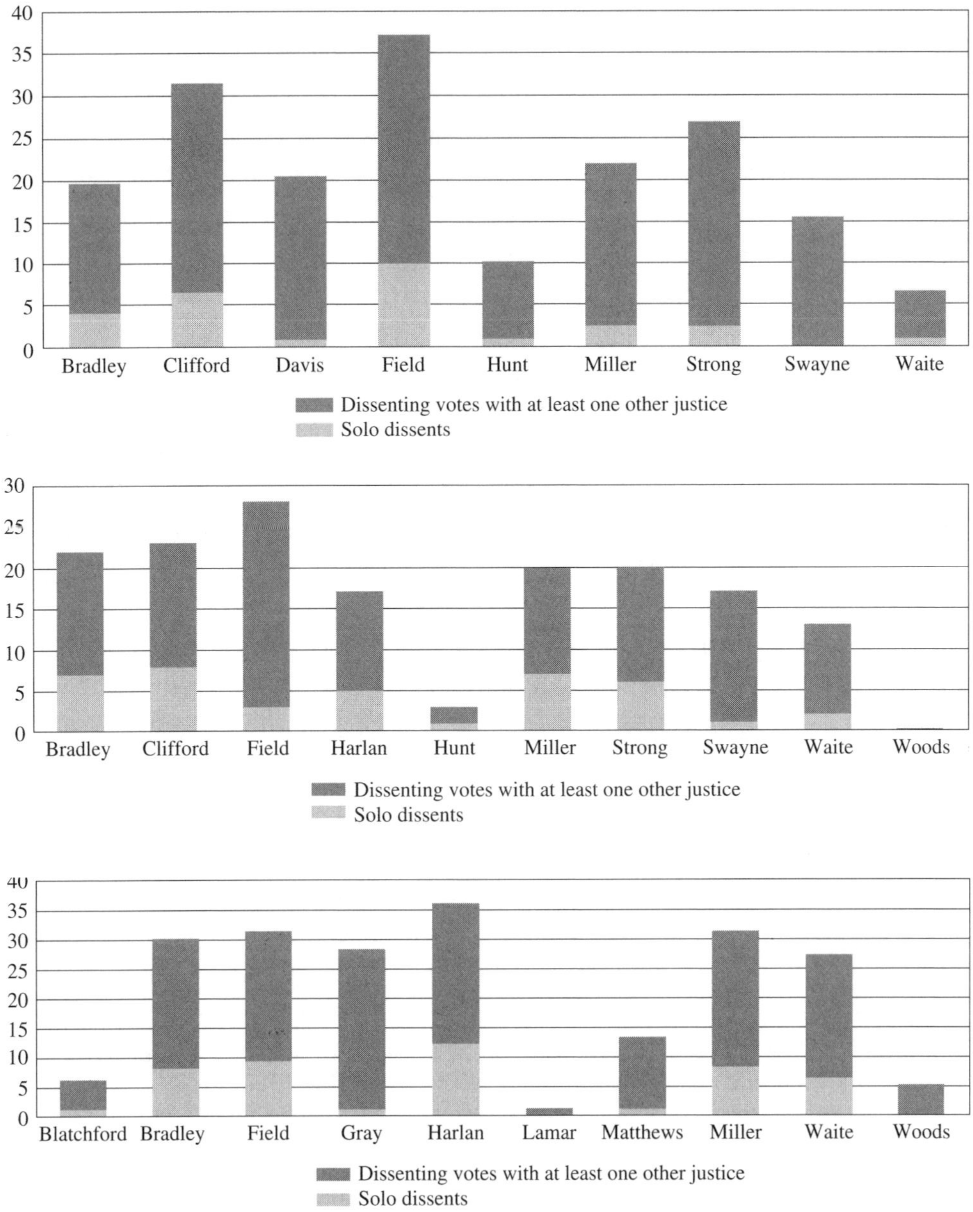

Figure 1.3 Dissenting votes, by Justice, in the First, Middle, and Last Waite Courts

nonetheless, the data allow some general observations. First, with a handful of exceptions that will be discussed in Chapter 2, pairings or groupings of dissenting justices ranged across issues, that is, one justice's tendency to dissent with another justice was usually not confined to a single issue. Second, noticeable pairings between justices in one court did not always persist into the next court. In the first court, Bradley's dissenting votes were cast most frequently with Miller's; Clifford, Davis, Hunt, and Strong associated most often with Field; and Swayne aligned himself most closely with Clifford in dissent. Waite's dissents highly correlated with Strong's, and somewhat less often with Bradley's and Miller's. In the middle Court, Bradley's dissents were cast most often with Field, and then secondarily with Miller and Waite. Clifford was also prominently aligned with Field, while Harlan displayed no pronounced affinity for any other dissenting justice. Swayne and Strong were paired in dissent more frequently than with anyone else. In the last court, Bradley was found in dissent most commonly with Gray and Waite. Field and Harlan dissented together far more often than they dissented with others. When dissenting, Matthews found himself with Waite nearly two-thirds of the time, and about half the time with Gray. Dissenting votes by Miller, Waite, and Woods were cast most often with Gray. When Blatchford dissented, he was aligned with Gray or Matthews more than twice as often as he was with any other justice.

However, the actual number of dissenting votes initially cast by Waite Court justices was considerably greater than the published record reveals. That is, many seemingly unanimous decisions were in fact initially decided with one or more dissenting votes; likewise, decisions reporting only one or two dissents may have been reached initially with three or four dissents. This is known not merely anecdotally but because of very precise records that Chief Justice Waite maintained in his docket books that indicate the vote among the justices at the conference where each case was decided. Waite's data can then be compared to data drawn from the *U.S. Reports*. The most thorough study of this phenomenon finds that dissenting votes at conference were recorded in 40 percent of the cases (Epstein, Segal, Spaeth 2001, 366), or about four times the percentage indicated by the *U.S. Reports*.

For example, consider the bridge factory and gristmill bond cases discussed in the previous section. When the Court took its initial vote in *Topeka City*, Hunt joined Clifford in dissent, yet the published reports show only a dissent by the latter. In *Beasley*, the shift was even more pronounced. At conference, five justices (Hunt, Clifford, Swayne, Strong, and Waite) voted to uphold the validity of the bonds, while Field, Davis, Miller, and Bradley thought them invalid. Yet the Court's vote in the gristmill case is reported as 8–1, with only Justice Field dissenting without opinion (Fairman 1987, 313).

In trying to account for such divergence between the conference tally and the *U.S. Reports*, the study by Epstein, Segal, and Spaeth considers the Waite Court's pattern as part of a trend in judicial behavior during the past two centuries. Until 1940, the Supreme Court's public dissent rate never exceeded 30 percent and usually hovered between 5 and 10 percent. Since 1940 the public dissent rate has almost never been below 50 percent. Some scholars have argued that the sharp increase in dissents in the modern era is a function of the Court's increasing control over its docket. That is, in Waite's time the Court was obliged to decide every case that qualified jurisdictionally. The Court, in a small step after 1891 and in a giant leap after 1925, found itself able to select cases for decision, and to refuse the rest. The abundance of routine and easy cases therefore disappeared from the docket, and hard cases, with a greater tendency to provoke disagreement, took their place.

That may explain some of the contrast between the fourth quarter of the nineteenth- century and the last half of the twentieth century, but it does not account for the many instances in which Waite Court justices dissented at conference, only later to join with the majority. If the bulk of nineteenth-century cases were easy, involving only perfunctory appellate review of correctly decided cases from courts below, that presumably would have been apparent at conference. So, what else could account for the divergence between the private/public dissent rate among the Waite Court justices?

Using various statistical tools, Epstein, Segal, and Spaeth prefer an alternate explanation: a prevailing norm of consensus that discouraged the public display of a divided bench. So a justice who indicated disagreement at conference would later typically acquiesce in what the majority decided. It is that norm, the authors contend, that collapsed in the twentieth century.

An additional factor should be considered as well. As already noted, the number of cases on the Court's docket mushroomed during Waite's tenure, due both to congressional expansion of federal jurisdiction and to increasing economic and social changes. By the time of Waite's death, the Court had fallen more than four years behind in its work. This was also a time when the justices had practically no support staff. The justices truly did their own work. (Justice Gray was the first justice with a law clerk; in 1882 he hired a recent law school graduate and paid him out of his own salary. Not until 1922 would Congress appropriate money to provide a clerk for each justice.) Even manual typewriters were not widely marketed until after Waite's tenure began.

Although a growing backlog itself might not discourage dissent, the number of opinions the justices had to write might do so. As Table 1.7 shows, the number of opinions issued after the 1878 term tended to be considerably greater than the number issued during the preceding five terms that roughly corresponded to the first Waite Court. And it is in this first court that the rate of public dissents was highest. More significantly, the first five terms displayed the highest rate of published dissenting opinions, averaging 10 percent. In contrast, during the remaining terms, dissenting opinions were attached to only 5 percent of majority opinions (Epstein, Segal, Spaeth, and Walker 1994, 160). Then there were the occasions when illness prevented one or more justices from shouldering a normal share of opinion writing. Waite, for instance, was absent from the Court between December 1884 and March 1885 while recuperating in Florida (Magrath 1963, 272–274). With added work to do because of another's incapacity, a justice might conclude that prudence, including a wariness of trying to do too much, advised writing a dissent only in exceptional circumstances.

Measured by demands and output, Waite Court justices were the most burdened, the hardest working, and the most productive in Supreme Court history. No other bench in U.S. history had to endure such an avalanche of cases for so long. The chapters that follow explore the collective and individual achievements of these men as well as their impact on constitutional law.

References

Abraham, Henry J. 1992. *Justices and Presidents.* 3rd ed. New York: Oxford University Press.

Atkinson, David N. 1999. *Leaving the Bench.* Lawrence: University Press of Kansas.

Basler, Roy P. 1953–1955. *The Collected Works of Abraham Lincoln.* Vol. 5. New Brunswick, NJ: Rutgers University Press.

Conkling, Alfred R. 1889. *The Life and Letters of Roscoe Conkling.* New York: C. L. Webster.

Epstein, Lee, Jeffrey A. Segal, and Harold J. Spaeth. 2001. "The Norm of Consensus on the U.S. Supreme Court." *American Journal of Political Science* 45: 362–377.

Epstein, Lee, Jeffrey A. Segal, and Thomas G. Walker. 1994. *The Supreme Court Compendium.* Washington, DC: Congressional Quarterly Press.

Fairman, Charles. 1939. *Mr. Justice Miller and the Supreme Court: 1862–1890.* Cambridge, MA: Harvard University Press.

———. 1941. "Mr. Justice Bradley's Appointment to the Supreme Court and the Legal Tender Cases." *Harvard Law Review* 54: 977–1034, 1128–1155.

———. 1987. *Reconstruction and Reunion 1864–88, Part Two. History of the Supreme Court of the United States.* Vol. 7. New York: Macmillan.

Frankfurter, Felix, and James M. Landis. 1928. *The Business of the Supreme Court.* New York: Macmillan.

Friedman, Leon. 1969. "Joseph P. Bradley." In *The Justices of the United States Supreme Court 1789–1969*, vol. 2, ed. Leon Friedman and Fred L. Israel. New York: Chelsea House.

Gillette, William. 1969a. "John A. Campbell." In *The Justices of the United States Supreme Court 1789–1969*, vol. 2, ed. Leon Friedman and Fred L. Israel. New York: Chelsea House.

Gillette, William. 1969b. "Noah H. Swayne." In *The Justices of the United States Supreme Court 1789–1969*, vol. 2, ed. Leon Friedman and Fred L. Israel. New York: Chelsea House.

Howard, John R. 1999. *The Shifting Wind.* Albany: State University of New York Press.

Kens, Paul. 1997. *Justice Stephen Field.* Lawrence: University Press of Kansas.

Magrath, C. Peter. 1963. *Morrison R. Waite.* New York: Macmillan.

Maltese, John Anthony. 1995. *The Selling of Supreme Court Nominees.* Baltimore, MD: Johns Hopkins University Press.

Mason, Alpheus Thomas, and Donald Grier Stephenson, Jr. 2002. *American Constitutional Law.* 13th ed. Upper Saddle River, NJ: Prentice Hall.

Meador, Daniel J. 1986. "Lamar to the Court: Last Step to National Reunion." *Supreme Court Historical Society Yearbook:* 27–47.

Silver, David M. 1998. *Lincoln's Supreme Court.* (Reissue of 1956 edition.) Urbana: University of Illinois Press.

Stephenson, D. Grier, Jr. 1973. "The Chief Justice as Leader: The Case of Morrison Remick Waite." *William and Mary Law Review* 14: 899–927.

Swisher, Carl B. 1935. *Roger B. Taney.* Washington, DC: Brookings Institution.

Warren, Charles. 1926. *The Supreme Court in United States History.* Rev. ed. Boston: Little, Brown.

Yarbrough, Tinsley E. 1995. *Judicial Enigma: The First Justice Harlan.* New York: Oxford University Press.

2

The Justices

The Supreme Court matters in U.S. government because of the cases it decides. Yet behind every Supreme Court case are people: litigants whose lives, liberties, property, or other interests will be directly and immediately affected by the decision; attorneys who argue the case in the Court; judges who decide the case in the lower courts; the Supreme Court justices themselves; and of course the class of those who will be indirectly touched by the outcome. This chapter examines the fifteen individuals who comprised the Waite Court (1874–1888), as shown in Table 2.1.

The Supreme Court was established in 1789 and held its first session in 1790, meaning that the fourteen years of the Waite Court span less than 7 percent of the years the High Court has been in existence. However, the fifteen Waite Court justices account for 14 percent of the 108 persons who, as of mid-2003, have sat since the Court's beginning. Moreover, a study commissioned in 1970 to rank the ninety-six justices who served between 1789 and 1967 suggests that the Waite Court justices were, as a group, unusually capable (Abraham 1992, 412–413). John Marshall Harlan (I) is counted among the twelve that the study deemed "great," and Samuel Miller, Stephen Field, Joseph Bradley, and Morrison Waite are among the fifteen "near greats." Nine are among the fifty-five receiving an "average" mark, and only Woods is lodged among the six with the grade of "below average." None were among the eight judged "failure." Few periods of Supreme Court history fare as well or better in the survey. This chapter will show that Woods deserves to have his grade moved up a notch. His evaluation probably results more from general unfamiliarity than from a careful appraisal of his work.

Whatever their standing, the fifteen justices reached the Supreme Court only after experience in a variety of arenas: private practice, judicial, legislative, and executive. Several of them would have been worthy of study by later generations even had they never been appointed to the Supreme Court. Several followed circuitous paths to the Court, reminding us that there is no fixed route to the bench. In every instance, these were people of considerable accomplishment. Each fits Justice Sandra Day O'Connor's 1983 observation about judicial selection: one must be "the

Table 2.1 Justices of the Waite Court (1874–1888)

	Appointed by	Nominated on	Confirmed on	Takes Judicial oath	Service Ends
Clifford	Buchanan	12-9-1857	1-12-1858	1-21-1858	7-25-1881
Swayne	Lincoln	1-21-1862	1-24-1862	1-27-1862	1-24-1881
Miller	Lincoln	7-16-1862	7-16-1862	7-21-1862	10-13-1890
Davis	Lincoln	12-1-1862	12-8-1862	12-10-1862	3-4-1877
Field	Lincoln	3-6-1863	3-10-1863	5-20-1863	12-1-1897
Strong	Grant	2-7-1870	2-18-1870	3-14-1870	12-4-1880
Bradley	Grant	2-7-1870	3-21-1870	3-23-1870	1-22-1892
Hunt	Grant	12-3-1872	12-11-1872	1-9-1873	1-27-1882
Waite	Grant	1-19-1874	1-21-1874	3-4-1874	3-23-1888
Harlan (I)	Hayes	10-16-1877	11-29-1877	12-10-1877	10-14-1911
Woods	Hayes	12-15-1880	12-21-1880	1-5-1881	5-14-1887
Matthews	Garfield	3-14-1881	5-12-1881	5-17-1881	3-22-1889
Gray	Arthur	12-19-1881	12-20-1881	1-9-1882	9-15-1902
Blatchford	Arthur	3-13-1882	3-27-1882	4-3-1882	7-7-1893
Lamar, L.	Cleveland	12-6-1887	1-16-1888	1-18-1888	1-23-1893

right person in the right spot at the right time. Stated simply, you must be lucky" (Abraham 1992, 7).

As the Waite Court justices advanced professionally, all found themselves caught up in tumultuous times. No other U.S. generation has experienced quite the same degree of change. The political world that the justices knew while coming of age turned upside down in less than a decade. The accepted political party system that pitted Democrats against Whigs collapsed in the mid-1850s over the question of slavery. The Democratic Party was badly tainted once the Civil War began because of its identity with slavery. The Republican Party displaced the Whigs, the only time in U.S. history that an upstart third party has taken the place of a major party. Many Waite Court justices had to rethink their party loyalties and determine, once the North's victory settled the question of slavery and secession, how in fact and in law the United States had changed. The justices were faced with three post-war constitutional amendments ratified between 1865 and 1870. In interpreting the Thirteenth, Fourteenth, and Fifteenth Amendments, the Waite Court confronted significant new questions of federal power. Among the issues the justices encountered were protecting the rights of newly freed slaves, the place of the states in the federal system, the authority of government over a growing population and a new industrial capitalism, and the role of the Supreme Court in determining such issues.

Seven Waite Court personalities also played roles in the great Hayes-Tilden presidential election controversy of 1876–1877 that threatened to paralyze the government and rekindle civil strife. Justices Bradley, Clifford, Field, Miller, and Strong served on the electoral commission that decided the election, Matthews (appointed a few years afterwards) presented the Republican Party's case to the commission, and Lamar (appointed in 1888) helped to fashion the terms of the compromise that assured acceptance of the commission's decision. (To avoid repetitive accounts in this chapter, this episode is, aside from an occasional reference, treated in Chapter 4.)

During the days of the Hughes Court, forty-four years after Chief Justice Waite's death, a Harvard Law School professor named Felix Frankfurter (whom President Franklin Roosevelt would name to the Supreme Court in 1939) lamented the fact that more was not known about individual Supreme Court justices. "The formal remoteness of their labors has largely conspired to consign [them] to the limbo of impersonality. From this fate only Marshall has been adequately rescued. . . . The Court's prestige and American history both would be gainers by . . . studies of other great judges" (Frankfurter 1932, vi). Fortunately the intervening years have witnessed publication of a number of biographies and biographical essays not only about the great judges but others too. This chapter hopes to continue this task of rescuing the Waite bench, at least, from any remaining "limbo of impersonality."

The Buchanan Appointment

Nathan Clifford

When Morrison Waite became chief justice, Nathan Clifford had been senior associate justice only since the retirement in November 1872 of Justice Samuel Nelson. Nominated by President Buchanan in late 1857, Clifford was also the only member of the bench in 1874 not appointed by either President Lincoln or President Grant. Not only was he the surviving justice from the pre–Civil War Court, but he was the remaining link to Jacksonian Democracy. Also of the fifteen justices of the Waite Court, he was one of only three to have also served in the executive and legislative branches of the federal government.

Buchanan had named Clifford to fill the seat vacated by Benjamin R. Curtis of Massachusetts. Curtis had been blessed with the finest training for a lawyer then available on the U.S. side of the Atlantic Ocean and quickly earned a reputation as one of the country's preeminent attorneys. Warm with family and close friends but cool and detached toward others, he was identified with Boston's social elite. Curtis was also a Whig, owing his appointment to Millard Fillmore, the last Whig to occupy

Nathan Clifford (Matthew Brady, Handy Studios, Collection of the Supreme Court of the United States)

the White House. Although he sat on the Court for not quite six years, even that short tenure allowed Curtis to write a telling dissent in *Dred Scott v. Sandford* (1857), opposing the majority's view that Congress and territorial legislatures lacked authority to ban slavery in the territories. He also authored one of the Court's most important nineteenth-century opinions in *Cooley v. Board of Wardens* (1851), a decision with lasting impact that began to clarify the respective authorities of state and nation over interstate commerce.

However, except for their common regional link Curtis and Clifford were a study in contrasts. Curtis's successor had a skimpy formal education and was largely self-taught. A warm and outgoing person who made friends easily, Clifford established a successful legal practice in rural Maine and had extensive office-holding experience at both the state and national levels. Clifford was also a faithful and lifelong Democrat. As Chapter 1 discussed, it was that party tie and the fact that he was the choice of a Democratic president who supported the *Dred Scott* decision that nearly derailed his confirmation in the Senate. As a justice, Clifford served for over twenty-three years, earning a reputation as a workhorse and a master of detail. Yet in all that time he authored no constitutional opinion of lasting significance.

Clifford's ancestors immigrated to the New World in 1644, casting them among the earliest settlers of New Hampshire. The only son of seven children, Nathan was born on August 18, 1803, just outside the village of Rumney where his father was a deacon in the Congregational Church and, like Nathan's grandfather, a farmer of modest means. After attending the village school, Nathan entered Haverhill Academy at age fourteen. During the next several years he seems to have devised his own work-study program: he taught school to help cover expenses, at least when he could find the time. After an additional year at New Hampton Institute, his formal education ended when he realized he had insufficient funds to attend Dartmouth College. As his grandson later wrote, "Nathan was not brilliant. . . . The child had something better than genius. He possessed the ability for hard work and the slow, plodding retentive mind. . . . It is to this characteristic of dogged determination to stick to a thing till mastered . . . that must be attributed the success which came to him . . ." (Clifford 1922, 5).

At eighteen he began to read law under the tutelage of Josiah Quincy, the most prominent attorney in the area. By 1827 he was admitted to the New Hampshire bar. Looking for a promising location to open his practice, Clifford chose Newfield, Maine, a lawyerless community of some 1200 about thirty miles northwest of Portland, near the New Hampshire border. Family tradition reports that Clifford literally walked to Newfield with all his worldly possessions on his back. He soon established himself professionally as well as personally, although probably at no time in his life would he ever think of himself as financially comfortable and independent. Within a year he married Hannah Ayer, the seventeen-year-old daughter of Newfield's most prominent family. Their marriage was long, happy, and close, yielding four sons and two daughters. Clifford was a faithful correspondent during the many times in his life when they would be apart. Occasionally his letters began "Dear Hannah," but more often the salutation was "Dear Wife" or "My Dear Wife."

Clifford directed his energies toward a public career. In 1830 he was elected as a Jacksonian Democrat to the Maine legislature, no small achievement in a state that had voted by a ratio of 3:2 for Adams over Jackson in the presidential election of 1828. Within two years he was selected speaker of the state house of representatives, a position he held until his appointment in 1834 as state attorney general.

In 1832 Clifford was named one of Maine's delegates to the Democratic Party's first presidential nominating convention. This required first a journey from Maine to "Washington City" in May, where he met President Jackson "at his house." He then took a much shorter ride from the capital to Baltimore, where the convention renominated Jackson by acclamation. As a measure of the speed of travel in that day even in the most developed region of the country, the segment of the trip from Providence, Rhode Island, to Washington consumed sixty-six hours. As the future justice wrote Hannah, "I have seen most of the great men of our country, Jackson, Calhoun, Clay, Webster, . . . Woodbury, Cass, Wirt, . . . Hayne, . . . to most of whom I was introduced. . . . We have had green peas several times. . . . We board at Mrs. Lenchenbergs, a fashionable house. It is expensive travelling. I shant buy much" (Clifford 1922, 49–50).

In the midterm election of 1838, voters sent Clifford to Congress and reelected him in 1840 even though William Henry Harrison, the Whig candidate, carried Maine over incumbent Democrat Martin Van Buren. His Washington legislative career ended at the next election, however, after reapportionment cost Maine a seat.

It was during his state and national legislative service that Clifford articulated a Jacksonian political vision, which guided him for the rest of his life. He favored hard currency and was opposed to renewal of the charter of the Second Bank of the United States, seeing it not only as a threat to state banks but a big money threat to democracy. Representing a part of New England not yet caught up in the industrial revolution, he opposed the protective tariff. He opposed a national uniform policy on slavery, viewing it as a local institution that should be governed by the laws of each state. Later he would fear for the future of the Union as the newly emerging Republican Party sought to nationalize the slavery question. Internal improvements, financed by the national government, were also suspect, not only on constitutional grounds but because the tariff would invariably be the source of revenue.

James K. Polk's election as president in 1844 resulted in Clifford's nomination as U.S. attorney general in 1846. Yet despite the president's support and the prospects of little opposition in the Senate, Clifford had serious misgivings about his own capabilities, particularly as the government's counsel at the Supreme Court. As Polk recorded in his diary on December 13, Clifford called on the president and delivered a letter of resignation. "I told him if he resigned now it would be assumed by his political opponents that he was not qualified, & that it would ruin him as a public man," the president recorded. "In the course of the conversation he dropped a remark to the effect that perhaps I had some other person in my mind who could perform the duties better than he could. I told him I had not, and that if he were to resign it would greatly embarrass me. . . . He finally concluded not to tender his resignation. . . ." Ten days later, the Senate confirmed Clifford unanimously. As he wrote Hannah, "I have had many anxious hours but begin to feel more at home" (Clifford 1922, 150–151). Ironically, the first case he argued before the Court involved dividend payments from the old Bank of the United States.

Polk's diary also reveals that Clifford was an important adviser to the president during the war with Mexico. That would explain his appointment as minister to Mexico in 1848, a position he held until the fall of 1849 after a change in administrations. Mexico was then a dangerous place, especially for a representative of the U.S. government. On one occasion bandits set upon Clifford's coach, whereupon he jumped outside and fired his pistol at the apparent ringleader, and the attackers fled. On his return to the United States, Clifford reentered private practice, although, to advance himself financially, he relocated from Newfield to Portland where he remained until his nomination to the Supreme Court.

Clifford's Supreme Court service was marked by several characteristics. First, probably because most of his colleagues were considerably older during his early years on the bench, he quickly became known as a workhorse who wrote numerous opinions when others could not. His total output reached nearly 400, although the pace diminished considerably in the 1870s with a mental slowdown. For example, Clifford once voted with the majority in a case, and Waite assigned the opinion to him. He later returned the slip to the chief justice, saying that he was unprepared. Waite wrote the opinion himself. In another instance in 1878, Clifford had been upset by something and notified Waite: "I am not willing to write an opinion in No. 93 and therefore return it. If you want No. 99 for any of your friends you may have that also" (Stephenson 1973, 910). Clifford's decline partly explains why Waite assigned him almost no opinions in constitutional cases. In some 72 cases Waite deemed of constitutional significance between 1874 and 1881, Clifford and Ward Hunt were each asked to write only one opinion (Magrath 1963, 263).

Second, most of his opinions were ponderously written. As his grandson explained, "He began at the beginning, and marched by careful stages through every possible phase or contingency. The result was that when he arrived at his conclusion, there was no point which had not been covered" (Clifford 1922, 87). Waite no doubt agreed. As the chief commented in a letter about one opinion, "It will take a good while to find out *all* there is in it. Bro. Clifford is never very short" (Stephenson 1973, 910).

Third, Clifford's opinions and his votes, whether for the majority or the minority, usually reflected his Jacksonian Democrat views. According to one account, "the most distinctive characteristic . . . is their deference to legislative decisions, both state and federal" (Clinton and Walsh 1999, 49). But that assessment must be qualified. Of his opinions in constitutional cases, Clifford was proudest of his dissent of about 18,000 words in *Knox v. Lee* (1871), when the Court reversed itself on legal tender and upheld congressional authority. Belief in hard currency trumped deference to Congress. Clifford also was not always solicitous of state, as opposed to federal, authority. In his partial dissent in the important jurisdictional case *Murdock v. Memphis* (1875) discussed in Chapter 1, Clifford argued for Supreme Court review of state court decisions on all implicated matters of state law if the state court had decided the federal question in the case incorrectly. Neither was he supportive of state policy in *Hall v. DeCuir* (1877), which invalidated on commerce clause grounds a Louisiana statute that banned racial discrimination on public conveyances. In a concurring opinion more than twice the length of Waite's majority opinion, Clifford went out of his way to explain that separate accommodations for persons based on race were no more unreasonable than those based on gender. "[E]quality is not identity," he wrote. The phrase and the reasoning behind it foreshadowed the Fuller Court's separate but equal doctrine of *Plessy v. Ferguson* (1896). Yet, apparently believing that states retained full control over their judicial systems despite the Fourteenth Amendment, he dissented in *Strauder v. West Virginia* (1880) in which the Court struck down a state law that excluded African Americans from jury service. Moreover, his concurring opinion in *United States v. Reese* (1876) emphasized that the Fifteenth Amendment and its Enforcement Act barred only laws based on race, not laws that had only a racially discriminatory effect—a perspective the full bench adopted in *Williams v. Mississippi* (1898).

Fourth, aside from his essential and workmanlike part in coping with an expanding docket, Clifford tended to speak for the Court most often in three categories of cases. As Table 1.7 in Chapter 1 shows, admiralty and maritime cases were a staple of the Court's work. Clifford became the bench's shipwreck expert. For example, during the first Waite Court he authored eighteen such opinions for the Court; no other justice authored more than four. He led the field in the number of patent opinions and argued for expanded protection for intellectual property. In cases in commercial law and bankruptcy, his opinions numbered close to the average for each member of the bench, but within this broad category, he specialized in those dealing with bills and notes. Resolution of such issues was crucially important in the latter half of the nineteenth century.

Finally, if Clifford's pre-Court political experience did little to prepare him for some of the legal challenges he faced as a justice, it certainly prepared him well for his role in the electoral vote dispute of 1877. Part of the minority when the commission voted 8–7 for the Hayes electors, Clifford nonetheless earned praise for his evenhandedness as presiding officer. He signed the order for Hayes's inauguration under circumstances where a lesser person might have capitalized on the opportunity for obstruction to further partisan ends. That high-minded conduct, however, never hid the fact that he henceforth regarded Hayes as illegitimate. Wanting to outlast Hayes and to see a Democrat in the White House, Clifford clung to his seat even after a stroke in 1880 kept him from the bench until his death in Cornish, Maine, on July 25, 1881.

The Lincoln Appointments

Aside from his selection of Salmon P. Chase to be Chief Justice in 1864, President Abraham Lincoln named four associate justices to the Supreme Court: Noah H. Swayne, Samuel F. Miller, David Davis, and Stephen J. Field. All were "westerners" as the term was then used, and all four associate justices were still sitting when Morrison Waite succeeded Chase in 1874.

Noah Haynes Swayne

If Clifford was the last addition to the Court by the pre–Civil War regime, Noah Swayne was the first by the new Republican regime. In January 1862 Swayne filled the vacancy created by the death of Jackson appointee Justice John McLean in the cataclysmic month of April 1861. Both McLean and Swayne were Ohioans and had been close friends, and McLean made it known to the newly elected President Lincoln that he wanted Swayne to succeed him. Like McLean, the fifty-eight-year-old Swayne was politically astute; as described in Chapter 1, upon McLean's death he set in motion an extensive lobbying campaign that all but smothered Lincoln in accolades for himself. Like his predecessor, Swayne did not forsake politics once becoming a justice. However, unlike McLean he never craved the presidency. He instead coveted the Court's center chair, actively foraging for the position in 1864 and again in 1873.

Swayne was born December 7, 1804, in the uppermost reaches of the Shenandoah Valley in Frederick County, Virginia, about 100 miles northwest of Washington, D.C. Noah was the youngest of the nine children in the pious home of Joshua and Rebecca (Smith) Swayne, of Quaker stock from Chester County, Pennsylvania. After Noah's father died in 1809, his mother was able to educate Noah locally until he was thirteen. He then enrolled in Jacob Mendenhall's Academy, a respected Quaker school in Waterford, Virginia. At age fifteen Noah ventured to Alexandria to study medicine but abandoned this pursuit when his teacher, Dr. George Thornton, died,

Noah Swayne (Matthew Brady, Handy Studios, Collection of the Supreme Court of the United States)

and when he learned that no family funds remained for his education. Undeterred, he read law under the tutelage of John Scott and Francis Brooks in Warrenton and was admitted to the Virginia bar in 1823.

Opposition to slavery prompted Swayne to move to the free state of Ohio. He settled first in Zanesville, but relocated his law office to Coshocton in 1825. A physically imposing person above six feet in height, Swayne also was warm, outgoing, and affable. Such attributes and qualities, combined with a good legal mind—his Court colleague David Davis later said that he was "by all odds the best *lawyer*" of Lincoln's five appointees (Fridlington 1987, 176, emphasis added)—brought him quick success as an attorney. Indeed, Swayne's career seemed to be on a fast track. An enthusiastic Jacksonian Democrat, he was named prosecuting attorney for Coshocton County in 1826 and elected to the state legislature in 1829. President Jackson appointed him U.S. attorney for Ohio in 1830, a position Swayne held until 1841 when the Whigs gained control of the White House.

With this appointment Swayne moved to the state capital of Columbus, about sixty miles southwest of Coshocton. A romance with Sarah Ann Wager, of Harpers Ferry, Virginia, led to their marriage in 1832 and the prompt manumission of the slaves she owned. Their union yielded one daughter and four sons, including Wager Swayne, who was to become a Union general in the Civil War and a prominent New York attorney.

Being U.S. attorney did not preclude other political and legal activities. Swayne was elected to the Columbus city council in 1834 and to a second term in the state legislature in 1836. A law partnership that he established in 1839 with James Bates lasted until 1852; this was followed by a seven-year partnership with Llewellyn Taber. During these years Swayne not only expanded his practice but served his state in several important ways. As one of three specially appointed state fund commissioners, he did much to put Ohio's credit on firmer footing after the panic of 1837 ("panic" being the nineteenth-century term for a sudden and severe economic downturn). He helped to settle a potentially violent boundary dispute between Ohio and Michigan (with the disputed land remaining in Ohio), and spoke out for the creation of state-supported institutions to care for those with mental, vision, and hearing disabilities. His practice included some high-profile cases that heightened his reputation as one of the state's leading trial attorneys. One involved a four-day cross-examination that yielded the acquittal in U.S. circuit court of the owners of the steamboat *Martha Washington* who had been accused of setting the vessel ablaze in order to collect the insurance. In a few cases he worked on behalf of fugitive slaves.

Swayne's long-standing antislavery views eventually eroded his loyalty to the Democratic Party. He joined the ranks of the newly formed Republican Party in time to back its presidential nominee, John C. Fremont, in 1856. With war on the horizon in 1860, Swayne stood firmly on the side of Lincoln and union. Given his stature within Ohio, it was hardly a surprise when Governor William Dennison named Swayne as his assistant for statewide mobilization once fighting began. The link with Dennison proved providential. As explained in Chapter 1, the governor became one of Swayne's most enthusiastic allies as Swayne waged his successful campaign for McLean's seat.

Swayne served nineteen years as a Justice, with the last seven as a member of the Waite Court. Yet his accomplishments in political life and as a leader of the Ohio bar did not foreshadow an outstanding judicial career. He may have been, as Davis said, the best lawyer of the five men Lincoln sent to the Supreme Court. But he proved to be the weakest jurist. It may be just as well that his strivings to become chief justice did not succeed. His judicial ambitions seemed to have outrun his abilities. He wrote about 350 opinions for the Court during his nineteen years, but only a few were of lasting value. (In terms of number of opinions, his per term output was similar to Miller's, who wielded one of the fastest pens on the bench.) His principal achievement lay in faithfulness to the president who nominated him and the party that confirmed him. Of Lincoln's five, none surpassed Swayne in support for the war, the Union, and the administration's policies, as his votes in the *Prize Cases* and the *Legal Tender Cases*, reviewed in Chapter 1, illustrate. As for Reconstruction-era statutes guaranteeing federal protection for the civil rights of the newly freed slaves, a topic to be addressed in Chapter 3, his votes generally aligned with most of the Lincoln and post-Lincoln appointees: defending those rights on occasion, but withholding federal protection in other instances.

Among his strongest supporters at the time of his appointment were financial and other business interests who considered the Ohioan sound on matters important to them. Their trust was well-placed, as *Gelpcke v. Dubuque* (1864) illustrates. The case presented the Court with a dispute, all too common in the 1860s and 1870s, concerning the validity of municipal bonds and the obligation of a government to make good on its debt. But *Gelpcke* was different in one important respect. In earlier litigation in the case, the Supreme Court of Iowa had upheld the validity of the bonds that had been floated to finance railroad construction. But in a later ruling the same court changed its mind and held that the law authorizing the bonds violated the state constitution; hence, the bonds were invalid and no repayment was due. In the U.S. Supreme Court, Swayne for the majority rejected the Iowa high court's later construction of its own constitution and reinstated the earlier and "correct" holding that the bonds were valid. Not only was the city of Dubuque thus required to make payment, but the Court departed from the rule that a state court was the final authority on the meaning of its state's own laws and constitution. "We shall never immolate truth, justice, and the law, because a state tribunal has erected the altar and decreed the sacrifice." The significance of *Gelpcke* did not go unnoticed by sole dissenter Justice Miller: "[T]he Court has . . . taken a step in advance of anything theretofore decided . . . in the direction of a usurpation of the right, which belongs to the state courts, to decide as a finality upon the construction of state constitutions and state statutes."

Such unwavering and sometimes creative defense of creditors made Swayne the "judicial patron of the bondholding class" (Fairman 1950, 61). It also earned Miller's lasting condescension. When Miller heard attorney and brother-in-law W. P. Ballinger speak highly of Swayne in 1869, Miller was quick to reply. "The impression which Judge Swayne seems to have made on you, is the same first impression that he makes on every one. . . . [I]t does not last. So much of it is found to be mere courtesy, parade of learning, . . . with an absence of any real sincerity, and the presence of an ever watchful selfishness . . ." (Fairman 1939, 234). As it was, the *Gelpcke* doctrine "took this court a good while to explain," Justice Holmes acknowledged much later in *Muhiker v. N.Y. and Harlem R.R. Co.* (1905). It was not implicitly interred until *Erie Railroad v. Tompkins* (1938).

If Swayne led this expansion of federal judicial power, he also found himself in the minority in the *Slaughterhouse Cases* (1873), when a five-justice majority emasculated the newly ratified Fourteenth Amendment as a federal shield against abuses of individual rights by state governments. For reasons that combined both greed and public health concerns, Louisiana chartered a new slaughterhouse company and required all slaughtering of animals in three parishes, including New Orleans, to be done only at the company's facility for a fee. Over 1,000 butchers were adversely affected. Yet according to Justice Miller, the aggrieved butchers asserted no right protected by the Fourteenth Amendment. The amendment was held to protect only rights adhering in national, rather than state, citizenship even though the latter included most of the important rights, such as that of being able to engage in an occupation.

In what was surely his most important dissent, Swayne contended that the Fourteenth, along with the Thirteenth and Fifteenth Amendments, "rise to the dignity of a new Magna Charta. Property is everything which has an exchangeable value, and the right of property includes the power to dispose of it according to the will of the owner. Labor is property, and as such merits protection. A more flagrant and indefensible invasion of the rights of many for the benefit of a few has not occurred in the legislative history of the country." The majority's construction "defeats, by a limitation not anticipated, the intent of those by whom the instrument was framed . . . turn[ing], as it were what was meant for bread into a stone." A statute restricting property in that manner could not be said to accord with "due process of law." Swayne's reading of the Fourteenth Amendment, combined with the posture of judicial activism reflected in *Gelpcke*, would characterize the Court a quarter century later.

Yet Swayne was by no means an enemy of government regulation. In 1877 he was firmly in the majority of seven in *Munn v. Illinois*. In that landmark decision, the Court upheld state regulation of grain warehouse and railroad rates against challenges that such legislation was a plain violation of the due process clause of the

Fourteenth Amendment. A year later, Swayne spoke for the Court in another Illinois case. A charter issued by the state in 1867 authorized a company to manufacture fertilizer from offal, manure, and dead animals in the Village of Hyde Park. The village banned such shipments through the village because of the stench from the animal matter as it moved slowly by rail. The company contended that the restriction would put it out of business and violated its charter (a contract). Swayne found no impairment of a contractual right, but rather the lawful exercise of a local government's power to quell nuisances. "We cannot doubt that the police power of the State was applicable and adequate to give an effectual remedy" (*Northwestern Fertilizing Co. v. Hyde Park*, 1878).

Neither was Swayne averse to political intervention on the side. One might think today that the Fifteenth Amendment, ratified in 1870 to remove race as a criterion for voting, was a foregone result of the Civil War. It was not. Ohio had rejected black suffrage in 1867, and in 1869 the Democrat-controlled legislature refused to ratify the amendment. Black suffrage was not entirely an altruistic goal on the part of Republicans. It was their ticket to a continued hold on power. (Swayne identified the Republican Party with the national interest.) So Swayne was enlisted early in 1870 to help pressure the Ohio legislature to do what it had failed to do in 1869. In an understatement, he wrote the governor in January that "I have had the subject a good deal in my thoughts" (Gillette 1969, 998). With all persuasion and patronage stops pulled out by everyone from President Grant on down, the state senate approved the amendment by a one-vote margin, as did the state house by two votes.

By 1879, Swayne's mental faculties were in decline. "But as the old fox don't want to go," said Miller, "he readily seizes on the objection that the business of the court might be suspended to delay action" (Fairman 1939, 380). Not until President Hayes prevailed upon Swayne to retire by assuring him that Swayne's friend and fellow Ohioan Stanley Matthews would have his seat did Swayne agree to step down.

The most important constitutional decision in which Swayne spoke for the Court came down on his last day as a justice, January 24, 1881. *Springer v. United States* (1881) challenged the constitutionality of a tax on incomes enacted during the Civil War. (The tax expired in 1872 when Congress declined to renew it.) William Springer, himself an attorney, refused to pay, contending that the tax was direct (as opposed to indirect) and therefore should have been apportioned among the states according to population as stipulated by Article I, section 9 of the Constitution. In a rambling and disjointed opinion that quoted at length from statements by Alexander Hamilton, James Madison, and other founding fathers, Swayne accepted the intimation in *Hylton v. United States* (1796) that direct taxes included only taxes on land and capitation taxes. Because "evils would attend the apportionment of a tax [on incomes], the Constitution could not have intended that an apportionment should be made." The Court would totally reject *Springer* only fourteen years later, but the position taken by the unanimous bench in *Springer* was vindicated by ratification of the Sixteenth Amendment in 1913.

Swayne lived three years in retirement and apparently enjoyed them immensely. As he wrote Justice Joseph P. Bradley, "You need have no apprehension that you will not find enough to do. . . . You will be brighter and happier . . ." (Atkinson 1999, 59). After his wife died, Swayne moved to New York to live with his son Wager. He died there on June 8, 1884.

Samuel Freeman Miller

In July 1862, the swearing-in of the second of the Lincoln justices filled a seat that had been vacant since the death of Justice Peter V. Daniel in May 1860. In several important respects, Samuel F. Miller's Supreme Court career of twenty-eight years differed markedly from Daniel's of nineteen years. Daniel was named to the bench in early 1841 during the closing days of Martin Van Buren's administration. This "last Jeffersonian to hold public office in the United States" (Frank 1964, vii) wrote no opinions of lasting importance, defended slavery, expounded secession, and was hostile to congressional power. In contrast, Miller spoke for the Court more frequently in significant constitutional cases than any other Lincoln appointee, opposed slavery, defended the Union, and generally looked to Congress as lawmaker for the nation. Yet, like Daniel he distrusted corporations and respected states' rights.

Among the Waite Court justices, there were a few like Clifford who had little formal education; there were a handful like Horace Gray who claimed little in the way of nonjudicial public service; and there were some like L. Q. C. Lamar who had no prior judicial experience. But none combined so shallow a formal educational preparation for the bench and so skimpy a political and judicial resume as did Samuel Miller in July 1862. Yet, as Chief Justice Chase observed, Miller became "beyond question the dominant personality upon the bench, whose mental force and individuality [were] felt by the Court more than any other" (Fairman 1939, 3).

Samuel Miller was born on April 5, 1816, on a farm near Richmond, Kentucky, about thirty miles south of Lexington. His father, Frederick, was of German stock and had been reared in Berks County, Pennsylvania; Patsy, his mother, was the daughter of Samuel Freeman who was of English descent and had moved to Kentucky from North Carolina in the late 1700s. The first of eight children, Samuel attended an academy in Richmond until he was fourteen. He then began working in a relative's pharmacy. This experience apparently sparked an interest in medicine. With some self-study and a handful of courses at Transylvania University (now the University of Kentucky), he was awarded an M.D. degree in 1838.

For about a decade Miller practiced medicine in Barbourville in Knox County, barely twenty miles north of Kentucky's borders with Tennessee and Virginia. He was

Samuel Freeman Miller (Handy Studios, Collection of the Supreme Court of the United States)

a founding member of a debating society that assembled on Saturdays in this mountain village of 200 to consider the great questions of the day. These meetings provided not only an opportunity for Miller to display his intellect and to polish his public speaking but also a forum for his progressive views. He was a Whig in his politics and a supporter of Henry Clay, who called for federally sponsored internal improvements. He was a Unitarian, believed in public education, opposed capital punishment, advocated the gradual manumission of slaves, was highly suspicious of money's influence in politics, and flirted with female suffrage. Miller would later exhibit tendencies toward agrarian radicalism that made him appealing in Midwestern farm states as a possible presidential candidate in 1880 and 1884. In his dissent against Swayne's opinion in *Gelpcke v. Dubuque* (1864), he made no effort to hide his antipathy for the "gambling stockbroker of Wall Street." "I have met with but few things of a character affecting the public good of the whole country," he commented privately in 1878, "that has shaken my faith in human nature as much as the united, vigorous, and selfish effort of the capitalists . . .—I mean those who live solely by interest and dividends. . . . They engage in no commerce, no trade, no manufactures, no agriculture. They produce nothing" (Fairman 1939, 67). In Barbourville as on the Court, Miller was unafflicted with self-doubt. Indeed, he was supremely confident of his sagacity and the correctness of his opinions and could be openly impatient with those whom he considered narrow-visioned adversaries.

Miller's growing passion for public issues paralleled a growing disillusionment with medicine as it lagged well behind progress in other sciences. The result was a career change. He became a justice of the peace (a lay office) in 1844 and was chosen president of the county court in 1846. At about the same time he began to read law on the side and was admitted to the bar in 1847. He then resigned his position as magistrate and decided to devote himself fully to his new calling.

It was also in Barbourville that he met and married Lucy Ballinger, a union that yielded three children. Lucy introduced Miller to her brother William Pitt Ballinger, a Texas lawyer, with whom Miller developed the closest friendship of his life. Miller later brought Ballinger's name to President Hayes's attention as a contender for the seat vacated in 1877 by Justice Davis.

However, the doctor-turned-lawyer soon left the Bluegrass State. Miller had been a candidate in 1849 to a state constitutional convention, but withdrew in favor of a friend to avoid splitting the antislavery vote. After the newly ratified constitution of 1850 strengthened slavery's grip on the state, Miller accepted the inevitable and moved west with his family to the thriving Mississippi River town of Keokuk, in southeastern Iowa. He entered into a partnership with Lewis Reeves, who already had an established practice. Miller was a nearly instant professional success. Within a year he was widely known and highly regarded in legal circles throughout Iowa. Yet tragedy followed his relocation to Keokuk. Both Lucy and Reeves died. In 1854 Miller joined in partnership with John Rankin, another leading attorney, and in 1857 married Elizabeth Winter Reeves, widow of his former partner, who survived Miller by a decade.

When the Republican Party was organized in 1854, Miller was attracted by its free-soil principles and was elected the party's county chairman. There followed two unsuccessful races for public office: for state senator in 1856 and for governor in 1861. Miller enthusiastically and fortuitously supported Abraham Lincoln, whose views on slavery were identical to his own, for the Republican presidential nomination in 1860. Following the judicial reorganization of 1862, discussed in Chapter 1, Miller's renown made him the most visible prospect to represent the new trans-Mississippi circuit and to fill Daniel's seat at the Supreme Court.

Miller's Supreme Court career was marked by several themes. As noted in Chapter 1 in connection with the *Slaughterhouse Cases* (1873), he prevailed against a reading of the privileges and immunities clause in section one of the recently ratified Fourteenth Amendment advocated by colleagues Chase, Swayne, Stephen J. Field, and Joseph P. Bradley. This interpretation would have given citizens federal constitutional protection when states had allegedly violated fundamental rights, such as the right to labor or to engage in an occupation. Miller insisted that "one pervading purpose" lay at the heart of the Fourteenth Amendment as well as the Thirteenth (which abolished slavery) and the Fifteenth (which removed race as a criterion for voting). This purpose was "the freedom of the slave race, the security and firm establishment of that freedom, and the protection of the newly-made freeman and citizen from the oppressions of those who had formerly exercised unlimited dominion over him." The result was that, in most other circumstances, citizens were left with protections afforded by their state laws and constitutions. Miller reasoned that to hold otherwise "would constitute this court a perpetual censor upon all legislation of the States, on the civil rights of their own citizens. . . ." Miller so effectively constricted the meaning of this clause that since 1873 the Supreme Court has relied on it as a source of federally protected rights only twice. His interpretation, however, had an ironic result. States remained free to regulate commercial matters, but it became more difficult, as explored in chapter 3, to sustain federal legislation designed to protect the very persons who were presumably the intended beneficiaries of the amendment.

Miller was equally cool to use of the Fourteenth Amendment's due process clause as a substantive limit on the police (or regulatory) power of the states. In an opinion in 1878, he went out of his way to admonish future litigants, counsel, and lower courts about what he considered an ominous trend.

> It is not a little remarkable, that while [the due process clause] has been in the Constitution . . . as a restraint upon the authority of the federal government, for nearly a century, . . . this special limitation upon its powers has rarely been

> invoked in the judicial forum. . . . But while it has been a part of the Constitution, as a restraint upon the power of the States, only a very few years, the docket of this court is crowded with cases in which we are asked to hold that . . . State Legislatures have deprived their own citizens of life, liberty or property without due process of law. There is here abundant evidence that there exists some strange misconception of the scope of . . . the XIVth Amendment. In fact, it would seem . . . that the clause under consideration is looked upon as a means of bringing to . . . this court the abstract opinions of every unsuccessful litigant in a State Court . . . of the merits of the legislation on which such a decision may be founded. (*Davidson v. New Orleans*, 1878)

Miller believed instead litigants should look to the political process and state courts for redress. The Court did not repudiate this hands-off approach until Miller's death in 1890. However, Justice John Marshall Harlan had by then already forecast its demise in dictum: "The courts . . . are at liberty—indeed, are under a solemn duty—to look at the substance of things" (*Mugler v. Kansas*, 1887).

A general predisposition toward state authority, however, did not necessarily include laws that regulated commerce among the several States. That authority, according to the Constitution, lay expressly with Congress. At least since Justice Curtis's opinion in *Cooley v. Board of Wardens* (1851), however, the Court had recognized that states could control some local aspects of interstate commerce in the absence of congressional legislation and in situations where no uniform rule was needed. For example, in one of the *Granger Cases* of 1877, the Court had upheld the right of states to set railroad rates (*Chicago, B. and Q. R.R. v. Iowa*). Within a decade a crazy quilt of regulation resulted, causing the Court to rethink the matter. Justice Miller's opinion for the Court in *Wabash, St. Louis and Pacific Railway Co. v. Illinois* (1886) illustrated the quandary. The railroad charged 15 cents per 100 pounds from Peoria, Illinois, and 25 cents per 100 pounds from Gilman, Illinois, on shipments of similar goods to New York City. Because Gilman was 86 miles closer to New York, the rate scheme ran afoul of an Illinois statute banning long-haul/short-haul rate discrimination. With most of the distance for each shipment lying outside Illinois, the state was effectively regulating the rates of interstate shipments. "This is commerce of national character," declared Miller in invalidating the statute, "and national regulation is required." The ruling spurred Congress into action to fill the void. The Interstate Commerce Act of 1887 created the Interstate Commerce Commission, the second permanent federal regulatory agency with broad quasi-legislative, executive, and judicial powers.

Indeed, Miller had long supported Congress's power under the commerce clause, as one would expect from a former Whig. On circuit in the *Clinton Bridge Case* (1867), Miller rejected a claim that Congress lacked authority to regulate bridges over navigable streams. "The power to regulate commerce is one of the most useful confided to the federal government; and its exercise has done as much as that of any other to create and foster that strongest bond of nationality—a community of interests among the States. The want of it was one of the most pressing necessities which led to the formation of the Constitution" (Fairman 1939, 311, quoting the *Clinton Bridge Case,* 1867).

Yet Miller was hostile to perceived abuses of power by the national government. His opinion for the Court in *Kilbourn v. Thompson* (1881) overturned a conviction for contempt of Congress and established the important principle that any congressional investigation must be related to a valid legislative purpose. The next year Miller authored what he regarded as his greatest opinion. In contention was the validity of the seizure of the Robert E. Lee estate at Arlington, Virginia, during the Civil War following nonpayment of a tax imposed by Congress in 1862. (President Lincoln ordered the seizure after the Board of Tax Commissioners had cunningly ruled that the owner was required to pay the tax in person.) The government then allocated part of the property for a cemetery for Union soldiers in 1864 and the rest for an Army post. For a bare majority of five, Miller rejected the government's position that it was protected from suit by the doctrine of sovereign immunity. "No man in this country is so high that he is above the law. No officer of the law may set that law at defiance with impunity. All the officers of the government, from the highest to the lowest, are creatures of the law, and are bound to obey it" (*United States v. Lee,* 1882).

The life of the Waite Court's most prominent justice ended in the fall of 1890. Returning from the Capitol on October 10, the senior associate justice suffered a paralytic stroke and collapsed at Thomas Circle, within sight of his home at 1415 Massachusetts Avenue, N.W. A day later he sank into a coma and died on October 13.

David Davis

The third of Lincoln's appointees to the Supreme Court was one of only two with prior judicial experience. His appointment remains unprecedented: no one since David Davis has been elevated from a state trial court of general jurisdiction directly to the High Court. Moreover, he enjoyed a relationship with Lincoln that none of the other Lincoln justices could claim. Just as Davis would almost certainly never have been placed on the Supreme Court without Lincoln, it is highly probable that Lincoln would never have been elected president without Davis.

In October 1862 Davis filled the last of the three vacancies Lincoln confronted early in his first year in office. Justice John Archibald Campbell of Alabama had resigned in April 1861 and soon became the Confederacy's assistant secretary of war. Davis too would eventually leave the Court to accept another position. Indeed, his departure in 1877 created the first vacancy on the Waite Court. If the selection of Davis was very much the handiwork of the president himself, Franklin Pierce's nomination

David Davis (Unknown, Collection of the Supreme Court of the United States)

of Campbell in 1853 was not. In a bold and still unique step, eight justices dispatched a bipartisan delegation to inform the clueless new president that he should appoint Campbell to fill the existing vacancy. Pierce did as he was told. A thoroughgoing states-rights Democrat, Campbell in his postwar law practice nonetheless was the first to deploy the Fourteenth Amendment, a symbol of Union victory, in the Supreme Court in the *Slaughterhouse Cases* (1873) in an unsuccessful attempt to invalidate a Louisiana statute. Among the first to align himself with the new Republican Party in the 1850s, Davis not only joined Miller's opinion in the *Slaughterhouse Cases* that severely crippled the amendment but displayed a streak independent of the party to which he owed his appointment.

Davis was born on March 9, 1815, in Cecil County on Maryland's Eastern Shore. He was named for his father, a physician, who had died eight months earlier. In 1820, his mother, Ann Mercer Davis, married Franklin Betts and moved to Baltimore. David's stepfather sent him to Annapolis to live with an uncle, Dr. Henry Lyon Davis, who was rector of St. Anne's Episcopal Church and president of St. John's College. A custody struggle promptly ensued. Dr. Davis, who became a father figure to David, challenged Betts's guardianship by accusing him of misappropriating estate funds left for the boy; Betts claimed that Davis drank too much. Betts prevailed, and David was dispatched to New Ark Academy in Delaware. In 1828, he enrolled at Ohio's Kenyon College and graduated in 1832. Now seventeen, David traveled to Massachusetts, read law under the guidance of Lenox attorney Henry W. Bishop, and courted Sarah Woodruff Walker, daughter of the local judge. He capped his study of law with courses at the New Haven Law School in Connecticut in 1834.

The turmoil of his childhood left few, if any, long-term negative effects. Davis moved to Illinois, was admitted to the bar, and opened an office in the town of Pekin, some 60 miles north of Springfield. He soon met a state legislator named Abraham Lincoln, and the two attorneys (and fellow Whigs) became lifelong friends. A bout with malaria in 1836 and dissatisfaction with Pekin motivated Davis to relocate his practice to Bloomington, a thriving community of nearly 1,500 about thirty miles to the southeast. He soon prospered professionally, and displayed skills as a land speculator. In 1838 Judge William Walker of Lenox grudgingly gave his consent for his daughter Sarah to move west to become Mrs. Davis. As evidence of the appalling mortality rates of that day, a son (George Perrin), born to the couple in 1842, was the only one of their four children to survive infancy.

By 1839 it was clear that Davis had political aspirations. He made two unsuccessful bids for public office, first as district attorney and then as a Whig candidate for state senate. But he won election in 1844 to the Illinois legislature, served a term, and then was elected to the state constitutional convention of 1847 where he was partly responsible for abolishing legislative election of judges in favor of a system of popular election. Davis benefited nearly instantly from this change. He was elected judge of an eighteen-county circuit in 1848, a trial court position he held for fourteen years. Lincoln often traveled with Davis as the judge rode the courthouse circuit. Of the eighty-seven nonjury cases that Davis heard in which the future president appeared as counsel, he ruled against his friend in forty-seven (Niehoff 1993, 183).

The Whig Party disintegrated over slavery in the 1850s. Davis opposed the expansion of slavery in the western territories and so was against the Kansas-Nebraska Act, although he was equally opposed to his party's "being abolitionized," as he wrote his brother-in-law Julius Rockwell in Massachusetts in 1854 (Kutler 1969a, 1046). (The Kansas-Nebraska Act repealed the Missouri Compromise's limited ban on slavery and permitted residents of the Kansas and Nebraska Territories to decide whether their territories would allow slaveholding or not.) Furthermore, Davis was attracted by Lincoln's political ambitions, energetically campaigning for him in unsuccessful campaigns for the U. S. Senate in 1854 and again in 1858. By this time each man had joined the ranks of the newly organized Republican Party. It was the 1858 contest against incumbent Democrat Senator Stephen A. Douglas that earned Lincoln a national reputation, as Davis was quick to discern. "The prairies are on fire," commented a New York newspaper in describing the heated Illinois race (Holzer 1993, 1).

When Lincoln sought the Republican presidential nomination in 1860, Judge Davis was campaign strategist. With the convention conveniently meeting in Chicago, "Lincoln's manager" (King 1960) made sure that his candidate avoided offending leading contenders such as William Seward, Simon Cameron, Edward Bates, and Salmon Chase. The stratagem was as simple as it was efficacious: Davis secured second-choice pledges for Lincoln. When Seward failed to receive a majority vote on the second ballot, Lincoln won it on the third. After the election Davis advised Lincoln on patronage, reviewed a draft of the president-elect's inaugural address, and traveled with Lincoln on the train from Springfield to Washington in February 1861. It was more than puzzling to observers that Davis did not receive tangible reward for such faithful service until a year and a half later.

With two exceptions, Justice Davis supported Lincoln's policies and tended to align himself with Chase Court and Waite Court majorities on most questions. He cast a vital fifth vote in the *Prize Cases* (1863) that upheld the federal blockade of Southern ports in the absence of a declaration of war. With the rest of the bench, he agreed to sidestep a potentially explosive executive-judicial confrontation during wartime over the authority of military tribunals in *Ex parte Vallandigham* (1864), although he led the Court in revisiting that matter two years later. He joined the decisions in *Georgia v. Stanton* (1867) and *Ex parte McCardle* (1867) that declined to interfere in the operation of Reconstruction policies. Unlike his colleagues who struck down the statutes, he accepted the constitutionality of state and federal test oaths that blunted access of ex-Confederates and their supporters to licensed professional and government jobs

(*Cummings v. Missouri* and *Ex parte Garland*, 1867). He was in the majority in *Texas v. White* (1869) that, among other things, sustained Lincoln's theory of secession and the Union. Later, in both rounds of the legal tender litigation in 1870 and 1871, he backed the constitutionality of paper currency. He sided with the majorities in both the *Slaughterhouse Cases* (1873) and *Munn v. Illinois* (1877) that, for the time being at least, denied use of the recently ratified Fourteenth Amendment as a federal shield to protect property rights. He also seemed as disinclined as most of his Court brethren to lend a broad reading to Reconstruction statutes to protect the civil rights of the newly freed slaves (*United States v. Reese*, 1876, and *United States v. Cruikshank*, 1876).

Davis parted company with Lincoln on the Emancipation Proclamation and trial of civilians by military tribunals. The first, superceded by the Thirteenth Amendment, never came before the Court for review. But Davis's views on the matter were clear. He told the president that it was bad politically because of resentment that might be felt in Illinois. It was also bad policy: Because the proclamation purported to end slavery only in areas of the South still held by Confederates, it would unduly prolong the fighting. "If this war is not wound up this winter," he wrote in 1863, "I dread the next Presidential election" (Silver 1998, 81).

Davis's objection to the trial of civilians by military tribunals led to his only enduring opinion in a constitutional case. Lambdin P. Milligan was a resident of Indiana, an antiwar Democrat, and a leader of the Sons of Liberty, a paramilitary organization that operated in Indiana on behalf of the Confederacy. Captured by federal troops in Indiana in 1864 and charged with plotting acts of mayhem and fomenting insurrection, Milligan was tried before a presidentially authorized military commission and sentenced to be hanged. Counsel petitioned the U.S. circuit court in Indiana for a writ of habeas corpus, claiming that Milligan had been tried illegally. The bench consisted of Davis, sitting as circuit judge, and the district judge. By agreeing to divide on the questions raised by the litigation, they thus certified the case and assured a Supreme Court hearing on the authority of military tribunals.

Davis spoke for a unanimous Court on the central point of the case. "[T]he main question presented by this record cannot be overstated; for it involves the very framework of the government and the fundamental principles of American liberty. . . . The Constitution . . . is a law for rulers and people, equally in war and in peace, and covers with the shield of its protection all classes of men, at all times, and under all circumstances," he insisted in an emotionally laden assertion of judicial authority and plea for the civil liberties of civilians. "No doctrine, involving more pernicious consequences, was ever invented by the wit of man than that any of its provisions can be suspended during any of the great exigencies of government." When civilian courts were open and functioning, as they were in Indiana in 1864 and 1865, civilians could not be tried by military commission. Davis and four colleagues went further to address a point not actually before the Court and concluded that even Congress could not authorize such trials, although Chief Justice Chase and Justices Wayne, Swayne, and Miller disputed that point (*Ex parte Milligan*, 1866).

Although later generations have widely hailed Davis's defense of liberty, the Republican press and leading Republican lawmakers soundly chastised him at the time. "This constitutional twaddle of Mr. Justice Davis," editorialized the *New York Herald*, "will no more stand the fire of public opinion than the *Dred Scott* decision. . . . [The Court] is a relic of the past, nine old superior pettifoggers, old marplots, a formidable barrier to the consummation of the great revolution" (Warren 1926, II, 432). Critics feared that *Milligan* would deny the authority of military commissions in the occupied states of the old Confederacy and thus undermine Reconstruction. The criticism mystified Davis. There was "not a word said in the opinion about reconstruction, & the power is conceded in insurrectionary States," he wrote in 1867 (Kutler 1968, 67). Nonetheless, even though the Court never ruled on that aspect of Reconstruction policy, it seemed incompatible with the *Milligan* doctrine.

Davis's *Milligan* opinion typified his writing style. Probably reflecting his eighteen years' experience rendering charges to Illinois juries, his opinions were clear and direct, briefer than most of those penned by his colleagues, and unburdened by a wealth of citations. In short, they were most un-Clifford-like, although Davis at 300 pounds and Clifford shared the distinction of being the most physically massive members of the Waite Court. "I believe I write the shortest opinions of any one on the bench," Davis confided in 1870, "& if I had to elaborate opinions & write legal essays as some Judges do, I would quit the concern. I like to hold trial court, but this work on an appellate bench is too much like hard labor" (Fairman 1971, 1461).

These qualities served him well in *United States v. Union Pacific Railroad Company* (1875). The railroad had been congressionally chartered during the Civil War to complete a transcontinental line and bind the westernmost states with the rest of the Union. Financing came in part from U.S. bonds given to the company that would be repaid with interest at a later time. The government in turn could withhold half of the money it would otherwise have paid the company for transporting mail, troops, and supplies. When the withheld sums fell well short of the interest the government was paying on the bonds, it held out the remaining half, and the Union Pacific sued to recover. The case was a public relations nightmare for the Court. The country was still in an uproar over the Crédit Mobilier scandal of 1872. In that episode, top executives of the Union Pacific had created a construction company, with which several members of Congress were involved, through which they diverted some $20 million into their own pockets. In the unrelated 1875 case, the Court held unanimously for the railroad. Anxious that a justice such as Field or Bradley who had connections with railroad interests not author the opinion, Waite turned to Davis who was at his best when circumstances dictated plain speaking:

> This enterprise was viewed as a national undertaking for national purposes. . . . The difficulties in the way of building it were great, and by many intelligent persons considered insurmountable. . . . The project was not conceived for private ends; and the prevalent opinion was that it could not be worked out by private capital alone. It was a national work, originating in national necessities, and requiring national assistance. [Thus,] the Act itself was an experiment. . . . If enlisted at all, it could only be on conditions which would insure, in case of success, remuneration proportionate to the risk incurred.

Despite these skills at laying out a complex dispute in terms most could understand, Davis was temperamentally ill-suited for the Supreme Court. Not only did he seem to prefer the work of the trial judge, but he could not stay out of politics. This put him on the path to resignation. As a justice, Davis did not hesitate to offer Lincoln political advice and to intervene with the president to promote certain individuals for office and to obtain favors for friends. In 1864 he vocally supported Lincoln's renomination at the Republican convention in Baltimore as Davis began to cultivate presidential aspirations of his own. In 1872, Davis received the presidential nomination of the Labor Reform (or National Labor Union) Party but he declined it in hopes of a bigger prize: nomination by the Liberal Republicans, a reform movement. However, that nomination went to newspaper publisher Horace Greeley. In 1876 Davis unsuccessfully courted Democrats, but their choice to challenge Republican Rutherford Hayes was New York attorney and governor Samuel J. Tilden.

In 1877 Congress created a commission, with members coming from the House, Senate, and Supreme Court, to resolve the undecided presidential election of 1876. Democrats, who held an edge in the popular vote, agreed to the commission on the expectation that Davis, "whose political sympathies at the moment were supposed to be in a state of equipoise" (Fairman 1939, 286), would be the fifteenth and deciding member of the commission. The commission already consisted of seven Republicans and seven Democrats. Meanwhile, independents and Democrats in the Illinois legislature elected Davis to the U.S. Senate. He accepted, declined consideration for the commission, and resigned from the Court effective March 4, 1877. Justice Bradley became the fifth judicial commissioner and voted with other Republican members to award the contested electoral votes (and hence the election) to Hayes. Outraged Democrats, assuming that Davis would have tilted toward Tilden, heaped invective on him for quitting. Yet Davis presumably would have backed Hayes: "No good lawyer, not a strict partisan, could decide otherwise," he later explained (King 1960, 292–293). In a strategic ploy with unintended consequences, Tilden's nephew William Pelton had a large hand in inducing Davis's Senate election as a way of engendering a feeling of obligation (Fairman 1987, 173).

Davis served one term in the Senate, but presidential ambitions evaporated after his wife died in 1879. Admired for his independence, Republicans elected him president pro tem in 1881. With Garfield's assassination, that placed him second in line to the presidency, the closest he came to the highest office in the land. What seemed to matter most to him at this point of his life was reconciliation between North and South. "When the rude voices of faction which for fifteen years . . . have disturbed the national fellowship . . . shall be silenced, this country will bound forward in a career of grandeur and glory that will astonish mankind" (King 1960, 302). Just prior to leaving the Senate in 1883, Davis married Adeline Burr of Fayetteville, North Carolina. The newlyweds retired to Bloomington where the judge died on June 26, 1886.

Stephen J. Field

The last of the Lincoln associate justices was the first named from a West Coast state and the first in over a generation to occupy a new seat. In 1863 Stephen Johnson Field became the (temporary) tenth justice after Congress and the president concluded that an additional vote was needed to shore up the Union cause in the Supreme Court. Besides, complicated California land cases on the Court's docket and the need to cement that state firmly into the Union counseled that a new circuit be created and assigned to a Supreme Court justice from California. With the selection of Field, Lincoln reached far into the future. Until outstripped by William O. Douglas in 1974, Field's tenure of thirty-four years, six months, and eleven days stood as the longest in Supreme Court history. Furthermore, with the exception of Chief Justice John Marshall, the Californian's impact on U.S. constitutional law arguably surpassed that of any other nineteenth-century member of the Supreme Court.

The sixth of the nine children of the Reverend David Dudley and Submit Dickinson Field, Stephen was born on November 4, 1816, in Haddam, a village in Connecticut some twenty-five miles southeast of Hartford. Descended from old-line Puritan stock, both parents instilled in their offspring abundant self-discipline and a drive for success. Stephen's brother David Dudley became a prominent New York attorney and law reformer; his friendship with Abraham Lincoln would later help to convince the sixteenth president that the new tenth seat belonged to his brother. Cyrus, another brother, excelled in business and promoted the laying of the trans-Atlantic telegraph cable. Brother Henry followed his father into the clergy and achieved fame as an author. Stephen's sister Emilia was the mother of David J. Brewer, who became Field's colleague on the Supreme Court during the last eight years of his tenure.

In 1819 Stephen's father accepted the call of the Congregational Church in Stockbridge, Massachusetts, a small town in the Berkshires about 45 miles west of Springfield, where Jonathan Edwards had once held forth from the pulpit. The children heard their father preach three sermons each Sunday, and Stephen learned early that

Stephen J. Field (Handy Studios, Collection of the Supreme Court of the United States)

eternal verities tolerated no enfeebling doubt. This outlook permeated his many years of public service. In the Field household one person on God's side was a majority.

At age thirteen Stephen embarked on an adventure that few youngsters of his day could match. He traveled abroad with Emilia and her minister husband Josiah Brewer, spending two and one-half years in Greece and Turkey and acquiring fluency in French, Italian, Turkish, and Greek. Enrolling in Williams College upon his return, Stephen graduated in 1837 as class valedictorian. With law as his chosen calling, he studied first under brother David's tutelage in New York City and then in Albany with John Van Buren, the New York attorney general and brother of the president. Field seemed to have learned early the advantages of what in a later century would be called networking. Admitted to the bar in 1841 he practiced with David in a partnership until 1848. He then sailed abroad again, this time to England, with side trips to Vienna and Rome. Enticed by news in 1849 of the discovery of gold in California, he departed for the United States. By this time he had no doubt become fully aware of the revolutionary sentiment that had gripped the European continent, emphasized by publication of Karl Marx's *Communist Manifesto* in 1848. He retained an interest in European affairs for the rest of his life.

That was also the year of the cession from Mexico of most of the territory that now constitutes the states of California, Arizona, and New Mexico. The discovery of gold at Sutter's Mill that so captivated Field made California the destination of thousands. However, getting there entailed considerable risk and required extraordinary stamina. Field chose to sail to Panama where he crossed the isthmus in a variety of conveyances. He then sailed north along the Pacific coast to California.

Field reached San Francisco in December 1849 and proceeded inland to the confluence of the Feather and Yuba rivers where he helped to found the town of Marysville, about forty-five miles north of Sacramento. In law as well as in the expanse of territory, far more was unsettled than settled in California in the transition from Mexican to U.S. rule. It was a place for the intrepid, risk takers, gamblers, and adventurers. Field made the most of his opportunities. Although he arrived with no more than ten dollars in his pocket, he leveraged that sum to claim title to sixty-five lots worth at least $16,000 (and within a short time his holdings would be worth ten times that amount). He became the town's alcalde, a minor magisterial office retained from Mexican rule, that Field fashioned into Marysville's chief judge and municipal administrator.

California attained statehood and received a new constitution in 1850. The office of alcalde was abolished, and a system of county and district courts was imposed. At this point some of Field's life-defining traits and personal qualities became pronounced. Replacing Field as the highest judicial authority in Marysville was a southerner named William Turner, who was as strong-willed, short-tempered, controversy-prone, and grudge-bearing as Field. Pleading a case in Turner's court,

Field offended Turner who then jailed Field for contempt. Field obtained a release from another judge, but in the rancor that followed Turner disbarred Field. When the state supreme court overturned the disbarment, Turner disbarred Field again, only to have Field prevail once more in the high court. Turner meanwhile publicly threatened to cut off Field's ears, and the transplanted New Englander purchased a pair of pistols that he brandished in self-defense. The tumult subsided only after Field was elected to the state house in 1850. He pushed through legislation that dispatched Judge Turner to a wilderness district where "only grizzly bears" and Native Americans lived (Field 1893, 77).

After a failed campaign as a Democrat for the California senate in 1851, Field practiced law until his election in 1857 to the state supreme court. In 1859 he married Sue Virginia Swearingen. Field became chief justice the same year and remained on the bench until Lincoln elevated him to the U.S. Supreme Court in 1863. Both another feud and genuine accomplishment marked his tenure on the state bench. The feud involved a colleague named David Terry, who much later would cross paths with Field in an episode that made constitutional law. The genuine accomplishment built on Field's previous leadership as a single-term legislator in drafting civil and criminal codes for California. Accordingly, he labored as a justice to bring clarity to a state plagued by disputes over land titles, many of which were complicated by Mexican origin and the arrival of gold-seeking hordes.

Field was initially as faithful as any justice on the U.S. Supreme Court to the sixteenth president's policies. Yet once peace arrived, it seemed from some of his positions that the Civil War had never happened. He spoke for a 5–4 bench in the *Test Oath Cases* that invalidated federal and state laws that imposed professional disabilities on ex-Confederates (*Ex parte Garland*, 1867, and *Cummings v. Missouri*, 1867). Field and Justice Robert Grier protested the postponement of a case that challenged Reconstruction policy when their colleagues prudently waited to see if Congress would repeal their jurisdiction. Congress did, the Court dutifully acknowledged as much, and both Grier and Field, now less intrepid if wiser, silently acquiesced (*Ex parte McCardle*, 1869). Field also was rabid in his opposition to the constitutionality of legal tender legislation that had in large measure financed the war. Not only did he side with the four-justice majority in *Hepburn v. Griswold* (1870) against legal tender and dissent the following year in the *Legal Tender Cases* when five justices upheld the greenbacks, but he tenaciously held his ground. He later was the sole dissenter when the Court affirmed Congress's power to issue paper currency in peacetime (*Juilliard v. Greenman*, 1884).

In contrast to his defeat on legal tender, Field's headstrong persistence eventually paid off in molding the new Fourteenth Amendment into a formidable shield against undue state regulation. Ratified in 1868, the amendment's section one imposed new but undefined restraints on the states. This was potentially a highly significant development in U.S. government because states had been left largely unrestrained by the Constitution. The Constitution had always forbidden states from impeding interstate commerce, from passing ex post facto laws, from impairing the obligation of contracts, and from doing a few other things. But in terms of most social and economic regulation, states did as they pleased. To what extent had the Fourteenth Amendment altered this picture? The question was important because, in the last third of the nineteenth century, the bulk of U.S. public policy was enacted at the state and municipal and not the federal level.

The Court first confronted the Fourteenth Amendment in the *Slaughterhouse Cases* in 1873. As earlier noted, butchers in and around New Orleans objected to a Louisiana statute that required them to slaughter animals at a single facility and to pay a fee for doing so. They argued that by restricting how they earned a living, the regulation infringed one of the privileges and immunities of citizens of the United States the new amendment was intended to protect. Led by Miller, five justices concluded that the right allegedly violated—as well as almost all other important rights—was one the butchers possessed by virtue of their state, not national, citizenship, and so lay outside the amendment's protection.

By the majority's construction, Field wrote in a blistering dissent, the Fourteenth Amendment "was a vain and idle enactment, which accomplished nothing, and most unnecessarily excited Congress and the people on its passage." In his view, consistent with his pre-Fourteenth position in the *Test Oath Cases*, "the privileges and immunities designated are those *which of right belong to the citizens of all free governments.* Clearly among these must be placed the right to pursue a lawful employment in a lawful manner, without other restraint than such as equally affects all persons. . . ." This was "the distinguishing privilege of citizens of the United States. To them, everywhere, all pursuits, all professions, all avocations are open without other restrictions than such as are imposed equally upon all others of the same age, sex, and condition." Field was among a growing minority not only suspicious of majority rule but also willing to interpret the Constitution to restrain majorities from roughshod trampling of minority rights. For him the Constitution protected fundamental rights and chief among them were a right of property and a right to pursue a calling. Attuned to events in Europe, he would have been aware of the Paris Commune in the spring of 1871 and generally to the appeal of socialism. Field faced a dilemma of nineteenth-century democracy: whether economic inequality could coexist with political equality. So expansive a view of the Fourteenth Amendment, however, did not prevent him from voting in the same year to uphold an Illinois rule that barred women from the practice of law (*Bradwell v. Illinois*, 1873).

Four years later, disgruntled grain warehouse owners in Chicago challenged Illinois's scheme of rate regulation as a violation of Fourteenth Amendment due process. Seven members of the Court held the warehouses to be property "affected with a public interest" and so subject to government regulation. Moreover, the reasonableness of such rates was not a question for courts to decide (*Munn v. Illinois*, 1877). "If this be sound law," countered Field, "all property and all business in the State are held at the mercy of a majority of its legislature. I deny the power of any legislature under our government to fix the price which one shall receive for his property of any kind."

Field's longevity bolstered the power of his arguments. He outlasted many of his *Slaughterhouse Cases* and *Munn* colleagues, and some of the newer justices were more inclined to read the Constitution Field's way. In 1886 the Court adopted Field's contention that corporations were persons and so protected by the due process clause (*Santa Clara County v. Southern Pacific R.R.*). In 1887, *Mugler v. Kansas* hinted, contrary to *Munn*, that the Court would begin to assess the reasonableness of state regulations, and in 1890 six justices decided that rates set by a commission were judicially reviewable (*Chicago, Mil. and St. Paul R.R. Co. v. Minnesota*). Thus before Field retired, the Court was well on the way to becoming what Justice Miller had feared in the *Slaughterhouse Cases* —a "perpetual censor" of state legislation. This was a role the Court embraced with respect to economic and social regulations until 1937. Field cast a long shadow.

However, anyone assessing Field finds an anomaly. Although insistent that the Court defend rights he regarded as fundamental, he was among the least inclined to read broadly congressional statutes designed to protect African Americans from discrimination. Nor was he as willing as others to find racially discriminatory state laws a violation of the Fourteenth Amendment's equal protection clause. The picture becomes more complicated because he was more inclined, especially on circuit, to strike down discriminatory California statutes that targeted the thousands of Chinese in that state, although even there his record is erratic. The most charitable explanation for this pattern derives from a combination of Field's deeply held beliefs. He was suspicious of federal intrusions into the internal workings of state government. For example, he dissented in a case that invalidated a state's exclusion of nonwhites from juries (*Strauder v. West Virginia*, 1880). Yet he had no problem with federal judicial interference with the affairs of state governments in other contexts. He was constitutionally skeptical of legislation that seemed to single out a class for favored treatment; hence, his dissents in *Slaughterhouse* and *Munn*. However, he dissented in the *Sinking Fund Cases* (1879), when the Court upheld Congress's stipulation that western railroads set aside a fraction of their earnings as insurance against an inability to repay their federal debt. He objected to state-imposed discrimination, not discrimination by individuals. This explains his ruling in the *Queue Case* invalidating San Francisco's ordinance that required jailers to crop the hair of inmates (*Ah Kow v. Nunan*, 1879). It also illustrates his dissent in *Ex parte Virginia* (1880), which upheld the conviction of a state judge who had systematically excluded black citizens from the jury list. Particularly in the Chinese cases, he regarded some state and local laws as interfering with the federal treaty-making power (Kens 1997, 211).

Field's positions in such cases both helped and hurt his political aspirations. His stand in the *Test Oath Cases* led the California delegation to promote him for the Democratic presidential nomination in 1868. His position on legal tender allied him with stalwart Democrats. The first draft of his *Reminiscences* of his days in California appeared in 1877 and can be read as a campaign autobiography. A member of the Electoral Commission of 1877, he voted for the Tilden electors, and expressed his disdain for Hayes by refusing to attend the inauguration. His votes in civil rights cases made him popular with southern Democrats, but his hostility to some anti-Chinese legislation in California turned many Golden State Democrats against him. His identification with business interests (particularly his friendship with railroad magnate Leland Stanford) made him suspect among the agrarian-minded. Aspirations for the White House in 1880 and 1884 were therefore highly unrealistic. His final disappointment for advancement came when Democratic president Grover Cleveland failed to nominate him for the chief justiceship in 1888 after Morrison Waite's death. Field had nothing to do with Cleveland from that day forward (Fairman 1939, 298). As one contemporary observed, "When Field 'hates,' he hates 'for keeps'" (McCloskey 1969, 545).

That quality of stubborn antipathy may explain Field's behavior in one of the most remarkable episodes in a truly remarkable life. It involved David Terry who, as chief justice when Field joined the California Supreme Court, had been Field's nemesis. Terry also had killed one of Field's friends in a duel. During the 1880s, a woman named Sarah Hill claimed to have been married to William Sharon, a wealthy U.S. senator from Nevada. A state court decree granted her a share of Sharon's property, even though Sharon claimed that she had only been his mistress. Sharon died, and Mrs. Sharon (or Miss Hill) married David Terry. Field as circuit judge then held that no wedding contract existed between Hill and Sharon. Terry acted as his claimed wife's attorney in Field's courtroom. Field ordered the surrender of the marriage contract, but not before making gratuitous comments about her character. Terry interrupted the proceedings with insults, and Field ordered a marshal to remove him from the room. When Terry struck the marshal, Field jailed the Terrys for contempt. Because of David Terry's subsequent threats on Field's life, a federal marshal named David Neagle accompanied Field on his circuit trip west in 1889. At a railroad restaurant stop, the antagonists happened to meet. After Terry struck Field twice, Neagle shot and killed Terry on the spot. Neagle was arrested and charged with murder in state court, but Judge Lorenzo Sawyer of the U.S. circuit court (who with Field had invalidated the disputed marriage between Hill and Sharon) ordered his release. Neagle had been carrying out his federal duty, and Sawyer's court had jurisdiction because the state prosecution interfered with a federal law. On appeal, the U.S. Supreme Court held that the definition of federal law included any act (such as the order assigning protection to Field) done under the authority of the United States (*In re Neagle*, 1890).

By 1896, even though Field's dissent in the first income tax case of 1895 had been entirely lucid, Field's colleagues were trying various means of encouraging retirement because of apparent mental decline. But Field wanted to serve longer than record-holder Chief Justice Marshall. In April 1897 Field submitted his resignation to President William McKinley (who had succeeded Cleveland), but Field arranged for it to take effect on December 1, a date that placed him comfortably beyond Marshall's thirty-four years, five months, and two days. Death came after a brief illness on April 9, 1899.

The Grant Appointments

William Strong

For reasons explored in Chapter 1, President Lincoln's selection of Salmon Chase as the fifth chief justice in 1864 was the only addition to the Supreme Court between Field's appointment in 1863 and William Strong's arrival on March 14, 1870. Strong took the seat held since 1846 by Justice Robert C. Grier of Pennsylvania, the second of two appointments made by President James K. Polk. By the late 1860s, Grier's mental and physical infirmities had become so pronounced that even he could no longer ignore them.

Lincoln had considered Strong as he searched for someone to fill the center seat after the death of Chief Justice Taney. A gentle person and a gentleman, Strong was the antithesis of the tempestuous Field, who for seven years had been the Court's junior associate justice. Moreover, in contrast to Field's record-breaking and consequential tenure, Strong's ten years and nine months of service illustrate a factor in judicial influence. Although longevity in office hardly guarantees renown, such extended service almost always makes it possible. Except for a handful of individuals such as Chase, who was both a wartime and Reconstruction chief justice, hardly any justice with less than a decade on the bench has been ranked among the notable. True, Strong was widely respected in his time as an especially intelligent and talented jurist. Indeed, he was something of a perfectionist. A seat on the Supreme Court surpassed all his aspirations, he acknowledged to President Grant in a note of gratitude, "except to perform . . . [my] duties well" (Kutler 1969c, 1154). Yet Strong's abbreviated career on the Court, coupled with only a handful of opinions in cases of lasting importance, minimized the opportunities for influence enjoyed by justices such as Miller and Field who served far longer and who wrote disproportionately fewer time-bound opinions.

William Strong (Matthew Brady, Handy Studios, Collection of the Supreme Court of the United States)

Born May 6, 1808, William was the first of the eleven children of the Reverend William Lighthouse and Harriet Deming Strong. With New England roots dating to 1630, the family made its home in the hill country of northern Connecticut, in the village of Somers in Tolland County, about fifteen miles southeast of Springfield, Massachusetts. William's father drew a meager salary, as did most clergy of that day, but his parents prized learning. William attended Monson and Plainfield Academies and graduated from Yale College in 1828. From 1828 until 1832 William taught school in New Haven, Connecticut, and Burlington, New Jersey, to pay off college debts. While in Burlington he studied law with Garret D. Wall, a future U.S. senator, and then returned to Yale for six months of law courses that qualified him for a master's degree in 1831.

Soon after his admission to the bars in Connecticut and Pennsylvania in 1832, Strong opened an office in Reading, a growing manufacturing town and the seat of Berks County, Pennsylvania, some forty-five miles northwest of Philadelphia along the Schuylkill River. The county was also the center of a prosperous agricultural region with a large German-speaking population. Quickly becoming fluent in their language, Strong transformed obstacle into opportunity. His practice flourished. Sociable, athletic, and an outdoors person, he made friends easily. These qualities may help explain his election to the city council and the board of education. He became a director of the Farmer's Bank and the Lebanon Valley Railroad and counsel to the recently organized Philadelphia and Reading Railroad Company that ambitiously sought to link the nearby anthracite coal fields with lucrative markets in Philadelphia and later New York. He also found time for a courtship with Priscilla Lee Mallery of Easton, Pennsylvania, the daughter of the presiding judge of the court of common pleas, the commonwealth's court of general jurisdiction. Their marriage in 1836 yielded a son and two daughters. Following Priscilla's premature death in 1844, Strong married Rachel Davies Bull, a widow from Churchtown, Pennsylvania, and daughter of a former member of Congress. From this second union came two sons and two daughters. The second Mrs. Strong lived until 1887.

In 1846 Strong was elected as an antislavery Locofoco Democrat to the U.S. House of Representatives, where he met a member from Illinois named Abraham Lincoln, one from Georgia named Alexander H. Stephens, and another from Tennessee named Andrew Johnson. (Locofoco was the name of a match introduced in the 1830s. When a faction of radical Democrats was about to wrestle control of the New York City Democratic Party apparatus from the conservative "hunkers," the latter turned off the gas to the building, extinguishing the gas lights, and plunging the caucus room into darkness. The radicals deployed Locofoco matches, lit candles, and continued with the meeting. Hence the more progressive members of the party became known as Locofocos, also sometimes called "barnburners." Hunkers in turn backed the regular party organization and were so named because they wanted the whole "hunk" of patronage.) After reelection in 1848 Strong chaired the committee on elections in the Thirty-first Congress. Declining renomination in 1850, he resumed full-time law practice in Reading, where the population had just passed 16,000. He won election in 1857 as a Democrat to a fifteen-year term on the Supreme Court of Pennsylvania, but resigned his seat in 1868 and moved his practice to Philadelphia, apparently to shore up his sagging finances.

Always a firm unionist and an opponent of slavery, Strong joined the new Republican Party at some point before the outbreak of war in 1861. Strong additionally had long been active as an elder and in other leadership positions in the Presbyterian Church (U.S.A.). It was during his service on the state bench that he was president of a national association to add religious content to the preamble of the U.S. Constitution. The organization's proposed amendment would have recognized "the Lord Jesus Christ as the ruler of all nations, and his revealed will as the supreme law of the land" (Fairman 1939, 167–168). Fortuitously, it was also during Strong's judicial tenure that the Pennsylvania Supreme Court had occasion to rule on the constitutionality of the legal tender laws Congress had passed to finance the war. It fell to Strong to write the majority opinion upholding the legislation (*Shollenberger v. Brinton*, 1866).

Fourteen months after taking the oath as an associate justice on the U.S. Supreme Court, Strong wrote the majority opinion in the 5–4 ruling in the *Legal Tender Cases* (1871). The decision overruled Chase's 4–3 opinion in *Hepburn v. Griswold* (1870), which struck down the contentious legislation just as Grant was submitting Strong's name (and Joseph P. Bradley's) to the Senate. The Court's speedy change of mind gave rise to accusations of court packing, but as noted in Chapter 1, nearly any Republicans Grant might have appointed would have voted just as Strong and Bradley did.

Strong's opinion was direct, cognizant of wartime emergency, and deferential to national power. The cases "affect the entire business of the country and take hold of the possible continued existence of the government." To deny the authority to enact legal tender legislation would be to declare that "the government is without those means of self-preservation which . . . become indispensable." Countering Chase's contention in *Hepburn* that the laws violated the spirit of the Constitution, Strong found sufficient basis in the doctrine of implied powers: the necessary and proper clause of Article I, section 8, gave Congress "the right to employ freely every means, not prohibited, necessary for [the nation's] preservation."

The concept of incidental (or resulting), rather than implied, powers lay at the heart of Strong's equally firm and nationalistic majority opinion in *Kohl v. United States* (1876). For the first time the Court acknowledged that the federal government could exercise eminent domain, a power that is not expressed in the Constitution. "If the right to acquire property for [various public] uses may be made a barren right by the unwillingness of property holders to sell, or by the action of a State prohibiting a sale to the Federal Government, the constitutional grants of power may be rendered nugatory, and the Government is dependent for its practical existence upon the will of a State, or even upon that of a private citizen. This cannot be." In Strong's view, the ban in the Fifth Amendment on the taking of property for public use without just compensation was as much an enabling as a disabling provision.

In contrast to most of the bench, Strong was willing to strike down laws that seemed to work an unfair hardship on an industry. Although he joined the majority in the *Slaughterhouse Cases* (1873) that found no Fourteenth Amendment right implicated by a state-imposed monopoly, he joined Justice Field's dissent in *Munn v. Illinois* (1877) that the same amendment made rate regulation judicially reviewable. In the *Sinking Fund Cases* (1879), Strong, Field, and Bradley objected on constitutional grounds to Congress's 1878 stipulation that certain western railroads deposit part of their income in the U.S. treasury as surety against repayment of principal and interest on government loans. "It is absurd to say," Strong argued, "this is not practically a radical change in the relations between the parties established by the contract. And it is equally impossible to maintain that it is not depriving the debtors of their property without due process of law."

Strong was also sensitive to the dangers that state regulations posed to interstate commerce. After Pennsylvania imposed a tonnage levy of two to five cents on railroads doing business within its borders, Strong wrote for the majority against the statute's constitutionality in a case brought by his former client: *Philadelphia and Reading Railroad Co. v. Pennsylvania* (1873a). It was apparently the first time that the Court had invalidated a state law solely on commerce clause grounds. "It is of national importance," Strong explained, "that . . . there should be but one regulating power, for if one State can . . . tax persons or property passing through it, . . . every other may, and thus commercial intercourse between States remote from each other may be destroyed. . . . [F]or though it might bear the imposition of a single tax it would be crushed under the load of many." Strong's reasoning would undergird the position the Court took thirteen years later with respect to state regulation of interstate rail rates. However, Strong had no objection to Pennsylvania's 0.75 percent tax on the gross receipts of railroads incorporated within the state, implicitly because the tax avoided the defect of the tonnage tax: the risk of multiple taxation on the same assets (*Philadelphia and Reading Railroad Co. v. Pennsylvania*, 1873b).

A small but crucial part of the Court's docket during Strong's tenure involved the scope of Reconstruction-era statutes and the Thirteenth, Fourteenth, and Fifteenth Amendments in protecting blacks from various predations. Civil rights triumphs were few, but Strong spoke for the majority in two such victories during his last year on the Court. *Strauder v. West Virginia* (1880) invalidated a state law that excluded African Americans from jury service. The Fourteenth Amendment, said

Strong, created a "right to exemption from unfriendly legislation against them distinctively as colored; exemption from legal discriminations, implying inferiority in civil society, . . . and discriminations which are steps towards reducing them to the condition of a subject race." On the same day the Court upheld a criminal provision of the Civil Rights Act of 1875 that prohibited racial discrimination in the selection of jurors (*Ex parte Virginia*, 1880). A state judge who had been convicted under the statute argued that his actions were distinct from those of a state that Congress could properly restrain. "We do not perceive how holding an office under a State, and claiming to act for the State," Strong declared in rejecting that contention, "can relieve the holder from obligation to obey the Constitution . . . or take away the power of Congress to punish his disobedience." Yet the Court through Strong was unwilling to conclude that racial discrimination by jury commissioners (not by statute) allowed removal of cases with black criminal defendants from state to federal court (*Virginia v. Rives*, 1880).

Strong retired from the bench on December 14, 1880, with more than 250 opinions of the Court to his credit. In a unique action by a Supreme Court justice, he aimed to set an example for three infirm colleagues (Clifford, Swayne, and Hunt), even though Strong at age seventy-two remained mentally sharp and physically fit (Fairman 1987, 527). A daughter later explained that he preferred the question "Why does he?" to "Why doesn't he?" leave (Fairman 1939, 381–382). Strong's plan was only partly successful. Swayne soon took the hint and retired, but Clifford died a sitting justice in the summer of 1881, and Hunt held on until Congress conferred a special pension in 1882.

In retirement the Strongs remained at their residence two blocks from the White House they had purchased for $40,000 in 1871. In May 1881 he addressed "The Needs of the Supreme Court" in the *North American Review*, one of the most influential periodicals of the day. Among other things Strong advocated creation of a system of intermediate appellate courts between the federal trial courts and the Supreme Court as a way of coping with the High Court's ballooning docket. The idea was not original with Strong, but what mattered most in the piece was the identity of the author. Something very similar to Strong's plan became law a decade later.

As he had been not slothful in business Strong was ever fervent in spirit, remaining active in the Presbyterian Church and in other religious endeavors. He had been vice president of the American Bible Society since 1871 and president of the American Tract Society since 1873. To these in 1883 he added the presidency of the American Sunday School Union. His death came on August 19, 1895, in his eighty-eighth year, at Lake Minnewaska in the Shawangunk Mountains of New York. He was interred at the Charles Evans Cemetery in Reading.

Joseph P. Bradley

President Grant's nomination of Joseph P. Bradley was sent to the Senate on February 7, 1870, the same day as Strong's. Bradley, who had never held public office, filled a new seat on the bench created by Congress in 1869 that strategically followed Andrew Johnson's departure from the White House. The seat restored the Court's roster to nine, where it has remained ever since. Bradley was no stranger to the Court when he was sworn in on March 23. His legal career had already brought him before the bench as counsel on six occasions, beginning in the 1850s.

Together with Lincoln appointees Miller and Field, Joseph P. Bradley completed a trio of justices who dominated the Supreme Court intellectually during the Waite era and beyond. Less ideologically disposed than Field, Bradley could nonetheless be almost as irascible and impatient. Lacking the degree of ambition Miller and Field displayed either for the chief justiceship or for high elective office, Bradley surpassed even them in his knowledge of the law and in his scholarly inquisitiveness. Energized by the Protestant ethic, his life had a Horatio Alger quality, apparent proof of the rewards of discipline, piety, and perseverance. It was as if the future justice had already taken to heart a precept that Justice Louis D. Brandeis later expounded: make each task preparation for the next.

The eldest of twelve children, Joseph was born on March 14, 1813, about two years after his parents, Philo and Mercy Gardner Bradley, had married, each at the age of 17. (Joseph much later added the middle initial "P" to his name, although it stood for nothing. A reasonable guess is that he did so in respect for his father.) The family had Connecticut roots that dated to 1660, although Joe's arrival marked the fourth generation of Bradleys living on adjacent farms near the village of Berne in the Helderberg Mountains, some sixteen miles west of the state capital of Albany, New York. Joe would later recall the stories his great-grandfather told about the French and Indian War. He never forgot the labors involved in growing up in a nearly self-sufficient farm community: the homespun clothing, the plowing, the grain cutting with a scythe, and the wood burning to make the charcoal he peddled in Albany. Rigors of rural life meant that attendance at the nearby country school was irregular at best; most book learning occurred at home. At age fifteen he augmented his farm chores with school teaching on the side. It was then that he was first exposed to algebra, after walking five miles to borrow a text from an uncle.

By age eighteen Bradley became convinced of the need for further and formal education and persuaded his father to excuse him from the farm. He planned to travel to New York City to earn money as a clerk. Providentially, the last boat south for the winter departed about ten minutes before he arrived at the dock in Albany. Stranded in the capital city for a few days, he spent time observing the state legislature and that quickened an interest in law. Making his way back to Berne, he shared his hopes with

Joseph P. Bradley (Vic Boswell, National Geographic, Collection of the Supreme Court of the United States)

the local Dutch Reformed Church pastor (or dominie) who agreed to tutor Joseph in Greek and Latin to prepare him for a Dutch Reformed college in New Brunswick, New Jersey, recently renamed Rutgers.

At age twenty Bradley enrolled at Rutgers. Some four to six years older than most of the other students, he completed his degree in three years with high marks. Classmates included Frederick Frelinghuysen, who as a U.S. senator would serve with Bradley on the Electoral Commission of 1877, and Cortland Parker, who would be a president of the American Bar Association. Bradley later said that had he caught the boat at Albany on that cold December day, he would probably have spent the rest of his life as a grocer.

Frelinghuysen and Parker introduced Bradley to Archer Gifford, who was the collector for the Port of Newark and who agreed to oversee Bradley's study of law. Bradley was admitted to the New Jersey bar on November 14, 1839. A year later, he took the first step in establishing himself as one of the preeminent railway lawyers in the nation by becoming an associate with John P. Jackson, the attorney for the New Jersey Railroad and Transportation Co. To have a railroad for a client meant involvement in one of the fastest growing industries of the day. As with telecom and Internet companies 165 years later, fortunes could be made and lost in short order. Railroad cases also were a staple on the dockets of state and federal courts.

Bradley's work for Jackson led to a lengthy association with New Jersey's infamous Camden and Amboy Railroad. The railroad enjoyed a craftily guarded state monopoly, and in the 1850s and 1860s Bradley served as general counsel, director, member of the executive committee, and occasional lobbyist. As Chapter 1 explained, this work for the Camden and Amboy both gave Bradley the visibility to be considered for the Supreme Court and nearly proved fatal to his nomination. Interspersed among his railroad clients, perhaps as much for diversion as for income, Bradley also solved novel actuarial and other statistical problems as the chief mathematician for Newark's Mutual Benefit Co.

As he built his practice in Newark in 1844, he married Mary Hornblower, daughter of the chief justice of the New Jersey Supreme Court. Their union yielded seven children, four of whom lived into adulthood. As appalling as the loss of three offspring in childhood might seem today, the Bradleys were fortunate by mid-nineteenth-century standards. Others endured even greater loss.

A manufacturing city for southern markets, Newark lay in a heavily Democratic region. Bradley by contrast was a Whig who became a Republican as his old party faded in the late 1850s. In 1860 he advocated two constitutional amendments that might have avoided war. Once hostilities began he became an unequivocal supporter of both the Union cause and ratification of the Reconstruction amendments. In 1862 he made his single unsuccessful try for elective office as a Republican candidate for Congress.

The Bradleys arrived in Washington well-heeled. His prosperous railroad practice had enabled him to invest widely in Newark real estate and in other ventures. Presumably out of a sense of propriety, he promptly sold the stock he owned in the Camden and Amboy and other client roads to Frelinghuysen for about $27,000. Consequently, he could easily make do on the relatively modest annual salary of $10,000 paid to associate justices during most of his tenure. Soon after his confirmation, Bradley purchased a house for $40,000 at I Street and New Jersey Avenue that had been built in 1856 by Senator Stephen A. Douglas. The residence was spacious by Washington standards. It had to be: toward the end of his life Bradley's library numbered more than 16,000 volumes, on subjects ranging from mathematics and science to history and theology, as well as law.

Once on the bench Bradley was quickly involved in the most pressing constitutional questions of the day. He joined Strong in the slimmest of majorities in upholding the contentious legal tender acts. He appended his own views in a concurring statement: "It would be sad, indeed, if this great nation were now to be deprived of a power so necessary to enable it to protect its own existence, and to cope with the other great powers of the world."

Bradley was among the first to confront the meaning of the potentially revolutionary Fourteenth Amendment. Assigned initially to the Fifth Circuit that encompassed Louisiana, Bradley, with Circuit Judge William B. Woods, heard arguments in the *Slaughterhouse Cases.* In those cases the Louisiana Supreme Court had upheld a law that conferred monopolistic privileges on a newly chartered slaughterhouse by requiring all other butchers in the New Orleans area to do their slaughtering on its premises. Although the substantive constitutional question in the litigation was not technically before the circuit panel, Bradley addressed it just the same. The privileges and immunities clause of section one shielded at least "the right to pursue, unmolested, a lawful employment in a lawful manner," declared the farm boy from Berne turned railroad lawyer from Newark. When the litigation reached the Supreme Court in 1873, Bradley was among the four justices dissenting against Miller's position that the monopoly implicated no federally protected right. Joining Field's proclamation of economic liberty, Bradley added: "[T]he right of any citizen to follow whatever lawful employment he chooses to adopt (submitting himself to all lawful regulations) is one of his most valuable rights and one which the legislature of a state cannot invade. . . ."

That defense of equal access to occupations did not extend, however, to Myra Bradwell's attempt to practice law in Illinois after the state supreme court denied her admission to the bar because of gender. The exclusion was entirely reasonable and not a violation of the Fourteenth Amendment, Bradley wrote in a concurring opinion to *Bradwell v. Illinois* (1873). "The paramount destiny and mission of woman are to fulfill the noble and benign offices of wife and mother. This is the law of the Creator. . . . [I]n view of the peculiar characteristics, destiny, and mission of woman, it is within the province of the legislature to ordain what offices, positions, and callings shall be filled and discharged by men. . . ."

Any expectations by former railway clients that in Bradley they now had a friend in court proved unfounded. Although he sided with the Union Pacific and Central Pacific Railroads in the *Sinking Fund Cases* (1879), he frequently took the other side in railroad litigation. He spoke for the Court in *New York Central v. Lockwood* (1873), which denied the right of a railroad to contract away its liability for damages caused by the negligence of an employee. Bradley must have had his years of professional work in mind as he wrote, "It is a favorite argument in the cases . . . that men may be permitted to make their own agreements, and that it is no concern of the public on what terms an individual chooses to have his goods carried. . . . The carrier and his customer do not stand on a footing of equality. . . . The business of common carriers is mostly concentrated in a few powerful corporations, whose position in the body politic enables them to control it."

Moreover, Bradley consistently defended the authority of state governments to set rates that railroads could charge their customers. Indeed, he provided the intellectual underpinnings for Chief Justice Waite's opinion in the landmark case of *Munn v. Illinois* (1877), one of the *Granger Cases*, which rejected arguments that such regulations violated the due process clause of the Fourteenth Amendment. Several months before the cases came down, Bradley forwarded to Waite an outline of views in which he stated: "I have reduced my notes in the Granger cases into a sort of general [outline] on the questions involved. The authorities referred to . . . may be of service to you. Make just such use of it as you please. . . . [W]herever a particular employment, or a business establishment becomes a matter of public consequence so as to affect the whole public and to become a 'common charge,'" Bradley continued, "it is subject to legislative regulation and control . . . otherwise, the very object of legislative power—the consulting of the general good—would be subverted" (Stephenson 1973, 922–923). This was the source of Waite's reference in *Munn* to property "affected with a public interest." The chief justice's opinion cited a treatise by Lord Chief Justice Hale (perhaps a volume in Bradley's library) as authority for the concept. Bradley's opinions routinely traced legal principles as far back as could be done.

After *Munn*, Bradley tenaciously held to the position that rate regulation was not a matter of judicial concern, even as the Court abandoned the principle near the end of his tenure. When the Court invalidated state railroad regulation of interstate rates in *Wabash, St. Louis and Pacific Railway v. Illinois* (1886), Bradley insisted that, in the absence of congressional legislation, states should be allowed to do so. The Court four years later decided in *Chicago, Milwaukee and St. Paul Railway Co. v. Minnesota* (1890) that the reasonableness of rates was judicially reviewable. Bradley dissented: the ruling "practically overrules *Munn v. Illinois*. . . . The governing principle of those cases was that the regulation and settlement of . . . fares . . . is a legislative prerogative and not a judicial one. This is a principle which I regard as of great importance."

However, such deference to legislatures did not extend to many of the racial equality cases the Court decided. Although Bradley dissented in the notorious *Blyew v. United States* (1872) discussed in Chapter 1, he spoke for the Court in the *Civil Rights Cases* (1883). The decision invalidated a part of the Civil Rights Act of 1875 that forbade racial discrimination in hotels, theaters, and other privately owned places of public accommodation. Because the Fourteenth Amendment was directed to actions by states, Congress could not reach action by private individuals. At most, the amendment authorized only national legislation that superseded discriminatory state laws. In a lapse of immense proportions, Bradley and all justices save Harlan naively assumed that state laws already required innkeepers and public carriers to furnish accommodations to all unobjectionable persons, and that anyone refused service had an adequate remedy under state law. It was not until 1964 that Congress, relying mainly on the commerce clause, reenacted similar legislation to forbid racial discrimination in hotels, theaters, and other places of public accommodation.

That ruling aside, to the end Bradley could not abide ineptitude in himself or in others, as illustrated by a letter written from New Orleans to his daughter Caroline in 1871. "I started to go to Church at Savannah . . . and not being able to walk the distance, took the horse car. I requested the driver to put me down at Broad Street (in which the best Presbyterian preaching was to be had); but the stupid fool . . . put me out at Broughton Street, which had nothing but an Episcopal Church in it. . . . This accident had such an effect on my temper, that I have not made the attempt to go to church since." This may explain why the scholar who knew Bradley best concluded that "Mrs. Bradley devoted her life to protecting the Justice from irritation" (Fairman 1964, 81).

An entry from Bradley's diary on March 14, 1891, reflects his disciplined life and devotion to his work: "5 1/2 A.M. My birthday. 78 years completed. I rise early this morning to make up for lost time; as being conference time, I have many cases to master and decide. I have now been 21 years on the bench . . . and begin to be pretty tired with the awful hard work of the court" (Atkinson 1999, 65–66). Complications from a cold the following winter weakened him seriously, and he died in Washington on January 22, 1892.

Ward Hunt

The third of the Grant appointees, Hunt filled the vacancy in January 1873 caused by the retirement of Samuel Nelson of New York in November 1872. Nelson, who had served for nearly twenty-eight years, was the only justice named by President John

Ward Hunt (Matthew Brady, Handy Studios, Collection of the Supreme Court of the United States)

Tyler. Hunt is most often remembered for remaining on the bench totally incapacitated for the last three years of his nine-year tenure. His elevation to the Supreme Court is an example of the combined advantages of having a friend (Roscoe Conkling) in high places (the Senate) and a pliable president in the White House.

Ward was born on June 14, 1810, to Montgomery and Elizabeth Stringham Hunt, who lived in Utica along the Mohawk River in Oneida County, New York. His father, a bank cashier, had ancestors who had settled in Connecticut as early as 1650. After instruction in the nearby Geneva and Oxford Academies, Ward spent a year at Hamilton College in Clinton but completed his degree at age eighteen at Union College in Schenectady, some fifteen miles northwest of Albany. He studied law at the Tapping Reeve School in Litchfield, Connecticut, before returning to Utica as clerk to Judge Hiram Denio.

Soon after admission to the bar in 1831, Hunt opened a law office in his parents' home in a partnership with Denio. In 1837, he married Mary Ann Savage, a judge's daughter, who bore three children. (She died in 1845; Hunt's marriage to Marie Taylor followed in 1853.) By 1838 Hunt was sufficiently well known and highly regarded to win election as a Van Buren Democrat to the state legislature, where he served one term. He was elected mayor in 1844, by which time Utica boasted more than 9,000 residents and was an important stop on the Erie Canal that had opened in 1825.

Hunt's practice continued to prosper, but he became disillusioned with Democrats over slavery and Texas annexation. Accordingly, he backed Martin Van Buren's Free-Soil candidacy for the presidency in 1848. He left the Democratic Party for good in the mid-1850s, and was one of the founders of the Republican Party in New York in 1856. By this time he was already a close friend of fellow attorney and Utica native Roscoe Conkling, nineteen years Hunt's junior, who was elected to the U.S. Senate in 1866 and was the undisputed boss of the Republican Party in the state. During the Grant administration Conkling controlled federal patronage across the Empire State.

Hunt's judicial career began in 1865 when he was elected as a Republican to the New York Court of Appeals, the state's highest tribunal. This must have been satisfying to Hunt; not only had he endured two unsuccessful races for the same court as a Democrat in the late 1840s and early 1850s but also succeeded his mentor Judge Denio. After becoming chief judge in 1868, an amendment to the state constitution in 1869 reorganized the judiciary. Hunt stayed on as commissioner of appeals until Conkling orchestrated his appointment to the U.S. Supreme Court.

Any appraisal of Hunt's Supreme Court career must begin with the fact that it was short. Even before the paralytic stroke in January 1879 that effectively ended his judicial career, his health had begun to deteriorate with gout and related ailments. As early as 1877 these problems caused him to miss several sessions. Thus, for only about five terms was Hunt able to shoulder his share of the workload. Second, Hunt rarely spoke for the Court in cases of great public importance; the bulk of his opinions dealt with commercial, admiralty, and patent law. Although those decisions were of obvious importance to the litigants involved, they did little to shape or reshape the law. Indeed, perhaps the most memorable opinion Hunt wrote was a lone dissent. That in itself remains noteworthy because his dissenting opinions totaled only seven.

United States v. Reese (1876) involved the validity of indictments under sections three and four of the Enforcement Act of 1870 that were intended to put the teeth of criminal sanctions behind the Fifteenth Amendment. William Garner, a black man, claimed that election inspectors in Kentucky had refused to accept his poll tax, making him ineligible to vote. For the Court, Chief Justice Waite explained that the Fifteenth Amendment did not grant the right to vote to anyone, but granted the right to vote free of discrimination based on race. Therefore, to qualify as appropriate legislation under the Fifteenth Amendment, sections three and four had to refer to denial of the right to vote on account of race. Unlike earlier provisions of the statute, sections three and four lacked any explicit mention of race, and the Court held them unconstitutional. The Waite Court was slightly ahead of the curve, constitutionalizing the normalcy that would be enshrined in the Compromise of 1877.

Hunt's bold dissent was a distant echo of Republican ideology that had been ascendant only a few years earlier. He noted that the contested sections included words such as "aforesaid," which made it clear that Congress was referring in particular to the racially based predations of previous sections. Congress's "intention . . . on this subject is too plain to be discussed," he contended. "Just so far as the ballot to . . . the freedmen is abridged, in the same degree is their importance and their security diminished." The motivating idea behind the Fifteenth Amendment had been to give the freedmen the power to protect their own rights. "Punishment is the means, protection is the end," he continued. "The arrest, conviction and sentence to imprisonment, of one inspector, who refused the vote of a person of African descent on account of his race, would more effectively secure the right of the voter than would any number of civil suits in the state courts, prosecuted by timid, ignorant and penniless parties against those possessing the wealth, the influence and the sentiment of the community." The majority, Hunt concluded, had brought "to an impotent conclusion the vigorous amendments on the subject of slavery."

In his capacity as circuit judge assigned to the litigious Second Circuit, Hunt had already confronted a related issue involving voting rights of women. Ironically, his position on the locus of the right to vote followed Miller's reasoning in the *Slaughterhouse Cases* and was identical to what Waite would articulate in *Reese*. Soon after his confirmation he presided over the trial of suffragette Susan B. Anthony, accused of illegally voting in a federal election in New York. Excluding women from the franchise did not violate the Fourteenth Amendment, Hunt explained, because voting was a right that derived from state, not national, citizenship. "If the state of New York should provide that . . . no person having gray hair, or who had not the use of all his limbs, should be entitled to vote, I do not see how it could be held to be a violation of any right derived or held under the Constitution of the United States [even though] [w]e might say that such regulations were unjust, tyrannical, unfit for the regulation of an intelligent state . . ." (Kutler 1969b, 1225). Accordingly, Hunt directed the jury to find her guilty and imposed a fine of $100 (*United States v. Anthony*, 1873).

In other instances Hunt could be as ambivalent about federal power as his colleagues. Consider *Home Insurance Co. v. Morse* (1874) and *Doyle v. Continental Insurance Co.* (1877). A Wisconsin statute of 1870 required out-of-state insurance companies doing business in Wisconsin to forego the right to remove state court suits to federal court. In *Morse*, Home Insurance had removed a suit, and the state courts proceeded as if they still had jurisdiction. The U.S. Supreme Court found the state court judgment against the company illegal. A citizen, Hunt explained for the majority, "may omit to exercise his right to remove his suit to a Federal tribunal, as often as he thinks fit. . . . He cannot, however, bind himself in advance by an agreement . . . thus to forfeit his rights at all times and on all occasions, whenever the case may be presented." In *Doyle*, the company had removed a case to federal court after the ruling in *Morse*. Wisconsin authorities then revoked the company's license to do business within the state. Hunt for the majority reaffirmed but distinguished *Morse*, saying that the facts in *Doyle* presented a question not decided in the first case. A greater power included the lesser: if a state could bar an out-of-state corporation from doing business within the state (as was conceded), it could do so for a bad reason. "If the Act done by the State is legal," Hunt wrote, "is not in violation of the Constitution or laws of the United States, it is quite out of the power of any court to inquire what was the intention of those who enacted the law." Bradley's pointed dissent maintained that the Court was indirectly sanctioning what it had condemned when done directly—compelling an out-of-state company to forfeit its right to resort to the federal courts.

The Court reflected a tendency to defer to state power by exempting states and their instrumentalities from federal taxation. In *Collector v. Day* (1871) the Court barred application of a federal income tax to the salaries of state judges. In 1873 Hunt spoke for the Court in *United States v. Baltimore and Ohio Railroad Co.* and extended the exemption from federal taxation to a railway that had been financed by bonds issued by the city of Baltimore. The effect was to treat the railroad, for tax purposes, as if it were a municipality. "If they may be taxed lightly, they may be taxed heavily; if justly, oppressively. Their operation may be impeded and may be destroyed. . . ."

In the flood of municipal bond cases in the 1870s, Hunt was as inclined as most justices to side with bondholders against local governmental entities disinclined to pay their debts. In contrast to the tendency in this period to construe civil rights legislation narrowly, Hunt seemed to go out of his way to find sufficient statutory authorization for issuance of the bonds, and hence a federal constitutional obligation to repay (*Randolph v. Post County, Commissioners v. Thayer*, 1877).

The pattern seems clear. With a bare handful of exceptions, Hunt was a team player and a follower, not a leader. He added his vote to the dominant judicial opinion of the day. He must also have received high marks for collegiality—so one may conclude from comments by Justice Miller—who was rarely effusive with kind words about others—as Hunt's health took its downward turn in 1879. "He is not a very strong man in intellect, but he is a cultivated lawyer and a gentlemen. A Warm hearted courteous man [and] one of the most agreeable men on the bench" (Fairman 1939, 377).

Hunt clung to his seat after his paralytic stroke in January 1879 probably because he had not served long enough to qualify for a pension. There is also some evidence that he held on in deference to his friend Conkling who was quarreling with President Rutherford Hayes over patronage. Whatever the reason, the absentee jurist was a heavy burden for the other justices to bear. The impasse was broken when Senator and former Justice David Davis pushed through a private bill three years later. The bill made Hunt eligible for his pension at full salary, provided he retire within thirty days. Hunt stepped down on January 27, 1882, just as the bill became law. He died on March 24, 1886, in Washington, D.C.

Morrison R. Waite

The first six chief justices of the United States were named by presidents of stature: Washington, John Adams, Jackson, and Lincoln. One would struggle to find a more impressive executive quartet. In contrast, the least auspicious aspect of the arrival of the seventh chief justice was the appointing president. By 1874 it was clear that Grant's dominance of southern battlefields had not assured his control of the White House. Grant seemed to much prefer smoking a cigar or sipping whiskey at the nearby Willard Hotel. Additionally, his administration had become the most corrupt in U.S. history. As detailed in Chapter 1, Grant replaced Chase by a long, roundabout, stop-and-go process. Waite was at best Grant's fifth and probably even seventh choice. It was therefore a surprise the decision turned out so well.

Born on November 27, 1816, Morrison Remick Waite was the eldest child of Henry Matson and Marie Selden Waite. With roots in New England dating to the 1600s, the Waite household was devoutly Episcopalian. Waite's father was a gentleman farmer and lawyer in Lyme, Connecticut, a village at the mouth of the Connecticut River, between New Haven and New London. When he was chosen chief justice of the state supreme court, Henry Waite had earned a reputation for charging modest fees, which his eldest son would later take to heart. As Morrison Waite's wife recalled many years later, Henry told his children "that he never charged but one one hundred

Morrison R. Waite (Library of Congress, Collection of the Supreme Court of the United States)

dollar fee in his life, and felt ashamed of it for years, but it was for saving a man's neck from the gallows" (Magrath 1963, 24).

Like several of his forebears, "Mott" (as he had come to be called) enrolled at Yale College. He graduated with high marks in 1837. In 1838 he ventured west to Maumee, in northwestern Ohio, along the Maumee River south of Toledo, and studied law with Samuel Young with whom he established a partnership upon admission to the bar in 1839. Within two years he married Amelia Champlin Warner of Lyme, a second cousin whom he had courted while at Yale. Their union blessed them with three sons and a daughter who grew into adulthood. Waite's practice initially involved many minor land cases to which he later added cases for the many railroads that crisscrossed the Buckeye State. Throughout, he heeded his father's counsel and earned a reputation for his modest fees. He argued the first of a career total of thirty cases before the Ohio Supreme Court in 1844. In 1850 the Waites moved to the Lake Erie port of Toledo after it had become the seat of Lucas County. In 1856, with Waite's income at about $7,000 annually, his partner left the practice to pursue some business interests. Waite entered into a new partnership with his younger brother Richard, with the firm reorganized under the name "M. R. & R. Waite." By this time he had become a director of the Bank of Toledo and president of the Young Men's Association.

Morrison might never have become chief justice had he been more successful in politics. He lost a bid as a Whig candidate for Congress in 1846 but three years later won a term in the lower house of the Ohio legislature. By the mid-1850s, with the Whig party disintegrating, he helped to organize the Republican Party in Ohio. Strongly antislavery, Waite was not pro-black. That distinction separated him from the more zealous members of the new party and would perhaps account for some of his later jurisprudential stances on the supreme bench. A year after the firing on Fort Sumter, Waite ran unsuccessfully for Congress, this time as a Lincoln Republican. More successful was John Brough in 1863, an ex-Democrat and now the Unionist candidate for governor whom Waite backed enthusiastically. Brough offered a seat on the Ohio Supreme Court that Waite declined, preferring an informal advisory role to the governor instead. Thus, as of 1870, Waite was well respected in Ohio, but barely known beyond its borders.

It was therefore fortuitous when Interior Secretary Columbus Delano, also from Ohio, suggested to Grant that Waite be named one of the three U.S. counsel to the Geneva Arbitration in 1871. So unknown was Waite along the Potomac that Delano wrote to Secretary of State Hamilton Fish that "'Morrison R. Waite Toledo Ohio' gives you name and address" (Magrath 1963, 78). The appointment proved propitious. The arbitration had been set up to settle claims that England had violated neutrality principles during the Civil War by outfitting Confederate cruisers on its territory. After months of arguments and deliberations in 1872—which allowed the Waites their first trip abroad—the arbiters awarded the United States $15.5 million. Waite returned to Toledo a hero. There was a parade, Yale followed with an honorary doctorate, and the

Democratic and Republican Parties stumbled over themselves to nominate Waite as a delegate to Ohio's constitutional convention. At the convention, where Waite served as president, he received word on January 19, 1874, of his nomination as chief justice. He hardly had time to react before the Senate confirmed him two days later.

The chief justice of the United States is often said to be primus inter pares (first among equals). Although the Court's presiding officer, the chief justice's vote counts no more than the vote of an associate justice. But the chief often leads the Court in one or more of several ways: managerially, intellectually, and socially. Waite's leadership skills as chief justice will be assessed in greater detail in chapter 4. It suffices here to note that from the outset the lawyer from Toledo confronted several imposing challenges. First, his relative obscurity was compounded by the fact that he had never argued a case before the tribunal that he was now to head. Moreover, every Republican member of the bench except Davis and the recently appointed Hunt had coveted the center chair and had campaigned for it. Third, Waite had to preside over a bench populated by several strong-willed and intellectually gifted colleagues—Bradley, Field, and Miller—who doubted that the new chief was equal to the task. "We have had our new Chief Justice with us now three weeks, twice in conference," Miller wrote in a letter. "He is pleasant, a good presiding officer, *mediocre*, with a fair amount of professional learning" (Fairman 1939, 349). "We have a Chief Justice," heaved Field in a letter, "that would never have been thought of for the position by any person except President Grant. . . . He is gentlemanly . . . [b]ut how much of a lawyer remains to be seen. . . . My objection to the appointment is that it is an experiment whether a man of fair . . . abilities may make a fit Chief Justice of the United States—an experiment which no President has a right to make with our Court" (Magrath 1963, 107). Fortunately Waite was a quick study. "I got on the box as soon as I arrived there this morning," he confided to a friend, "gathered up the lines and drove, and I am going to drive and those gentlemen know it" (Trimble 1938, 135). Finally, burdening his Court within a very few years would be the various infirmities of a full one-third of the bench: Clifford, Swayne, and Hunt.

Waite did not arrive in Washington as financially comfortable as, say, Bradley in 1870. Probably because of Waite's custom of charging only modest fees, a biographer estimates that his annual earnings in Toledo never exceeded $25,000. Contemplating his new salary of $10,500 as chief justice, Waite wrote to his wife: "We shall have to pull in the purse strings somewhat, but I hope they will leave a little play" (Fairman 1987, 538). That goal proved elusive. He and Mrs. Waite initially lived in two rental properties in Washington, and it was not until 1883 that they had a house of their own, in the 1400 block of I Street. Social demands and the increased cost of living in the capital pushed Waite into debt. Samuel Young, his former law partner, quietly advanced him nearly $3,000 between 1876 and 1877 to help make ends meet. Waite eventually repaid the sum, but at his death only a small estate remained for his widow.

The Court in Waite's time confronted two novel constitutional questions that the Chase Court had only begun to address. To what extent and under what circumstances did the Thirteenth, Fourteenth, and Fifteenth Amendments, all adopted within five years of the end of the Civil War, grant Congress authority to protect the civil rights of the newly freed slaves and their children? To what extent, if any, did the Fourteenth Amendment impose new limitations on run-of-the-mill economic and social legislation in the states? The two questions were related in that each involved federal limitations on state power. (A third question, that of Congress's authority to legislate for a national economy, began to surface late in the Waite era but did not fully manifest itself until the 1890s and after.) In general, the Waite Court's answers to the first two questions were "marginally at most" and "hardly at all." Waite was closely identified with both answers.

As noted in the previous discussion of Justice Hunt, Waite spoke for the Court in *United States v. Reese* (1876). Reese and another election inspector in Kentucky had been indicted under the Enforcement Act of 1870, which had been designed to protect black voting rights, for refusing to accept a poll tax payment from William Garner. Garner therefore was ineligible to vote. But in Waite's view, the sections of the law on which the indictments were based were constitutionally flawed. The Fifteenth Amendment itself granted no one the right to vote but only disallowed a state denial of the vote based on race. Because sections three and four of the Enforcement Act did not expressly mention denials of the vote based on race, they were not appropriate legislation within the meaning of the Fifteenth Amendment. The government argued unsuccessfully against the majority's insistence on clarity in the criminal law (convincing only Hunt) that the applicable sections were simply the next steps to cope with the racially discriminatory acts described in earlier sections.

Events in *United States v. Cruikshank* (1876) were far more tragic. Following a disputed election in Louisiana, a white mob attacked and killed at least sixty blacks. Indictments were returned against eight defendants under an Enforcement Law provision that criminalized the banding together of persons for the purpose of denying others their constitutionally protected rights. Waite explained for the Court that the indictments were flawed even though the defendants had allegedly violated the victims' constitutional right to peaceably assemble. Although the First Amendment secured that right from infringement by Congress, it did not create the right. "For their protection in its enjoyment, . . . the people must look to the States." Nor was there sufficient evidence that the right to vote had been interfered with on account of race. "We might suspect that race was the cause of the hostility; but it is not so averred." Even though *Ex parte Yarbrough* (1884) would later affirm federal authority to protect voting rights against racial discrimination, *Reese* and *Cruikshank* made it exceedingly difficult to obtain constitutionally acceptable indictments and convictions in defense of voting rights. The decisions no doubt demoralized federal prosecutors. Similar reasoning led to the defeat of a claim of women's suffrage on Fourteenth Amendment grounds (*Minor v. Happersett*, 1875). Because women had always lacked the vote, Waite reasoned, it was not one of the privileges and immunities of citizenship that the amendment secured against infringement by the states. Waite's position in most of the civil rights cases may have reflected less a hostility toward the claimant and more a fear of centralized power. It was a matter of priorities; for Waite, civil rights only rarely trumped competing values.

The previous section on Justice Bradley recounted the important role that he played in providing the legal underpinnings for Waite's opinion for the Court in *Munn v. Illinois* (1877). *Munn* upheld a state legislature's setting of rates for grain warehouses (and, in companion cases, railroads). Declaring that such property was "affected with a public interest," Waite rejected a claim that such regulations were both judicially reviewable and that they violated the due process clause of the Fourteenth Amendment. Despite Bradley's undoubted influence in the case, much of the opinion reflects the views that Waite maintained through his tenure. After all, the more significant aspect of the holding was not that rates could be set by the state. Rather, the aspect that most troubled foes of regulation was Waite's announcement that rate regulation was almost entirely a matter for the legislature, not the courts. "For our purposes we must assume that, if a state of facts could exist that would justify such legislation, it actually did exist when the statute now under consideration was passed. . . . We know that this is a power which may be abused, but that is no argument against its existence. For protection against abuses by legislatures the people must resort to the polls, not to the courts. . . ."

This is not to say that Waite endorsed an "anything goes" position or that he was antiproperty. To the contrary, he supported Justice Miller's hypothetical characterization of a violation of the due process clause in *Davidson v. New Orleans* (1878) ["a statute which declared . . . that the full and exclusive title of a described piece of land, which is now in A, shall be and is hereby vested in B. . . ."]. He also announced eight years later that the "Court does not wish to hear argument on the question whether the [equal protection clause] applies to . . . corporations. We are all of opinion that it does" (*Santa Clara County v. Southern Pacific Railroad Co.*, 1886).

Nonetheless, Waite remained generally disposed toward state power throughout his career. In *Stone v. Farmers' Loan and Trust Co.* (1886), the Mobile and Ohio Railroad challenged railroad rate setting by Mississippi on contract and due process grounds, citing a provision in its charter to set rates "free of all legislative control." Over dissents by Field and Harlan, Waite contended that the "power of regulation is a power of government, . . . and if it can be bargained away at all it can only be by words of positive grant. . . . If there is reasonable doubt, it must be resolved in favor of the existence of the power." Because the charter also required the railroad to operate in a manner consistent with the laws of the state, the railroad was subject to the rates set by the commission. Later in the same year Waite joined Bradley's dissent in *Wabash, St. Louis and Pacific Railway v. Illinois* when the majority forbade state laws that set interstate rail rates.

No chief justice has worked harder at the job than Waite. He had the misfortune both to lead the Court when its workload became almost unbearable, and then to die before Congress provided relief. Moreover, Waite added to his own burden by assigning himself more than one-quarter of the opinions of the Court over the fourteen years of his tenure. The load took its toll. Waite suffered a breakdown in 1885 and recuperated in Florida for a month before returning to the Court. In early 1888, Waite's coachman fell ill, and the chief walked to and from a reception. He was left with a chill that probably turned into pneumonia. Waite insisted on going to the Court anyway to read an opinion. Since Waite was not strong enough to speak, Justice Blatchford read it for him. "It was evident to the observer that death had almost placed its hand upon him," Attorney General Alexander Garland later wrote (Garland 1898, 35–36). Waite died on March 23, 1888, and was interred at Woodlawn Cemetery in Toledo.

The Hayes Appointments

John Marshall Harlan

The roster of the Waite Court remained stable after the new chief's arrival until 1877 when the Illinois legislature elected Justice David Davis to the United States Senate. As described in Chapter 1, President Rutherford B. Hayes used this vacancy to repay political debts he owed to John Marshall Harlan. Time was on Harlan's side: He survived two chief justices, served with a third, and, with the exception of Field, sat longer (thirty-three years, ten months) than any other Waite Court justice. A tall, large-framed redhead with a flair for finger-wagging dissents, this kind and deeply religious man displayed enigmatic qualities that have challenged biographers. He was a person who would rather be right than consistent. A skilled polemicist, he believed in a moral dimension to U.S. constitutionalism. Harlan "goes to bed every night," observed his colleague Justice Brewer probably only half-jokingly, "with one hand on the Constitution and the other on the Bible, and so sleeps the sweet sleep of justice and righteousness" (Yarbrough 1995, viii).

On June 1, 1833, John became the sixth of the nine children born to James and Eliza Shannon Davenport Harlan (one of the three daughters died in infancy). The family home was in Boyle County in central Kentucky, near the headwaters of the Salt River, about seven miles from what is now the town of Harrodsburg. The Harlan (originally spelled Harland) family had originally settled in southeastern Pennsylvania in 1687. John's grandfather had been among the first pioneers to venture west into

John Marshall Harlan (Matthew Brady, Collection of the Supreme Court of the United States)

what is now the Bluegrass State in the 1770s. John grew up in a slave-owning family. His father's slaves, all assigned to the household, numbered fourteen in 1850, and ranged in age from three months to seventy years. His father had a busy law practice and was a Whig in the Henry Clay mold. (He named John after Chief Justice John Marshall; another son bore the name of the Great Compromiser himself, Henry Clay.) John absorbed both politics and Presbyterianism at home and watched as his father pursued public service, serving as a member of Congress, as Kentucky's secretary of state, as a state legislator, state attorney general, and finally as U.S. attorney before his death in 1863.

John graduated from Centre College in nearby Danville in 1850 and then studied law at Transylvania University in Lexington. In 1852 he joined his father's law office in Frankfort and was admitted to the bar in 1853. He promptly won three elections in succession: as city attorney of Frankfort in 1854 and 1856 and a highly contested seat on the Franklin County trial bench in 1858, a post he held until 1861. These years on the local judiciary comprised his total judicial experience at the time of his appointment to the U.S. Supreme Court in 1877.

A courtship with Malvina (Mallie) French Shankin that had begun in 1853 when she was fifteen led to the couple's marriage in the Shankin home in Evansville, Indiana, on December 23, 1856. Strongly antislavery and predisposed against everything involved with the "peculiar institution," Mallie later recorded in her memoirs that she was nonetheless impressed that all the Harlan slaves were "carefully looked after, not only physically but morally" (Harlan 1999, 115). John and Mallie had three daughters and three sons, all of whom lived to adulthood. In 1899, one of the sons—John Maynard Harlan—became the father of John Marshall Harlan II, who was an associate justice on the U.S. Supreme Court from 1955 until 1971. Mallie survived her husband by five years.

Harlan's political life began its strange odyssey in the mid-1850s. With the Whig party disintegrating nationally, he found the Democratic and the newly organized Republican Parties equally unacceptable because of what he regarded as their extreme, nation-rending positions on slavery. Accordingly, he reluctantly and briefly aligned himself with the American Party (the Know-Nothings), apparently believing that its nativist and anti-Catholic message could smother the slavery question and unify old-stock Protestants. In the presidential election of 1860 he again rejected the Democratic and Republican candidates and supported the hastily arranged Constitutional Union ticket of John Bell of Tennessee and Edward Everett of Massachusetts that carried only Virginia and Bell's and Harlan's home states of Tennessee and Kentucky.

As war broke out, Harlan paradoxically remained both proslavery and fiercely loyal to the Union. Soon after moving both his practice and his family to Louisville, he accepted appointment as a colonel and outfitted the Tenth Kentucky Volunteers that became a unit in a division commanded by General George H. (Old Pap) Thomas. Harlan saw service in Kentucky and in other states as well. Encamped outside Florence, Alabama, on one occasion, Harlan and his officers attended Sunday services at the local Presbyterian church. At the conclusion of an invocation in which the pastor earnestly beseeched the Almighty to smite the invading hordes, the Union officers quickly left. After consulting with General Thomas, Harlan arrested the cleric in the midst of his sermon and had him transported to St. Louis for the duration of the war. The future justice later recalled a young woman in the congregation who, trying to block the minister's removal from the sanctuary, "called me a red-whiskered Yankee. I disclaimed being a Yankee, saying that I was a Kentuckian" (Yarbrough 1995, 49).

Harlan resigned his commission on his father's death in 1863 to take over the practice. He spoke out against Lincoln's Emancipation Proclamation, was elected state attorney general on a moderate Union ticket, and backed Democrat George McClellan's campaign for the White House in 1864. Harlan strongly opposed ratification of the Thirteenth Amendment, which banned slavery in 1865. However, by 1867, Colonel Harlan, as he was now called, had joined the Republican Party. He campaigned for Grant in 1868, and supported all three Reconstruction constitutional amendments. Although he lost gubernatorial campaigns as the Republican nominee in 1871 and 1875 as well as a bid for the U.S. Senate in 1872, he was widely mentioned in the press as a vice-presidential prospect for the 1872 election.

In the late 1860s Harlan became friends with Benjamin Bristow. The two men established a law partnership in 1870 just before Grant named Bristow as the first solicitor general of the newly established Department of Justice. Bristow later served as secretary of the treasury. His reform policies in that position lay the basis for Bristow's presidential bid in 1876 that Harlan orchestrated. As Chapter 1 explained, once Bristow's nomination appeared doomed, Harlan was able to deliver key Bristow delegates to Hayes at a critical moment of the convention. The Ohioan was forever grateful to Harlan. Harlan had been thinking about a seat on the Supreme Court as early as 1870. "I know of no more desirable position . . .," he wrote Bristow, "especially if the salary should be increased to $10,000.—It lifts a man high above the atmosphere on which most public men move, and enables him to become in every sense, an independent man, with an opportunity to make a record that will be remembered long after he is gone" (Beth 1992, 90).

Indeed, Congress had set the salary for associate justices at $10,000 by the time the Harlans moved to Washington, but that proved greatly insufficient. Harlan had debts he had difficulty repaying. He and Mrs. Harlan had to live in a series of rental properties, one of them sixteen miles away in Rockville, Maryland, because they could not afford to purchase a home. They built a house on Washington, D.C.'s Euclid Avenue in the 1880s, but only after their three sons assisted with the financing. However, differences over the terms under which they were to occupy this new house led to considerable strains within the family that were hardly eased when Justice Harlan fell behind on his share of the mortgage payments.

But Harlan made "a record" in two senses of the word. During his judicial career of nearly thirty-four years, one scholar has estimated that Harlan participated in 14,226 cases and authored a total of 1,161 written opinions (majority, dissenting, and concurring). This is probably still a Supreme Court record (Filler 1969b, 1284). Furthermore, from this impressive body of work a distinct, if not entirely consistent, theme emerges: nationalism, perhaps derived from his formative years as a Whig. This theme seems clearest in three categories of cases: racial justice, the Bill of Rights and the states, and the economy

More than any justice with whom he served, Harlan understood the Reconstruction amendments to establish a nationally protected right against racial discrimination, although it is a measure of the Court that he frequently articulated those promises in dissents. For example, in the *Civil Rights Cases* (1883), the Court invalidated the provision of the Civil Rights Act of 1875 that criminalized racial discrimination in privately owned places of public accommodation such as hotels and theaters. The Court reasoned that because the Fourteenth Amendment banned discriminatory state action, Congress was powerless to prevent discriminatory actions by private persons. Yet for Harlan the statute was valid under both the Thirteenth and the Fourteenth Amendments. Discrimination was "a badge of servitude" that Congress could address under the former. Because the latter made the former slaves "citizens of the United States" and authorized Congress to enforce the amendment with appropriate legislation, the act was valid because it guaranteed equal treatment for blacks in the commercial life of the nation. The drafters of the Fourteenth Amendment must have known "that the great danger to the equal enjoyment by citizens of their rights, as citizens, was to be apprehended, not altogether from unfriendly state legislation, but from the hostile action of corporations and individuals in the states." Harlan may have had special pleasure in writing this dissent: Harlan's wife recorded that he used the same quill pen and ink well to compose it that Chief Justice Roger Taney had used in writing his 1857 opinion in the *Dred Scott* case.

Harlan's most masterful dissent in defense of the legal (but not social) equality of black Americans came in *Plessy v. Ferguson* (1896). With Justice Brewer not participating, seven justices denied an equal protection challenge to Louisiana's 1890 statute requiring racial segregation on trains. "[I]n view of the Constitution, in the eye of the law," Harlan declared, "there is in this country no superior, dominant, ruling class of citizens. There is no caste here. Our Constitution is color-blind, and neither knows nor tolerates classes among citizens." With foresight he perceived accurately what was to come. "In my opinion, the judgment this day rendered will, in time, prove to be quite as pernicious as the decision made by this tribunal in the Dred Scott case."

A second manifestation of Harlan's nationalism was his conclusion that the

Fourteenth Amendment protected citizens from state infringement of rights guaranteed by the Bill of Rights. At least since *Barron v. Baltimore* (1833), the Court had held that the Bill of Rights limited what the federal government, not the states, could do. Had the Fourteenth Amendment's due process clause changed that? In *Hurtado v. California* (1884), Justice Matthews rejected a challenge to a murder conviction in a California state court that had not been based on indictment by grand jury, as required in federal courts by the Fifth Amendment. The Fifth Amendment contained a due process clause identical to that of the Fourteenth Amendment. Therefore, Matthews reasoned that the meaning of due process could not include specific rights also mentioned in the Fourteenth Amendment; otherwise, the additional reference to due process in the Fifth Amendment would be superfluous. Harlan dissented, insisting that the majority's position proved too much. If one thought of due process of law as enshrining basic rights, the majority's logic led to the conclusion that due process could not encompass the most important rights. In later cases Harlan insisted that the Fourteenth Amendment protected all Bill of Rights guarantees from state infringement (*O'Neil v. Vermont,* 1892; *Maxwell v. Dow,* 1900; *Patterson v. Colorado,* 1907; *Twining v. New Jersey,* 1908). It was not until the late 1960s that the Supreme Court arrived practically by piecemeal at Harlan's constitutional destination.

Consistent with this view of the Fourteenth Amendment was Harlan's acceptance of what came to be called substantive due process—an understanding that the due process clause required courts to examine the content of laws regulating property rights to ascertain that the resulting restrictions on liberty were justified. Harlan was more disposed than some of his colleagues to accept state regulations (unless they impeded unduly on interstate commerce). He nonetheless gravitated toward those on the bench who believed the Fourteenth Amendment imposed greater limits on a state's police power than those Chief Justice Waite had acknowledged in *Munn v. Illinois* (1877). In upholding a prohibition on the production of alcoholic beverages within a state, even those manufactured for out-of-state use, Harlan addressed the judge's task: "The courts are not bound by mere forms, nor are they to be misled by mere pretenses. They are at liberty—indeed, are under a solemn duty—to look at the substance of things. . . . If, therefore, a statute purporting to have been enacted to protect the public health, the public morals, or the public safety, has no real or substantial relation to those objects, or is a palpable invasion of rights secured by the fundamental law, it is the duty of courts to so adjudge." (*Mugler v. Kansas,* 1887). Harlan thus saw the judiciary as an arbiter between public need and private rights. This is indicated in his opinion for the Court in *Smyth v. Ames* (1898), in which he laid out a formula to determine whether rates set by a government agency were reasonable. The Court had indeed come a long way since *Munn.*

In his third demonstration of nationalism, Harlan believed that the Constitution through the contract and commerce clauses established a national economy that

Congress was endowed with ample authority to protect. The Court in *Antoni v. Greenhow* (1883) allowed Virginia to make changes in the administration of its bonds despite a claim that the legislation violated the contract clause. Harlan in dissent despaired of the "disastrous consequences which would result both to the business interest and to the honor of the country" if other states acted similarly. When the majority defanged the Sherman Anti-Trust Act by distinguishing commerce, which Congress could regulate, from manufacturing, which it could not, Harlan was the sole dissenter (*United States v. E. C. Knight Co.*, 1895). "The common government of all the people," wrote Harlan, "is the only one that can adequately deal with a matter which directly and injuriously affects the entire commerce of the country. . . . Its authority should not be so weakened by construction that it cannot reach and eradicate evils that, beyond all question, tend to defeat an object which that government is entitled by the Constitution, to accomplish." Harlan's views on antitrust prevailed to break up a railroad combination in *Northern Securities Co. v. United States* (1904). *Northern Securities* came a year after Harlan had spoken for a slim majority in *Champion v. Ames* (1903), defending Congress's power to prohibit the interstate shipment of lottery tickets. "We should hesitate long before adjudging that an evil of such appalling character," Harlan admonished, "carried on through interstate commerce, cannot be met and crushed by the only power competent to that end." Yet even in cases involving interstate commerce power, Harlan believed the Court had a supervisory role to play. For example, in *Adair v. United States* (1908) Harlan for the majority was unwilling to accept the Erdmann Act, which barred railroads from resorting to yellow dog contracts and firing workers who joined a union. Assuming a fictional equality in bargaining position between employer and employee and finding no real connection between the firing and commerce, Harlan borrowed from the Fourteenth Amendment and applied notions of substantive due process and liberty of contract to the due process clause of the Fifth Amendment.

Off the bench, Harlan was a busy man. He was a lecturer (often on Saturday nights) for nearly two decades at the Columbian (now George Washington) Law School in Washington, D.C. Long a lay leader in the Presbyterian Church (U.S.A.), he was an elder and taught a Sunday school class at the New York Avenue Presbyterian Church. He served as vice moderator of the General Assembly (his denomination's highest adjudicatory) and led an unsuccessful fight in 1905 against a proposal to allow individual congregations to adopt racially exclusive membership policies. On one occasion he had to miss a Court session to attend a church conference. "You are such a good Presbyterian, Harlan," said Justice Rufus Peckham, "that I don't see why you are afraid to die." According to a newspaper account, Harlan responded: "I would not be afraid if I were sure that in the next world I would not turn up at Democratic headquarters" (Atkinson 1999, 83).

When the Court's term opened in the fall of 1911, Harlan was seventy-eight and had served longer than all justices except John Marshall and Stephen Field. Moreover, he generally had enjoyed robust health. But on October 13 a cold from which he was suffering progressed rapidly into bronchitis. He died on the morning of October 14 and was laid to rest in Rock Creek Cemetery in Washington.

William B. Woods

Justice Strong's resignation in 1880 opened a pair of opportunities. Assigned since 1870 to the extensive Fifth Circuit that ranged from Georgia and Florida west through Texas, Justice Bradley sought reassignment to the more compact, familiar, and easily managed Third Circuit. The Third Circuit that had been Strong's encompassed Pennsylvania, New Jersey, and Delaware, as it does today. Bradley's transfer would be easy to arrange if President Hayes replaced Strong with someone from Bradley's old circuit. For Hayes, in turn, naming a justice from the Fifth Circuit would be mortar that might more firmly rejoin the states of the former Confederacy to the Union.

The swearing-in of William Woods of Georgia on January 5, 1881, only two months before the end of the Hayes administration, gave the bench not only its second Civil War veteran but a Whig-turned-Democrat-turned-Republican and a former Union army general who now claimed the South as his home. He also proved to be an extraordinarily productive colleague at a time when the Court needed all the help it could get. Yet with a tenure of not quite six and one-half years, Woods, who thus far ranks last alphabetically on the roster of justices, also remains among the most obscure. Very much a team player and overshadowed in historical accounts by luminaries such as Miller, Field, Bradley, and Harlan, he was ironically only slightly more noticed when he sat. At his death newspaper accounts devoted more space to speculation about a successor than to his considerable service to the nation.

William Burnham Woods was born on August 3, 1824, in Newark, Ohio, the seat of Licking County, about thirty miles east of Columbus. His father, Ezekiel S. Woods, was a farmer and merchant with roots in Kentucky. His mother, Sarah Judith Burnham Woods, was from New England. After a childhood on the farm, Woods attended Western Reserve College in Hudson, Ohio, for three years. He then transferred to Yale College where he graduated in 1845 as class valedictorian. Returning to Newark, he studied law with S. D. King, was admitted to the bar in 1847, and established a partnership with his mentor. His marriage to Anne E. Warner of Newark in 1855 yielded a son and a daughter and was later a key factor in his advancement.

Initially a Whig, Woods by the mid-1850s had become an ardent Democrat. He was elected mayor of Newark in 1856 and a delegate to the state legislature in 1857. His oratorical skills may have contributed to his later election as speaker of the house. When Republicans took control of the chamber after the 1860 elections, Woods as minority leader initially led his party in opposing the majority party's sup-

William B. Woods (Collection of the Supreme Court of the United States)

port for the Lincoln administration. Yet after the attack on Fort Sumter in April 1861 he reversed himself and led the Democrats in support of the Union.

Woods committed himself personally as well as with his vote. In November 1861, he became a lieutenant colonel in the Seventy-sixth Ohio Volunteer Infantry, organized by his younger brother Charles. The unit was placed under General William T. Sherman's command in the West. Woods saw action at Shiloh and Vicksburg and was wounded at least once. Promoted to colonel in 1863, he was with Sherman on the infamous March to the Sea from Atlanta to Savannah in 1864. He traveled northward with Sherman to Durham Station, North Carolina, for General Joseph E. Johnston's surrender on April 26, 1865. By this time, on the recommendation of Generals Sherman, U. S. Grant, and John A. Logan, he had been made brigadier general.

Mustered out of the service in February 1866 as a breveted major general, Woods settled in Bentonville (now called Elba) in Coffee County, Alabama, some 40 miles west of Dothan. He planted cotton, operated an iron foundry, and practiced law. He was also a Republican who seemed to make friends easily among both those who had been on the losing side in the war and those of the newly arrived carpetbag class. In 1867 he was elected judge on a state chancery (or equity) court. He was sitting in that capacity when President Grant named him in 1869 as U.S. circuit judge for the Fifth Circuit, following congressional creation of those new judgeships in the same year. Exactly why Grant chose Woods is not entirely clear. To be sure, Grant knew him, but he surely also knew other former officers who were attorneys. The answer may lie in the quip that a federal judge is a lawyer who knows a U.S. senator. Willard Warner, Woods's brother-in-law, had moved to Alabama as a carpetbagger and was soon elected to the U.S. Senate. Warner had also served with Grant, was one of the new president's faithful allies, and no doubt brought the name of his sister's husband to Grant's attention.

Woods maintained his home in Alabama until 1877 when he moved to Atlanta, but his new job required holding court in each state in the circuit. It was on circuit that he became close friends with Justice Bradley. Bradley was so impressed with Woods that he submitted his name to President Hayes in 1877 for the Supreme Court seat that went to Harlan. Perhaps part of the scholarly Bradley's admiration stemmed from Woods's success in collecting and publishing decisions by the Fifth Circuit in a four-volume set known as *Woods Reports* (1875–1883).

Woods was among the first federal judges to confront the Fourteenth Amendment and prosecutions under the Enforcement Acts. In *United States v. Hall* (1871), for example, he upheld the indictment under the Enforcement Act of 1870 of white men who had broken up a political meeting of blacks. The question was whether the Fourteenth Amendment protected freedom of speech and assembly. If so, Congress could validly protect those rights from abridgement. "What are the privileges and immunities of citizens of the United States [protected by the Fourteenth Amendment]?" Woods asked. "They are undoubtedly those which may be denominated fundamental; which belong of right to the citizens of all free states. . . . Among these . . . are the right of freedom of speech, and the right peaceably to assemble." This of course was opposite the position later taken by Justice Bradley on circuit (where he disagreed with Woods). It also differed from the view of the Supreme Court in *United States v. Cruikshank* (1876), where such rights were seen as deriving from state, not federal, citizenship, and so outside the Fourteenth Amendment's protection. However, when the circuit court had heard arguments in the *Slaughterhouse Cases* in 1870, Woods and Bradley had agreed that the state-imposed butchering monopoly violated the Fourteenth Amendment. With John A. Campbell as attorney for the aggrieved butchers, this surely must be one of the few occasions where a former justice, a sitting justice, and a future justice were all involved in the same case.

As a Supreme Court justice, the "Yankee from Georgia" (Baynes 1978, 31) did more than his share of the work. His first of well over 100 opinions for the Court was issued on January 31, 1881, and his last came on May 10, 1886, by which time he had been laid low by illness. Despite this heavy production, Woods was and is a relatively obscure justice. In addition to the handicap that a clipped tenure nearly always imposes, nearly all of his labors were on the mundane cases that crowded the docket at the time—disputes important to the litigants, to be sure, but with little or no importance to the growth of the law. Yet even in minor cases his dry wit could surface. "Pensions are the bounties of the Government," Woods mused in *United States v. Teller* (1883), "which Congress has the right to give, withhold, distribute or recall, at its discretion."

Woods furthermore was among the least likely of the Waite justices to express himself independently through dissents. One must search long and hard for a dissenting Woods vote, although one can be found in *Elk v. Watkins* (1884), when Woods joined Justice Harlan's vigorous dissent. The majority in that case excluded Indians from Fourteenth Amendment citizenship even when they had left the reservation and assimilated themselves into the white community. Such departures by Woods from the prevailing view on the bench were rare. For instance, he forsook his broad Fifth Circuit interpretation of the Reconstruction amendments for the Waite Court's more restricted view. To know the Waite Court's decisions between 1881 and 1886, therefore, is also to know Woods's position in nearly every case. He played not only a supporting role but a role set well in the background.

Indeed, Woods spoke for the Court in only six constitutional cases, and only three of these were important. His opinion in *United States v. Harris* (1883) invalidated part of the Enforcement Act of 1871 that criminalized conduct by any two persons that deprived another of "equal protection of the laws." Applying the Court's thinking from *Cruikshank*, Woods explained that Congress could prohibit only discriminatory action by the state, not by private persons. To hold otherwise would be to "accord to Congress the power to punish every crime by which the right of any person to life, property or reputation is invaded. . . . A construction . . . which leads to such a result is clearly unsound." However, Woods seemed to leave open the significant possibility that Congress could act if a state failed to protect its citizens.

Over its entire history, the Supreme Court has decided only a handful of Second Amendment cases. It is therefore an anomaly that one of the tiny number of constitutional opinions that Woods authored dealt with this right-to-bear-arms provision. In *Presser v. Illinois* (1886), the state had banned any unlicensed drilling or parading while armed. Herman Presser, a member of the Lehr und Wehr Verein (Education and Defense Association), a cultural and paramilitary organization of mainly working-class Germans with socialist leanings, was convicted of violating the law. Presser challenged his conviction, claiming that the state had violated his Second Amendment right to bear arms. The amendment did not grant such a right, Woods countered, but only limited Congress's authority to take it away. In addition, it placed no limitations on the states. Additionally, individuals had no right, independent of government, to organize their own militias (Spitzer 2001, 14). "The exercise of this power by the States is necessary to the public peace, safety and good order," Woods wrote. "To deny the power would be to deny the right of the State to disperse assemblages organized for sedition and treason, and the right to suppress armed mobs bent on riot and rapine."

On the same day that *Presser* came down, Woods spoke for the Court in *Mobile v. Watson* (1886). In 1879 the Alabama legislature dissolved the city of Mobile and reincorporated a smaller area as the Port of Mobile, with the latter claiming that it was not responsible for bonds and other financial obligations of its predecessor city. The Port of Mobile, Woods decreed, "is the successor in law of the former and liable for its debts. . . . Where the resource for the payment of the bonds of a municipal corporation is the power of taxation existing when the bonds were issued, any law which withdraws or limits the taxing power and leaves no adequate means for the payment of the bonds is forbidden by the Constitution of the United States. . . ."

Presser and *Watson* were decided just a few months before Woods became incapacitated. After an extended absence from the Court for recuperation in California that did little to improve his condition, he returned to Washington. He died on May 14, 1887. Burial was in Newark where his life had begun.

The Garfield Appointment

Stanley Matthews

Justice Swayne's none-too-soon retirement in January 1881 opened the door to another appointment by Hayes in the waning weeks of his administration. His choice

Stanley Matthews (Matthew Brady, Collection of the Supreme Court of the United States)

on January 24 was college friend Stanley Matthews. The president and Matthews were also related by marriage: Lucy Webb Hayes's brother and Matthews's sister were husband and wife (Roper 1993, 228). But the Judiciary Committee pigeonholed the nomination and let it die as the session ended. James Garfield, the new president, resubmitted Matthews's name on March 14. The confirmation vote of 24–23 on May 12, after considerable acrimony in the Senate, stands as a record for a Supreme Court justice. No other successful nominee has been met with a higher percentage of nays. (Second place on the roster of close calls is held by Justice Clarence Thomas, who was confirmed 52–48 in 1991.) As explained in Chapter 1, Matthews's razor-thin confirmation reflected associational liabilities, not a talent deficiency. He came to the bench as a highly intelligent and able attorney and a skilled political operator. He might have had a larger presence and impact on the Court had he, like Woods, not had an abbreviated tenure.

Born July 21, 1824, in Lexington, Kentucky, Thomas Stanley Matthews (he dropped the "Thomas" as an adult) was the eldest of eleven children born to Thomas J. and Isabella Brown Matthews. The Matthews household also contained five children from Thomas's first marriage, so Isabella must have been a very busy woman. Stanley's father was a mathematics professor at Transylvania University in Lexington, but the family moved to Cincinnati when he was made principal of the city's Woodward High School. Stanley was schooled at Woodward and then enrolled at Kenyon College where he became close friends with Rutherford B. Hayes. Graduating in 1840, he studied law for two years in Cincinnati, mainly under the tutelage of Salmon P. Chase, the future chief justice. Now age eighteen, Stanley fell three years shy of Ohio's minimum age for admission to the bar. However, Tennessee was more lenient in its rules, so he taught school and opened a law practice in Maury County, the home of James K. Polk in central Tennessee. He also took a strong interest in political journalism, helping to edit the *Tennessee Democrat.* This affiliation did not dampen his courtship of Mary Ann (Minnie) Black, daughter of a prominent Whig politician. Stanley married Minnie in 1843, and the couple had ten children. (Minnie Matthews died in 1885, and her husband was remarried in 1887 to Mary Theaker of Washington.)

In 1844, Matthews returned to Cincinnati, by now an important port city of over 25,000, just across the Ohio River from the slave state of Kentucky. Because of its economic ties to the South, Cincinnati was the state's most pro-slavery city but, with James G. Birney's abolitionist newspaper *Philanthropist* published there, it was also a center of antislavery ferment. Admitted to the Ohio bar in 1845, Matthews caught the abolition fever and followed Gamaliel Bailey as editor of the city's antislavery *Morning Herald.* He took the U.S. Supreme Court to task in one editorial for its pro-slavery decision in *Jones v. Van Zandt* (1847), in which Matthews's former tutor Chase had defended the underground railroad member. Matthews's work with the *Herald* gave him connections with Liberty and Free-Soil activists in Ohio and was probably responsible for his selection as clerk of the state house of representatives during the 1848–1849 session. There followed a series of political sorties interspersed within a law practice that quickly identified him as a capable railroad attorney. He served as judge on the court of common pleas for Hamilton County from 1851 until 1853, and was elected to the state senate in 1855. By this time Matthews must have been perceived as a mainstream Democrat, less militant on the slavery question. Otherwise it would be hard to account for his appointment by President James Buchanan in 1858 as U.S. attorney for southern Ohio. As U.S. attorney, he was charged with enforcement of the recently enacted fugitive slave law that was a key element of the Compromise of 1850 and anathema to abolitionists.

A year later tragedy struck the Matthews family when four children died quickly in a scarlet fever epidemic that swept Cincinnati. Their deaths had a profound impact on Matthews. He renewed his Christian faith and became a devout lay leader in the Presbyterian Church, attending the meeting of its highest adjudicatory (the General Assembly) in 1864 and drafting the denomination's formal condemnation of slavery.

When Lincoln became president in 1861, Matthews resigned his office as U.S. attorney, although by this time he had become a Republican. He was appointed a lieutenant colonel in the Twenty-third Ohio Infantry where he served with Hayes. In 1862 he became a colonel and was shifted to the Fifty-first Ohio Volunteers, part of the Army of the Cumberland. Injured during a battle when he was thrown from his horse, Matthews left the army in 1863. He ran successfully for superior court, a position he held until 1865 when he resumed his railroad practice. (He thus missed by a few months sitting with Alfonso Taft, father of a future president and chief justice.) Matthews earlier had made enemies by enforcing the law against fugitive slaves and those who aided them. Again, Matthews found himself the object of scorn when he defended the Cincinnati School Board after it ordered an end to the regular morning reading of the Bible in the city's schools in the interest of protecting religious diversity. Matthews eventually won the case before the Ohio Supreme Court, but the local reaction against him was so severe that he had to resign the office of elder in the Presbyterian Church in 1869 (*Minor v. Board of Education*, 1873).

Matthews remained connected politically. He was a presidential elector for Lincoln in 1864 and for Grant in 1868. Yet by 1872 he had become disillusioned with scandals in the latter's administration and veered into the Liberal Republican reform alternative. He acted as temporary chair when that party held its convention in Cincinnati. Aside from his identity with railroad interests, Matthews's politics could be described as liberal, at least as that term was used then. He was concerned about continued federal occupation of the South, he favored an inflated currency through silver coinage (an issue on which he and Hayes flatly disagreed), and he opposed a high protective tariff (Stevens 1999, 55). So he was understandably dismayed when the Cincinnati convention nominated Horace Greeley, a staunch protectionist, for president. His consorting with the anti-Grant movement no doubt kept him off the short list for the chief justiceship after Chase's death in 1873.

Matthews was a close adviser as the Hayes campaign for the White House gained momentum in 1876. It was also the year of his defeat, by seventy-five votes, for a seat in Congress. The presidential election handed Democrat Samuel Tilden the popular vote and left Hayes's presidential future teetering on disputed electoral votes in four states. Matthews was named one of the Republican counsel to press the party's case before the electoral commission Congress had established. One tightrope that Matthews had to walk was to convince the commission not to scrutinize the officially certified (Republican) votes from Florida, yet to examine votes certified by the Democratic governor in Oregon. Matthews's reasoning prevailed, and Hayes won the White House by one electoral vote. But his work for Hayes was not yet done. It was Matthews who took the lead in negotiating the Compromise of 1877 with disgruntled Democrats, whereby the last of the federal troops would be withdrawn from the South if Democrats acquiesced in the commission's vote.

Hayes picked Ohio senator John Sherman (younger brother of the general) to be secretary of the treasury, and the Ohio legislature elected Matthews to fill out the two years remaining in Sherman's term. Matthews campaigned in the Senate to place silver on a parity with gold, and advocated both silver coin and greenbacks as legal tender. He also took sides with railroad magnate Jay Gould by strenuously opposing passage of the Thurman Act. He thereby added to the ranks of those who would try to block his appointment to the Supreme Court in 1881. The Thurman Act that the Court upheld in the *Sinking Fund Cases* (1879) imposed substantial obligations on the Pacific railroads to make good on repayment of enormous loans the government had extended to them in the 1860s. As a justice, Matthews lived long enough to vote with the majority in *Juilliard v. Greenman* (1888), which upheld greenbacks as legal tender even outside the exigencies of wartime. To his credit he seemed no more inclined than most of his colleagues to unduly favor the railroads, as the bias of his earlier professional years might have promised and as his opponents in 1881 certainly feared. In *Smith v. Alabama* (1888), for example, he rejected a challenge on commerce clause grounds to a state requirement that locomotive engineers, even those on trains traveling interstate, be examined and licensed.

In his less than eight years on the bench, Matthews authored more than 200 opinions of the Court, and he was almost as infrequent a dissenter as Woods. So, as with Woods, Matthews's views are nearly coterminous with those of the Waite Court majority; he departed from the majority on no major question of the day. His legacy on constitutional questions rests primarily on three cases in which he spoke for the Court.

Hurtado v. California (1884) was the Court's first landmark ruling that expressly addressed whether the due process clause of the Fourteenth Amendment encompassed any of the procedural guaranties of the Bill of Rights. California allowed a felony prosecution to proceed on the filing of information by the prosecutor, rather than on the basis of a grand jury indictment as long required under English common law and as required for federal courts by the Fifth Amendment. Writing for all but Justice Harlan, Matthews rejected Hurtado's contention that his conviction for murder was therefore faulty on Fourteenth Amendment due process grounds. Because the Fifth Amendment also contained a due process clause it could not be supposed that the Fourteenth Amendment's reference to due process included the Fifth Amendment's guaranty of grand jury indictment. Instead Matthews gave due process a different meaning: protection against arbitrary power. Accordingly due process under the Fourteenth Amendment did not require states to adhere to particular procedures in order to be fair. The Supreme Court later abandoned the view that Fourteenth Amendment due process excluded specific protections of the Bill of Rights. But the Court has never tied states otherwise to late eighteenth-century common law practices and has steadfastly adhered to Matthews's conception that, at least, due process is a barrier against arbitrary policies and treatment.

A year later in 1885, *Poindexter v. Greenhow* presented the Court with a dilemma that juxtaposed the contract clause limitation on the states with the Eleventh Amendment's limitation on the federal judicial power. A Reconstruction-era government in Virginia had floated bonds, promising not only to repay the principal but to accept the bondholders' interest coupons as payment for taxes. A later administration reneged, refused to accept the coupons in place of taxes, and began seizing the assets of bondholders. Admittedly the contract had been broken, but the Eleventh Amendment made the state immune to nonconsensual suits in the federal courts. Yet the same could not be said for the agents of the state (the tax collectors) when they acted illegally. "This distinction," wrote Matthews, "is essential to the idea of constitutional government. To deny it or blot it out obliterates the line of demarcation that separates constitutional government from absolutism. . . ."

Perhaps Matthews's most durable opinion was in *Yick Wo v. Hopkins* (1886). The case provided a window into the rampant discrimination in California against Asians, Chinese in particular. A San Francisco ordinance, ostensibly enacted to promote public health and safety, required anyone operating a laundry in a wooden structure (most buildings in the city were constructed of wood) to obtain a license. Licenses were denied to more than 200 laundry operators, nearly all of whom happened to be Chinese subjects, while some 80 licenses were issued to others, only one of whom was arguably Chinese. Did this facially neutral law with racially unequal impact violate the Fourteenth Amendment's equal protection clause? "Though the law itself be fair on its face and impartial in appearance," Matthews concluded, "yet, if it is applied and administered by public authority with an evil eye and an unequal hand, . . . the denial of equal justice is still within the prohibition of the Constitution." The "conclusion cannot be resisted," he added, "that no reason for it exists except hostility to the race and nationality to which the petitioners belong." A later generation would label Matthew's perspective an exercise in judicial realism. One can only speculate whether, had he remained on the Court another eight years, he would have joined Harlan's dissent to the transparency in *Plessy v. Ferguson* (1896).

Justice Matthews's health went into sharp decline in 1888. Exposure in the blizzard of 1888 in New York City may have contributed to chills and fever that led to a serious rheumatic condition. He died in Washington on March 22, 1889, and was buried in Cincinnati.

The Arthur Appointments

Horace Gray

Before he was shot in July 1881, President Garfield considered Massachusetts chief justice Horace Gray as a possible successor to the rapidly deteriorating Justice Clifford. Gray's college classmate, George Hoar, now U.S. senator from Massachusetts, had made sure of that. After Clifford's death on July 25 and Garfield's on September 19, Hoar successfully pressed Gray's case with the new president, Chester A. Arthur. Gray's swearing-in on January 9, 1882, began a Supreme Court career of nearly twenty years that, across some 450 opinions, displayed a wealth of legal knowledge that earned him recognition as a prodigious scholar-in-residence. Yet this brilliant master of juristic acumen fashioned only a single new doctrine and was not disposed toward articulating a constitutional vision for the Court or the nation.

Probably none of the nineteenth-century justices was born into more comfortable circumstances as was Horace Gray on March 24, 1828, in the Beacon Hill section of Boston. Although his great-grandfather had been a poor shoemaker, his grandfather William Gray had made a fortune in the import trade and shipbuilding businesses, which Gray's father, Horace, Sr., continued. Horace, Jr.'s mother was Harriet Upham, whose father Jabez Upham was an attorney and member of the U.S. House of Representatives. At age six, the younger Horace's mother died, and his father remarried. A half-brother from this second marriage was John Chipman Gray, later a professor at Harvard Law School and a noted scholar. Educated in private schools in Boston, the younger Horace enrolled at Harvard College at thirteen, by which age he had spectacularly reached his full adult height of six feet, six inches. Although he demonstrated a strong interest in natural history and botany, he graduated with an average record in 1845. Gray was traveling in Europe when he learned that the family wealth had been decimated because of bad investments his father had made in iron smelting.

Nothing focuses the mind on the future like the prospect of impecunity, and Gray chose law as a safe route to financial security. Despite lax standards at Harvard

Horace Gray (Harris & Ewing, Collection of the Supreme Court of the United States)

Law School (payment receipts for three terms apparently entitled one to a diploma), Gray dived into the subject and in the process helped to change the way in which law would be taught in the United States. With another Harvard student named John Felton, Gray decided that knowledge of the law was best learned by tracing legal principles through their application in various cases, rather than merely from reading treatises. They shared their approach with another student named Christopher Columbus Langdell. Langdell as dean of Harvard Law School later would establish the case study method as standard pedagogy for Harvard Law's curriculum. Eventually, law schools across the nation adopted the method. After clerking for a Boston firm and reading law under John Lowell, Gray gained admission to the bar in 1851 and opened his own practice. An attraction to the Free-Soil Party led him to become a Republican after the latter party's formation in the mid-1850s.

Gray soon was handed a life-changing opportunity. Luther S. Cushing, reporter for the Supreme Judicial Court of Massachusetts, became ill, and Gray received a temporary appointment to prepare a volume of reports. When Cushing died in 1854, Gray was named in his place. Within seven years he produced sixteen volumes of reports, all while carrying on his own practice that included arguing cases before the state's high court. An 1857 article he wrote for the *Monthly Law Review* undercut a main point of Chief Justice Taney's opinion in *Dred Scott v. Sandford* that even free blacks were not intended to be citizens of the United States. The essay vindicated the dissent of Justice Curtis of Massachusetts, Justice Clifford's predecessor and soon to be Gray's friend and professional associate in Boston's legal circles.

Gray's vehement antislavery views were probably too extreme for mainstream Republicans in 1860, when he lost a convention nomination to be state attorney general. Instead he became an unofficial adviser on war-related legal questions to Governor John A. Andrew. Andrew in turn recognized the thirty-six-year-old's talents and services with an appointment to the Supreme Judicial Court in 1864, making Gray the youngest justice in Bay State history. Elevation to chief justice followed in 1873. In addition to sitting as a trial judge (like the high courts of some other states, the Massachusetts court still retained what was called a *nisi prius* jurisdiction in certain matters), Gray wrote a total of 1,367 opinions for the court in appellate cases. Firmly believing that dissents were to be avoided in almost all instances because they weakened the force of a decision, Gray authored only one dissent in these cases. This was a perspective he would adjust only marginally at the U.S. Supreme Court, where in twenty years he recorded only fifty-one dissenting votes.

Gray brought to Washington a custom that eventually was institutionalized at the Supreme Court. As early as 1875 he began hiring a recent Harvard Law School graduate as a law secretary to help him with research. (His first secretary on the Massachusetts bench was Louis D. Brandeis, whom President Woodrow Wilson would name to the Court in 1916.) Congress eventually provided funds to pay the justices' law clerks, and today they are fixtures at all federal courts, all state appellate courts, and most state trial courts.

Gray would also carry a distinctive manner and bearing with him to Washington. A bachelor until June 4, 1889, when he married Jane Matthews, daughter of the late Justice Matthews and thirty years Gray's junior, Gray was a fussy, punctual, refined, and occasionally imperious person who insisted on proper etiquette, decorum, and appearance. Certainly when he was on the state bench, an attorney or witness would enter his courtroom improperly attired only once. It was as if he wanted no one to forget his Beacon Hill upbringing. Once when there was little precedent on which to draw in a dispute over the tariff status of tomatoes (duty was owed on fruit but not on vegetables), he drew on his experiences at the table. Tomatoes "are usually served at dinner in, with, or after the soup, fish, or meats which constitute the principal part of the repast, and not, like fruits generally, as dessert" (*Nix v. Hedden*, 1893). Hence, tomatoes were taxable. Yet he also loved outdoor adventure. In 1883, he, Waite, and General William T. Sherman went on a camping expedition in Montana. Imagine the genial chief justice from Toledo, the fastidious jurist from Boston, and the conquistador of Georgia (who had provided a list of the items his comrades would need to pack) all sitting around a campfire enjoying coffee, eggs, and lamb chops on a crisp morning. The scene strains credulity.

Gray's Supreme Court opinions tended to read like academic papers, as they had on the Massachusetts bench. If Clifford's opinions had been ponderous, Gray's were meticulous and exhaustive. Gray's first opinion in 1864 was in a suit to reclaim a heifer. Within five pages, he cited a "textbook several times, eight English cases going back to . . . Henry VIII, twenty-six state cases from five jurisdictions, one federal case, and twenty-one statutes going back to the Body of Liberties of 1641 and forward to the 1836 revisions" (Filler 1969a, 1382). Gray's sixty-seven-page opinion for the U.S. Supreme Court in *Liverpool and Great Western Steam v. Phoenix Insurance* (1889), which involved the liability of a common carrier for employee negligence, displayed citations to more than eighty cases from U.S., British, French, Dutch, and Italian courts. Sometimes relevancy became lost in antiquity. *Hilton v. Guyot* (1895), which determined how U.S. courts should accept findings of French courts, resulted in a 100-page opinion that traced the application of a 1629 French ordinance across 250 years in cases from 22 countries (Nash 1994, 1999). His new colleagues in Washington took notice. Waite coveted Gray's writing abilities. "Can't you tell me the secret of your *style*. I wish I had it. . . ." Joking once with Waite about the vacations of various colleagues, Harlan speculated that "Gray is, at this time, examining into the Precedents in British Columbia" (Magrath 1963, 185, 301).

Gray's marshaling of precedent was comforting to those on his side, but discomforting to those who were not. Once when Gray was vacationing in Europe, Field wrote to Bradley concerning what he regarded as Gray's dangerous toleration for state regulation of commerce, pledging "to co-operate with you . . . to defeat the manifest purposes of Gray to overturn our interstate commerce decisions." Field even said he might "purchase a one-horse landau" to give the two of them time together to plot tactics en route to and from judicial conferences.

One analysis of Gray's dissents (Nash 1994, 199, 201) suggests that he was influential especially in the Court's cases that involved the fellow-servant rule, one of the most contentious issues of the day, especially in an increasingly industrial economy. This was a judicially crafted rule that exempted employers from liability when one employee had caused harm to another employee in a workplace accident. (The employee would usually be judgment-proof, lacking the financial resources to cover an injured worker's loss, thus leaving the latter without compensation.) As a state judge Gray had narrowed the rule, but on the Supreme Court he resisted efforts by Field and others to do the same. By the 1890s, Gray's dissents in such cases declined; the bench, apparently, was moving more in his direction. For example, in *Alaska Mining Co. v. Whelan* (1897), Gray deemed a foreman the equivalent of a regular employee, and even though the former's action had caused a serious accident, the company could not be held financially accountable.

On constitutional issues, Gray is perhaps best remembered as an advocate of federal power. In *Juilliard v. Greenman* (1884) he spoke for the Court in upholding Congress's authority to issue greenbacks as legal tender even outside the exigencies of wartime. The case is usually cited as the origin of the theory of resulting powers—powers that Congress possesses because of other powers expressly granted. "Congress is vested with the exclusive exercise of the analogous power of coining money and regulating the value of domestic and foreign coin, and also with the paramount power of regulating foreign and interstate commerce. Under the power to borrow money . . . and to issue circulating notes for the money borrowed, its power to define the quality and force of these notes as currency is as broad as the like power over a metallic currency. . . . Under the two powers, taken together, Congress is authorized to establish a national currency, either in coin or in paper and to make that currency lawful money for all purposes." Similarly, in *Logan v. United States* (1892) he held that the implied powers of Congress justified application of the Enforcement Act to lawless action by a mob against someone in the custody of a federal marshal.

In *Fong Yue Ting v. United States* (1893) Gray virtually declared that the extent of Congress's authority over aliens was a political question and therefore not appropriate for judicial decision. Reaffirming the constitutionality of the Chinese Exclusion Act, Gray not only upheld the deportation of Chinese aliens who ran afoul of an early treaty but ruled that Congress was not obliged to extend any procedural guaranties to assure fairness. "Congress, having the right, as it may see fit, to expel aliens of a particular class, or to permit them to remain, has undoubtedly the right to provide a system of registration and identification of the members of that class within the country, and to take all proper means to carry out the system which it provides." However, children of Chinese aliens born on U.S. soil raised a different question, as he explained in *United States v. Wong Kim Ark* (1898). Those children were citizens under the Fourteenth Amendment's definition of citizenship. The ruling seemed to conflict with Gray's opinion in *Elk v. Watkins* (1884) excluding Indians from citizenship even when they had assimilated themselves into the white community. As a measure of popular attitudes of the day, the holding in *Wong Kim Ark* caused Finley Peter Dunne's barroom newspaper character Mr. Dooley to ask, "If cats were born in an oven wud they be biscuits?" (King 1950, 237–238).

Gray, however, balked at the federal income tax. His role in *Pollock v. Farmers' Loan and Trust Co.* (1895) poses a question that has yet to be convincingly answered. On the first hearing in the case, the majority invalidated the tax as applied to income from municipal bonds and, as a nonapportioned direct tax, as applied to rents on land. Justice Howell Jackson was absent because of illness, and the bench split 4–4 on whether the tax could be constitutionally applied to income from personal property such as stocks and bonds. On the second hearing, with Justice Jackson present and voting to sustain the tax, the Court ruled 5–4 against the tax. This meant that one of the four justices on the first hearing had switched sides. Some Court lore has long accorded that distinction to Justice George Shiras. However, Edward Corwin, the late great constitutional scholar at Princeton, believed that Gray, not Shiras, had changed his vote. His explanation, written some forty-three years after *Pollock*, bears repeating. "Gray was for years, except for Bradley, the strongest nationalist on the bench. . . . Furthermore, Gray was an old-school judge, a product of the Civil War, and not especially alert to the property question. . . . Also, Gray was a very learned man and a great precedent judge, whereas the Pollock Case played 'ducks and drakes' with the precedents. For all which reasons, the surprising thing would be not that Gray was the last Justice to line up against the act, but that he should have done so at all" (Corwin 1938, 199–200).

Although usually a nationalist, Gray was also generally disposed to accept state regulation. He dissented in *Poindexter v. Greenhow* (1885) when Matthews for the majority circumvented the Eleventh Amendment to hold a state to its contract with bondholders. Moreover, he did not share the substantive due process inclinations of some of his colleagues, as reflected by a distinct impatience in his opinion in *Head v. Amoskeag Manufacturing* (1885). Indeed, he dissented in the *Minnesota Rate Case* (1890) that, contrary to *Munn v. Illinois* (1877), refused to accept commission-set rates without judicial review. Yet the Court seemed to come back to his way of thinking in *Budd v. New York* (1892) when it accepted a legislatively determined rate as satisfying the demands of due process.

Gray's last day at the Court was February 3, 1902. His health had been in decline for at least two years, but on that evening he suffered a paralytic stroke. Recuperative time at his home on the Massachusetts coast (he also still maintained a home in Boston as well as one in Washington) did little to improve his condition. He submitted his letter of retirement to President Theodore Roosevelt on July 9, to take effect on the appointment of a successor, and died on September 15 at Nahant, northeast of Boston. His successor on the Supreme Court was the same person who had taken his seat on the Massachusetts bench: Oliver Wendell Holmes, Jr.

Samuel Blatchford

Ward Hunt was the last of three debilitated justices to leave the bench within the span of a year. With the appointment of Samuel Blatchford in the spring of 1882 the Court had nine able-bodied and mentally alert members for the first time since 1878. The tradition of a New York seat continued, barely. Except for the period from 1795 until 1806, one of the Court's seats had always been filled by a New Yorker. President Arthur's third choice for the position (his second choice had been a Vermonter), New Yorker Blatchford was the first person named to the Court with experience as both a federal district and circuit judge. He also may still be the only justice whose hobby was collecting almanacs. During his eleven years of service Blatchford earned a reputation as a workhorse, a moderate, and a consensus builder. Of the 3,237 signed opinions issued by the Court during his tenure, he churned out 430, about a fifth more than his proportionate share, with only two dissenting ones. Yet his opinions too often consisted of long and rambling recitations of cases instead of analysis and articulation of principle, making them both less accessible and less useful to later generations.

Samuel was born on March 9, 1820, into the conventionally distinguished New York City family of Richard Milford and Julia Ann Mumford Blatchford. Richard Blatchford was an attorney who counted the Bank of England and the Bank of the United States among his clients and who also served as a Whig in the New York legislature, where he developed a close friendship with William H. Seward. Samuel's mother was the daughter of publicist John R. Mumford. At thirteen Samuel enrolled at Columbia College and graduated at the top of his class four years later.

Blatchford read law at his father's office and became private secretary to Seward who was by then governor of New York. Admitted to the bar in 1842, Blatchford went into practice with his father. In 1844 he married Caroline Appleton of Lowell, Massachusetts. Seward, now out of office, took Blatchford into his Auburn firm as a partner, a relationship that lasted until the practice was dissolved in 1854. Blatchford moved to New York City and established a new partnership with Seward's nephew. By this time Blatchford was well connected politically and professionally. Clients included Samuel F. B. Morse, Cyrus McCormick, and Charles Goodyear.

Having turned down a seat on the state bench in 1855, he accepted appointments as U.S. judge for the case-clogged Southern District of New York in 1867 and

Samuel Blatchford (Handy Studios, Collection of the Supreme Court of the United States)

U.S. judge for the maritime and patent-rich Second Circuit in 1872. Even after his appointment to the U.S. Supreme Court, he continued a project he had begun in 1852: editing and publishing twenty-four volumes of *Blatchford's Circuit Court Reports.* The volumes included cases decided in the circuit since 1845 and a series of maritime reports as well. This was an important contribution, just as Woods's was for the Fifth Circuit. There was no standardized national reporter system as yet to make decisions accessible across a region, much less across the nation.

As a justice, Blatchford was widely regarded among experts in his day for his opinions on maritime and patent law. Indeed, with the latter he rivaled Justice Bradley. One of his opinions illustrated not only his legal perceptiveness but his practical knowledge of manufacturing, design, and the mercantile business generally. In *Dobson v. Hartford Carpet Co.* (1885), the holder of a patent on a carpet design objected to the appropriation by others of a design in the weaving of inferior, less expensive carpets. This in turn negatively affected sales of the holder's more expensive carpets. Assuming patent infringement, the question was how to determine an award for damages. "Approval of the particular design or pattern may very well be one motive for purchasing the article containing it," he reasoned, "but the article must have intrinsic merits of quality and structure, to obtain a purchaser, aside from the pattern or design; and to attribute in law the entire profit to the pattern . . . confounds all distinctions between cause and effect." A second decision on the same question followed in *Dobson v. Dornan* (1886). Blatchford's rules outlining infringement of design patents shaped subsequent congressional legislation on the subject.

Blatchford's opinion for the Court in *Ex parte Boyer* (1884) extended admiralty jurisdiction for the federal district courts to canals. These waterways were entirely intrastate but they connected bodies of water (in this instance Lake Michigan and the Chicago River to the Illinois and Mississippi Rivers) that were routes of interstate commerce. "Navigable water situated as this canal is, . . . a highway for commerce between ports and places in different States, . . . is public water of the United States, and within the legitimate scope of the admiralty jurisdiction . . . even though the canal is wholly artificial, and is wholly within the body of a State, and subject to its ownership and control."

As his paucity of dissenting votes demonstrates, Blatchford moved with the Waite Court as it gravitated away from the holding in *Munn v. Illinois* (1877) that rate setting was a legislative, and not a judicial, concern. True, Blatchford did not participate in *Stone v. Farmers Loan and Trust Co.* (1886), which announced that an unreasonably low rate, which the Court did not find in that instance, would be a denial of due process. Yet it would have been surprising had he parted company with the majority on that point. This seems clear from his opinion four years later in the *Minnesota Rate Case* (1890). In that case six justices rejected on due process grounds rate setting by a railroad commission that was not judicially reviewable. Minnesota's system deprived "the Company of its right to a judicial investigation, by due process of law, under the forms and with the machinery provided by the wisdom of successive ages for the investigation judicially of the truth of a matter in controversy, and substitutes therefor, as an absolute finality, the action of a Railroad Commission which . . . cannot be regarded as clothed with judicial functions or possessing the machinery of a court of justice." Blatchford was not prepared to believe that the procedures of a commission or administrative agency—a recently invented governmental entity—could embody essential fairness. He therefore found the Milwaukee Railroad Company was denied the "process" that it was "due." The occasion was historic: it was the first time the Court had used the Fourteenth Amendment to invalidate a rate regulatory scheme.

Blatchford must have been one of the more moderate members of the majority in the *Minnesota Rate Case.* So it would seem from *Budd v. New York* (1892), in which Blatchford spoke for a different configuration of six justices that rate setting by the state legislature, without judicial review of the reasonableness of the rates, did not violate due process. In a delicate tightrope act, Blatchford distinguished the 1890 ruling and expressly reaffirmed *Munn.* "What was said in the [earlier] opinion, as to the question of the reasonableness of the rate of charge being one for judicial investigation, had no reference to a case where the rates are prescribed directly by the legislature." Blatchford conceded that a legislative finding of reasonableness might still be challenged in the courts as an unconstitutional taking of property if the rates were too low. But the regimen put in place by New York did not intrinsically offend the due process clause, as had Minnesota's. Blatchford's position in the two cases understandably perplexed both advocates and opponents of rate regulation.

With respect to the second holding in the *Granger Cases* that states could set railroad rates for routes stretching across state lines, Blatchford was in the majority in the *Wabash Case* (1886). (*Munn* was the lead case of the *Granger Cases.*) The *Wabash Case* effectively reversed *Munn* with respect to rates applied to interstate shipments. Blatchford also wrote for the Court in *Pickard v. Pullman Southern Car Co.* (1886), which invalidated as a burden on interstate commerce Tennessee's assessment on sleeping cars owned by an out-of-state company and operating on interstate trains passing through the state.

Yet Blatchford was as inclined as most Waite era justices to accept state regulations if there was no demonstrable burden on, or discrimination against, interstate commerce, and if Congress had not legislated on the matter (as it rarely did in that day). *Turner v. Maryland* (1883) challenged the state's comprehensive inspection system for tobacco that was grown within the state for shipment outside the state. Section 10 of Article I of the U.S. Constitution prohibited a state, without the consent of Congress, from laying "any Imposts or Duties on Imports or Exports, except what may be absolutely necessary for executing its inspection Laws. . . ." To qualify for the inspection Maryland required payment of a fee. Was this in effect a tax on exports or a bona fide inspection fee? The answer to that question turned on whether the Maryland requirement was truly an inspection, especially in light of counsel's contention that the actual tobacco did not have to be examined. "Recognized elements of inspection laws," Blatchford wrote for a unanimous bench, again drawing on his experience with mercantile matters, "have always been: quality of the article, form, capacity, dimensions and weight of package, mode of putting up, and marking and branding of various kinds, all these matters being supervised by a public officer having authority to pass or not pass the article as lawful merchandise. . . . It has never been regarded as necessary, and it is manifestly not necessary, that all of these elements should coexist in order to make a valid inspection law. . . . When all are prescribed, and then inspection as to quality is dropped out, leaving the rest in force, it cannot be said to be a necessary legal conclusion that the law has ceased to be an inspection law." The Court found the inspection law did not burden commerce among the states.

Perhaps Blatchford's most far-reaching, if not entirely durable, constitutional opinion has been in *Counselman v. Hitchcock* (1892), which fully extended the Fifth Amendment's protection against self-incrimination to testimony before a grand jury. In this case, Counselman, a Chicago grain warehouse owner, was being questioned concerning alleged violations of the Interstate Commerce Act of 1887 (passed as a result of the *Wabash Case*). On Fifth Amendment grounds Counselman declined to answer whether he had ever received any rebate, drawback, or commission from the Rock Island Railroad. He was then held in contempt of court. A federal statute conferred a limited immunity by barring the government's use of the immunized person's testimony against that person in any federal proceeding. But it did not bar the use of the testimony to search out other evidence on which the same person could be convicted. Blatchford announced that the statutory immunity was inadequate; it had to be as broad as the privilege itself: "no statute which leaves the party or witness subject to prosecution after he answers the criminating questions put to him, can have the effect of supplanting the privilege conferred by the Constitution of the United States." In more modern language, Blatchford insisted on transactional, as opposed to use, immunity. Much later the Supreme Court found the more prosecutorially friendly use immunity unobjectionable under the Fifth Amendment in *Kastigar v. United States* (1972).

Not long after *Counselman* was decided, Blatchford suffered a stroke. He was able to resume his duties at the Court, but in the spring of 1893 he was further incapacitated by three lesser strokes. He hoped to recuperate during his summer vacation at Newport, Rhode Island, but this was not to be. He died on July 7, 1893, some three weeks after a fifth stroke, and was buried in Brooklyn, New York.

The Cleveland Appointment

L. Q. C. Lamar

Justice Wood's death in 1887 ended a five-year period of unusual stability in the membership of the Waite Court, and gave President Grover Cleveland the only opportunity in his first administration to make an appointment to the Supreme Court. It also ended a three-decade Republican monopoly on judicial nominations. However, L. Q. C. Lamar, Woods's successor, barely counts as a member of the Waite bench. Lamar was sworn in on January 18, 1888, less than nine weeks before Waite's death on March 23. By then his name had appeared on opinions only five times in the *Reports*. Yet Lamar merits at least abbreviated treatment here. A cousin of former Justice John A. Campbell and of future Justice Joseph R. Lamar, he was one of only three Waite justices who served in all three branches of the federal government. His judicial career was the climax to an already eventful, extraordinary, and consequential public life.

Lucius Quintus Cincinnatus Lamar was born into well-to-do plantocracy near Eatonton, in Putnam County, Georgia, on September 17, 1825. (An uncle was Mirabeau Buonaparte Lamar, the second president of Texas.) Lamar's father, who bore the same name as his son, was an attorney and later a state circuit judge who committed suicide when the younger L.Q.C. was nine. His mother, Sarah Williamson Bird Lamar, then moved the family to Covington, a thriving cotton town in Newton County, thirty-five miles east of what is now Atlanta. L.Q.C. was enrolled in the experimental Georgia Conference Manual Labor School that Methodists had established just west of Covington. He continued his education at Emory College in nearby Oxford, into which the manual labor school was folded, and graduated in 1845. He read law with cousin Absalom Chapell and was admitted to the bar in 1847. After a brief partnership with Chapell, he opened a law office in Covington on a site 500 feet east of where the present 1884 courthouse stands. Also in 1847 Lamar married Virginia Longstreet, the daughter of Emory's president, Augustus B. Longstreet. Their union yielded one son and three daughters. Lamar and Augustus Longstreet had established a lasting bond during the former's student days at Emory. Longstreet's son had died some years before. Lamar became the son he lost, and Longstreet became the father Lamar truly needed.

In 1849 Lamar followed Longstreet to Oxford, Mississippi after the latter accepted the presidency of the state university and hired his son-in-law to teach mathematics. Lamar returned to Covington in 1852 to resume his law practice and was elected to the state legislature as a Democrat (in a Whig-dominated county) in 1853, but he returned to Mississippi in 1855. A gifted orator and debater, he soon developed a large political following and was elected to Congress as a Democrat in

L. Q. C. Lamar (Matthew Brady, Handy Studios, Collection of the Supreme Court of the United States)

1856. He was reelected without opposition in 1858. By 1860 Lamar had become a strong advocate of a southern republic, and as a delegate to the Democratic national convention in April he led the Mississippi and Alabama delegations out of the hall when Stephen Douglas was nominated. Lamar drafted Mississippi's Ordinance of Secession in January 1861, and with the outbreak of war became a lieutenant colonel in the Confederate army. When spells of vertigo and probably epilepsy eliminated any chance for a battlefield command, Jefferson Davis designated him the Confederacy's commissioner to Russia, but Lamar was recalled before traveling further than London and Paris. By the end of the war he was judge advocate and a colonel in Lee's Army of Northern Virginia. After Lee's surrender at Appomattox Courthouse, Lamar returned to Oxford to teach ethics and metaphysics and then law at the University of Mississippi.

Politics again beckoned, and Lamar was elected to the U.S. House of Representatives as a Democrat in 1872. He was able to take his seat after the chamber voted a special pardon. He quickly became known as an advocate of sectional reconciliation, realistically the only way that the former ruling class in the South could hope to reestablish itself. In exchange for southern acquiescence in northern victory, the North would return control of local institutions to southern whites. The most memorable articulation of this theme was his eulogy in 1874 on the death of Charles Sumner of Massachusetts, the hater of all things southern. Regarded as one of the most moving speeches ever given in Congress, it held the chamber spellbound and earned for Lamar a nearly instant national reputation and later merited a chapter in John F. Kennedy's *Profiles in Courage* (1956). Yet the "Great Pacificator," a designation that a biographer describes as a "more or less self-consciously prepared image" (Murphy 1973, 273), was also a cagey dialectician. Woven within the praise for Sumner was a defense of what Sumner detested. Elected to the Senate in 1876, Lamar had a major hand in shaping the Compromise of 1877, and was in his second term when President Cleveland named him secretary of the interior in 1885.

The only justice to come to the Court from that cabinet department, Lamar stood out from some of his colleagues in a way one might not expect from a justice whose tenure was barely five years. Not only did he craft concise and readable opinions, but those opinions reflected a constitutional vision and a judicial role. That vision might best be described as balanced government. Lamar was experienced in state government, the cauldron of civil war, and across the branches of the federal government. Perhaps as a result, Lamar seemed to perceive that the Court's tasks were to prevent either states or the national government from becoming too powerful and to maintain the separate integrity of the legislative, executive, and judicial branches.

For instance, Lamar filed a lone dissent in *In re Neagle* (1890). That case arose from the feud between Justice Field and David Terry and the writ of habeas corpus that freed from custody Field's bodyguard, David Neagle, after Neagle killed Terry.

Lamar was troubled by the absence of a congressional statute authorizing the deputy federal marshal to protect Field. Without a statute Neagle could not be acting "in pursuance of a law of the United States" and so could not qualify for habeas relief. "Waiving the question of the essentiality of any such protection to the existence of government," Lamar insisted, "the manifest answer is, that the protection needed and to be given must proceed not from the President, but primarily from Congress. Again, while it is the President's duty to take care that the laws be faithfully executed, it is not his duty to *make* laws or a law of the United States."

In other arenas, Lamar was prepared to allow the states ample governing authority, and was wary of assuming a larger role for the Court under the Fourteenth Amendment. Thus he joined both Bradley's dissent in the *Minnesota Rate Case* (1890), which undercut *Munn v. Illinois*, and Blatchford's majority opinion in *Budd v. New York* two years later, which reaffirmed *Munn*. Yet he wrote the majority opinion in *McCall v. California* (1892), which invalidated as an interference with interstate commerce a state tax on the California office of a Chicago–New York railway. If the commerce clause "prohibits a state from taxing interstate commerce as it passes through its own territory, *a fortiori*, the prohibition will extend to such commerce when it does not pass through its territory."

In *Kidd v. Pearson* (1888) neither the commerce clause nor the Fourteenth Amendment was a bar to Iowa's extensive prohibition on the manufacture or importation of alcoholic beverages. However, Lamar digressed into a seemingly unnecessary but perhaps strategic discussion of the distinction between commerce and manufacturing. The commerce clause was the constitutional guarantor of a national market, but within the clause were limits on the powers of Congress. "No distinction is more popular to the common mind, or more clearly expressed in economic and political literature, than that between manufactures and commerce. . . . If it is held that the term [commerce] includes the regulation of all such manufactures as are intended to be the subject of commercial transactions in the future, . . . Congress would be invested, to the exclusion of the States, with the power to regulate, not only manufacture but also agriculture, horticulture, stock raising, domestic fisheries, mining—in short, every branch of human industry." The distinction Lamar drew became central in 1895 when the Court clipped the wings of the Sherman Anti-Trust Act (*United States v. E. C. Knight*) and fueled commerce clause debates for nearly a half-century afterward.

Lamar began to suffer cardiovascular problems as early as 1889, but he continued to do his work. By 1892 he also had symptoms of tuberculosis and kidney problems. Returning to Mississippi by train for Christmas, he had a heart attack near Atlanta. He died on January 23, 1893, in Macon, Georgia, where he was buried along with a small copy of the United States Constitution that he routinely carried in his pocket (Kammen 1986, 197).

References

Abraham, Henry J. 1992. *Justices and Presidents: A Political History of Appointments to the Supreme Court.* 3rd ed. New York: Oxford University Press.

Atkinson, David N. 1999. *Leaving the Bench: Supreme Court Justices at the End.* Lawrence: University Press of Kansas.

Baynes, Thomas E. 1978. "Yankee from Georgia." *Supreme Court Historical Society Yearbook* 1978: 31–42.

Clifford, Philip G. 1922. *Nathan Clifford, Democrat.* New York: G. P. Putnam's Sons.

Clinton, Robert Lowry, and Kevin Walsh. 1999. "Judicial Sobriety: Nathan P. Clifford." In *Sober as a Judge: The Supreme Court and Republican Liberty,* ed. Richard G. Stevens and Matthew J. Franck. Lanham, MD: Lexington Press.

Corwin, Edward S. 1938. *Court over Constitution.* Princeton, NJ: Princeton University Press. (Reissued by Peter Smith in 1957.)

Fairman, Charles. 1939. *Mr. Justice Miller and the Supreme Court: 1862–1890.* Cambridge, MA: Harvard University Press.

———. 1950. "What Makes a Great Justice? Mr. Justice Bradley and the Supreme Court, 1870–1892." *Boston University Law Review* 30: 49–102.

———. 1964. "Mr. Justice Bradley." In *Mr. Justice,* rev. and enl. ed., ed. Allison Dunham and Philip B. Kurland. Chicago: University of Chicago Press.

———. 1971. *Reconstruction and Reunion 1864–1888, Part One. History of the Supreme Court of the United States.* Vol. 6. New York: Macmillan.

———. 1987. *Reconstruction and Reunion 1864–1888, Part Two. History of the Supreme Court of the United States.* Vol. 7. New York: Macmillan.

Field, Stephen J. 1893. *Personal Reminiscences of Early Days in California.* Washington, DC: privately published (reissued by Da Capo in 1968).

Filler, Louis. 1969a. "Horace Gray." In *The Justices of the U.S. Supreme Court 1789–1969: Their Lives and Major Opinions,* vol. 2, ed. Leon Friedman and Fred L. Israel. New York: Chelsea House.

———. 1969b. "John M. Harlan." In *The Justices of the U.S. Supreme Court 1789–1969: Their Lives and Major Opinions,* vol. 2, ed. Leon Friedman and Fred L. Israel. New York: Chelsea House.

Frank, John P. 1964. *Justice Daniel Dissenting.* Cambridge, MA: Harvard University Press.

Fridlington, Robert. 1987. *The Reconstruction Court, 1864–1888.* Millwood, NY: Associated Faculty Press.

Garland, Augustus H. 1898. *Experience in the Supreme Court of the United States.* Washington, DC: J. Byrne.

Gillette, William. 1969. "Noah H. Swayne." In *The Justices of the U.S. Supreme Court 1789–1969: Their Lives and Major Opinions,* vol. 2, ed. Leon Friedman and

Fred L. Israel. New York: Chelsea House.

Harlan, Malvina Shanklin. 1999. "Some Memories of a Long Life, 1854–1911." *Journal of Supreme Court History* 26: 109–211.

Holzer, Harold, ed. 1993. *The Lincoln-Douglas Debates.* New York: HarperCollins.

Kammen, Michael. 1986. *A Machine That Would Go of Itself: The Constitution in American Culture.* New York: Knopf.

Kens, Paul. 1997. *Justice Stephen Field: Shaping Liberty from the Gold Rush to the Gilded Age.* Lawrence: University Press of Kansas.

King, Willard L. 1950. *Melville Weston Fuller.* Chicago: University of Chicago Press.

———. 1960. *Lincoln's Manager: David Davis.* Cambridge, MA: Harvard University Press.

Kutler, Stanley I. 1968. *Judicial Power and Reconstruction Politics.* Chicago: University of Chicago Press.

———. 1969a. "David Davis." In *The Justices of the U.S. Supreme Court 1789–1969: Their Lives and Major Opinions,* vol. 2, ed. Leon Friedman and Fred L. Israel. New York: Chelsea House.

———. 1969b. "Ward Hunt." In *The Justices of the U.S. Supreme Court 1789–1969: Their Lives and Major Opinions,* vol. 2, ed. Leon Friedman and Fred L. Israel. New York: Chelsea House.

———. 1969c. "William Strong." In *The Justices of the U.S. Supreme Court 1789–1969: Their Lives and Major Opinions,* vol. 2, ed. Leon Friedman and Fred L. Israel. New York: Chelsea House.

McCloskey, Robert G. 1969. "Stephen J. Field." In *The Justices of the U.S. Supreme Court 1789–1969: Their Lives and Major Opinions,* vol. 2, ed. Leon Friedman and Fred L. Israel. New York: Chelsea House.

Magrath, C. Peter. 1963. *Morrison R. Waite: The Triumph of Character.* New York: Macmillan.

Murphy, James B. 1973. *L. Q. C. Lamar: Pragmatic Patriot.* Baton Rouge: Louisiana State University Press.

Nash, A. E. Keir. 1994. "Horace Gray." In *The Supreme Court Justices: A Biographical Dictionary,* ed. Melvin I. Urofsky. New York: Garland.

Niehoff, Leonard M. 1993. "David Davis." In *The Supreme Court Justices: Illustrated Biographies, 1789–1993,* ed. Clare Cushman. Washington, DC: Congressional Quarterly Press.

Roper, Donald. 1993. "Stanley Matthews." In *The Supreme Court Justices: Illustrated Biographies, 1789–1993,* ed. Clare Cushman. Washington, DC: Congressional Quarterly Press.

Silver, David M. 1998. *Lincoln's Supreme Court* (reissue of 1956 edition). Urbana: University of Illinois Press.

Spitzer, Robert J. 2001. *The Right to Bear Arms.* Santa Barbara, CA: ABC-CLIO.

Stephenson, D. Grier, Jr. 1973. “The Chief Justice as Leader: The Case of Morrison Remick Waite.” *William and Mary Law Review* 14: 899–927.

Stevens, Richard G. 1999. “Due Process of Law: Stanley Matthews.” In *Sober as a Judge: The Supreme Court and Republican Liberty*, ed. Richard G. Stevens and Matthew J. Franck. Lanham, MD: Lexington Press.

Trimble, Bruce R. 1938. *Chief Justice Waite: Defender of the Public Interest.* Princeton, NJ: Princeton University Press (reissued by Russell and Russell in 1970).

Warren, Charles. 1926. *The Supreme Court in United States History.* 2 vols., rev. ed. Boston: Little, Brown.

3

Major Decisions

Three broad and significant questions stand out in the Supreme Court's constitutional business between 1874 and 1888. The answers that the justices provided influenced public policy and the quality of life in the United States for decades to come. One—the constraints imposed by the commerce clause on the states—had been a staple of the Court's constitutional docket since the middle of the Marshall era. Yet the emergence after 1869 of a truly national economy, bound together by a network of railroads and telegraph (and, soon, telephone) wires, intensified the importance of the question. Another question—the meaning of certain provisions of the Bill of Rights—confronted the Waite justices to a degree previously unknown at the Court and foreshadowed cases that would consume a major share of the Court's time in the twentieth and twenty-first centuries. The third question was related to the second and proved to be both foundational and far-reaching: what changes in U.S. government had been wrought by the three Reconstruction amendments to the Constitution? Embedded in this third question were at least four additional inquiries: (a) Especially for newly freed slaves and other African-Americans in the 1870s and 1880s, what rights did the amendments directly confer? (b) How severely did the amendments curtail state authority? (c) To what extent did the amendments augment the powers of Congress? (d) Did the amendments limit government in any way outside the context of the end of slavery? The Waite Court was not the first to engage the Reconstruction amendments and statutes derived from them; indeed, it was in the waning hours of the Chase Court that the bench first construed them. But it was the Waite Court that first engaged the legal legacy of the Civil War and Reconstruction on a sustained basis.

Prelude: The Reconstruction Amendments and the Slaughterhouse Cases

The Civil War (1861–1865) provided a military answer to questions about the legitimacy of secession and the supremacy of the national government. A long-running debate in U.S. federalism thus was settled, if not entirely silenced. Generated but not resolved by the war were many other issues. Chief among them was the status of the newly freed slave population that numbered about 4 million. Along with a series of statutes, the Thirteenth, Fourteenth, and Fifteenth Amendments—ratified between December 1865 and March 1870—addressed the matter of status directly. These enactments remain today the constitutional legacy of the Republic's greatest domestic crisis. Some attention to the scope of those amendments, as well as to the circumstances of their creation, will help in understanding the Waite Court's civil rights decisions. Excepting possibly the Thirteenth, the amendments were as restrained as they were ambitious. They reflected a wariness of going too far, an attitude largely shared by the Supreme Court. A broad consensus at the close of the war that slavery should be abolished soon dissipated as the discussion shifted to other aspects of the status of African Americans under the law.

The Thirteenth Amendment, which ended slavery, was therefore the least surprising of the three amendments, even if its human consequences were vast. In granting freedom to one class, it imposed a huge and unprecedented economic disadvantage on another. No compensation was paid to slave owners, most of whom lived in the states of the late Confederacy and now faced financial ruin. "The legal authority of the United States was thus used for an annihilation of individual property rights without parallel (outside of modern communism) in the history of the Western world" (Palmer 1960, 543). Proposed four months before General Robert E. Lee's surrender at Appomattox Courthouse in April 1865, ratification of the Thirteenth in December made permanent and national a major Union war objective born in President Lincoln's Emancipation Proclamation two years earlier. The amendment quickly accomplished its immediate objective, as slavery vanished from the fields and from the political agenda.

More than either of the other two amendments of this period, the Fourteenth Amendment, proposed in June 1866 and ratified in July 1868, signaled a new relationship between federal and state governments that had been decreed by the Union victory. In contrast to the single objectives of the Thirteenth and Fifteenth Amendments, the Fourteenth was actually five amendments rolled into one. The first sentence of section one addressed citizenship: "All persons born or naturalized in the United States and subject to the jurisdiction thereof, are citizens of the United States and of the State wherein they reside." Those twenty-eight words utterly abrogated the Supreme Court's holding in *Dred Scott v. Sandford* (1857) that African Americans were never intended to be "citizens" and so could "claim none of the rights and privileges which that instrument provide[d] for and secure[d] to citizens of the United States." The second sentence of section one proclaimed new, broad, but undefined restrictions on state power. "No State shall make or enforce any law which shall abridge the privileges or immunities of citizens of the United States; nor shall any

State deprive any person of life, liberty, or property, without due process of law; nor deny to any person within its jurisdiction the equal protection of the laws."

The first clause of the second sentence borrowed language from Article IV of the Constitution: "The Citizens of each State shall be entitled to all Privileges and Immunities of Citizens in the several States." The second clause drew verbatim from the due process limitation on the national government in the Fifth Amendment. The words of the third clause were new to the Constitution, and seemed to tweak the guaranties of the first and second clauses. Taken together, the three evidenced a strong antidiscriminatory purpose.

That second sentence of section one has long made the amendment routinely the most litigated provision of the Constitution as measured by the number of cases on the Court's docket. More immediately, both parts of section one erased any lingering doubts about the constitutionality of the Civil Rights Act of 1866. This comprehensive statute, designed to augment the Thirteenth's abolition of slavery, had declared all persons born in the United States to be national citizens.

> Such citizens, of every race and color, without regard to any previous condition of slavery or involuntary servitude . . . shall have the same right, in every State and Territory . . ., to make and enforce contracts, to sue, be parties, and give evidence, to inherit, purchase, lease, sell, hold, and convey real and personal property, and to full and equal benefit of all laws and proceedings for the security of persons and property, as is enjoyed by white citizens, and shall be subject to like punishment, pains, and penalties, and to none other, any law, statute, ordinance, regulation, or custom, to the contrary notwithstanding.

By constitutionalizing as well as codifying both these guaranties and a new relationship between national and state governments, Congress greatly reduced the chance that lawmakers of a later day might undo its work. Little wonder that the Fourteenth Amendment has sometimes been called the "Second Constitution."

Section three of the Fourteenth Amendment politically disabled former Confederate leaders, section four foreclosed any attempt by a state or the nation to assume the Confederate debt or to pay compensation to ex-slave owners, and section five empowered Congress to enforce the terms of the amendment. It is only in section four that an oblique and curious reference to voting rights appears. Section four eliminated the Three-Fifth's Compromise (the 1787 political agreement that counted three-fifths of the slave population for purposes of determining representation in the House of Representatives and votes in the Electoral College). It further dictated that a state's representation in Congress would be reduced in proportion to the number of males twenty-one years of age and older who were denied the right to vote. Although that penalty was never exacted from a state, the amendment directly anticipated, and indirectly allowed, racially based disfranchisement. The origins of the Fifteenth

Amendment ("The right . . . to vote shall not be denied or abridged by the United States or by any State on account of race, color, or previous condition of servitude") thus rest in the Fourteenth. The Fifteenth also derived from complex political realities at a time when the future of the Republican Party was at stake.

With the prospect of Democratic political inroads in the North, Republican control of the White House and Congress was in danger, especially in view of an increase by some fifteen seats in southern representation as a result of the elimination of the Three-Fifths Compromise. Blacks in the South would surely vote Republican if they were allowed to vote. Yet the difficulty in 1866 in providing security for black voters in the South was compounded by the fact that blacks in northern states voted freely only in New England. Indeed, voters in eleven northern states expressly rejected black suffrage between 1865 and 1869 (Gillette 1965, 25–26). Any extension of the vote to blacks by constitutional amendment at the time the Fourteenth Amendment was proposed was doomed to failure and might have been costly to Republicans at the polls. This probably would explain the complete absence of the word race in the Fourteenth Amendment. Section two thus represented a compromise between doing a lot for black suffrage and doing nothing. If southern states excluded blacks from the polls, they did so at the risk of losing representation in the House and in the Electoral College, thereby diminishing somewhat the impact of a Democratic resurgence in the old Confederacy. The Fourteenth Amendment thus recognized not only the practical importance of southern black votes to the Republican Party but also the widespread unacceptability among whites, almost everywhere, of voting by black men (Keyssar 2000, 89).

The equation that yielded the Fifteenth Amendment also included a series of 1867 congressional enactments requiring black suffrage in some territories and the District of Columbia and as a condition for Nebraska's admission to the Union. In addition, the Reconstruction Act of that year required black voting as a precondition to readmission to the Union of the former Confederate states and seating their delegations in Congress. An ironic double standard was now in place. Black voting was the law of the land except in most northern states.

Republican setbacks among northern white voters in the elections of 1868, however, stimulated a rethinking of this policy of incrementalism with respect to voting. If there were political risks in stressing black voting, there were perhaps greater risks in failing to ensure it. Only a constitutional amendment would open the polls fully to blacks in the North. "You need votes in Connecticut, do you not?" asked Massachusetts Republican senator Charles Sumner. "There are three thousand fellow-citizens in that State ready at the call of Congress to take their place at the ballot box. You need them also in Pennsylvania, do you not?" he went on. "There are at least fifteen thousand in that great State waiting for your summons. Wherever you most need them, there they are; and be assured they will all vote for those who stand by them in the assertion of Equal Rights" (Stephenson 1988, 51).

Various congressional versions of what became the Fifteenth Amendment would have guaranteed the right to hold political office, directly conferred the vote on all males twenty-one years of age and older, and eliminated poll taxes, literacy tests, and property qualifications. In the interests of passage and ratification, all were eliminated from the final version that was proposed to the states on February 26, 1869—not an affirmative extension of the franchise but an injunction against the use of race in setting voting qualifications. Questionable prospects for ratification—some West and East Coast Republicans feared it would give Chinese and too many Irish access to the polls—may explain why there was so little discussion in the Fortieth Congress on section two, the enforcement clause of the amendment. That involved the consensus-splitting issue of federal control over state election laws, best left unmentioned. As it was, Tennessee, Kentucky, Delaware, and Maryland (former slave states not covered by the Reconstruction Acts) rejected the amendment, as did California and Oregon. Ohio rejected it initially, until Republican leaders, including Justice Noah Swayne, intervened and persuaded enough state legislators to change their minds. New York rescinded its ratification. Nonetheless, the requisite number of states signed on to make the amendment officially a part of the Constitution on March 30, 1870.

These were unmistakably ambitious amendments. As the first shots were fired in the Civil War in April 1861, hardly anyone imagined either the severity or the length of the ensuing conflict or the changes the war's outcome would bring. The Thirteenth Amendment abolished an economic system that had existed in many areas of the country since the earliest colonial days. The Fourteenth Amendment promised federal protection of undefined rights against state interference where no federal recourse had existed before. The Fifteenth Amendment barred states from excluding persons from the polls on account of race. In a departure from most direct limitations on the states found in the main body of the Constitution, each amendment contained a section authorizing Congress to enforce its terms through "appropriate legislation." Thus, within only fourteen years, the Republican Party had gone from calling for a ban on slavery in the territories to the achievement of unanticipated goals. The party's center could not have contemplated such accomplishments when Republicans ran their first candidate for president in 1856 and when their second candidate won the presidency in 1860.

But each amendment was also restrained. Given the total collapse of the Confederacy and the unconditional surrender by the South, much that might have been done in the wake of so great a defeat was not. None of the amendments provided for reparations to former slaves or guaranteed a redistribution of land to them. No revolutionary new political system was enshrined. Federal power could now check state power in certain new respects, but it did not truly displace it. States still retained the primary responsibility for governing their citizens, including matters of voting and elections. The exact balance to be struck between the competing objectives of ambition and restraint would be left to the Supreme Court.

Three weeks before the death of Chief Justice Salmon Chase and barely eleven months before Chief Justice Morrison Waite's arrival, the Supreme Court examined the Thirteenth and Fourteenth amendments for the first time in the *Slaughterhouse Cases* (1873). The circumstances of the cases seemed about as remote as could be from the presumed purpose of the amendments: racial justice. Moreover, the tight 5–4 decision symbolized the lack of consensus over precisely what the amendments, especially the Fourteenth, were supposed to accomplish. The case warrants attention here for two reasons: it cast a long shadow not only on the Waite Court but on U.S. constitutional law to follow; second, it was rendered by a bench of which eight members made up the first Waite Court.

In 1869 the carpetbag legislature of Louisiana chartered the Crescent City Live-Stock Landing and Slaughter-House Company. The company received a monopoly over the slaughtering of animals in three parishes, including the city of New Orleans. Barred from slaughtering on their own premises, butchers had to use the Crescent City facilities for a fee. In three separate cases, the Butchers' Benevolent Association and others unsuccessfully sought an injunction in the state courts to block the monopoly. When the cases reached the U.S. Supreme Court, their attorney, former justice John A. Campbell, argued that the legislation was constitutionally defective on four counts: it created "an involuntary servitude forbidden by the thirteenth article of amendment," it abridged "the privileges and immunities of citizens of the United States," it denied the butchers "the equal protection of the laws," and it deprived them "of their property without due process of law; contrary to the provisions of the first section of the fourteenth article of the amendment."

"This court," Justice Samuel Miller momentously observed for the majority, "is thus called upon for the first time to give construction of these articles." "On the most casual examination of the language of these amendments," Miller continued, "no one can fail to be impressed with the one pervading purpose found in them all, . . . and without which none of them would have even been suggested, we mean the freedom of the slave race, the security and firm establishment of that freedom. . . . It is true that only the fifteenth amendment, in terms, mentions the negro by speaking of his color and his slavery. But it is just as true that each of the other articles was addressed to the grievances of that race, as designed to remedy them as the fifteenth. . . ."

As for the constitutional objections alleged by the aggrieved butchers, Miller thought counts one, three, and four merited only the briefest attention. To regard the Louisiana regulation as "involuntary servitude" within the meaning of the Thirteenth Amendment "requires an effort, to say the least of it." Ignoring Chief Justice Roger Taney's arguably analogous use of Fifth Amendment due process in *Dred Scott* (1857) and Chief Justice Chase's similar deployment of it in *Hepburn v. Griswold* (1870), Miller perfunctorily dispensed with the butchers' due process objection. "[U]nder no construction of that provision that we have ever seen, or any that we deem admissible, can the restraint imposed by . . . Louisiana . . . be held to be a deprivation of property within the meaning of that provision." Not clear was whether he meant that no deprivation had occurred or that no property was involved. In either event, he closed the due process door. As for the equal protection claim, Miller "doubt[ed] very much whether any action . . . not directed by way of discrimination against the negroes as a class, or on account of their race [neither of which applied in this instance], would ever be held to come within the purview of this provision."

Regarding the second count, Miller seized on the first sentence of section one to virtually dispatch the privileges and immunities clause from the Fourteenth Amendment. That sentence spoke of state citizenship and national citizenship. The second sentence spoke of "the privileges and immunities of citizens of the United States." This led Miller to conclude that one possessed certain privileges and immunities by virtue of state citizenship and others by virtue of national citizenship. The latter consisted of rights created by the federal government. The former (and larger) category of rights either flowed from state citizenship or predated formation of the federal government. These were "fundamental" rights that belonged "to the citizens of all free governments," as Justice Bushrod Washington had written in an 1823 circuit court opinion construing the privileges and immunities clause of Article IV. Although declining to enumerate them, Washington suggested "several general heads: protection by the government, with the right to acquire and possess property of every kind, and to pursue and obtain happiness and safety, subject, nevertheless, to such restraints as the government may prescribe for the general good of the whole." Accordingly, Miller insisted that any liberties claimed by the butchers—such as a right to pursue a lawful calling—derived from state citizenship and so fell outside the protection of the Fourteenth Amendment. To read the clause more generously, Miller contended, would make the Supreme Court "a perpetual censor upon all legislation of the States" and "radically change the whole theory of the relations of the State and Federal governments to each other and of both these governments to the people. . . ."

Of the three dissenting opinions published in the *Slaughterhouse Cases*, Justice Stephen Field's was the most virulent. Miller's construction of the privileges and immunities clause converted the amendment "into a vain and idle enactment, which accomplished nothing, and most unnecessarily excited Congress and the people on its passage." Furthermore, under Miller's reading, the clause was entirely superfluous. If all it did was to prevent states from infringing rights established by the national government, the supremacy clause of Article VI "always controlled any State legislation of that character." Instead, Field opted for a broad fundamental rights construction of the amendment. "[I]f the amendment refers to the natural and inalienable rights which belong to all citizens, the inhibition has a profound significance and consequence." Seen from that perspective, the Louisiana monopoly was defective because it denied "the distinguishing privilege of citizens of the United States. To them, everywhere, all pursuits, all professions, all avocations are open without other restrictions, than such as are imposed equally upon all others of the same age, sex, and condition."

Justice Joseph Bradley's dissent called for an even more expansive reading of the amendment than Field's. His dissent reflected the views of some congressional sponsors of the amendment that it was intended to nationalize all rights deemed fundamental, including provisions from the Bill of Rights. This notion was itself an offshoot of the prewar abolitionist movement. Chief Justice John Marshall in *Barron v. Baltimore* (1833) had reiterated the prevailing view that the Bill of Rights restrained the national government, not the states. By the mid-1850s, however, abolitionist authors in the South found themselves under indictment because, to local authorities, their thinking presented a public danger. Similarly, the newly established Republican Party found its message against the expansion of slavery muffled in the South, hence its slogan of 1856: "Free Speech, Free Press, Free Men, Free Labor, Free Territory, and Frémont." In an example of necessity begetting invention, clever theorists had combined Article IV's privileges and immunities clause with the same article's guaranty of a republican form of government for each state as a way of asserting a federally protected right of free speech against invasion by the states. Thus, when a privileges and immunities clause was inserted into the Fourteenth Amendment after the war, Bradley concluded that it encompassed at least some provisions of the Bill of Rights (Curtis 2000, 281, 360–368).

If shoring up constitutionally the Civil Rights Act of 1866 was the most widely understood purpose of the Fourteenth Amendment when it was proposed and ratified, as seems today to be generally conceded (Currie 1985, 347), the Court surely missed the mark. Miller undershot and Field and Bradley overshot that target. Miller resisted a broader reading to avoid altering the federal balance, but a strong case can be made that the amendment was indeed supposed to alter that balance. The framers and ratifiers of the amendment may not have had local monopolistic legislation in mind when they used the words "privileges and immunities." But they presumably intended the amendment to prevent states from penalizing their residents' exercise of basic rights, just as Article IV had always enjoined a state from denying basic rights to nonresidents that it afforded to its own residents. Additionally, by emphasizing the racial purpose of all three amendments, Miller made abundantly clear what the authors of the amendments had sought to obscure for partisan reasons. In contrast, Field's and Bradley's fundamental-rights approaches would have brought about an immediate and substantial enlargement of federal jurisdiction. Their view would have given judges vast discretion in identifying Fourteenth Amendment rights, particularly in the contexts of property and occupation. Yet it would be Miller's far more constricted view that frequently dictated the Waite Court's application of the Reconstruction amendments in civil rights and other kinds of cases.

Civil Rights

The *Slaughterhouse Cases* revealed a bench sharply divided over the breadth of the Fourteenth Amendment. As racially tinted civil rights cases involving one or more of the Reconstruction amendments arrived, one might have expected the Waite Court to remember what Justice Miller had called the "persuasive purpose" of the amendments. But the Court had no easier time deciding them than the Chase Court had with the *Slaughterhouse Cases*. As it happened, dissents were few, but racially driven civil rights claims only sometimes prevailed.

United States v. Reese and *United States v. Cruikshank*, both decided in 1876, involved the Enforcement Act of 1870 that Congress passed soon after ratification of the Fifteenth Amendment. Both cases tested the meaning of this newest amendment as well as Congress's authority to make that meaning a reality.

Section one of the Enforcement Act declared a right to vote free from racial discrimination. Section two made it unlawful for an official, on account of race, to refuse to permit citizens to perform actions required for voting. Section three specified that if an official violated section two, the citizen could present an affidavit of the violation to those in charge of an election, and the affidavit would qualify the citizen to vote. Section four made it unlawful for any person to prevent another from voting or from doing those things necessary to qualify for voting. When *Reese* reached the Supreme Court in January 1875, arguments centered on indictments arising under sections three and four.

William Garner, a black man residing in Lexington, Kentucky, was denied the right to vote in January of 1873. The city charter required payment of a head tax of $1.50 before one could vote. The tax was due on or before January 15, but when Garner attempted to pay the tax, the collector refused to accept it. When Garner later produced the affidavit as set forth in section three, Hiram Reese and Matthew Foushee, two of the three election inspectors in Lexington, refused to allow him to vote. Garner claimed that the tax collector and the inspectors acted as they did solely because of his race.

According to Chief Justice Waite, the Court's principal task was to determine at the outset what the Fifteenth Amendment had done. It "does not confer the right of suffrage upon anyone," he wrote. Rather, it prevented states from conditioning the vote on race. "It follows that the amendment has invested the citizens of the United States with a new constitutional right which is within the protecting power of Congress." But the right granted was not the right to vote, but the right to vote free of discrimination based on race. Therefore, to be "appropriate legislation" within the meaning of the amendment, sections three and four of the Enforcement Act needed to refer to "wrongful refusal . . . because of race." However, unlike the first two sections of the statute, sections three and four did not explicitly refer to race when criminalizing the refusal to accept the affidavit or the obstruction of someone's attempt to vote. The Court refused to accept the government's contention that section three was merely the next step to cope with the racially discriminatory act described in section two. Moreover, even though both sections three and four contained the word "aforesaid," referring presumably to the racially based denial of the vote in sections one and two, the Court concluded that the sections on which the indictments were based were severed from the Fifteenth Amendment. The sections omitted reference to race and because the amendment authorized no general protection of the right to vote, only protection of the right to vote free of racial discrimination, sections three and four of the Enforcement Act of 1870 were deemed inappropriate and therefore unconstitutional.

Only Ward Hunt, the most junior associate justice, dissented. He rejected outright the reading the majority gave to the 1870 act. The "intention of Congress on this subject is too plain to be discussed. . . . Just so far as the ballot to . . . the freedmen is abridged, in the same degree is their importance and their security diminished. . . . Punishment is the means, protection is the end," he continued. "The arrest, conviction and sentence to imprisonment, of one inspector, who refused the vote of a person of African descent on account of his race, would more effectively secure the right of the voter than would any number of civil suits in the state courts, prosecuted by timid, ignorant and penniless parties against those possessing the wealth, the influence and the sentiment of the community." For Hunt, the law in question was not only appropriate under the Fifteenth Amendment but the most effectual means of achieving its objective: a franchise free of racial discrimination. He also perceptively identified the implications for power and personal security that accompanied access to the ballot. Conversely, those denied the vote were at the mercy of everyone else.

What seemed implausible about *Reese* was not the majority's reading of the Fifteenth Amendment. Theirs had become the mainstream Republican view. It conformed to what Waite had written a year earlier in *Minor v. Happersett* (1875), which tested whether the privileges and immunities clause of the Fourteenth Amendment barred states from excluding women from the polls. The provision "did not add to the privileges and immunities of a citizen," he wrote. "It simply furnished an additional guaranty for the protection of such as he already had." Except by conferring national and state citizenship on those who lacked it, "no new voters were necessarily made by it." The Fourteenth Amendment, then, did not make voting a privilege and immunity of citizenship. *Reese* instead seemed implausible because of the majority's reading of the statute. Not only did Hunt make the stronger argument, but the concurring opinion by Nathan Clifford, a Democrat and the sole surviving prewar justice, found the racial nexus obvious between the first and last pair of sections. But Clifford concluded that the indictments were defective not on constitutional, but on factual, grounds.

Why might the Court have resorted to such a tortured reading of the statute? One explanation is partisan politics. According to this view, the six Republican justices in the majority reacted to Republican losses in the congressional elections of 1874, in which Democrats gained a majority in the House of Representatives for the first time since the Buchanan administration of the late 1850s. By largely annulling a prominent piece of Reconstruction legislation, the bench did the party a favor by distancing Republicans from civil rights. This made the party more appealing to white voters, while providing Congress an opportunity to correct the statutory deficiencies if the political climate changed (Maltz 1996, 76–77). Yet party leaders and Republican legislators would evidently be more attuned to that need than the Court. Besides, *Reese* would appear to be a circuitous method for assisting Republicans. Furthermore, such partisan motivation seemed wholly out of character for at least some of the majority, including Miller and Joseph Bradley, and of course Waite himself. In addition, if the *Reese* Court was moved mainly by partisan concerns, why was Justice Field, a Democrat, in the majority? A more probable explanation was that the attitude underlying the *Slaughterhouse Cases* had evidently enveloped most of the bench: suspicion of an enlarged federal authority, unless both the Constitution and the relevant statute spoke unequivocally. *Reese* also served a related objective: insisting on specificity and clarity in the criminal law, and construing criminal statutes narrowly. This insistence had long been seen as a way to avoid injustice. Among other things, the Waite bench seemed to be reminding Congress to pay attention to detail.

At about the same time that Garner was denied the right to vote in Kentucky, a violent event occurred in Louisiana. Because of a disputed election, Democrats and Republicans both laid claim to local offices. A posse composed of black men authorized by the state's carpetbag Republican governor occupied the Grant Parish Courthouse in Colfax. (In Louisiana, the parish is comparable to the county in other states.) Whites representing the rival Democratic group stormed the building, and at least sixty blacks were killed. The Justice Department sought to indict more than 100 whites under section six of the Enforcement Act of 1870. Section six prohibited the banding together of persons "with the intent to violate any provision of this Act, or . . . to prevent or hinder [an individual's] free exercise and enjoyment of any right or privilege granted or secured to him by the Constitution or laws of the United States." Indictments were returned against only eight whites, including William Cruikshank, charging that they had conspired to deprive two citizens "of African descent and persons of color" of a number of rights, all of which "were secured to them by the constitution and laws of the United States."

At the trial in circuit court, Justice Bradley sat with Circuit Judge (later Justice) William Woods, but the two disagreed over the validity of the indictments. Woods saw ample federal authority; Bradley did not. In his circuit opinion, Bradley, who had dissented in the *Slaughterhouse Cases*, now professed a more constricted view of national power. Protection of fundamental rights "does not devolve upon . . . [the federal government], but belongs to the state government as a part of its residual sovereignty." Although the Fifteenth Amendment admittedly created a right to be free from racial discrimination in voting and provided for congressional enforcement of this right, the indictments in the Colfax killings were flawed because neither state action nor a racial basis for the attack was shown. Because of the division between Bradley and Woods, the case was certified to the Supreme Court. Certification had been the grounds for the Court's consideration of *Reese* as well. Otherwise the High Court in the 1870s would have had no appellate jurisdiction over an ordinary federal criminal case.

For the full Court (with Clifford again concurring, but on different grounds), Chief Justice Waite adopted Bradley's view of the case. It was not Bradley's dissent reasoning from the *Slaughterhouse Cases* but Justice Miller's majority opinion from that case that carried the day. Cruikshank also profited from effective advocates. Counsel included former Justice John Campbell, who had advocated an enlarged national jurisdiction on behalf of the Louisiana butchers in the *Slaughterhouse Cases*. Also present was David Dudley Field, brother of sitting Justice Stephen Field. Justice Field, who had been swayed by Campbell's earlier advocacy on behalf of the butchers, was persuaded by Campbell again, and adopted the restricted understanding of national rights shared by his brethren.

"To bring a case within the operation of that statute," Waite explained, "it must appear that the right, the enjoyment of which the conspirators intended to hinder or prevent, was one granted or secured by the Constitution or laws of the United States." So, when the indictments read that the defendants had hindered others in their right peaceably to assemble, Waite was quick to point out that the First Amendment secured that right against infringement by Congress but the amendment did not create the right. "For their protection in its enjoyment, . . . the people must look to the States. The power for that purpose was originally placed there, and it has never been surrendered to the United States." Because the rights allegedly violated did not inhere in national citizenship, they lay outside the amendment's purview and the statute's protection. Consistent with the doctrine laid down in the *Slaughterhouse Cases*, the Reconstruction amendments had not given the national government a new responsibility in protecting those rights. Nor was there sufficient basis to charge the Colfax defendants with interfering with the right to vote. According to Waite, "the right of suffrage is not a necessary attribute of national citizenship [but] exemption from discrimination in the exercise of that right on account of race . . . is. The right to vote in the States comes from the States; but the right of exemption from the prohibited discrimination comes from the United States. The first has not been granted or secured by the Constitution; but the last has been." Waite drew a distinction between private action that was under state but not federal control, and state action in violation of federally protected rights. The Colfax case was not state action and so fell outside of federal jurisdiction.

Because the indictments in *Cruikshank* did not rest on racially motivated conduct, whatever had occurred did not interfere with a right protected by the federal government. "We may suspect that race was the cause of the hostility; but it is not so averred." Consistent with *Reese*, the Waite Court would not infer even that which seemed plainly apparent. Yet, without a racial component, it is doubtful there would have been a riot.

Taken together, *Reese* and *Cruikshank* are an astounding pair of decisions. By voiding two sections of the Enforcement Act of 1870 and dismissing indictments under another section, the Court in effect said that the Reconstruction amendments had amended very little—that Congress had acquired no general authority to protect the civil and political rights of Americans. Recall that the minimal common ground among the justices in the *Slaughterhouse Cases* had been that the amendments were intended to guard the rights of African Americans. Thanks to *Reese* and *Cruikshank*, that objective now seemed largely out of reach. Fearing the consequences of momentous change, the Court held fast when it came to acknowledging that radical alterations in the nature of the Union had occurred.

Viewed narrowly, the two decisions alone did not have to cripple civil rights enforcement. Congress might have corrected the deficiencies in sections three and four of the Enforcement Act of 1870 that had proven fatal in *Reese*. Indeed, the Senate did so in 1876, but a Democratic House refused to go along. Likewise, more carefully drafted indictments were surely possible. But already the conviction rate for prosecutions brought under the Enforcement Act had dropped sharply, from about 74 percent in actions brought in 1870 to less than 10 percent in 1874 and thereafter (Cummings and McFarland 1937, 238). These figures, coupled with a growing local hostility to prosecutions, made indictments rare even as violations were on the rise. Practically, the 1870 act had become nearly dead law by the time *Reese* and *Cruikshank* were decided (Swinney 1962, 217–228). The decisions of 1876 obviously compounded the difficulty of obtaining both indictments and convictions and no doubt further demoralized federal prosecutors.

However, the Court was not prepared to negate federal supervision entirely. Perhaps the consequences of a diminished federal presence were becoming more obvious. In a nonracial voting fraud case that came before the Justices in 1880 (*Ex parte Siebold*), Justice Bradley went out of his way to mention federal authority. "It seems to be often overlooked that a National Constitution has been adopted in this country, establishing a real government therein, operating upon persons and territory and things. . . ." That was an astonishing statement, more of a confession of weakness than a reminder of strength. There was evidently no large or effective federal presence in voting rights disputes.

Justice Bradley's concern bore fruit four years later in *Ex parte Yarbrough* (1884). This was the primary nineteenth-century Court decision involving race that fully supported federal protection of voting rights. Jasper Yarbrough and eight other white men in Georgia had beaten a black man named Berry Saunders because he had voted in a congressional election. Incarcerated in the Fulton County jail in Atlanta after their convictions, they could not employ a writ of error (by which the Court routinely examined decisions of U.S. circuit courts in noncriminal cases) because of the Supreme Court's lack of jurisdiction to review federal criminal convictions. Instead, they petitioned the Court for a writ of habeas corpus to ascertain the lawfulness of their confinement. Even so, Justice Miller acknowledged that this form of pleading allowed only a narrow examination of the case. The Supreme Court had no authority, he explained, to "convert the writ of habeas corpus into a writ of error, by which the errors of law committed by the court that passed the sentence can be reviewed here; for if that court had jurisdiction of the party and of the offense for which he was tried and has not exceeded its powers in the sentence which it pronounced, this court can inquire no further."

Whether the U.S. circuit court for the northern district of Georgia that had tried and convicted the defendants had jurisdiction depended on the validity of their indictments. That question, in turn, rested on the constitutionality of two sections of the Enforcement (or Ku Klux Klan) Act of 1871, which, among other things, banned various forms of voter intimidation. However, neither section referred to intimidation based on race. To suggest that the government "has no power . . . to secure this election from the influence of violence, of corruption, and of fraud, is a proposition so startling as to arrest attention and demand the gravest consideration," declared Miller. *Reese* was not to be read, he said, as arguing otherwise. The Fifteenth Amendment "does . . . substantially confer on the negro the right to vote, and Congress has the power to protect and enforce that right." Neither was congressional power confined to cases of racial discrimination. "The principle . . . that the protection of the exercise of this right is within the power of Congress, is as necessary to the right of other citizens to vote as to the colored citizen, and to the right to vote in general as to the right to be protected against discrimination." He was at pains to sidestep the formal state action doctrine that lay at the core of the *Civil Rights Cases* (1883), decided the year before.

> While it may be true that acts which are mere invasions of private rights, which acts have no sanction in the statutes of a State, or which are not committed by any one exercising its authority, are not within the scope of [the Fourteenth] amend-

> ment, it is quite a different matter when Congress undertakes to protect the citizen in the exercise of rights conferred by the Constitution of the United States essential to the healthy organization of the government itself.

Without such authority, Miller declared, "the country [is] in danger." Thus Yarbrough and his cohorts could constitutionally be tried because they interfered with another's exercise of the right to vote, even though the interference lacked a racial predicate. Regardless of Miller's insistence to the contrary, the basis of the holding in *Yarbrough* did seem difficult to square with *Reese.*

Despite the potentially broad sweep of *Yarbrough,* it was abundantly clear that the Court maintained a highly circumscribed view of the power of Congress under the Reconstruction amendments to punish conduct by private individuals. This appears true because of two cases decided in 1883.

United States v. Harris challenged the constitutionality of a section of the Enforcement Act of 1871 that made it a crime for any two persons to conspire to deprive another of "the equal protection of the laws." Harris and nineteen others had forcibly seized four African American prisoners from the custody of a Tennessee deputy sheriff and severely beaten them. Siding against the government, the nearly unanimous opinion by Justice Woods receded from the far more expansive view of federal authority that he had entertained as a circuit judge in *Cruikshank.* Woods bluntly reasserted the proposition that the Fourteenth Amendment, the only amendment deemed even remotely applicable in the case, did not empower Congress to criminalize private conduct. It seemed to make no difference to the Court that the private conduct in this instance was interference with a state's criminal justice system. *Harris* appeared to disregard Justice Miller's statements in the *Slaughterhouse Cases* that attributed the origins of the Fourteenth Amendment to the failure of states after ratification of the Thirteenth Amendment to provide sufficient safeguards for blacks against discriminatory treatment. Perhaps the preferred course, which Woods's opinion did not rule out, was for Congress to direct legislation against states that failed to provide equal protection to their citizens, rather than legislating against private individuals themselves. Yet even that might not have done much to alter the outcome in *Harris,* as there had been no substantiated allegation that Tennessee authorities had been derelict in their duty to protect the four men in custody.

Harris came down on January 22, 1883. It practically dictated the outcome in the *Civil Rights Cases* decided almost ten months later. In dispute this time was the validity of a provision of the Civil Rights Act of 1875 in which Congress banned racial discrimination in places of public accommodation, such as hotels and theaters, and on public conveyances. Challenges to prosecutions in four cases and to a civil action for damages in a fifth—from Kansas, California, Missouri, New York, and Tennessee—were joined for decision.

Speaking for every member of the Court except John Marshall Harlan, Justice Bradley insisted that Congress lacked authority under the Fourteenth Amendment to reach individuals or businesses that engaged in racial discrimination. "[C]ivil rights," he said, "such as are guarantied by the constitution against state aggression, cannot be impaired by the wrongful acts of individuals, unsupported by state authority in the shape of laws, customs, or judicial or executive proceedings. The wrongful act of an individual, unsupported by any such authority, is simply a private wrong, or a crime of that individual; an invasion of the rights of the injured party, it is true, whether they affect his person, his property, or his reputation; but if not sanctioned in some way by the state, or not done under state authority, his rights remain in full force, and may presumably be vindicated by resort to the laws of the state for redress."

Neither was the Thirteenth Amendment a sufficient basis for the Civil Rights Act of 1875. True, congressional authority to enforce the amendment extended to "all [of slavery's] badges and incidents." However, "[i]t would be running the slavery argument into the ground to make it apply to every act of discrimination which a person may see fit to make as to the guests he will entertain, or as to the people he will take into his coach or cab or car, or admit to his concert or theater, or deal with in other matters of intercourse or business." Racial discrimination was presumably neither a badge nor an incident of slavery. Moreover, Bradley intimated that the 1875 act extended favored treatment to blacks. They should instead be patient. "When a man has emerged from slavery, and by the aid of beneficent legislation has shaken off the inseparable concomitants of that state, there must be some stage in the progress of his elevation when he takes the rank of a mere citizen, and ceases to be the special favorite of the laws, and when his rights as a citizen, as a man, are to be protected in the ordinary modes by which other men's rights are protected."

Going even further, Bradley insisted that, were the Court to uphold the act, Congress would be empowered to "establish a code of municipal law regulative of all private rights between man and man in society. It would be to make congress take the place of the State legislatures and to supersede them." Rather, in light of the principle that the Fourteenth Amendment reached state action only, Congress's authority in this realm was limited to legislation that focused on state laws. Congress could either require states to make the common law right of access to common carriers, inns, and similar facilities a reality, or it could target state laws that required racial discrimination in such places. In the latter, or indirect, mode, Congress would exercise a kind of legislative, as contrasted with judicial, audit of state laws.

Neither course of action—direct or indirect—was any longer probable. By 1883, the chances that Congress would enact additional civil rights legislation to meet the Court's objections were slim. Bradley's opinion was consistent with mainstream opinion. *Harper's Weekly* approvingly editorialized that because the "long and terrible Civil War sprang from the dogma of State sovereignty, invoked to protect and perpetuate slavery, it was natural that, at its close, the tendency to magnify the National authority should have been very strong, and especially to defend the victims of slavery. . . . In a calmer time, the laws passed under the humane impulse are reviewed, and when found to be incompatible with strict constitutional authority, they are set aside." "The Court has been serving a useful purpose in thus undoing the work of Congress," added the *New York Times*. "The fact is, that, so long as we have State governments, within their field of action we cannot by National authority prevent the consequences of misgovernment. The people of the State," the *Times* concluded, "are dependent on their own civilized ideas and habits for the benefits of a civilized administration of laws" (Mason and Stephenson 2002, 649). In fact, Congress did not again pass a civil rights bill of any kind until 1957, and it did not pass another public accommodations civil rights bill until 1964. When it did, Congress received the Supreme Court's approval, but the principle from the *Civil Rights Cases* remained good law: The Fourteenth Amendment covered state action only. Instead, because of the ill economic effects of racial discrimination, Congress could reach such discrimination by private individuals and businesses through its power to regulate commerce among the states (*Heart of Atlanta Motel v. United States*, 1964).

Justice Harlan authored a powerful solo dissent to Bradley's opinion. The dissent helped to establish the reputation of the Court's only former slave owner as the most vocal and frequent, if inconsistent, champion of civil rights on the Waite and, later, Fuller benches. Harlan maintained that either the Thirteenth or the Fourteenth Amendment provided ample constitutional footing for the Civil Rights Act of 1875. Noting that the majority acknowledged the former to encompass incidents and badges of slavery, Harlan argued that freedom from slavery "necessarily involved immunity from, and protection against, all discrimination against them, because of their race, in respect of such civil rights as belong to freemen of other races." Furthermore, the Fourteenth Amendment reached well beyond discriminatory state action because section one of the act conferred both national and state citizenship on the newly freed slaves. Citizenship brought with it inherent rights. "The citizenship thus acquired by that race, in virtue of an affirmative grant from the nation, may be protected, not alone by the judicial branch of the government, but by congressional legislation of a primary direct character; this, because the power of Congress is not restricted to the enforcement of prohibitions upon State laws or State action." Referring specifically to section five of the Fourteenth Amendment, Harlan insisted that Congress was empowered "in terms distinct and positive, to enforce 'the provisions of this article' of the amendment; not simply those of a prohibitive character, but the provisions—all of the provisions—affirmative and prohibitive, of the amendment."

Before concluding, Harlan also rejected Bradley's observation that the newly freed slaves had received preferential treatment or otherwise had improperly been made favored wards of the government.

> What the nation, through congress, has sought to accomplish in reference to that race is, what had already been done in every state in the Union by the white race, to secure and protect rights belonging to them as freeman and citizens; nothing more. The one underlying principle of congressional legislation has been to enable the black race to take the rank of mere citizen. The difficulty has been to compel a recognition of their legal right to take that rank. . . . At every step in this direction the nation has been confronted with class tyranny. . . . To-day it is the colored race which is denied . . . rights fundamental in their freedom and citizenship. At some future time it may be some other race that will fall under the ban. If the constitutional amendments be enforced, according to the intent with which, as I conceive, they were adopted, there cannot be, in this republic, any class of human beings in practical subjection to another class, with power in the latter to dole out to the former just such privileges as they choose to grant.

Thirteen years later, in *Plessy v. Ferguson* (1896), Harlan would return to that theme in another dissent when he declared that "there is in this country no superior, dominant, ruling class of citizens. There is no caste here. Our Constitution is color-blind and neither knows nor tolerates classes among citizens."

Thanks to Mrs. Harlan, later generations have learned the ironic circumstances under which her husband's dissent in the *Civil Rights Cases* was written. Harlan used the same inkstand Chief Justice Taney had used when writing the infamous *Dred Scott* opinion in 1857. When the Supreme Court handed down its decision in the *Civil Rights Cases* on October 15, Harlan indicated that he would file a dissenting opinion later. Apparently he was suffering from writer's block. As his wife Mallie recorded in her memoirs, her husband had "reached a stage when his thoughts refused to flow easily. He seemed to be in a quagmire of logic, precedent, and law." She remembered a small, old inkstand, hidden away in their home, that had belonged to Taney and that the Court's marshal had given to Justice Harlan some time before. On a Sunday morning after Harlan had left the house for church services—"Nothing ever kept *him* from church," she wrote—she recovered it, "gave it a good cleaning and polishing, and filled it with ink. Then, taking all the other inkwells from his study table, I put that historic and inspiring inkstand directly before his pad of paper." When Harlan found it upon his return, he was ecstatic. "The memory of the historic part that Taney's inkstand had played in the *Dred Scott* decision, in temporarily tightening the shackles of slavery upon the Negro race in the antebellum days, seemed that morning to act like magic in clarifying my husband's thoughts. . . . His pen fairly flew on that day and, with the running start he then got, he soon finished his dissent" (Harlan 2001, 166–167).

Jury service, together with voting, has long been the most common medium through which most citizens participate in government. Prior to the Reconstruction amendments, states were free, as most did, to exclude blacks from the ranks of jurors. As cases assailing this practice reached the Waite Court, the justices seemed generally more disposed to accept federal power in this context than in others. Three important rulings on jury discrimination were all decided on March 1, 1880, and Justice William Strong spoke for the Court in each.

Ex parte Virginia (1880) challenged a provision of the Civil Rights Act of 1875 that criminalized the exclusion of persons from the venire list on account of race. J. D. Coles, a judge in Pittsylvania County, along the central part of Virginia's southern tier, had been indicted under the act for systematically barring black men from consideration as grand and petit (trial) jurors. (The exclusion of women, black or white, was seen as unexceptionable in Virginia and elsewhere.) Implicit in the case was the question whether Congress could intrude into the operation of state judicial systems by requiring blacks to serve on juries. An additional question was whether congressional power to rectify discriminatory state action included punishing a judge for his official conduct. The bench split exactly along party lines: The seven Republican Justices answered both questions in the affirmative, finding sufficient authority in the Thirteenth Amendment and the Fourteenth Amendment's equal protection clause. The Court's two Democrats (Field and Clifford) dissented. "One great purpose of these Amendments," declared Strong, "was to raise the colored race from that condition of inferiority and servitude in which most of them had previously stood into perfect equality of civil rights with all other persons within the jurisdiction of the States. They were intended to take away all possibility of oppression by law because of race or color." Moreover, he continued, the amendments "were intended to be, what they really are, limitations on the power of the States and enlargements of the power of Congress. . . . Indeed, every addition of power to the General Government involves a corresponding diminution of the governmental powers of the States. It is carved out of them."

Given the enforcement provisions of both amendments, wrote Strong, Congress was fully within its authority in punishing exclusion of persons from this civic duty on account of race. Nor did it matter that the person charged was a state official. Even though the prohibitions of the Fourteenth Amendment are directed to state governments, it was also true, Strong explained, that "a State acts by its legislative, its executive or its judicial authorities. It can act in no other way. . . . [A]s he acts in the name and for the State, and is clothed with the State's power, his act is that of the State. This must be so, or the constitutional prohibition has no meaning. Then the State has clothed one of its agents with power to annul or to evade it." Finally, Strong did not understand "how holding an office under a State and claiming to act for the State can relieve the holder from obligation to obey the Constitution of the United States, or take away the power of Congress to punish his disobedience."

An attempt by a black man indicted for murder to have his trial removed from state court to federal circuit court presented the Waite Court an even more blatant example of racial discrimination in juror selection (*Strauder v. West Virginia*, 1880).

In contrast to Judge Coles who individually kept black men off the venire list, West Virginia barred blacks from juries by statute. The controlling question, wrote Strong on allowing the removal, was "whether by the Constitution and laws of the United States, every citizen of the United States has a right to a trial of an indictment against him by a jury selected and impaneled without discrimination against his race or color, because of race or color. . . ." An answer in the affirmative, with Clifford and Field again dissenting, followed from the common purpose of the Reconstruction amendments.

> At the time when they were incorporated into the Constitution, it required little knowledge of human nature to anticipate that those who had long been regarded as an inferior and subject race would, when suddenly raised to the rank of citizenship, be looked upon with jealousy and positive dislike, and that state laws might be enacted or enforced to perpetuate the distinctions that had before existed. . . . They especially needed protection against unfriendly action in the States where they were resident.

That protection was afforded in this context by the equal protection clause. "What is this but declaring that the law in the States shall be the same for the black as for the white?" Access to the jury box was a check on the evils of prejudice and was a bulwark of liberty. "[H]ow can it be maintained that compelling a colored man to submit to a trial for his life by a jury drawn from a panel from which the State has expressly excluded every man of his race, because of color alone, however well qualified in other respects, is not a denial to him of equal legal protection?" The West Virginia statute was constitutionally defective because it violated "*the right to exemption from unfriendly legislation against them distinctively as colored;* exemption from legal discriminations, implying inferiority in civil society, and discriminations which are steps towards reducing them to the condition of a subject race" (emphasis added). States remained free to set qualifications for jurors, but race could not be one of them.

Strauder v. West Virginia and *Ex parte Virginia* may be doubly important because they seem to have enlarged substantially the meaning of the Fourteenth Amendment beyond the intent of its framers. Considerable evidence exists that the amendment was designed to protect "civil" but not "political" rights (Currie 1985, 384). That point lay at the basis of Justice Field's dissent, which Clifford joined, in *Ex parte Virginia.* Rights deemed fundamental—such as the rights to contract and to buy, hold, and sell property—were to be guarded, but that objective fell short of assuring absolute equality by conferring equal political rights too. This explained why, although white women were deemed citizens, few men in that day argued that possession of citizenship entitled them to sit on juries or to vote. In removing doubts about the citizenship of blacks, the Fourteenth Amendment did not also confer a constitutional right to be eligible for jury service. Voting would be another political right—hence, the Fourteenth Amendment's oblique allowance for racial discrimination in voting in section two, and the subsequent need for the Fifteenth Amendment to correct the deficiency.

The Court's arguable stretching of the Fourteenth Amendment in these two jury cases, however, did not lead to a broad construction of a removal statute in a third (*Virginia v. Rives*, 1880). Burwell and Lee Reynolds, black men seventeen and nineteen years old respectively, were indicted for the murder of a white man in Patrick County, also along Virginia's southern tier. They petitioned the state court that their trials be removed to the federal circuit court because no blacks sat on the grand jury that indicted them nor on the jury impaneled to try them. They further asserted that blacks were regularly excluded from juries in the county. Their motions were denied, the trials proceeded, and they were found guilty. After the verdicts were set aside, a jury convicted one defendant on retrial, and there was a hung jury for the other. At this stage of the proceedings, the federal court ordered removal on the authority of section 641 of the Revised U.S. Statutes (the same provision that Taylor Strauder successfully deployed in his case). Both men were then placed in custody of the U.S. marshal. The commonwealth of Virginia petitioned the U.S. Supreme Court to direct U.S. District Judge Alexander Rives to return the defendants to the custody of the commonwealth.

A unanimous Court ruled that the defendants could not avail themselves of section 641. Writing for the Court, Justice Strong reasoned the removal statute did not apply to all situations in which "equal protection of the laws may be denied. . . . The statute authorizes a removal of the case only before trial, not after a trial has commenced. . . . It does not embrace a case in which a right may be denied by judicial action during the trial, or by discrimination against him in the sentence. . . ." Redress in those instances would be left "to the revisory power of the higher courts of the State and ultimately to the review of this court." Strong continued that section 641 would apply if there were a discriminatory state law or constitutional provision in existence that made it plain before trial began that a federally protected right was threatened. No such law or provision existed in this instance. Virginia law was racially neutral on the subject of selection of jurors. Prejudicial conduct or procedure at the trial did not qualify under section 641. Nor was the Court persuaded by the assertion of a pattern and practice of discrimination as a qualifying condition. That was a question altogether different from the selection of jurors for this case. "The assertions . . . fall short of showing that any civil right was denied, or that there had been any discrimination against the defendants because of their color or race. The facts may have been as stated, and yet the jury which indicted them, and the panel summoned to try them, may have been impartially selected."

Strong's construction of section 641 seemed as unyielding and stingy as the Court had given the Enforcement Act in *Reese*. But the outcome in *Rives* may have been dictated by a quirk. The 1866 removal statute and all other federal statutes were reformulated when Congress enacted the Revised Statutes in 1875. The compilers had been instructed to systematize, but not substantively to change, the laws Congress had passed. However, although the 1866 version allowed for both pretrial and postjudgment removal, the postjudgment provision was inexplicably dropped in the 1875 compilation (Maltz 1996, 81).

Ex parte Virginia, *Strauder*, and *Rives* were among Strong's last opinions for the Court. One wonders whether he might have joined Harlan's dissent in the *Civil Rights Cases* had he remained on the bench. According to one of Harlan's biographers, evidence points in that direction. After Harlan's dissent was published, Strong wrote Harlan indicating that his first inclination was to have sided with the majority. But in light of Harlan's "very able opinion—the best you have ever written"—Strong had second thoughts. "It may be that you are right. The opinion of the Court, as you said, is too narrow—sticks to the letter, while you aim to bring out the spirit of the Constitution" (Yarbrough 1995, 152).

Indeed, a majority opinion by Harlan in *Neal v. Delaware* (1881) drew heavily upon Strong's opinions in *Ex parte Virginia*, *Strauder*, and *Rives* and largely seemed to close the door to rampant discrimination in juror selection that *Rives* left open. The facts in *Neal* were similar to those in *Rives*. A black man had been indicted in a Delaware court for rape. Relying on section 641, he petitioned for his trial to be removed to federal circuit court because of the exclusion of blacks from the jury pool. The state court denied his request, the trial proceeded, and he was found guilty and sentenced to death. In the U.S. Supreme Court, Neal's reliance on 641 was predicated on the fact that jurors were drawn from the list of eligible voters and that the Delaware Constitution still contained a provision granting the franchise to white men only. That would have made it parallel to *Strauder v. West Virginia*, not *Virginia v. Rives*. However, Harlan sided with the state's contention that the Fifteenth Amendment had, practically speaking, negated the discriminatory constitutional provision and that "the State Court did not err in disregarding the petition for removal." Although this language would seem to have dictated an outcome identical to that in *Rives*, such was not to be. Harlan's opinion did not mention *Rives*.

Although Field predictably dissented on the now familiar ground of the limited scope of the Fourteenth Amendment in such matters, and although Chief Justice Waite was convinced that *Rives* was controlling, the Court this time focused on the pattern-and-practice argument. Even though blacks by law could serve on juries, they did not serve in fact. That fact surely accounted for the all-white jury that convicted Neal. An indiscreet comment by one of the Delaware judges helped the bench to that conclusion: "That none but white men were selected is in nowise remarkable in view of the fact—too notorious to be ignored—that the great body of black men residing in this State are utterly unqualified by want of intelligence, experience or moral integrity, to sit on juries." Exceptions, he added, were rare. Reversing the judgment and quashing the indictment, Harlan was indignant.

"It was, we think, under all the circumstances, a violent presumption which the State Court indulged, that such uniform exclusion of that race from juries, during a period of many years, was solely because, in the judgment of those officers, fairly exercised, the black race in Delaware were utterly disqualified . . . to sit on juries. The action of those officers in the premises is to be deemed the act of the State; and the refusal of the State Court to redress the wrong by them committed, was a denial of a right secured to the prisoner by the Constitution and laws of the United States." Thus in proving violations of the equal protection clause, Harlan was perhaps suggesting that, in similar instances, circumstantial evidence of juror discrimination would be sufficient.

The Court's understanding of the Fourteenth Amendment's use of the word "equal" extended just so far, however. It was Justice Field who spoke for a unanimous bench in 1883 in *Pace v. Alabama.* Although the Court, even Field, would doubtless have struck down a law that imposed a greater penalty for blacks than on whites committing the same offense, *Pace* presented a different challenge. Legislators in Alabama had decided that adultery and fornication, on the first offense, merited a fine of at least $100 and time in the county jail not exceeding six months. A second offense called for a fine of at least $300 and a jail sentence of no more than twelve months. However, if partners of different races engaged in the same conduct (or if they should intermarry), the penalty was a minimum of two years and a maximum of twelve years in prison for each person. In a very brief three paragraph opinion for a unanimous Court, Justice Field turned back an equal protection challenge to the two-year sentences imposed on Tony Pace (a black man) and Mary Cox (a white woman) "for living together in a state of adultery or fornication." To Field, it was dispositive that there was no discrimination against either race. A white person living in a state of adultery with a black person was punished just as severely as the latter. Field refrained from saying what the state had concluded: that fornication and adultery were seen as more harmful offenses when committed by persons of different races than by persons of the same race. That was doubtless a proposition with which each member of the Court could agree.

Yick Wo v. Hopkins (1886) arose from a different context, and stands today as one of the Waite Court's most insightful civil rights decisions. The case was different because it involved San Francisco's Chinese population, not the recently freed slaves of southern and border states. Indeed, California's treatment of persons of Asian origin in the last half of the nineteenth century and well into the twentieth century rivaled the mistreatment southern whites visited upon blacks at the same time.

The 1880 census indicated that approximately 75,000 Chinese lived in California, about 10 percent of the state's population. About half of the Chinese lived in San

Francisco, and most of the laundries in the city were owned and operated by Chinese. For at least ten years the city had been trying to discourage settlement by Chinese. An ordinance in 1870 applied to apartments inhabited by Chinese imposed rules on maximum occupancy; the infamous queue ordinance of 1876 called for snipping the hair of Chinese prisoners; and an ordinance in 1878 denied police protection to the Chinatown section of the city. In 1880 San Francisco enacted what was ostensibly a fire-safety ordinance stipulating that laundries could operate only if licensed by the board of supervisors. The ordinance did not apply to laundries in brick buildings. Only one Chinese laundry operator received a license, and she may not have been perceived as Chinese. Some 240 Chinese operators, including Yick Wo, who had been in business since 1861, were denied licenses. Eighty other laundry operators, none of whom were Chinese, received licenses. The effect was clear: The ordinance as applied was about to eliminate a large share of the Chinese economic presence in San Francisco. When Yick Wo and another operator named Wo Lee continued to do business, both were jailed for washing clothes without the required permit.

What was especially amazing in *Yick Wo* was that every member of the Court joined Justice Stanley Matthews's conclusion that the ordinance, even though racially neutral in its language, violated the equal protection clause. First, the clause applied to aliens and citizens alike. (Recall that the equal protection clause uses the word "person," not "citizen.") Second, what mattered were the facts: not the language of the ordinance, but how the ordinance worked in practice. This was not an ordinary health and safety ordinance but something considerably more sinister. "The fact of this discrimination is admitted. No reason for it is shown, and the conclusion cannot be resisted, that no reason for it exists except hostility to the race and nationality to which the petitioners belong. . . ."

The Waite Court's record on civil rights from *Reese* and *Cruikshank* to *Yick Wo* was decidedly mixed. However, the record suggests a theme. Although suspicious of expanded congressional authority to protect civil rights, the Court was prepared to accept the Fourteenth Amendment on its own terms as a restraint on racial discrimination by the states. Oddly, therefore, in spite of the express language in section five of the amendment, it restrained the states but correspondingly did little to empower Congress. The Court was inclined to see the amendment negatively as a check on state laws more often than it was inclined to accept the amendment positively as a grant of authority to Congress. One wonders whether concerns about a rapacious Congress in the post–Civil War era influenced the justices as they considered civil rights legislation, especially in light of a near subjugation of the presidency following Lincoln's death. Protecting the federal system and the carefully constructed system of separation of powers from a dominant Congress may have seemed more urgent than facilitating congressional protection of civil rights.

The Bill of Rights

Decisions defining and applying the first eight amendments to the Constitution, commonly known as the Bill of Rights, are hallmarks of the contemporary Supreme Court. These amendments, along with the more general Ninth and Tenth amendments, were proposed by the First Congress in 1789 after critics of the Constitution (called antifederalists) charged that the 1787 document left basic freedoms unprotected. Ratified by the requisite number of states in 1791, the Bill of Rights, among other things, secures freedom of religion, speech, press, assembly, and petition and sets basic procedural standards to be followed in law enforcement and the criminal justice system. The drafters of the Bill of Rights knew firsthand the dangers that government-as-prosecutor could pose to personal liberty. Common-sense limits on government's crime-fighting powers help safeguard democracy. Yet such civil liberties questions came before the nineteenth-century Supreme Court only occasionally.

Four factors tended to make the Bill of Rights so judicially invisible. First, and most important, the Bill of Rights initially limited only the federal and not state governments. As noted earlier in this chapter, this was the prevailing view that Chief Justice Marshall reiterated in *Barron v. Baltimore* (1833). In this landmark case, the city of Baltimore, under acts of the Maryland legislature, had diverted the flow of several streams. The diversion deposited silt around Barron's wharf in Baltimore harbor, making it unfit for shipping. Barron claimed that the city had deprived him of his property without the just compensation required by the Fifth Amendment. This was a question "of great importance," Marshall acknowledged, "but not of much difficulty." He and the rest of the Court never touched the question of whether such circumstances amounted to a taking of property that required the city to compensate Barron. Instead the Court held it lacked jurisdiction to decide the question because the Fifth Amendment (along with other amendments in the Bill of Rights) did not apply to the actions of state and local governments.

Second, because the Bill of Rights did not apply to the states, most government actions and policies in the nineteenth century were not subject to its restraints. This is why *Barron* was so significant. Well into the twentieth century, when a person talked about government doing something, it usually meant activity of state governments and their local subdivisions such as counties, cities, and towns. Moreover, only rarely was federal government action perceived to implicate Bill of Rights provisions such as the First Amendment's guaranty of freedom of expression.

Third, Congress did not give the Supreme Court jurisdiction in criminal cases from the U.S. circuit courts until 1889 (a year after Chief Justice Waite's death). Even then the jurisdiction was in capital cases only. Review of other felonies from lower federal courts was allowed in 1891. This exclusion over the course of a century nearly completely denied the Court any opportunity to construe the procedural commands of the Bill of Rights. Other than a challenge to a person's confinement through a writ of habeas corpus, the only way around the exclusion was by a certification of a division of opinion by the circuit court on a question of law (Frankfurter and Landis 1928, 79, 109). However, the Supreme Court could receive appeals from certain territorial courts. There, unlike in state courts, the Bill of Rights applied because Congress had established the territorial governments (Fairman 1987, 730). However, the number of territorial cases was very small.

Fourth, a culture of rights featuring judicial vindication of liberties enshrined in the Bill of Rights, did not mature in the United States until the twentieth century. This is not to suggest that Americans of the nineteenth century did not think in terms of rights. They did. However, other than seeking judicial protection of contractual and property-related rights, Americans generally had not yet linked state or federal courts with a defense of civil liberties. Americans of course thought they had a right of free speech, and they would be quick to protest when they thought that right had been abridged. But it would be a while before they routinely thought of turning to the courts for protection of such rights. To be sure, the Bill of Rights was more than a "certain number of amendments on comparatively unimportant points," as Sir Henry Maine disparaged it in the late nineteenth century (Maine 1886, 243). But it remained more within the realm of first principles, lore, platitudes, and aspirations, instead of the more familiar substance of day-to-day courtroom business.

By Waite's day there were at least two signs that the Bill of Rights might become juridically prominent through the newly ratified Fourteenth Amendment. Both indicated that the idea of rights for all Americans, regardless of the state in which they lived, had become more elevated in the public consciousness. First, as noted, the prewar antislavery movement had inspired belief that section two of the Constitution's Article IV ("The Citizens of each State shall be entitled to all Privileges and Immunities of Citizens in the several States") included freedom of speech and perhaps other fundamental rights. Later, Democratic Party critics of the Civil War had protested the various and sometimes highhanded attempts by the Lincoln administration to squelch dissent against administration policies as a violation of basic rights.

Second, John Bingham and at least some other congressional Republicans, in introducing the resolution that became the Fourteenth Amendment, clearly believed the amendment would subject the states to the Bill of Rights, thus accomplishing what *Barron v. Baltimore* had not. The words they chose to express this point were "privileges or immunities of citizens of the United States." Madison had introduced the proposed Bill of Rights in the First Congress seventy-seven years earlier. Ironically, he had advocated an amendment that would restrain states from violating "the equal right of conscience, freedom of the press, or trial by jury in criminal cases; because it is proper that every Government should be disarmed of powers which trench upon those particular rights." Madison referred to the rights as "invaluable privileges." However, the second piece of Madison's double safeguard—limiting state as well as federal governments—was not included in the package of amendments that Congress sent to the states for ratification in 1789. That was perhaps understandable. As Marshall explained in 1833, "In almost every convention by which the constitution was adopted, amendments to guard against the abuse of power were recommended. These amendments demanded security against the apprehended encroachments of the general [federal] government, not against those of the local [state] governments." Thus Bingham and others hoped that the Fourteenth Amendment would correct that omission. According to one study, the Fourteenth Amendment was the centerpiece of the Republicans' congressional campaigns of 1866. Party leaders "referred to the amendment as securing freedom of speech, the right to bear arms, all rights of American citizens, and all constitutional rights" (Curtis 2000, 362–363). Whether standing for or against the amendment, many in 1866 thought that the application of the Bill of Rights to the states was one of the amendment's principal objectives.

If that was the intent, it was quickly stifled. As described earlier in this chapter, the decision in the *Slaughterhouse Cases* (1873), in the dim twilight of the Chase Court, essentially neutralized the privileges and immunities clause of the Fourteenth Amendment. The amendment's reference to citizens of the United States and to citizens of the states where the former resided led Justice Miller to conclude that the clause protected from state infringement only those rights created by national citizenship. All other rights, including virtually all the important ones, predated the Constitution and adhered in one's state citizenship. It was to the state alone that a citizen was to look for his or her protection. Little wonder that Justice Field in his dissent thought that Miller was turning recent history on its head.

With the privileges and immunities clause of the Fourteenth Amendment lying dormant after 1873, could other provisions of the amendment accomplish the objective Bingham and others sought? The third of the three restraints—the equal protection clause—probably would not do. Justice Miller in his *Slaughterhouse* opinion had doubted that the clause would ever be applied outside the context of discrimination "against the negroes as a class, or on account of their race." Even as late as 1927, Justice Oliver Wendell Holmes characterized the same enfeebled provision as the "last resort of constitutional arguments" (*Buck v. Bell*).

But there was still the second provision: "nor shall any State deprive any person of life, liberty, or property, without due process of law." Could those words somehow substitute for the privileges and immunities clause? As explained in the next section, one response by some litigants to the *Slaughterhouse Cases* was to turn to the due process clause as protection for the kind of occupational and property interests threatened by the butchering monopoly in Louisiana. If successful, the Court would become Miller's feared perpetual censor upon all legislation of the States. A nearly parallel movement looked to the due process clause as a vehicle for applying some provisions of the Bill of Rights to the states. If successful, it would also vastly expand the Supreme Court's jurisdiction, allowing review of even the most common state criminal convictions.

The possibility posed by the latter movement received its first full attention in *Hurtado v. California* (1884). The district attorney in Sacramento County, California, through a written accusation called an "information," charged Joseph Hurtado with murder in 1882. Hurtado was found guilty and sentenced to death. In the Supreme Court Hurtado challenged the legality of the trial on the grounds that, by substituting an information for indictment by a grand jury, California had deprived him of due process of law in violation of the Fourteenth Amendment. The Fifth Amendment called for a grand jury indictment in serious federal criminal cases, as did most state constitutions for state trials. The question became whether the Fourteenth Amendment mandated grand jury indictments for the states' criminal justice systems. "The question is one of grave and serious import, affecting both private and public rights and interests of great magnitude . . . ," wrote Justice Stanley Matthews for the majority (Justice Field did not participate). Matthews found no right to a grand jury indictment. He rejected the view that "any proceeding . . . not . . . sanctioned by usage, or which supersedes and displaces one that is, cannot be regarded as due process of law. . . . [T]o hold that such a characteristic is essential to due process of law, would be to deny every quality of the law but its age, and to render it incapable of progress or improvement. It would be to stamp upon our jurisprudence the unchangeableness attributed to the laws of the Medes and Persians."

Besides, the fact that the Fifth Amendment contained a due process clause, alongside a series of procedural guaranties including the right to indictment by grand jury, meant that due process was not intended to encompass specific safeguards of the Bill of Rights. If the Fourteenth Amendment required grand jury indictments, "it would have embodied, as did the Fifth Amendment, express declarations to that effect." Thus, the words "due process" could not have been intended to be a kind of legal shorthand for other rights mentioned elsewhere. Instead, Fourteenth Amendment due process "refers to the law of the land in each State, which derives its authority from the inherent and reserved powers of the State, exerted within the limits of those fundamental principles of liberty and justice which lie at the base of all our civil and political institutions. . . ." What, therefore, did "due process" allow? "[A]ny legal proceeding . . . whether sanctioned by age and custom, or newly devised . . . in furtherance of the general public good, which regards and preserves these principles of liberty and justice, must be held to be due process of law. . . ." Thus, if a procedure was traditional it ordinarily would be compatible with due process. If a procedure was new, that fact alone would not invalidate it under the due process clause. The tilt of the opinion was clearly toward innovation. Nonetheless, the Court placed itself in the position of being the final judge concerning "those fundamental principles of liberty and justice which lie at the base of all our civil and political institutions. . . ." The *Hurtado* Court was both tolerant of diversity in policies among the states and highly protective of judicial prerogative as expositor of the Constitution.

The theory that Matthews articulated in *Hurtado* about Fourteenth Amendment due process was consistent with less systematic and scholarly statements the Waite Court had already made on the subject. Chief Justice Waite had explained in *Walker v. Sauvinet* (1876) that the Seventh Amendment right of a jury trial in most civil cases did not apply to state courts because it was not a privilege or immunity of national citizenship. *Davidson v. New Orleans* (1878) had intimated that the just compensation clause of the Fifth Amendment was also inapplicable to the states. "If private property be taken for public uses without just compensation," Justice Miller explained, "it must be remembered that, when the XIVth Amendment was adopted, the provision on that subject, in immediate juxtaposition in the Vth Amendment . . . was left out. . . ." The specter of the *Slaughterhouse Cases* still hovered over the bench.

The concept of due process that Matthews proclaimed in *Hurtado* bears comparison to an earlier construction of the same words in the Fifth Amendment. Probing the meaning of the Fifth Amendment's due process clause in 1856, Justice Benjamin Curtis explained that the "constitution contains no description of those processes which it was intended to allow or forbid. It does not even declare what principles are to be applied to ascertain whether it be due process." Yet it was "manifest that it was not left to the legislative power to enact any process which might be devised. The article is a restraint on the legislative as well as on the executive and judicial powers of the government, and cannot be so construed as to leave congress free to make any process 'due process of law,' by its mere will." How, then, was one to determine what process was constitutionally due? "To this the answer must be twofold. We must examine the constitution itself, *to see whether this process be in conflict with any of its provisions.* If not found to be so, we must look to those settled usages and modes of proceeding existing in the common and statute law of England, before the emigration of our ancestors, and which are shown not to have been unsuited to their civil and political condition by having been acted on by them after the settlement of this country" (*Murray's Lessee v. Hoboken Land and Improvement Co.*, emphasis added).

The italicized words partly explain Justice John Marshall Harlan's passionate and lengthy dissent in *Hurtado.* Under Matthews's reasoning, no right mentioned in the Bill of Rights could be encompassed by due process of law. Thus, the majority's argument proved too much by excluding from the due process clause the most fundamental protections. That "line of argument," Harlan insisted, "would lead to results which are inconsistent with the vital principles of republican government." He was unimpressed by Matthews's reasoning that the Fifth Amendment's protection of due process, alongside other procedural guaranties, meant that the latter were excluded from the former. Rather, according to Harlan, "it was deemed wise to avoid the possibility that Congress, in regulating the processes of law, would impair or destroy them." Hence their specific enumeration in several amendments of the Constitution. For Harlan there was no doubt that due process equaled at least the procedural safeguards of the Bill of Rights.

The Matthews construction of due process in relation to the Bill of Rights held fast until 1897, when the Court cast doubt on *Hurtado* by ruling that the due process clause of the Fourteenth Amendment limited the taking of property for public use without just compensation. It was beside the fact that the Fifth Amendment contained the same safeguard (*Chicago, B. and Q. R. Co. v. Chicago*). In 1908 the Court laid to rest the view that inclusion of a right in the Bill of Rights necessarily excluded that right from the protection of the due process clause. "[I]t is possible, acknowledged Justice William Moody, "that some of the personal rights safeguarded by the first eight Amendments against national action may also be safeguarded against state action. . . . If this is so, it is not because those rights are enumerated in the first eight Amendments, but because they are of such a nature that they are included in the conception of due process of law" (*Twining v. New Jersey*). But application of almost all the rest of the Bill of Rights to the states did not begin until the 1920s. The Court then proceeded on a case-by-case basis across some two dozen decisions until the late 1960s. Only then was Justice Harlan's dissent in *Hurtado* finally vindicated. Within this long succession of decisions was *Cantwell v. Connecticut* (1940), which applied to the states the First Amendment's guaranty of "free exercise of religion."

It fell to the Waite Court in *Reynolds v. United States* (1879) to offer the first authoritative interpretation of the free exercise clause. The reverberations of this decision are still felt today. The case was also the first of several decisions by the Waite Court delineating the authority of the federal government in what amounted to a war against the Church of Jesus Christ of Latter-Day Saints (the Mormons).

The national campaign against the Mormons began fifteen years after Brigham Young led his followers to the Utah Territory in 1847 where they established the theocratic community of Deseret. This settlement was the final stop in their persecution-beset trek from New York to Ohio in 1831, to Missouri in 1838, and to Illinois in 1840, where founder Joseph Smith was killed in an 1844 uprising against the sect. Once in Utah, Mormons were geographically well removed from most of the rest of the country, but distance did little to lessen the widespread and intense opposition to their distinctive, well-publicized practice of polygamy. Many U.S. citizens considered it as morally offensive as slavery. As the platform of the newly organized Republican Party proclaimed in 1856, "it is both the right and the imperative duty of Congress to prohibit in the Territories those twin relics of barbarism—Polygamy, and Slavery" (Stephenson 1999, 86).

Accordingly, in 1862 Congress made polygamy a crime in any U.S. territory, punishable by a fine and imprisonment up to five years; it revoked the territorially granted charter of the Mormon Church; and it annulled all acts passed by the Utah territorial legislature deemed protective of polygamy. Another congressional act in 1874 handed local jurisdiction in criminal and most civil cases to district courts, staffed by federal appointees, and limited other courts, controlled by Mormons, to cases involving estates, guardianships, or divorce. Congress also gave the U.S. Supreme Court jurisdiction over capital cases and bigamy convictions appealed from the Utah Territory's Supreme Court. Still more federal legislation came in 1882 in a serious effort to eradicate polygamy. Congress disfranchised polygamists and their wives (the territorial legislature had conferred the right to vote on women in 1870), set up a board of commissioners to oversee the work of election officials, and imposed other civil penalties. Laws also made it easier to obtain convictions for polygamy by criminalizing unlawful cohabitation as well, thus eliminating any prosecutorial need to show proof of marriage. Prosecutors had only to demonstrate that a man lived with two or more women who were neither his mother nor his sisters, not that they were formally married. In 1887 yet another statute directed the attorney general to seize all real property valued above $50,000 that belonged to the Mormon Church (Urofsky 2002, 119–121). Cumulatively, the statutes had one objective: to dissolve the church or at least to force it to abandon polygamy.

The Waite Court's direct involvement in this anti-Mormon crusade began after George Reynolds, Brigham Young's personal secretary, was convicted of polygamy in 1875, sentenced to five years at hard labor, and fined $5,000. When his appeal reached the U.S. Supreme Court, his principal argument was that the trial judge erred by not instructing the jury that his sincerely held religious belief in polygamy was a ground for acquittal. Thus Reynolds asked the Court not to invalidate Congress's criminalization of polygamy but in effect asked the Court to carve out a religiously based exemption, based on the free exercise clause, to an otherwise valid law of general application. His argument amounted to a claim that the free exercise clause placed religious practice in a preferred position. By his reasoning, a polygamous atheist or Presbyterian could lawfully be sent to jail under the statute, but a polygamous Mormon could not.

However, taking that step "would be introducing a new element into criminal law," Waite observed for the Court in rejecting Reynolds's contention. "Laws are made for the government of actions," explained the chief justice, "and while they cannot interfere with mere religious belief and opinions, they may with practices." "Suppose one believed that human sacrifices were a necessary part of religious worship," he inquired. "Would it be seriously contended that the civil government under which he lived could not interfere to prevent a sacrifice?" To excuse Reynolds "would be to make the professed doctrines of religious belief superior to the laws of the land, and in effect to permit every citizen to become a law unto himself. Government could exist only in name under such circumstances." In short, when the commands of the government collided with the dictates of religion, law trumped faith.

With government sovereign over actions and individuals sovereign over their beliefs, had Waite transformed the free exercise clause into merely a free belief clause? Was the chief justice suggesting that Congress could constitutionally criminalize actions involved in public worship? Probably not. In his opinion Waite quoted approvingly from the preamble to Virginia's statute for religious freedom, largely drafted by Thomas Jefferson slightly more than a year before the Philadelphia Convention of 1787 convened: "That to suffer the civil magistrate to intrude his powers into the field of opinion, and to restrain the profession or propagation of principles on supposition of their ill tendency, is a dangerous fallacy which at once destroys all religious liberty. . . . [I]t is time enough for the rightful purposes of civil government for its officers to interfere when principles break out into overt acts against peace and good order." From this Waite concluded that "Congress was deprived of all legislative power over mere opinion, but was left free to reach *actions which were in violation of social duties or subversive of good order*" (emphasis added). Thus, Waite's reading of the free exercise clause was that it barred discrimination because of religion (and there were plentiful examples of such religiously based targeting in early U.S. history). It did not create a sanctuary against laws furthering valid secular interests. Waite's construction also conformed to provisions in early state constitutions, as seen in this passage from the New York Constitution of 1777: "The free exercise and enjoyment of religious profession and worship, without discrimination or preference, shall forever hereafter be allowed . . . : *Provided*, That the liberty of conscience, hereby granted, shall not be so construed as to excuse acts of licentiousness, or justify practices inconsistent with the peace or safety of this State."

The U.S. Supreme Court generally followed Waite's construction of the free exercise clause for eighty-four years. However, in a 1963 about-face, *Sherbert v. Verner* required government to demonstrate a compelling interest before requiring believers to do something their faith forbade, or before forbidding them from doing something their faith required. In short, *Sherbert* held that sometimes faith could trump law. Then, in 1990, with four justices dissenting on the point, the Court generally reverted to Waite's interpretation in *Reynolds* (*Employment Division v. Smith*). Yet *Smith* has hardly ended the controversy George Reynolds ignited 125 years ago regarding the scope of the free exercise clause.

The Waite Court upheld other anti-Mormon/polygamy policies as well. These were not litigated in a First Amendment context, but the outcome in each directly affected the free exercise of religion allowed communicants of the Church of Jesus Christ of Latter-Day Saints. *Murphy v. Ramsey* (1885) upheld the disfranchisement of polygamists and their wives. Congress had plenary authority over how territories would be governed, explained Justice Stanley Matthews. "[N]o legislation can be supposed more wholesome and necessary in the founding of a free, self-governing commonwealth," he added, "than that which seeks to establish it on the basis of the idea of the family, as consisting in and springing from the union for life of one man and one woman in the holy estate of matrimony; the sure foundation of all that is stable and noble in our civilization, the best guaranty of that reverent morality which is the source of all beneficent progress in social and political improvement. And to this end, no means are more directly and immediately suitable than those provided by this Act, which endeavors to withdraw all political influence from those who are practically hostile to its attainment." A similar perspective probably explains *Clawson v. United States* (1885), in which the Court extended to grand juries an 1882 statute's creation of a cause for challenge excluding polygamists from juries in polygamy trials.

Furthermore, *Cannon v. United States* (1885) allowed trial courts to draw inferences about an earlier statute's prohibition of cohabitation. The defendant had married three women, but lived only with one. Another occupied separate quarters in Cannon's house, and the third lived in a separate house. Angus Cannon claimed that the law criminalized only multiple sexual relationships, but that he was living sexually only with one woman, having explained to the others that he had to abide by the law. Speaking for the Court, Justice Blatchford, over dissents by Miller and Field, gave the statute a broad interpretation against Cannon's defense. "Compacts for sexual nonintercourse, easily made and as easily broken, when the prior marriage relations continue to exist, with the occupation of the same house and table and the keeping up of the same family unity, is not a lawful substitute for the monogamous family which alone the statute tolerates." For a bench with Victorian sensibilities, Blatchford's language was about as sexually explicit as one finds in the *U.S. Reports* in this period.

The statutorily decreed confiscation of church property was upheld two years after Waite's death in *Late Corporation of the Church of Jesus Christ of Latter-Day Saints v. United States* (1890). With Waite-era justices Field and Lamar dissenting, Justice David J. Brewer—in language similar to contemporary opinions dealing with property seizures connected with racketeering and organized crime—decreed that the confiscation was lawful because the stance of the church in furtherance of polygamy was unlawful. Only after the church officially recanted doctrinally on polygamy in 1890 was Congress inclined to reciprocate, as it did in restoring church property by 1896.

This strategic switch by the church may have moderated extensive persecution elsewhere. As an indication of the extent to which the Court was prepared to approve anti-Mormon legislation, all seven holdover justices who had sat with Waite joined Field's opinion in *Davis v. Beason* (1890). The case upheld an Idaho territorial statute that effectively denied the vote to all Mormons. Bigamists and polygamists were barred from the polls, as well as those who were "members of an order that teaches the commission of those crimes." Field and others seemed to have forgotten Waite's carefully developed distinction in *Reynolds* between actions and beliefs.

Waite's bench was not only the first to address the First Amendment's free exercise clause but probably also the first to encounter the protections the same amendment afforded for speech and press. In contrast to *Reynolds*, neither of the two decisions yielded a systematic examination of the scope of the freedoms—that would not be seen until well into the twentieth century. Despite the general absence of such issues on the Court's docket at this time, however, each indicates that at least a few justices of the Waite era were giving thought to those freedoms.

Ex parte Jackson (1878) reached the Court as a habeas corpus petition after Orlando Jackson had been sentenced to jail for mailing a circular promoting a lottery in violation of an 1876 act of Congress. Although lotteries had been widely accepted early in the nineteenth century as a device to raise capital for various public and private projects, the tide of morality had turned against them. Indeed, *Champion v. Ames* (1903) would later reflect that change of attitude by upholding an act of Congress of 1895 that criminalized the interstate shipment (by any means) of lottery tickets.

Justice Field's opinion upheld the ban and hence the lawfulness of Jackson's conviction as an exercise of Congress's broad authority to operate a postal system. Just as Congress had barred obscene materials from the mails in 1873, Field concluded that Congress could now exclude materials encouraging legal or illegal lotteries because of their "demoralizing influence upon the people." Digressing well beyond what was necessary to decide the case, Field acknowledged the "difficulty attending the subject" that arose "not from the want of power in Congress to prescribe regulations as to what shall constitute mail matter, but from the necessity of enforcing them consistently with rights reserved to the People, of far greater importance than the transportation of the mail." Thanks to the Fourth Amendment's protection against "unreasonable searches and seizures," sealed letters were "fully guarded from examination and inspection, except as to their outward form and weight, as if they were retained by the parties forwarding them in their own domicils." These could be opened only upon issuance of a warrant. Otherwise, knowledge of the content of such communications could be legally ascertained only when revealed by the parties receiving the materials or through similar channels. Regulations on printed matter subject to inspection (and Field did not know whether Jackson's circular had been sealed or left open for inspection) also had to be carefully constructed. They could not be enforced "so as to interfere in any manner with freedom of the press. Liberty of circulating is as essential to that freedom as liberty of publishing; indeed, without the circulation, the publication would be of little value." Therefore, if Congress barred certain content from the mails, "its transportation in any other way [as by a private carrier] cannot be forbidden by Congress." Otherwise the "circulation of documents would be destroyed, and a fatal blow given to the freedom of the press."

Ex parte Curtis (1882), the second case, also reached the Court as a habeas corpus petition. Newton Martin Curtis, a federal worker, challenged the validity of an 1876 congressional act under which he had been convicted in New York. In sweeping language, the statute prohibited federal employees (except those appointed by the president with the advice and consent of the Senate) from "requesting, giving to or receiving from" any other officer or employee of the government "any money or property or other thing of value, for political purposes." Enacted in the twilight of the era of the spoils system, before creation of the protections afforded by the Civil Service Commission, the law was plainly aimed at curbing the corrupt practice of exacting payment from government workers as a condition for continued employment. Significantly, it did not cover assessments of federal workers by private individuals (such as an official of a political party).

Chief Justice Waite's opinion for the majority found the statute well within the lawful powers of Congress. "The evident purpose . . . in all this class of enactments has been to promote efficiency and integrity in the discharge of official duties, and to maintain proper discipline in the public service." The statute did not "prohibit them altogether from receiving or soliciting money or property for [political] purposes," Waite noted. "It simply forbids their receiving from or giving to each other. Beyond this no restrictions are placed on any of their political activities." Waite may have stressed what the statute did not prohibit because of Justice Bradley's solo dissent. Indicating the embryonic state of free speech doctrine in the late nineteenth century, only Bradley raised the First Amendment's guaranty of free speech. Waite ignored it completely, except possibly by his indirect reference to political avenues government employees were still free to pursue.

Bradley realistically assessed the statute in terms of its impact on political freedoms. It decreed "that a man shall not, even voluntarily, and of his own free will, contribute in any way through or by the hands of any other *employé* of the Government, to the political cause which he desires to aid and promote." That was beyond the power of Congress to impose on any citizen, regardless of his employer. The majority had overlooked an important reality of politics: that organization, money, and speech were interconnected. "Amongst the necessary and proper means for promoting political views, or any other views, are association and contribution of money or for that purpose, both to aid discussion and to disseminate information and sound doctrine. To deny to a man the privilege of associating and making joint contributions with such other citizens as he may choose, is an unjust restraint of his right to propagate and promote his views on public affairs. The freedom of speech and of the press, and that of assemblying together . . . are expressly secured by the Constitution." The First Amendment protected citizens in these activities from "inconvenient restrictions."

Bradley must have felt strongly about the matter. "The whole thing seems to me absurd. Neither men's mouths nor their purses can be constitutionally tied up in that way." The goal was laudable, but the means were not. "It is not lawful to do evil that good may come. . . . No doubt it would often greatly tend to prevent the spread of a contagious and deadly epidemic, if those first taken should be immediately sacrificed to the public good. But such a mode of preventing the evil would hardly be regarded as legitimate in a Christian country." True, a late twentieth-century court perhaps would have probed Congress's "compelling interests" that underlay the prohibition (drawing on points that Waite made) and perhaps would have determined whether the statute was overly broad. A later court would also have probed whether there were available means to accomplish the same objective with less damage to free speech. But for what is probably the first discourse on freedom of speech by a Supreme Court justice in an opinion, Bradley's analysis remains impressive.

Justice Field's opinion in *Ex parte Jackson* mentioned the Fourth Amendment, but it was not until *Boyd v. United States* (1886) that the Court focused systematically on that amendment's ban on unreasonable searches and seizures. Moreover, the Court did so in conjunction with the Fifth Amendment's command that a person not be "compelled in any criminal case to be a witness against himself."

The case involved an allegation by the U.S. attorney in New York City that E. A. Boyd and Sons had imported thirty-five cases of plate glass without paying the duty required by the Customs Act of 1874. The federal court directed the Boyds to produce the proper invoices. Failure to comply meant that the government's allegations would be assumed to be true, so there was a strong element of coercion present. The Boyds submitted the requested papers under protest, the jury found in favor of the government, and most of the cases of plate glass were forfeited.

For the Court, Justice Bradley held the statute unconstitutional: It authorized an unreasonable search and seizure in violation of the Fourth Amendment and compelled the owner of the plate glass to be a witness against himself in violation of the Fifth Amendment. Bradley thus became the first Supreme Court justice to link the one guaranty to the other. The statute violated the Fourth Amendment not because it involved "breaking into a house and opening boxes and drawers," but because it effected a "forcible and compulsory extortion of a man's own testimony or of his private papers to be used as evidence." Bradley reviewed the heritage of search and seizure law with which the framers of the Fourth Amendment were surely familiar. The infamous writs of assistance, or general search warrants, had allowed British customs agents to search homes and businesses in Boston and other colonial towns after 1767 looking for smuggled goods. An English court decision from 1765 (*Entick v. Carrington*)—"one of the landmarks of English liberty," Bradley contended—ruled that the searching of a person's papers was a trespass.

> The principles laid down in this opinion affect the very essence of constitutional liberty and security. They reach farther than the concrete form of the case there before the court, with its adventitious circumstances; they apply to all invasions on the part of the Government and its employés of the sanctities of a man's home and the privacies of life. It is not the breaking of his doors, and the rummaging of his drawers, that constitutes the essence of the offense: but it is the invasion of his indefeasible right of personal security, personal liberty and private property, where that right has never been forfeited by his conviction of some public offence. . . . Breaking into a house and opening boxes and drawers are circumstances of aggravation; but any forcible and compulsory extortion of a man's own testimony or of his private papers to be used as evidence of a crime or to forfeit his goods, is within the condemnation of that judgment. In this regard the Fourth and Fifth Amendments run almost into each other.

For Bradley, the framers of the Bill of Rights intended the Fourth Amendment to prohibit such actions in the New World. Not even a criminal warrant would justify the seizure of a person's papers, in Bradley's view. Property could be seized only if "the government is entitled to the possession of the property," as would be the case with stolen merchandise. But in this instance, the government had no proprietary claim on the Boyds's papers concerning the contested crates of plate glass.

Without saying so, Bradley's *Boyd* opinion introduced to the Supreme Court what later would be called the exclusionary rule. As the Court announced some twenty-eight years later in *Weeks v. United States* (1914), evidence obtained in violation of the Fourth Amendment was inadmissible against an accused in court. If the method of obtaining the evidence was illegal, then the fruits of the search had to be suppressed. Bradley's opinion was also noteworthy because he applied the constitutional guaranties in criminal cases to quasi-criminal civil proceedings. Equally important, he equated the compelled production of papers with compelled testimony of an accused in court. The reference in his opinion to the "privacies of life" may have planted the seeds for a constitutionally protected right of privacy that emerged in twentieth-century jurisprudence. Justice Hugo Black was never a friend of a judicially created and constitutionally based right of privacy. But he later echoed Bradley's reasoning to find that a constitutionally based exclusionary rule was necessary: "when the Fourth Amendment's ban against unreasonable searches and seizures is considered together with the Fifth Amendment's ban against compelled self-incrimination, a constitutional basis emerges which not only justifies but actually requires the exclusionary rule" (*Mapp v. Ohio*, 1961).

Bradley's opinion in *Boyd* is probably the most expansive reading of the unreasonable search and seizure and self-incrimination clauses of the Fourth and Fifth Amendments in Supreme Court history. Indeed, willing to invalidate the statute on Fifth Amendment grounds alone, Justice Miller, with Chief Justice Waite concurring, reminded Bradley that the Fourth Amendment did not forbid all searches and seizures of papers or effects, only unreasonable ones. Furthermore, twentieth-century Court rulings sharply curtailed the broad contours of these amendments that Bradley described. Nonetheless, Bradley might have been gratified by a later observation of Justice Louis Brandeis in a dissent in the Court's first wiretapping case: *Boyd* was "a case that will be remembered as long as civil liberty lives in the United States" (*Olmstead v. United States*, 1928).

Kilbourn v. Thompson (1881) did not expressly implicate the Bill of Rights, but posed a question—the extent of congressional investigatory power—that the twentieth-century Court often perceived in both Fifth and First Amendment terms. In January 1876 the U.S. House of Representatives, now with Democrats in the majority, passed a resolution creating a special committee to inquire into the collapse of Jay Cooke and Co., an overextended investment banking house then in federal bankruptcy. The failure of the company in 1873 had set off a chain reaction, including the closing of the New York Stock Exchange for ten days. Moreover, by the time the House passed its resolution, a fifth of the nation's railroads were in bankruptcy, and stocks had lost nearly a third of their value (Davis 2002, A1). Congressional curiosity had been understandably aroused. Jay Cooke also had a heavy interest in what the House called a "real estate pool" in the District of Columbia. The U.S. government also was one of the company's creditors, thanks to the secretary of the navy's improvident deposits with the firm's London office.

The committee issued a subpoena to a Jay Cooke employee named Hallet Kilbourn, commanding him to produce various documents and to answer questions. When Kilbourn refused to do either, the House held him in contempt and directed Sergeant at Arms John Thompson to arrest Kilbourn and jail him until he agreed to comply with the subpoena. After forty-five days behind bars, Kilbourn was released by a writ of habeas corpus by the chief justice of the Supreme Court of the District of Columbia. Kilbourn then sued the House committee members and Thompson for trespass and false imprisonment. The District's high court held for the defendants and dismissed Kilbourn's suit. In the U.S. Supreme Court, attorneys for Kilbourn and the House pressed sharply divergent theories. The first claimed that the House "has no power whatever to punish for a contempt of its authority," and the latter insisted "that such power undoubtedly exists, and when that body has formally exercised it, it must be presumed that it was rightfully exercised."

The House members rested their argument on three principal grounds: The British House of Commons had historically possessed the power; Article I of the Constitution expressly granted each house of Congress the power to discipline its members, to compel their attendance, and even to expel them; and the power to punish for contempt was inherent in the legislative function. Writing for a unanimous bench, Justice Miller rejected the first point because, historically, Parliament was a judicial as well as a legislative body. It was therefore inapposite to a political system marked by separation of powers in which legislative and judicial functions were exercised by different institutions. The second point was unpersuasive, Miller explained, because those clauses vesting each House with punitive powers were as disabling as they were enabling. That is, it was significant in his view that punishing nonmembers was not among the powers granted.

House attorneys must have felt confident about the third ground. In 1821 the Marshall Court, in an opinion by Justice William Johnson, had upheld the implicit power of the House of Representatives to punish nonmembers for contempt (*Anderson v. Dunn*). However, Miller reopened what *Dunn* had presumably settled, and came within a hairbreadth of flatly declaring that the power could not constitutionally exist at all. Punishment imposed by the House lacked the safeguards of due process of law. Furthermore, the House "assumed a power which could only be properly exercised by another branch of the government, because the power was in its nature clearly judicial." But in the end *Kilbourn* was decided on more narrow grounds. The House's hastily crafted and passed resolution failed to state the reasons why it needed the information Mr. Kilbourn might provide. Therefore, it lacked legislative pertinence. Instead, it looked more like a legislative fishing expedition. "[W]e are sure," said Miller, "that no person can be punished for contumacy as a witness before either House, unless his testimony is required in a matter into which that House has jurisdiction to inquire, and we feel equally sure that neither of these bodies possesses the general power of making inquiry into the private affairs of the citizen."

Even though the Court held that the House had proceeded improperly, Kilbourn received much less than he had asked for. The House committee members were protected by the speech and debate clause of Article I, and so were not answerable for Kilbourn's arrest. Mr. Thompson, however, was not so fortunate. Although as sergeant at arms he was only carrying out the orders of the House, he was not a member and so not entitled to the Article I immunity.

Why did the Court stop short of the full implication of its opinion? Justice Miller had even commented privately in November 1876 "that the House is gradually absorbing all the powers of government." He certainly rejected "the doctrine that Congress is *the grand inquest* of the nation." Approximately two months after *Kilbourn* came down, Miller revealed in a letter that the decision was framed on the more narrow ground in order to achieve a unanimous vote. "[T]here was a careful and avowed avoidance of . . . the power of one house to compel by punishment witnesses to appear and answer questions which may throw light on the legislative duties of those bodies. The reason of this was that on that point the court was not united, and dealing as we were with the asserted privileges of one of the most important coordinate branches of the government, it was very desirable to have unanimity in the court, as well as to decide no more than what was necessary. It was partly due to my conservative habit of deciding no more than is necessary in any case, that I was selected to write the opinion" (Fairman 1939, 332–334).

The Court much later upheld the broad investigatory powers of Congress in *McGrain v. Daugherty* (1927), but Congress did not acquire the authority to impose punishment directly on recalcitrant witnesses. Instead, contempt citations for failing to answer any question "pertinent to the question under inquiry" are now referred to the U.S. Department of Justice for prosecution in the federal courts. *Kilbourn's* emphasis on pertinence later lay at the heart of at least one major decision by the Warren Court reining in the House Un-American Activities Committee during the witch-hunt days of the Cold War (*Watkins v. United States*, 1957).

Waite Court jurisprudence touched the Eighth Amendment too. Litigation surrounding the death penalty has been a staple of the Supreme Court's docket since the early 1970s. But it was not until Waite's years as chief that the Court first encountered capital cases to any significant degree. Sixteen were decided between 1876 and 1888, as the bench reversed nine times and affirmed on seven occasions. The Waite Court's sixteen would pale beside the 136 such cases that the Fuller Court decided in the twelve years after 1888. However, the gravity with which the Waite justices approached their task set a compelling example and seemed largely to dictate how the Fuller bench would proceed (Harring and Swedlow 2000, 41). Three of the Waite Court's death penalty decisions merit attention here.

In *Wilkerson v. Utah* (1879), a convicted murderer challenged his sentence in part on the ground that execution by being "publicly shot until you are dead" infringed the Eighth Amendment's ban on "cruel and unusual punishments." The Court affirmed the judgment below. In an interpretation of the Eighth Amendment still cited occasionally today, Justice Clifford admitted for a unanimous bench that it would be difficult "to define with exactness the extent of the constitutional provision." Yet, after typical Clifford-like examination of all relevant (and many less relevant) authorities, he felt "safe to affirm" that it encompassed "torture . . . and all others in the same line of unnecessary cruelty," but not death by a firing squad.

The Waite justices split 5–4 in a case four years later involving Charles Kring, who had been before a St. Louis jury in four trials for the same murder, and on appeal before the state court of appeals and the state supreme court three times. In the most recent round of appeals, the Missouri Supreme Court had affirmed both his conviction for first-degree murder and a sentence that he be hanged. In an earlier proceeding he had been allowed to plead guilty to murder in the second degree, a noncapital offense. He maintained that acceptance of that plea by the prosecutor and the trial court constituted an acquittal of murder in the first degree. However, during the course of the proceedings, Missouri adopted a new constitution that allowed Kring's retrial. It was from his conviction for first-degree murder and sentence of death that he appealed to the U.S. Supreme Court. Kring contended that the change in Missouri law was an ex post facto law in contravention of the U.S. Constitution. This provision in section ten of Article I was one of the few direct prohibitions on the states prior to ratification of the Fourteenth Amendment. The Court's decision in Kring's case was one of the few rendered by the Supreme Court in the nineteenth century involving the Constitution's ex post facto clause. Against a dissent by Matthews that Waite, Bradley, and Horace Gray joined, Miller (the Waite Court's only professed opponent of capital punishment) led the majority in siding with Kring.

> The case rests . . . upon the proposition that, having an erroneous sentence rendered against him on the plea accepted by the court, he could only take the steps which the law allowed him, to reverse that sentence, at the hazard of subjecting himself to the punishment of death for another and a different offense of which he stood acquitted by the judgment of that court; that he prosecuted his legal right to a review of that sentence with a halter around his neck, when, if he succeeded in reversing it, the same court could tighten it to strangulation, and if he failed, it did him no good. And this is precisely what has occurred. His reward for proving the sentence of the court of twenty-five years' imprisonment (not its judgment of guilt) to be erroneous, is, that he is now to be hanged instead. . . . The whole error, which results in such a remarkable conclusion, arises from holding the provision of the new Constitution applicable to this case, when the law is *ex post facto* and inapplicable to it. (*Kring v. Missouri*, 1883)

Charles Kring may have been a frequent visitor to the appellate courts of Missouri, but Fred Hopt far surpassed him in resort to the U.S. Supreme Court. Between 1882 and 1887, Hopt's case was before the Supreme Court on four occasions, each involving the same crime. No other defendant in a capital case has so commanded the Supreme Court's plenary attention. He won reversals on his first three appeals. On the fourth try, when the Supreme Court finally affirmed the conviction and sentence of death, Justice Field observed that the "defendant has seemed to live a charmed life" (*Hopt v. Utah*, 1887).

A twenty-one-year-old man who had been born in Brooklyn, New York, Hopt and another man were convicted of killing a teamster named John F. Turner near Park City, Utah, on July 3, 1880. After burying his body in Echo Canyon, they sold his horses, freight wagon, and personal items a few days later in Wyoming. Hopt and his companion might have escaped detection altogether except for the fact that the victim was the son of John W. Turner, sheriff of Utah County (Utah). Hopt had twice served time in Turner's jail for less serious offenses, and the sheriff had been informed about the sale of his son's stolen property. Hopt was apprehended by railroad detective Thomas Carr at the depot in Cheyenne, Wyoming. A confession ensued just after Carr handed Hopt over to a local police officer, who spirited the suspect away from the clutches of a lynch mob (and out of range of Turner's drawn pistol).

In his first appeal to the Supreme Court, Justice Gray for a unanimous bench reversed the conviction on fairly minor grounds. Utah justice was crude; one did not have to look far into the record for defects. However, on his second conviction and appeal Justice Harlan for the full bench dealt with more weighty matters. It looked at five issues and concluded that three merited reversal. Two of these provide a window into the minds of the justices as they confronted the technicalities of criminal justice to a degree matched by no previous Court.

It may be significant that the second Hopt decision came down on the same day that *Hurtado v. California* was decided. As explained, Justice Harlan's expansive view of due process found him alone in that case. Harlan made no reference in *Hopt* to application of the Bill of Rights to the states via the Fourteenth Amendment's due process clause, but he nonetheless gave an expansive reading to what due process of law required. Some jurors in Hopt's trial had been selected outside his presence; territorial law required the defendant's presence at the trial. His absence was a fatal error, Harlan concluded. Due process required that the defendant be present, and "where the indictment is for a felony, the trial commences at least from the time when the work of impaneling the jury beings." It made no difference that Hopt did not object at the time. "We are of the opinion that it was not within the power of the accused or his counsel to dispense with the statutory requirement as to his personal presence at the trial. The argument to the contrary necessarily proceeds upon the ground that he alone is concerned as to the mode by which he may be deprived of his life or liberty. . . . The public has an interest in his life and liberty. Neither can be lawfully taken except in the mode prescribed by law. . . . If he be deprived of his life or liberty without being so present, such deprivation would be without that due process of law required by the Constitution" (*Hopt v. Utah*, 1884).

Hopt's confession itself did not constitute grounds for reversal. The trial judge had allowed Thomas Carr, the arresting officer, to relate Hopt's confession to the jury, even though Carr had been called as a defense witness. Had the confession been given voluntarily "uninfluenced by hope of reward or fear of punishment"? The trial judge accepted Carr's conclusion that it was voluntary without examining the police officer who actually received it. Should Hopt's confession have been made in open court instead? "[I]t is difficult, if not impossible, to formulate a rule that will comprehend all cases," Harlan began. "While some of the adjudged cases indicate distrust of confessions which are not judicial, it is certain . . . that the rule against their admissibility has been sometimes carried too far, and in its application justice and common sense have too frequently been sacrificed at the shrine of mercy." A confession was probative: "while from the very nature of such evidence it must be subjected to careful scrutiny and received with great caution, a deliberate, voluntary confession of guilt is among the most effectual proofs in the law. . . ." Against the presumption "that one who is innocent will not imperil his safety . . . by an untrue statement," Harlan acknowledged that the presumption ended when hopes or threats deprived the accused "of that freedom of will or self-control essential to make his confession voluntary within the meaning of the law" (*Hopt v. Utah*, 1884). Measured by that standard, the Court found no cause to believe that the confession in Cheyenne had been involuntary, even though there seems to have been no serious interest in having the trial judge probe more deeply into the record. Harlan's opinion in *Hopt II* broke no new ground in that it applied the then generally accepted standard from state courts for voluntariness of confessions. Nonetheless, the opinion was among the Supreme Court's first examinations of the admissibility of a confession. It would hardly be its last.

Among the Waite Court's decisions involving the Bill of Rights, cases like *Reynolds* were the rule, *Boyd* the exception. The civil liberty claimant rarely won. Moreover, Justice Harlan excepted, the Waite bench was indisposed to extend the protections of the Bill of Rights to the states, just as the bench was averse to read the Bill of Rights as placing broad limits on the power of the federal government. In the latter case, perhaps this was because a consensus prevailed about what those freedoms meant. If so, the executive and legislative branches were no more inclined to tread upon those defined freedoms than the judicial branch was to expand their reach.

Additionally, the Waite Court was less likely to enforce the Bill of Rights against federal actions than it was to apply the Fourteenth Amendment against actions by states in civil rights cases. The irony was, as the previous section showed, that the Court seemed as unreceptive to federal legislation promoting racial civil rights as it was to state legislation restricting such rights. It appears that obviously discriminatory state policies tended to fare poorly under the Fourteenth Amendment in the Waite Court because a class of people had been singled out officially for adverse treatment. The amendment embodied a right, as Justice Strong wrote in *Strauder v. West Virginia*, "to exemption from unfriendly legislation against them distinctively as colored." Moreover, there seemed to be little doubt in anyone's mind concerning Justice Miller's "one pervading purpose" of the Reconstruction amendments, even though justices could disagree among themselves whether Congress had appropriately pursued, or the states had complied with, that purpose.

In contrast, the freedoms under the Bill of Rights applied to everyone, whether the freedoms were broad or narrow. It was not as if one class or race was entitled to freedom of speech and another class or race was not. *Reynolds* was no exception to this principle. The Mormons' claim to a polygamous lifestyle was not part of the free exercise of religion that the First Amendment encompassed. Given the fact that the Waite Court justices had come of age politically during the years when Jacksonian ideas shaped the political culture, it is entirely understandable that they would exhibit a deference toward, even a faith in, the people's representatives. It was the political system they knew. As will be seen, this was a characteristic that permeated their outlook on the Fourteenth Amendment's due process clause in its noncriminal context as well. If so, rights shared by all usually meant for the Court what the people, through their representatives, wanted them to mean. Only after the Waite era would this nod toward government by the people give way to heightened judicial scrutiny of what the people had done.

Due Process of Law and the State Police Power

The phrase "due process of law" has an ancient origin. It first appeared in an English statute during the reign of King Edward III (1327–1377): "No man of what state or condition he be, shall be put out of his lands or tenements, nor taken, nor imprisoned, nor disinherited, nor put to death, without he be brought to answer by due process of law." The phrase in turn derived from the "law of the land" clause in the Magna Carta of 1215. Early U.S. state constitutions carried over parts of both and expanded on them, as illustrated by the Massachusetts Constitution of 1780: "No subject shall be arrested, imprisoned, despoiled, or deprived of his property, immunities, or privileges, put out of the protection of the law, exiled, or deprived of his life, liberty, or estate, but by the judgment of his peers or the law of the land." The thrust across the centuries was procedural. As it acted on the people, government was bound to follow custom or preestablished procedures and protocol. Otherwise individual liberty would be imperiled.

A major development in U.S. constitutional law in the late nineteenth and early twentieth centuries was the transformation of due process of law from a procedural limitation on government into a substantive one. Due process moved from being solely a restriction on the manner in which government proceeded against its citizens (how something could be done) to a restriction on policy choices themselves (what could be done). The significance of this shift can scarcely be exaggerated. Although the national government had been restrained by the due process clause of the Fifth Amendment since 1791, it was only with ratification of the Fourteenth Amendment in 1868 that an identical clause affected the states. The second sentence of section one of the amendment reads in part, "No State shall . . . deprive any person of life, liberty, or property, without due process of law." An expansion of the scope of due process would now give judges the final say on the acceptability of nearly every public policy, state or federal. Practically from its beginning the Waite Court was deluged with cases in which unhappy litigants sought to deploy due process as a shield against state legislation they considered undesirable. At heart they wanted to use due process to curb the state police power.

The police power of the states encompasses far more than ordinary criminal laws. It is that great mass of governing authority that the states did not surrender to the national government when the Constitution was ratified. Chief Justice Marshall referred to it in *Brown v. Maryland* (1827) as residual, comprising what was left over of the states' powers beyond those other great prerogatives of eminent domain and taxation. In the *License Cases* (1847), Chief Justice Taney referred to the police power as the "power to *govern men and things* within the limits of its own dominion." This power was considerable in scope because of the distinctly different bases of state and national legislative powers in federal constitutional law. Under the doctrine of reserved powers, states legislate at will unless prohibited by the U.S. Constitution or their own state constitutions. In contrast, under the doctrine of enumerated powers, Congress legislates only on the basis of express, implied, or resulting grants of power from the U.S. Constitution.

The scope of state police power was impressive because of the Constitution itself or, more accurately, because of what the Constitution did not say. Although concerns about state legislative abuses in part led to the Philadelphia Convention of 1787, the Constitution as authored by the framers contained only a trio of general limitations on state legislatures that might meaningfully limit the police power. Those were the two clauses in section ten of Article I banning "any . . . ex post facto Law, or Law impairing the Obligation of Contracts," and the implied limitations on state laws that were found unduly to interfere with interstate commerce, authority over which was an enumerated power of Congress. In *Calder v. Bull* (1798), the Supreme Court confined the meaning of ex post facto laws to retrospective criminal statutes that adversely affected a defendant. In *Dartmouth College v. Woodward* (1819) the Court decided that a corporate charter was among those contractual obligations states could not impair. But the Court largely enfeebled the contracts clause by making clear in 1837 that the contract rights protected against state impairment included only those that the contract expressly granted, not those that might be implied (*Charles River Bridge v. Warren Bridge*). The police power was so firmly entrenched that the Waite Court upheld Mississippi's ban on lotteries against a contracts clause challenge, even though the state had chartered a lottery for twenty-five years and had agreed not to suppress the lottery during that time. "All agree," wrote the chief justice, "that the legislature cannot bargain away the police power of the State. . . . No one denies . . . that it extends to all matters affecting the public health or the public morals." The charter held by the lottery was only a license to do business for a certain period of time or until the government changed its mind and rescinded the charter (*Stone v. Mississippi*, 1880).

As discussed in the next section, the police power also included considerable control of commerce-related matters. However, the power could not extend to regulation that needed to be national in scope, that was plainly a regulation of interstate commerce, or that conflicted with an existing act of Congress (*Cooley v. Board of Wardens*, 1851). Thus, by the time Waite became chief justice, states had long enjoyed ample discretion to enact laws on various subjects under their reserved police power.

This situation partly explains why, from 1810 (when the first state statute was invalidated on federal constitutional grounds in *Fletcher v. Peck*) through 1873 (the end of the Chase Court), the number of state laws declared unconstitutional by the Supreme Court averaged barely more than one per year.

The Constitution's nearly nonexistent limitations on state legislation became an acute concern in the last third of the nineteenth century. As described in chapter one, the nation was undergoing unprecedented economic and demographic changes. States responded with an equally unprecedented volume of legislation to cope with new conditions. Did states possess a nearly boundless discretion in their choice of policies? The tradition of popular sovereignty inherited from the Jacksonian heyday of the 1830s suggested that they did.

Thus, the question after 1868 was whether the Fourteenth Amendment made a difference on state police power. Were any substantive restrictions, beyond those protecting the newly freed slaves, concealed within the second sentence of section one? As explained early in this chapter, this was the sentence containing the privileges and immunities, due process, and equal protection clauses. Justice Miller's opinion for the Court in the *Slaughterhouse Cases* (1873) enervated the first and minimized the other two. Justice Field's passionate dissent focused nearly exclusively on privileges and immunities. He viewed that clause as a vehicle to provide national protection for "the common rights of the American citizens," but his opinion ignored the due process clause. Justice Swayne's dissent mentioned due process briefly, but it was Bradley's dissent that characterized the state-imposed monopoly as a violation of due process.

"Rights to life, liberty, and the pursuit of happiness [referring to the Declaration of Independence] are equivalent to the rights of life, liberty, and property," Bradley explained. "These are the fundamental rights which can only be taken away by due process of law, and which can only be interfered with, or the enjoyment of which can only be modified, by lawful regulations necessary or proper for the mutual good of all." He seemed to be suggesting that due process was something more (although not less) than proceeding according to the law. The statute challenged in the *Slaughterhouse Cases*, after all, had become law in Louisiana in the prescribed manner. No one maintained that it had not. The Fourteenth Amendment did not say that government could not take a person's life, liberty, or property, but only that when it did, the taking must adhere to due process. In Bradley's mind, the taking or sharp curtailment of the butchers' livelihood (liberty and property) was not "for the mutual good of all" and so could not be squared with due process. That is, not everything passed in the form of a law qualified as "the law of the land" referred to in the Magna Carta and early state constitutions. Instead, a fundamental requirement of legislation was that it be for the mutual good of all, a stipulation that, for Bradley, was totally absent in this instance. His was not an argument against the police power, but an argument that

Fourteenth Amendment due process imposed limits on that power. In Bradley's mind, it was for judges to decide when those limits should be applied. Bradley had taken an important step: With the privileges and immunities clause having been laid to rest, any further efforts to marshal the Fourteenth Amendment to substantively limit the police power would probably rely on the due process clause.

Where did this idea of a substantive aspect of due process originate? In his opinion for the Court in *Dred Scott v. Sandford* (1857), Chief Justice Taney declared that a congressional ban on slavery in the territories was a taking of property without due process of law in violation of the Fifth Amendment. Of course, no self-respecting Lincoln or Grant appointee to the Supreme Court would cite *Dred Scott* approvingly. For those hoping to give due process a substantive twist, there was fortunately a more respectable pedigree in *Wynehamer v. People* (1856). That New York Court of Appeals decision overturned a comprehensive state prohibition statute "for the prevention of intemperance, pauperism and crime." It forbade all owners of intoxicating beverages from selling them under any circumstances, except for medicinal purposes. According to the most thorough scholarly treatment of the subject, this decision "comprises a new starting point in the history of due process of law. . . . The main proposition of the decision . . . is that the legislature cannot destroy by any method whatever what by previous law was property" (Corwin 1987, 179). This was so, according to Judge George Comstock (one of several judges who wrote opinions in the case), even when the statute was for the "absolute benefit" of the people of the state. "In a government like ours," Comstock continued, "theories of public good or public necessity may be so plausible, or even so truthful, as to command popular majorities. But whether truthful or plausible merely, and by whatever numbers they are assented to, there are some absolute private rights beyond their reach, and among these the constitution places the right of property" (Mason and Stephenson 2002, 341).

On the same day that Waite became chief justice, the eight-justice bench decided *Bartemeyer v. Iowa* (1874), which challenged on Fourteenth Amendment grounds the state's ban on the sale of intoxicants. Although the statute was upheld unanimously, comments by several justices on the subject of due process echoed sentiments expressed in *Wynehamer*, indicating intellectual ferment was underway. Miller, as author of the majority opinion in the *Slaughterhouse Cases*, had denied the pertinence of due process for commercial regulations. In this case, he went out of his way to suggest that, had Iowa's ban applied to intoxicants Bartemeyer owned prior to enactment of the law (as in *Wynehamer*), "two very grave questions would arise, namely: Whether this would be a statute depriving him of his property without due process of law; and secondly, whether, if it were so, it would . . . call for judicial action by this court." Justice Bradley's concurring opinion revisited the *Slaughterhouse Cases*, noting that the Louisiana monopoly was not a police regulation, "intended for the preservation of the public health and the public order," but a violation of the due process clause. Justice Field addressed the due process question directly, forthrightly, and without Miller's equivocation, declaring that, applied to intoxicants owned prior to the law's enactment, the statute would be arbitrary and a confiscation of property without due process. Like Bradley, he contrasted a due process violation with one in which a less deficient regulation was protective of the "health and morals of the community. All property, even the most harmless in its nature, is equally subject to the power of the state in this respect with the most noxious." What no one acknowledged was the potential of this ruminating for expanded judicial oversight. Who decided whether a regulation furthered a community's health and morals or its mutual good? Was that a legislative or a judicial question?

That second question confronted the Waite Court soon after the new chief's arrival. Resolution of the question in *Munn v. Illinois* (1877) constituted the most important due process decision of the nineteenth century. Shortly before his own appointment to the Supreme Court, Felix Frankfurter exceeded even that accolade, placed the ruling "among the dozen most important decisions in our constitutional law" (Frankfurter 1937, 83). Its effects still reverberate in the twenty-first century.

"The country will look with deep interest to its decision in this case," editorialized *The Nation* ("The Right to Confiscate" 1874, 200). The case in reference was actually one of eight lawsuits, collectively known as the *Granger Cases*. The cases challenged state-set rates for warehouses and railroads, and the owners appealed to the Supreme Court in 1874 and 1875. Arguments in the railroad cases were heard between October 25 and November 4, 1875. Arguments in the warehouse case were heard on January 14 and 18, 1876. All were carried over to the following term and decisions in each were announced on March 1, 1877, practically on the eve of Rutherford B. Hayes's inauguration as the new president. This litigation entangled the Supreme Court in the most visible and vocal political movement of the immediate post–Civil War years.

At least two developments had allowed U.S. farmers, especially those in the Midwest, to become the most productive in the world: the revolution in agricultural machinery and an expanded, even continental, railroad network. The first was symbolized by the perfection of Cyrus McCormick's mechanical reaper in the 1850s. The reaper and other labor-saving equipment allowed farmers to cultivate greater acreage with greater grain yields than ever before. The second development was witnessed in the formation of new railroad companies and the construction of new rail routes. These gave farmers speedy and efficient access to far-flung markets and suppliers that had been largely out of reach of most producers in the prewar years. For example, rail shipments of wheat into Chicago by 1868 were counted in the tens of millions of tons, allowing the city to become the grain capital of the world. Thanks to the telegraph, commodity fluctuations in Chicago nearly instantly affected prices in New York, and, with the newly laid Atlantic cable, in England. With expanded opportunity, however, came increased dependency. Farmers were no longer self-sufficient or reliant on local markets alone. Agricultural prosperity hinged on continued access to distant markets at a reasonable cost.

Squeezed by declines in grain prices in the late 1860s and very early 1870s—thanks to overproduction during the war—farmers faced hikes in freight rates and complained about erratic and unresponsive service from the same railroads on which their livelihood now depended. Higher charges for transporting and storing grain, in turn, seriously and negatively impacted an industry in which a difference of a few cents in commodity prices could spell the difference between farm affluence and ruin.

The owners and operators of the large grain warehouses to whom farmers paid fees to store grain prior to sale compounded the farmers' potential hardships. Of thirteen such firms in Chicago, one of the biggest was the partnership of Munn and Scott with a storage capacity of nearly 3 million bushels. By 1868 Munn and Scott had formed an interlocking pool with four other large warehouse companies, allowing them to fix prices and raise fees. By 1870 various unscrupulous practices came to light, with the *Chicago Tribune* editorially describing the warehouse operators as "rapacious, blood sucking insects" (Magrath 1987, 124).

Farmers became convinced they were being victimized by powerful financial interests beyond their control. They vowed to take control. Founded in 1867 initially as a social and educational association of Midwestern farmers, the National Grange of the Patrons of Husbandry (the Grangers) turned to state governments for relief. "The State must either absorb the railroads or the railroads will absorb the State," the Grangers cried (Warren 1926, II, 574). In Illinois, the first state to act, the Grangers' efforts were aided by an unexpected alliance with grain merchants in the Chicago Board of Trade, who also had an interest in imposing controls on the predacious warehouses. The timing was perfect. A state constitutional convention was underway, and together the grain merchants and grain producers succeeded in obtaining a provision in the new 1870 constitution authorizing needed regulation. The legislature in 1871 then enacted a set of rate regulations and other restrictions for the railroads and warehouses, and established the Railroad and Warehouse Commission to enforce them.

Munn and Scott took the lead in defying the regulations by refusing to comply with the new licensing requirements and rates and by denying access to grain inspectors. The partnership challenged the regulatory regime on grounds including a violation of the Fourteenth Amendment's due process clause. After a delay due to the great Chicago fire in October 1871, the state won a $100 judgment against the firm in 1872. (Affected railroads put up similar resistance, but, as their legal attacks also involved the commerce and contracts clauses, theirs will be examined later in this chapter.) Ironically, Munn and Scott failed financially in the same year after the collapse of a highly speculative venture to corner the world's grain market. Ira Munn and George Scott declared personal bankruptcy and were expelled from the Board of

Trade. Their interests were purchased by George Amour and Company, and the case of *Munn v. Illinois* moved from the Illinois Supreme Court, which sustained the rate regulations, to the U.S. Supreme Court.

Munn and the railroad cases attracted nationwide attention. Much published commentary assured the business community that the laws would be struck down. Former Justice Benjamin Curtis was one of three attorneys who advised the Chicago and North Western Railroad that Wisconsin's rate statute (called the Potter Law) was unconstitutional. Supreme Court argument in *Munn* and the railroad cases pitted state attorneys general against some of the highest-priced and most sought-after courtroom advocates of the day. These advocates included former U.S. Senator and Interior Secretary Orville H. Browning of Illinois, who had been a candidate for Miller's seat on the Court; U.S. Senator Frederick Frelinghuysen of New Jersey; former U.S. Attorney General William Evarts; and Justice Field's brother David Dudley Field. They maintained that the regulations amounted to a confiscation of property. In incendiary language, they claimed that the statutes marked "the beginning of the operations of the [Paris] commune in the legislation of this country" (Magrath 1987, 132). Counsel for the states maintained that the regulatory schemes were reasonable responses to protect the public interest from predatory pricing and poor service. Months after oral argument, the justices decided the fate of the Granger laws when they met in conference on November 18, 1876.

When the cases came down on March 1, the states prevailed in each by a vote of 7–2. Surely realizing the momentous nature of the principal Fourteenth Amendment question involved, Chief Justice Waite had assumed the opinion-writing responsibilities in *Munn* and the railroad cases. Because *Munn* seemed the least encumbered by other federal constitutional issues, it became Waite's platform to explain why the regulations were compatible with due process of law and therefore why no judicial intervention was warranted. His opinion consumed about fourteen pages in the *Reports*—for Waite's time that was an unusually long opinion to develop what amounted to little more than a single point.

Noting that until 1868 the state could undoubtedly have enacted the legislation under its police power, the question was whether the Fourteenth Amendment imposed some new restriction. The due process clause, Waite explained, "prevents the States from doing that which will operate as . . . a deprivation." He looked to English law for guidance as to what had been accepted practice. Here Justice Bradley (a former railroad attorney) had come to his aid with considerable research, including a seventeenth-century treatise by Lord Chief Justice Hale from which Waite quoted: "[W]hen private property is 'affected with a public interest,' it ceases to be juris privati only. . . . Property does become clothed with a public interest when used in a manner to make it of public consequence, and affect the community at large." In such situations (Waite cited several examples from English practice and the early

United States), "the owner must submit to be controlled by the public for the common good. . . . He may withdraw his grant by discontinuing the use; but, so long as he maintains the use, he must submit to the control." Apparently Illinois Attorney General James Edsall had been thinking along similar lines. As his brief in defense of the statute argued, "Whenever any person pursues a public calling and sustains such relations to the public that the people must of necessity deal with him . . . , then in order to prevent extortion and an abuse of his position, the price he may charge for his services may be regulated by law."

That point established by Waite, it was necessary "to ascertain whether the warehouses of these plaintiffs . . . come within the operation of this principle." After reviewing the nature and scope of the warehouse business, he concluded: "Certainly, if any business can be clothed 'with a public interest, and cease to be juris privati only,' this has been. It may not be made so by the operation of the Constitution of Illinois or this statute, but it is by the facts." The warehouses "stand . . . in the very 'gateway of commerce,' and take a toll from all who pass."

The need for legislation thus derived from the specific facts at hand, and so one looked to the situation that confronted the state legislature. Little if any judicial second-guessing of the legislature about those facts was in order. "For our purposes we must assume," Waite explained, "that, if a state of facts could exist that would justify such legislation, it actually did exist when the statute now under consideration was passed. If no state of circumstances could exist to justify such a statute, then we may declare this one void, because it is in excess of the legislative power of the State. But if it could, we must presume it did." This point established the validity of the regulation in principle, but did the Court have a role in ascertaining the fairness of the rates that the legislature set?

The owners insisted that they were entitled to reasonable compensation and that the legislatively fixed rates were too low, the equivalent of taking of property without due process of law. "The controlling fact is the power to regulate at all," Waite replied. "If that exists, the right to establish the maximum of charge, as one of the means of regulation, is implied." Thus he denied that the reasonableness of the rates "was a judicial and not a legislative question." Courts had no role in overseeing that part of the legislative judgment. The power to set rates, Waite admitted, was subject to abuse, "but that is no argument against its existence. For protection against abuses by Legislatures the people must resort to the polls, not to the courts." That sentence must have seemed hollow, even mischievous, to those who challenged the law. After all, the people had successfully resorted to the polls for protection against abuses by the warehouse operators and the railroads, and the operators and railroad magnates had looked, in vain, to the courts for redress.

Waite's opinion was highly significant in emphasizing legislative power and minimizing the judicial role in at least two ways. First, legislatures had wide latitude in their judgment regarding the types of businesses for which rates could be set. Waite did not hand legislators a blank check, but he emphasized that if a state of circumstances could exist to warrant regulation, "we must presume that it did." That left a little room for judicial discretion, but not much. It was as if Waite was acknowledging the vast changes the country was undergoing. Such changes called for legislation, and because conditions were new, courts had to be tolerant of various legislative experiments. Perhaps he should have cited Justice Curtis's statement about "settled usage" and due process from *Murray's Lessee* (1856), but he did not.

Second, the rates that were set were not judicially reviewable. It would be up to the regulated business to work with its legislature to secure favorable rates. But once the rates were in place, there was no federal constitutional question left to pursue. The question that remains about Waite's opinion is whether property affected with a public interest was a category of property subject to rate regulation, or whether such regulation was justified only if the property was affected with a public interest.

Field's was the only dissenting opinion. In a short paragraph Strong indicated agreement with Field's position, and regretted not having had time to prepare his own. He as well as Field had been a member of the Electoral Commission of 1877 that was literally finishing its business as *Munn* was announced. Field had requested additional time to prepare and to file his dissent, and the Court acceded to his wishes. It is unfortunate that Strong did not do the same. Although Field had dissented in the *Slaughterhouse Cases*, Strong had been in the majority. It would therefore have been instructive to have had Strong's views plainly laid out in 1877. That might also have made him a more visible member of the Waite Court.

Field's dissent starkly restated the issue that the case raised: "whether it is within the competency of a State to fix the compensation which an individual may receive for the use of his own property in his private business, and for his services in connection with it." The fiery Californian refused to accept the applicability of Lord Hale's concept of property affected with a public interest. Hale and others had in mind "property dedicated by the owner to public uses, or to property the use of which was granted by the government, or in connection with which special privileges were conferred." None of those fit the warehouse operators. "[T]he storage of grain . . . is a private business, in which the public are interested only as they are interested in the storage of other products of the soil, or in articles of manufacture." If the owners had to submit to prices imposed by the legislature, "all property and all business in the State are held at the mercy of a majority of its Legislature. The public has no greater interest in the use of buildings for the storage of grain than it has in the use of buildings for the residences of families . . . ; and, according to the doctrine announced, the Legislature may fix the rent of all tenements used for residences, without reference to the cost of their erection." If all the owner retained was title and possession, then the guarantee of due process of law "does not merit the encomiums it has received." Field insisted that the concept had a "more extended operation."

So conceived, due process left ample room for the state police power. It was designed to protect "the peace, good order, morals and health of the community" and all that affected those ends came within its scope. For example, eight years after *Munn*, Field found "no rational ground" for considering as a violation of due process a state's insistence on double damages in tort actions if a railroad failed to fence its track (*Missouri Pacific Railway v. Humes*, 1885). But, as he insisted in his *Munn* dissent, "compensation which the owners of property, not having any special rights or privileges from the government in connection with it, may demand for its use, or for their own services in union with it, forms no element of consideration in prescribing regulations for that purpose." In short, rate fixing was something that the police power did not encompass. Field was being consistent. Just as he rejected the curtailment of livelihoods in the *Slaughterhouse Cases* as being within the police power, so also a confiscation of property via state-imposed rates was beyond legitimate state power.

Field predicted incorrectly that *Munn* would lead to publicly set prices for "everything, from a calico gown to a city mansion." But he correctly grasped the broad implications of Waite's opinion. As one commentator surmised in 1883, "No other decision has ever been made in the course of our judicial history—not even excepting the notorious *Dred Scott Case*—which threatens such disastrous consequences to the future welfare and prosperity of the country" (Warren 1926, II, 582). As late as 1890 another commentator still regarded the implications of *Munn* as terrifying. "Our boasted security in property rights," wrote Charles Marshall, "falls away for the lack of a constitutional guaranty against this sovereign power thus discovered in our legislatures. It is apparent," he continued, "that against the whim of a temporary majority, inflamed with class prejudice, envy or revenge, the property of no man is safe." Changing conditions made it more necessary to somehow dislodge *Munn*. "[T]he danger is even greater in an age teeming with shifting theories of social reform and economic science, which seem to have but one common principle—the subjection of private property to government control for the good—or alleged good—of the public" (Marshall 1890, 912).

Efforts to undermine *Munn* were already underway. A year after the decision in the *Granger Cases*, leading attorneys organized the American Bar Association (ABA). By 1881 the ABA had embarked on a deliberate and persistent campaign of education designed to change legal thinking about the police power in rate and nonrate regulation situations alike. Justice Miller in 1878 did not ease the fledgling ABA's sensibilities about the Waite Court's continued insistence that the Fourteenth Amendment's due process clause imposed few limitations on the states. In a barely veiled admonition to the profession, Miller seemed plainly exasperated about an unhappy litigant's due process objections to a land assessment. "While [due process] has been a part of the Constitution, as a restraint upon the power of the states, only a very few years, the docket of this court is crowded with cases in which we are asked to hold that State courts and State legislatures have deprived their own citizens of life, liberty, and property without due process of law. There is here abundant evidence," he continued, "that there exists some strange misconception of the scope of this provision . . . in the Fourteenth Amendment. In fact, it would seem from the character of many of the cases before us, . . . that the clause . . . is looked upon as a means of bringing to the test of the decision of this court the abstract opinions of every unsuccessful litigant in a State court of the justice of the decision against him, and of the merits of the legislation on which such a decision may be founded." There could be no taking of property without due process of law "when . . . he has, by the laws of the State, a fair trial in a court of justice, according to the modes of proceeding applicable to such a case" (*Davidson v. New Orleans*, 1878). The process that was due seemed thus to be whatever a state wished to provide.

Yet it was Miller's own words in *Davidson* that kept the flickering flame of substantive due process from being snuffed out altogether. "It seems to us that a statute which declares in terms, *and without more*, that the full and exclusive title of a described piece of land, which is now in A., shall be and is hereby vested in B., would, if effectual, deprive A. of his property without due process of law, within the meaning of the constitutional provision" (emphasis added). The suggestion in the addition of the words "and without more" seemed to be at odds with the rest of his opinion. Now it appeared that the legislature had to have a sound reason for its actions and that reason might be judicially reviewable. If so, the Court would find itself looking at the merits of legislation—exactly what Miller took pains to say that the Court did not want to do.

Less than three months after Miller's admonition in *Davidson*, Chief Justice Waite spoke for the Court in *R. F. and P. Railroad Co. v. Richmond* (1878) that upheld a ban on the operation of locomotives on city streets. "All property . . . ," wrote the chief, "is subject to the *legitimate* control of the government." Furthermore, "*[a]ppropriate* regulation of the use of property is not 'taking' property within the meaning of the constitutional provision" (emphasis added). The italicized words begged the question as to who would determine what control was legitimate and what regulation was appropriate.

That judges had a role to play was apparent in Justice Field's opinion for the Court in *Soon Hing v. Crowley* (1885). A San Francisco ordinance forbade the washing or ironing of clothes in a commercial laundry between the hours of ten at night and six in the morning, and all day on Sunday. The ban had the twin objectives of fire safety and public health, explained the Court's only Californian. "[I]t is of the utmost consequence in a city subject, as San Francisco is, the greater part of the year, to high winds, and composed principally . . . of wooden buildings, that regulations of a strict character should be adopted to prevent the possibility of fires. . . . [T]he municipal authorities are the appropriate judges," he explained. "Their regulations in the matter are not subject to any interference by the federal tribunals *unless they are made for the occasion for invading the substantial rights of persons*, and no such invasion is caused by the regulation in question" (emphasis added). The ban on Sunday labor was not a "promotion of religious observances, but [derived] from [the legislature's] right to protect all persons from the physical and moral debasement which comes from uninterrupted labor." In short, the ordinance made sense.

In fact, the Waite Court never held any state statute or state-imposed rate to be a violation of due process of law. Yet the progression of cases after *Munn* indicated that an increasing number of justices no longer perceived such a result to be the product of what Miller in *Davidson* had termed a "strange misconception." For later courts, case rulings would proceed along two parallel tracks: a declining hesitancy to consider the reasonableness of rates a judicial question, and a growing tendency to second-guess legislatures on the need for other forms of regulation of property.

That much seemed clear from the Waite Court's otherwise deferential decision in *Mugler v. Kansas* (1887), which upheld the state's ban on the brewing of beer, even for home consumption. "[I]t is difficult to perceive any ground for the judiciary to declare that the prohibition . . . is not *fairly adapted* to the end of protecting the community against the evils which confessedly result from the excessive use of ardent spirits" (emphasis added), wrote Justice Harlan, the Court's connoisseur of fine Kentucky whiskey. The ban seemed well within the police power. But Harlan emphasized that not every law purporting to be a health or safety measure would satisfy the standards of due process.

> The courts are not bound by mere forms, nor are they to be misled by mere pretenses. They are at liberty—indeed, are under a solemn duty—to look at the *substance of things*, whenever they enter upon the inquiry whether the Legislature has transcended the limits of its authority. If, therefore, a statute purporting to have been enacted to protect the public health, the public morals, or the public safety, has no *real or substantial relation* to those objects, or is a palpable invasion of rights secured by the fundamental law, it is the duty of the courts to so adjudge, and thereby give effect to the Constitution. (emphasis added)

Harlan had not joined the Court until shortly after *Munn* was decided, when he took the seat vacated by Justice David Davis. Other post-*Munn* additions to the Court who took part in *Mugler* included Justices Woods (1881), Matthews (1881), Gray (1882), and Samuel Blatchford (1882). Perhaps Field's dissent in the *Granger Cases*, like the proverbial water dripping on a stone, was beginning to have an effect.

The *Mugler* challenge to the Kansas law was no doubt more difficult because the subject was alcoholic beverages. The outcome perhaps would have been different had the prohibited commodity not been morally tainted. As already noted, lotteries were equally suspect, and the Fuller Court later would look kindly on legislation regulating other dubious products like oleomargarine. But in other situations lacking a moral overtone, a different bench staffed with justices less disposed to accept such legislation would have no difficulty in concluding that the prohibition was not fairly adapted to a goal such as public health or had no real or substantial relation to it.

Only a decade separated *Munn* and *Mugler*, yet in terms of constitutional interpretation and the Court's understanding of its role, they stand ages apart. Although the Waite Court professed belief in the breadth of the police power, it laid the foundation for its judicial transformation. Within two years of Waite's death, six justices repudiated the hands-off approach of *Munn*. (Bradley, Gray, and Lamar dissented.) An opinion by Blatchford, joined by Waite-era Justices Field and Harlan, with Miller concurring separately, held that the reasonableness of rates could not be left by the legislature to a state commission. The rate determination had to be subject to judicial review (*Chicago, Milwaukee and St. Paul Railroad Co. v. Minnesota*, 1890). That decision effected a judicial revolution. The Court was well on its way to becoming what Miller himself had feared in the *Slaughterhouse Cases*—a "perpetual censor" of state legislation.

The Commerce Clause

Waite Court justices were the first to encounter cases involving due process of law, civil rights, and the Bill of Rights on any significant scale. As discussed in the previous sections of this chapter, in many ways these elements of U.S. constitutional law literally began to take shape in the Waite Court. Another important category of Waite Court judicial business involved the commerce clause. Indeed, there were some fifty such cases, or slightly more than three per term on average. Yet cases under the commerce clause had been part of the Supreme Court's work for a solid half-century before Waite became chief justice. In this area of constitutional jurisprudence, Waite's bench was hardly writing on a blank slate. Given the importance and complexity of commerce clause cases, some background on this constitutional provision is a necessary first step in understanding the Waite Court's important decisions in this field.

"The Congress shall have Power . . . ," section 8 of Article I of the Constitution declares, "[t]o regulate Commerce with foreign Nations, and among the several States, and with the Indian Tribes. . . ." These twenty-one words have long been among the most important in the nation's fundamental charter, for both Congress and the states as well. This is because the commerce clause has two dimensions. In its active mode, it empowers Congress; in its dormant or negative mode, it is a self-executing limitation on the states, even in the absence of any legislation by Congress. "The desire of the Forefathers to federalize regulation of foreign and interstate commerce stands in sharp contrast to their jealous preservation of the State's power over its internal affairs," Justice Robert H. Jackson advised over a half century ago. "No other federal power was so universally assumed to be necessary. No other state power was so readily relinquished" (*Hood v. Du Mond*, 1949).

As a grant of authority to Congress, the commerce clause in its active mode did not become a constitutional battleground until the 1890s, soon after the Waite Court, as Congress took its first big steps in creating national economic policy. Thus, the Waite Court's commerce cases almost entirely involved the clause in its dormant mode. These were characterized by challenges to state laws that arguably interfered with commerce "among the several States." But this fact made the Waite bench's commerce clause decisions no less important.

As important as congressional enactments may be, measured by volume, most legislation in the United States, in Waite's day as in ours, originates from state and local governments. As explained in the previous section, these laws are examples of the police power, that general, residual, and regulatory power retained by the states under the Constitution. As also noted in the previous section, states in the last third of the nineteenth century were under increasing pressure to cope with problems arising from growing populations, burgeoning industrialism, and expanded financial and agricultural markets. Through a variety of laws they sought to protect the health and safety of their citizens and otherwise to foster a healthful economic climate. Frequently they taxed commercial activities as a way of raising revenue to pay for improvements to infrastructure and to compensate their treasuries for services rendered to those who profited from doing business within the state.

However, any of these categories of legislation could quickly generate constitutional controversies when parties disadvantaged by the regulations alleged either that they were out-and-out regulations of interstate commerce or that they had an adverse effect on interstate commerce. Moreover, as the century advanced an economy ever more interconnected and national in scope made it easier for such laws to be perceived as having an interstate impact. Reconciling the commerce clause with local authority therefore became an important judicial task. "The simple fact," Justice Anthony Kennedy has explained, "was that in the early years of the Republic, Congress seldom perceived the necessity to exercise its power in circumstances where its authority would be called into question. The Court's initial task, therefore, was to elaborate the theories that would permit the States to act where Congress had not done so" (*United States v. Lopez*, 1995).

Intriguing questions about the meaning of the commerce clause and the limits to state authority were first presented to the Supreme Court in 1824. *Gibbons v. Ogden* involved the steamboat monopoly, which the New York legislature had granted to Robert R. Livingston and Robert Fulton, their heirs, and others, bestowing on them an exclusive right to operate steamboats in the state's waters. Ex-governor Aaron Ogden of New Jersey held a license under the monopoly to operate a steam-powered ferry between New York and New Jersey. Thomas Gibbons, who possessed a coasting license under a congressional statute but no license from the monopoly, operated boats on the same route in competition with Ogden. New York's high court upheld the monopoly and maintained that Congress had no direct jurisdiction over internal commerce or waters. Daniel Webster, arguing for Gibbons on appeal to the U.S. Supreme Court, asserted that Congress alone could regulate high branches of commerce. Counsel for the monopoly claimed that a concurrent power existed whenever such a power was not clearly denied by the Constitution. Both sides agreed that if an actual collision of state and national power occurred the latter must prevail, but counsel for the monopoly held that state power gave way only to the extent needed to give effect to the federal law. Accordingly navigation on state waters was to remain under state control.

Chief Justice John Marshall could have decided the case on the narrow grounds that both state and nation had acted within their powers, and that because the state law conflicted with the federal licensing act it must yield. He chose instead to examine the nature of the commerce power before finding the existence of a conflict. Commerce was more than traffic; "it is intercourse," and comprehended navigation. He reiterated the point that commerce "among" the states did not stop at state lines but "may be introduced into the interior." The power to regulate was "complete in itself, may be exercised to its utmost extent, and acknowledges no limitations, other than are prescribed in the Constitution." Though the states retained authority to enact inspection, pilotage, and health laws, even here Congress could enter the field if it chose. Marshall suggested, but did not squarely hold, that the commerce power was vested exclusively in Congress.

Although Marshall described the subject matter of commerce to allow Congress to regulate it in the most sweeping terms, he did not overlook the tremendous power reserved to the states. But on what authority would state policy rest? Marshall's view on this question came out most clearly in *Willson v. Black Bird Creek Marsh Co.* (1829). The Delaware legislature had authorized the firm to build a dam across a creek for the purpose of reclaiming marshland. Willson, who owned a sloop licensed under national authority, broke through the dam and continued to navigate the creek. The company sued for trespass. Upholding the Delaware act, Marshall ruled,

> The act of assembly by which the plaintiffs were authorized to construct their dam, shows plainly that this is one of those many creeks, passing through a deep, level marsh, adjoining the Delaware, up which the tide flows for some distance. The value of the property on its banks must be enhanced by excluding the water from the marsh, and the health of the inhabitants probably improved. Measures

> calculated to produce these objects, provided they do not come into collision with the powers of the general government, are undoubtedly within those which are reserved to the states. . . .
>
> If Congress had passed any act which bore upon the case; any act in execution of the power to regulate commerce, the object of which was to control state legislation over those small navigable creeks into which the tide flows, and which abound throughout the lower country of the middle and southern states, we should feel not much difficulty in saying that a state law coming in conflict with such act would be void. But Congress has passed no such act. . . .
>
> We do not think, that the act empowering the Black Bird Creek Marsh company to place a dam across the creek, can, *under all the circumstances of the case*, be considered as repugnant to the power to regulate commerce in its dormant state, or as being in conflict with any law passed on the subject. (emphasis added)

This lengthy quotation illustrated the importance of facts, and a judge's perception of them, in the outcome of dormant commerce clause cases. Marshall was at pains to demonstrate the bearing of the dam on land values and the health of the community. As a health measure, enacted under police power, the act was valid until it collided with national authority. (Marshall conveniently ignored the fact that had been decisive in *Gibbons:* that Willson's sloop was federally licensed.)

During Roger B. Taney's tenure as chief justice (1836–1864), the Court confronted the issue Marshall had pointedly sidestepped in *Gibbons v. Ogden:* whether the states could regulate commerce in the absence of federal regulation. The concurrent commerce doctrine advocated by some justices held states could so act. The exclusive commerce doctrine held otherwise. The importance of the issue could not be overstressed. Because Congress was not likely to act positively during this period, an exclusive view of commerce would result in invalidation of any state laws regulating commerce, meaning that commerce would likely remain free from all regulation.

For a time, a consensus on this question eluded the Supreme Court. In a dispute similar to one the Waite Court would face, *New York v. Miln* (1837) generated a confused set of opinions. The case upheld a statute requiring the master on incoming ships to furnish information on passengers. (Some of the confusion in this and other cases was linked to the dispute over slavery, specifically whether persons were subjects of commerce.) In 1847, the even more confused opinions in the *License Cases* revealed the Court's apparent continued inability to settle on any one view of the commerce clause. Although the Court unanimously upheld the state laws in question that regulated imported liquor, it was difficult to understand why. Taney and at least three other justices reasoned that Congress's power over commerce was not exclusive. Others insisted that the laws affected only internal commerce and derived from the state police power, and so were not regulations of commerce among the states. In the *Passenger Cases* (1849), litigants challenged taxes on passengers on incoming vessels. The Court ruled 5–4 that the law conflicted with the Constitution, but the five justices in the majority split two ways on reasoning. For two, congressional power over foreign commerce was exclusive; three would only go as far as basing their votes on the fact the state act conflicted with existing national legislation. Indeed, Benjamin Howard, the official reporter of decisions, was at a loss in trying to characterize the basis of the majority's decision. All he could say as a headnote for the published case was that the statute was invalid.

The law was in this muddle when President Millard Fillmore appointed Benjamin R. Curtis to the Court in 1851. A brilliant Massachusetts lawyer, Curtis became a mediator of the judicial factions and the effective medium through whom a compromise could be reached. *Cooley v. Board of Wardens* (1851) upheld a Pennsylvania pilotage law of 1803 against the charge that the fee it imposed on vessels conflicted with the national commerce power. Clouding the picture was a congressional act of 1789 stating that pilots should be regulated in conformity "with such laws as the states may hereafter enact . . . until further legislative provision shall be made by Congress." "If the states were divested of the power to legislate on this subject by the grant of the commercial power to Congress," Curtis cautioned, "it is plain this act could not confer upon them power thus to legislate." In other words, Congress could not allow what the Constitution prohibited. Curtis then combined elements of the exclusive and concurrent commerce doctrines and fashioned a new formula that legal scholars have called "selective exclusiveness." His middle ground was this: Subjects national in scope demanded uniform regulation; these required congressional legislation, and in the absence of such legislation the states could not act. For subjects of a local character, not requiring uniform legislation, the states could legislate until Congress, by acting on the same subject, displaced or preempted the state law. Where national and state laws were in conflict, the federal rule would prevail.

However, substantial difficulties persisted despite the balanced nature of the *Cooley* doctrine. How did one decide whether a particular subject matter required a national (or uniform) regulation? Was congressional silence an implied declaration that the desired uniformity lay in no regulation? In the absence of a need for uniform regulation, would any state regulation be acceptable? If not, on what grounds would the state law be held to violate the commerce clause? These were some of the questions that awaited the Waite Court.

The fact that nearly all of the Waite Court's commerce cases involved the commerce clause in its dormant state spoke volumes about the Court's role during this period. First, because Congress exercised its active commerce power so infrequently (and then only rarely in a way likely to spark litigation), the U.S. Supreme Court was almost exclusively the only federal presence in the field of interstate commerce. Time and time again, the commerce cases of the Waite era referred to a particular state law's being considered "in the absence of" any national legislation at all on the subject. Second, whether the Court applied the *Cooley* doctrine or some other device to probe the contours of the commerce clause, the reality was that the Court—not Congress—determined the rules for the national commerce.

The *Cooley* doctrine lay at the heart of Justice Field's opinion for a unanimous bench in *Welton v. Missouri* (1876). A state law required peddlers (but no others) to pay a license fee if they sold goods grown, produced, or manufactured out of state. Peddlers dealing entirely in goods grown, produced, or manufactured within the state were exempt from the license. Claimed by the state to be a tax on a calling or occupation, the license, Field reasoned, was "in effect a tax upon the goods themselves." If Missouri could impose a tax on peddlers of out-of-state goods, it could "require such license tax as a condition of their sale from ordinary merchants." The matter was important because the amount of taxes a state could impose was "a matter resting exclusively in its discretion." That much established, Field asked whether discrimination in pricing against goods from outside the state was constitutional. Commerce in goods among the states was a subject "national in character" and so required uniform regulation. "The fact that Congress has not seen fit to prescribe any specific rules to govern interstate commerce does not affect the question. Its inaction on this subject, when considered with reference to its legislation with respect to foreign commerce, is equivalent to a declaration that interstate commerce shall be free and untrammeled." The Missouri law worked counter to that objective and was therefore invalid. Field's opinion was significant in that it drew from *Cooley* an important principal of commerce doctrine. The Constitution was designed to protect a national marketplace and to defeat protectionism: one state's discrimination against commerce from across its borders.

An altered regimen of taxation, however, could remove the commerce clause as an obstacle to state power. *Brown v. Houston* (1885) illustrated this point nine years after *Welton*. Coal shipped by a mining company in Pennsylvania to an agent in New Orleans was subjected to Louisiana's annual tax on movable property while the coal remained on flat boats in the Mississippi River awaiting sale. Justice Bradley reiterated the conclusion Field had drawn in the Missouri case that an absence of regulation by Congress was "indication of its will that the matter shall be left free . . . and any regulation of the subject by the State is repugnant to such freedom." But Bradley concluded that the state tax did not interfere with or restrict "the free introduction of the plaintiffs' coal from the State of Pennsylvania into the State of Louisiana." Unlike the situation in *Welton*, Louisiana's annual tax did not operate exclusively on goods from out of state or on goods in transit through the state to a destination in a third state. "The coal had come to its place of rest, for final disposal or use, and was a commodity in the market of New Orleans. It might continue in that condition for a year or two years, or only for a day." In any event, the coal "had become a part of the general mass of property in the state, and as such it was taxed . . . as all other property in the City of New Orleans was taxed." It was treated exactly like goods that had been produced within the state or were the property of the citizens of the state. There was thus no discrimination against interstate commerce as such.

Brown v. Houston was also noteworthy because it sharply broke with the "original package doctrine" Chief Justice Marshall had spelled out in *Brown v. Maryland* (1827). Marshall had been groping for a way to mark the point at which a state could constitutionally tax goods shipped into the state from a foreign country. That time came when the goods were no longer in their original packaging but had mixed with the interior commerce of the state. Although the 1885 case involved interstate, not foreign, commerce, Marshall had suggested in the 1827 case that the same rule would probably also apply to goods shipped into a state from another state.

"[A] most extraordinary statute" was Justice Miller's comment in *Chy Lung v. Freeman* (1876), decided on the same day as *Henderson v. Mayor of New York*. The latter case struck down a law requiring shipowners to post a bond to indemnify the state when an immigrant passenger became a public charge. The Taney Court had upheld a related statute in *New York v. Miln*, but Miller (with the Court now freed from the slavery controversy) based his claim to the law's unconstitutionality on the *Cooley* doctrine. However, the California law challenged in *Chy Lung* was more narrowly focused. It did not require a bond for all passengers, only those who seemed to pose special risks, such as "lewd and debauched women," among whom the plaintiff had been lumped. Miller worried about the power the statute vested in the port inspector who was entitled to 20 percent of the bond "to prevent entirely vessels engaged in a foreign trade . . . from carrying passengers, or to compel them to submit to systematic extortion of the grossest kind." The statute's "manifest purpose . . . is not to obtain indemnity, but money." Aside from the sordid operational details of the scheme, it violated the Constitution because it not only impeded commerce but infringed congressional authority.

> The passage of laws which concern the admission of citizens and subjects of foreign nations to our shores belongs to Congress, and not to the States. [Congress] has the power to regulate commerce with foreign nations: the responsibility for the character of those regulations, and for the manner of their executive, belongs solely to the national government. If it be otherwise, a single State can, at her pleasure, embroil us in disastrous quarrels with other nations.

Justice Field's emphasis in *Welton* concerning what one might conclude from congressional inaction, however, did not govern the Court's fleeting attention to the commerce clause in the *Granger Cases*. This was the name given to a group of cases presenting common questions that the Supreme Court decided on March 1, 1877. Chief Justice Waite spoke for the 7–2 Court in each one. Illinois had imposed rate regulation on the operators of grain warehouses and on railroads operating within the state. Iowa, Wisconsin, and Minnesota had set railroad rates. In total the Court decided the one warehouse case (*Munn v. Illinois*) and seven railroad cases, with the principal opinions for the latter appearing in *Chicago, Burlington and Quincy Railroad v. Cutts* and *Peik v. Chicago and Northwestern Railway.* All eight cases implicated the limits imposed on the states by the Fourteenth Amendment's due process clause and by the commerce clause. (The railroad cases also involved a third question, whether the rate setting amounted to state impairment of "the Obligation of Contracts," as prohibited by section ten of Article I of the Constitution. The Supreme Court had held in the *Dartmouth College* case of 1819 that a state-granted charter was a contract. *Munn*, the warehouse case, lacked the contract issue because Munn and Scott was a partnership and so had no corporate charter to impair. This aspect of the litigation will be examined below.)

Chief Justice Waite in the railroad cases invoked his *Munn* opinion to dispatch the due process objections. In these remaining seven cases he merely and briefly referred to *Munn* as authority for the principle that the railroads, as far as the Fourteenth Amendment was concerned, enjoyed no immunity from rate regulation. Perhaps surprisingly, especially in light of *Weston*, the commerce clause objection rated barely a single paragraph in any of Waite's opinions in this group of cases, and no mention in Field's dissents. (Justice Strong joined Field's dissent in the railroad cases as he had done in *Munn.*) Remarkably, the chief justice cited no authorities in his brief detour into the commerce clause, nor made any effort to connect the Court's decision with previous decisions.

The commerce clause argument the plaintiffs advanced was not aimed at the threat of protectionism—a state's advantaging its own producers at the expense of those outside the state. Instead, counsel took aim at the threat of what later generations would call "Balkanization"—that is, the phenomenon of states imposing their own regulations on interstate trade, with the cumulative effect being a quarrelsome hobbling of national commercial life. As counsel for Munn and Scott maintained in their brief to the Supreme Court, "If the Legislature of Illinois can thus make commercial rules, the Legislature of New York can do so too. A statute may be passed in regard to the grain elevators at Buffalo, and the farmers and dealers of the west will be subject to such rules as New York pleases to enact, as well as those of Illinois. Every other State may exercise the same power, and it is to be supposed that retaliatory legislation would be the sure result. The object of the union of these States, which was to remove just such a state of affairs in the confederation, would be defeated."

The chief justice was unimpressed. The warehouses "are used as instruments by those engaged in State as well as those engaged in interstate commerce, but they are no more necessarily a part of commerce itself than the dray or the cart by which, but for them, grain [could not] be transferred from one railroad station to another. Incidentally, they may become connected with interstate commerce, but not necessarily so." Their regulation was a matter for the state, and, "until Congress acts in reference to their interstate relations, the State may exercise all the powers of government over them, even though in so doing it may indirectly operate upon commerce outside its . . . jurisdiction" (*Munn v. Illinois*). Although the effects of the state laws on interstate commerce would seem to have been stronger in setting railroad rates, Waite applied the same reasoning and nearly the same language as in *Munn.* In the *Chicago and Northwestern* case, for instance, the rates imposed by Wisconsin governed "fare and freight upon the transportation of persons and property carried within the State, or taken up outside the State and brought within it, or taken up inside and carried without." In Waite's view, the law was "confined to state commerce, or such interstate commerce as directly affects the people of Wisconsin." The state had legislated in a field where Congress had not, and until "Congress acts in reference to . . . interstate commerce, it is certainly within the power of Wisconsin to regulate its fares, etc., so far as they are of domestic concern." This was true even if the effects of the regulations extended beyond Wisconsin's borders: The state "may provide for those within, even though it may indirectly affect those without" (*Peik v. Chicago and Northwestern Railway*).

Understandably perhaps, a bench otherwise disposed to accept state regulation of warehouses and railroads under the due process clause would not have taken seriously objections based on the commerce clause. The legislation in question was both new and experimental. The effects of various state regulations on rail networks in particular and on the national market in general were still dimly perceived. The emergence of Chicago as a rail and lake port center of commerce in the 1850s was well within the memories of each member of the Waite Court and of most opposing counsel in these cases. One wonders how many truly grasped both the causes and significance of the city's transformation—from a population of 4,000 upon its incorporation in 1837 to a population of 300,000 in 1870—as evidence of changes occurring in commerce across the nation. For the Waite bench, the alleged deleterious consequences of state-imposed regulations on commerce must have seemed more fanciful than probable.

There remained for Waite the contracts clause objection. This deserves mention here, not because it implicates the commerce clause, but because this claim by the railroads relied on a doctrine that had been a staple of U.S. constitutional law since the Marshall era. The railroads contended that the rate regulations impaired the contractual obligations contained within their state-granted charters of incorporation. As the chief justice explained in *Peik,* the "Company was by its charter authorized 'to demand and receive such sum or sums of money for the transportation of persons and property, and for storage of property,' as it shall deem reasonable." The Wisconsin Constitution, like the constitutions of many other states, contained a reservation clause, providing that charters could be later altered by the legislature. That of course was exactly what had happened next in Wisconsin. Thus, there had been no impairment of contract. In Illinois, where Waite made no mention of a reservation clause, he looked to the charter itself to see if the legislature had granted exclusive control over rates to the Chicago, Burlington, and Quincy Railroad. It had not. This was significant because of the Supreme Court's decision in *Charles River Bridge* (1837). Although corporate charters were to be judicially defended against legislative incursions, Chief Justice Taney explained that no special protections were to be inferred or implied from the charter. Any corporate rights—which in effect were grants of various privileges, powers, and/or exemptions by the people of the state to the corporation—had to be expressly stated. "But is was not;" Waite wrote, "and the company invested its capital, relying upon the good faith of the people and the wisdom and impartiality of legislators for protection against wrong under the form of legislative regulation."

Justice Field's dissent in the railroad cases, while briefly referencing his Fourteenth Amendment due process objections from his *Munn* dissent, sharply focused on the contracts clause. He admonished the majority for a missed opportunity, despite the efforts by counsel, "to define the limits of the power of the State over its corporations after they have expended money and incurred obligations upon the faith of the grants to them. . . . This has not been done." Even when a reservation clause governed the charter, "it should not, in common honesty, be so used as to destroy or essentially impair the value of mortgages and other obligations executed under express authority of the State. The reserved power has not generally been supposed to authorize the Legislature . . . to impair any vested rights acquired under them. But no considerations of this kind are of any weight under . . . Munn v. Illinois." As for situations in which no reservation clause applied, toward "what purpose can the constitutional prohibition upon the State . . . be invoked, if the State can, in the face of a charter authorizing a company to charge reasonable rates, prescribe what rates shall be deemed reasonable for services rendered? That decision will justify the Legislature in fixing the price of all articles and the compensation for all services" (*C. B. and Q. Railroad v. Cutts*).

Other than in cases holding states and municipalities to their financial obligations, as described in chapter one, the contract clause did not figure prominently in the Waite Court's constitutional jurisprudence. Indeed, as the nineteenth century neared its end, the clause was eclipsed in importance by increased judicial reliance on the due process clause as a check on state power. Moreover, the Waite bench was disinclined to construe the contract clause as a general limitation on the police power, as illustrated by *Butchers' Union Co. v. Crescent City Co.* (1884). Recall that the Crescent City Company had been chartered by the state of Louisiana in 1869 and, by its charter, possessed exclusive privileges as a slaughtering site. This monopoly gave rise to the *Slaughterhouse Cases.* But there was a sequel. The Louisiana Constitution of 1879 decreed that the "monopoly features of any corporation now existing in the State, save such as may be contained in the charters of railroad companies, are hereby abolished." After the butcher's union in New Orleans went back into the slaughtering business, Crescent City obtained an injunction, on contracts clause grounds, from the U.S. circuit court against their new competitors. Justice Miller for the Court upheld the state's authority on the premise that the police power interest in protecting public health could not be contracted away.

"While we are not prepared to say that the legislature can make valid contracts on no subject embraced in the largest definition of the police power, we think that, in regard to two subjects so embraced, it cannot, by any contract, limit the exercise of those powers to the prejudice of the general welfare. These are the *public health* and *public morals.* The preservation of these is so necessary to the best interests of social organization, that a wise policy forbids the legislative body to divest itself of the power to enact laws for the preservation of health and the repression of crime." Miller's view thus echoed Waite's, as expressed in *Stone v. Mississippi* (1880) and noted earlier in this chapter.

In fact, the commerce clause, in Waite's day and afterwards, proved to be a far more formidable check on the police power than the contracts clause. In *Hannibal and St. Joseph Rail-Road Co. v. Husen* (1878), for instance, the Court faced the Balkanization issue again. In contrast to the *Granger Cases*, *Husen* posed a more obvious threat to interstate commerce. To prevent diseased out-of-state cattle from infecting domestic cattle, a Missouri statute declared that no "Texas, Mexican, or Indian cattle shall be driven or otherwise conveyed into, or remain, in any county in this State, between the first day of March and the first day of November in each year." Cattle transported by rail or steamboat through the state were exempted from the ban, but the statute imposed "onerous liabilities" on such shipments. Ignoring *Cooley*, Justice Strong held that the commerce power lay exclusively with Congress. He then characterized Missouri's ban as "a plain regulation of interstate commerce; a regulation extended to prohibition" because it barred the movement of cattle into the state from the specified points of origin during two-thirds of the year. Accordingly, the statute could be upheld only as a legitimate exercise of the state's police power. Acknowledging the authority of the state to enact quarantine and inspection laws to deal with diseased cattle, the police power nonetheless could not be allowed to "interfere with transportation into or through the State, beyond what is absolutely necessary for its self-protection." The statute was thus constitutionally defective because it was overinclusive. Rather than block the movement of only diseased cattle into the state, Missouri blocked all cattle from the specified locales and sources. Perhaps well intended, the statute disrupted commerce itself. "To hold otherwise," said Strong, "would be to ignore one of the leading objects which the Constitution of the United States was designed to secure." The corresponding judicial duty was "to guard vigilantly against any needless intrusion."

Was there also a *Welton*-like antidiscriminatory or protectionism issue lurking within *Husen?* So far as the record indicates, Missouri's cattle law, however heavy-handed, was motivated by valid health concerns. But in operation the law surely provided some economic assistance to Missouri's cattle farmers, who were thereby shielded from competition and oversupply from major out-of-state producers during most of the year.

A week after *Husen* came down, the Court issued its opinion in *Hall v. De Cuir* (1878), which was actually a civil rights case wrapped in a commerce clause context. Implementing an equal rights provision of the state constitution, the Reconstruction legislature in Louisiana in 1869 prohibited operators of public conveyances in the state from discriminating on account of race or color. John Benson was the owner of *The Governor Allen*, a federally licensed steamboat that plied the Mississippi River between New Orleans in Louisiana and Vicksburg in Mississippi. Josephine De Cuir was a person of color who sought passage on *The Governor Allen* from New Orleans to Hermitage, Louisiana, but was denied accommodations "in the cabin set apart for white persons." As provided in the statute, she brought suit against Benson (whose interests after his death were represented by Eliza Jane Hall, his administrator), and won a judgment of $1,000 in the New Orleans parish court. Reviewing the state supreme court's holding in favor of De Cuir, the U.S. Supreme Court unanimously concluded that Louisiana's equal accommodations law as applied to carriers whose routes took them across state lines violated the commerce clause (even though De Cuir's passage was intrastate).

Beginning with the premise that the interstate commerce power was exclusive, Chief Justice Waite acknowledged the continuing judicial difficulty in determining "what is to be deemed an encroachment upon it." He rejected the suggestion that the Court should formulate and apply some overarching commerce theory to apply in every case. With unusual candor for the period, he said that would be a "useless task." It was "far better to leave a matter of such delicacy to be settled in each case upon a view of the particular rights involved." However, that observation did little to decide De Cuir's case. So Waite turned to the statute's impact on commerce. The law acted "directly upon the business as it comes into the State from without or goes out from within. While it purports only to control the carrier when engaged within the State, it must necessarily influence his conduct to some extent in the management of his business throughout his entire voyage. A passenger in the cabin set apart for the use of whites without the State must, when the boat comes within, share the accommodations of that cabin with such colored persons as may come on board afterwards, if the law is to be enforced." The mental image Waite conjured up in opposition to the statute was a nautical version of the game of musical chairs among passengers and cabins as the boat moved from the waters of one state to another. "Commerce," he declared, "cannot flourish in the midst of such embarrassments." Were the statute to be upheld, chaos and confusion would ensue, "productive of great inconvenience and unnecessary hardship. Each State could provide for its own passengers and regulate the transportation of its own freight, regardless of the interest of others." It "was to meet just such a case as that the commercial clause in the Constitution was adopted." Waite drew from Field's inference in *Welton:* "[C]ongressional inaction left Benson at liberty to adopt such reasonable rules and regulations for the disposition of passengers. . . ." What the chief justice did not explain was why the possible or even probable impact of Louisiana's law on travel outside the state differed so markedly from the impact of various state railroad rate regulations on out-of-state travel—an impact that Waite had tersely minimized in the *Granger Cases.* In any event, implicit in the chief's analysis was the view that racial segregation in public conveyances should be the rule, equal access the exception.

In the *U.S. Reports, De Cuir* appears as an ostensibly unanimous decision. Yet Chief Justice Waite's papers illustrate a behavioral phenomenon discussed in chapter one: the norm of public conformity or unanimity that pervaded the Court at this time. The norm of consensus was strong, and disagreements among justices about a decision only occasionally materialized as published dissents. So when *De Cuir* was submitted on April 17, 1877, and decided in conference, Miller, Strong, and Hunt initially dissented (Magrath 1963, 140). Yet when the case came down on January 14, 1878—an uncommonly long gestation for decisions at that time—they were silent.

As events unfolded, the Louisiana policy disallowed in *De Cuir* was followed by two great ironies. Five years later in the *Civil Rights Cases,* discussed earlier in this chapter, the Court denied Congress's authority under the Fourteenth Amendment to prohibit racial discrimination by private persons in places of public accommodation. Few if any in that day thought of deploying the commerce clause—it was still an amazingly underused power of Congress—as a tool to ensure equal rights. So no one knows whether the Waite Court would have allowed Congress (had it been willing) to accomplish through the commerce clause what it was barred from doing via the Fourteenth Amendment. Twelve years after *De Cuir* and after Melville Fuller had succeeded Waite as chief justice, the Court decided *Louisville, N. O. and T. Railway v. Mississippi* (1890). The decision rejected a commerce clause challenge to an 1888 Mississippi statute requiring railroads operating within the state to provide "equal, but separate, accommodations for the white and colored races, by providing two or more passenger cars for each passenger train, or by dividing the passenger cars by a partition so as to secure separate accommodations." Waite Court carryovers Harlan and Bradley dissented. A new day had dawned. Prohibiting racial segregation on steamboats violated the commerce clause; requiring it on trains did not. Forced separation of the races could thus prevail as the law of the state. Equal access as the law of the land could not.

De Cuir proved to be highly useful, however, in eventually unraveling that part of the holding in the *Granger Cases* of 1877 that minimized the constitutional significance of state-fixed rates for interstate commerce (*Wabash, St. Louis and Pacific Railway v. Illinois*, 1886). A provision of the Granger law enacted by Illinois in 1871 prohibited discrimination between long-haul and short-haul rates for similar goods shipped in similar carload units. Ignoring the ban, the Wabash Railway charged Elder and McKinney fifteen cents per 100 pounds to ship a carload of goods from Peoria, Illinois, to New York City. On the same day the railroad charged Isaac Bailey and F. O. Swannell twenty-five cents per 100 pounds to ship a carload of similar goods from Gilman, Illinois, to New York City, even though Peoria was eighty-six miles further from New York than Gilman.

Was a state-set rate applying to interstate shipment of goods compatible with the commerce clause? The Illinois attorney general argued that, even with an interstate effect, the law belonged "to that class of commercial regulations which may be established by the laws of a State until Congress shall have exercised its power on that subject." He confidently cited the *Granger Cases* as authority. "It cannot be denied that the general language of the court in these cases . . . may be susceptible of the meaning which the Illinois Court places on it," sheepishly acknowledged Justice Miller, who had been in the *Granger* majority. Backpedaling from Waite's *Granger* opinion, Miller "admitted that, in a general way, the court treated the cases then before it as belonging to that class of regulations of commerce which, like pilotage, bridging navigable rivers, and many others, could be acted upon by the States, in the absence of any legislation by Congress on the same subject." Miller candidly said he was prepared "to take his share of the responsibility for the language used in those opinions." However, rates now appeared in a different light. "By the slightest attention to the matter it will be readily seen that . . . the local rules which shall govern the conduct of the pilots of each of the various harbors of the coasts of the United States, depend upon principles far more limited in their application . . . than those which should regulate the transportation of persons and property across half or the whole of the continent, over the territory of half a dozen States. . . ." Yet why were they being seen as different in 1886 but not in 1877? Miller replied the emphasis in the *Granger Cases* had been on limits imposed on states by the due process clause; the commerce clause aspect of the litigation "did not receive any very elaborate consideration, either in the opinions of the court or in the arguments of counsel." In other words, the *Granger* majority (and the dissenters) had been more concerned about whether states were free of any Fourteenth Amendment restrictions on fixing rates—that being the novel question presented—than with other possible objections to the legislation. "The importance of that question overshadowed all others," Miller said.

Miller then looked to *Hall v. De Cuir*, decided a year after *Munn* and the seven railroad rate cases, for a more thorough analysis. As if attempting to rescue his chief from the embarrassing neglect of the commerce issue in 1877, Miller quoted from Waite's opinion in *De Cuir:* "[W]e think it may safely be said that state legislation which seeks to impose a direct burden upon interstate commerce, or to interfere directly with its freedom, does encroach upon the exclusive power of Congress." Was the Court's conclusion in *De Cuir* to dictate the outcome in *Wabash?* "It is not the railroads themselves that are regulated by this Act . . . , so much as the charge for transportation; and," Miller reasoned from the parallel considerations in *De Cuir,* "if each one of the States through whose territories these goods are transported can fix its own rules for prices, for modes of transit, for times and modes of delivery, and all the other incidents of transportation . . . , it is readily seen that the embarrassments upon interstate transportation . . . might be too oppressive to be submitted to." In that respect, the commerce clause "would be a very feeble and almost useless provision . . . if, at every stage of the transportation of goods and chattels through the country, the State within whose limits a part of this transportation must be done could impose regulations concerning the price, compensation, or taxation, or any other restrictive regulation . . . seriously embarrassing this commerce." Thus states were barred by the commerce clause from setting rates that applied out of state. "We must, therefore, hold," Miller declared in disowning part of the *Granger Cases,* "that it is not, and never has been, the deliberate opinion of a majority of this court that a statute of a State which attempts to regulate the fares and charges by railroad companies within its limits, for a transportation which constitutes a part of commerce among the States, is a valid law." Returning to the *Cooley* doctrine, Miller explained that an interstate rate was of "national character." Therefore, "regulation can only appropriately exist by general rules and principles, which demand that it should be done by the Congress . . . under the commerce clause. . . ."

Justice Bradley was joined by Justice Gray (who came to the bench after *Munn*) and Chief Justice Waite in dissent. Miller clearly had not won his chief's vote by quoting extensively from Waite's opinion in *De Cuir.* Indeed, Bradley—like Waite a part of the *Granger* majority—deemed Miller's opinion a clear and incorrect departure from settled law. Instead, he would "hold it to be a sound proposition of law, that the making of railroads and regulating the charges for their use is not such a regulation of commerce as to be in the remotest degree repugnant to any power given to Congress by the Constitution, so far as that power is dormant. . . . They affect commerce; they incidentally regulate it; but they are acts . . . which the State has a perfect right to do. . . ." Besides, the greater power includes the lesser: "It is only for the sake of convenience that the State lets out its railroads to private corporations. It might construct them itself." If the power to construct a railroad existed, then the power to impose rates existed as well. Moreover, *De Cuir* posed a different situation and was therefore inapposite. Louisiana had "attempted to regulate interstate commerce itself, directly, in a manner in which it had no special prerogative to legislate." That consideration, Bradley insisted, did not apply to a ban on long-haul/short-haul rate discrimination, or to rate setting generally. In his view the commerce clause allowed states to act with respect to rates. This was so even though the costs of interstate shipments were thereby affected. But the same clause did not allow states to make rules for the intrastate portion of an interstate journey that affected the quarters where passengers were accommodated.

The *Wabash* case had far-reaching consequences. It was a major factor in congressional passage of the Interstate Commerce Act in 1887 and establishment of the Interstate Commerce Commission (ICC), the nation's second independent regulatory commission that existed until Congress abolished it in 1996 as part of the deregulation movement. The 1887 law gave the ICC various oversight powers, mandated that rail rates be "reasonable and just," and prohibited various practices, including rate discrimination against short hauls.

The *Wabash* case and creation of the ICC eventually made state railroad rate regulation virtually meaningless. But state legislation affecting transportation continued unabated, as did review of such legislation by the Court. *Wabash*, it turned out, did not mean that the Court was hostile to all state laws that effectively reached across state lines, as *Smith v. Alabama* (1888) illustrated.

Joseph Smith was a locomotive engineer employed by the Mobile and Ohio Railroad, the main line of which extended from Mobile, Alabama, to St. Louis, Missouri. Smith was frequently assigned to passenger trains on the segment of the line between Mobile and Corinth, Mississippi, 60 miles of which lay in Alabama, and 265 miles in Mississippi. He was arrested in Mobile for failing to abide by an 1877 state law that prohibited engineers from operating locomotives within Alabama unless they first had been examined and licensed by the state.

Justice Matthews's opinion for the Court (Bradley dissented alone without opinion) made the now routine commerce case acknowledgment that the Court had faced difficulty in deciding whether the regulation was a permissible exercise of the state police power or an impermissible regulation of interstate commerce. "To draw the line of interference between the two fields of jurisdiction . . . is a judicial question often of much difficulty, the solution of which, perhaps, is not to be found in any single and exact rule of decision." However, in this instance the state's interest was very strong. The operation of railroads "requires the use of instruments and agencies attended with special risks and dangers, the proper management of which involves peculiar knowledge, training, skill, and care." States had ample discretion in rules imposed on the railroads and were "strictly within the limits of the local law. They are not per se regulations of commerce; it is only when they operate as such . . . that they can be required to give way to the supreme authority of the constitution." Alabama's licensing law was not such a regulation of commerce, he concluded, but part "of that body of the local law which . . . properly governs the relation between carriers . . . and the public who employs them. . . ." Insofar as the statute "affects transaction of commerce among the States, it does so only indirectly, incidentally, and remotely, and not so as to burden or impede them."

Still, one is left wondering about the impact of multiple licensing schemes enacted by the states through which a railroad might run. That had been enough to invalidate Louisiana's equal accommodations law when applied to steamboats. Why would it not also apply to a licensing regimen that "operate[d] as such" as a regulation of commerce? That had been enough to end state bans on long-haul/short-haul rate discrimination in interstate shipments. Why was the regulation in *Smith* incidental and remote, but not so in *De Cuir?* Perhaps the powerful interest in public safety, absent in the rate and segregation cases, was dispositive. The justices traveled by train, just like everyone else.

Waite's protestations in the *Wabash* case aside, his Court's stance on state regulations and the commerce clause by 1886 stood in sharp contrast to its view of state regulations and the due process clause. With the latter, the bench was highly deferential to legislative determination of the need to regulate; given that starting point, it is hardly surprising that during Waite's time no statute failed the due process test. However, with the former there was usually more probing of legislative purpose and need, as the Alabama engineer licensing case illustrates, and always reflection on the regulation's impact on commerce among the states. Stated differently, regulation in the absence of a nexus with the commerce clause was a legislative question. When a nexus with the commerce clause was present, regulation became a judicial question. With Congress opting not to exercise its commerce power, the Court assumed the role of guardian of the national market. This fact in turn left state legislatures in a perplexing position. On one hand, they did not share Congress's hesitancy to act with respect to commerce but instead were a continuing source of regulations. On the other hand, limits that the Constitution imposed on their discretion were far from clear. Given the Court's confessed inability to devise and to apply a one-size-fits-all doctrine, the breadth of the dormant commerce power was discernible only after cases had been decided. Legislatures had little to rely on but the examples of statutes that the Court had either upheld or rejected. Even the value of those precedents was compromised by changing judicial personnel and increasing judicial awareness of the complexity of commerce itself. How those factors played out would be anyone's guess, as the progression from the *Granger Cases* to *Wabash* illustrated.

In the few Waite Court cases testing the powers of the national government under the commerce clause, the justices were typically Congress-friendly. This was true despite a unanimous holding in the *Trade-Mark Cases* in 1879 that struck down a law because it was not confined to trademarks used in interstate or foreign commerce.

Yet in 1878 the Court broadly read a statute Congress enacted in 1866 that conditionally allowed telegraph companies to construct lines across public lands and streams and along designated post roads. Shortly after, Florida extended exclusive telegraph privileges in two northern counties to the Pensacola Telegraph Company, thus linking Florida to certain other states. Those two northern counties were strategically essential for any company desiring to build a line from east to west across the state because at some points in Florida's panhandle the state was no more than two counties wide, north to south. In 1873 and 1874, the state granted telegraph privileges to a railroad, including its rights-of-way in those same counties. As allowed by the federal statute of 1866, the railroad then assigned those privileges to the much larger and continental Western Union Telegraph Company. Western Union then claimed its rights to construct and operate telegraph lines under the federal statute, while Pensacola Telegraph clung to its 1866 state monopoly. These claims "gave rise to one of the most exciting contests over monopoly in the feverish economic development after the Civil War" (Frankfurter 1937, 102).

At the Supreme Court, the case pitted national power against state autonomy. The first rested on the commerce clause. The second derived in this context from *Bank of Augusta v. Earle* (1839), which affirmed a state's authority over corporations operating within its borders. But *Bank of Augusta* involved neither an interstate corporation nor a federal statute. Then the Chase Court had held in *Paul v. Virginia* (1869) that a state had full power over foreign insurance companies operating within the state because insurance was not commerce.

Waite's description in *Pensacola Telegraph Co. v. Western Union Telegraph Co.* (1878) of the commerce that Congress could validly regulate was plainly reminiscent of the expansive reading Marshall had given the commerce clause in *Gibbons v. Ogden* in 1821. "The powers thus granted are not confined to the instrumentalities of commerce . . . known or in use when the Constitution was adopted, but they keep pace with the progress of the country, and adapt themselves to the new developments of time and circumstances," wrote Waite. "They extend from the horse with its rider to the stage-coach, from the sailing vessel to the steamboat to the railroad, and from the railroad to the telegraph. . . ." It was the duty of Congress to see to it that "intercourse among the States and the transmission of intelligence" were not obstructed by the states. That duty had become all the more central because of the "electric telegraph," which marked "an epoch in the progress of time. In a little more than a quarter of a century it has changed the habits of business, and become one of the necessities of commerce" and a necessity for the work of the government.

The 1866 act of Congress allowed telegraph line construction "through and over any portion of the public domain of the United States, over and along any of the military or post-roads of the United States" now in existence or in the future. "There is nothing," Waite said, "to indicate an intention of limiting the effect of the words employed, and they are, therefore, to be given their natural and ordinary signification. Read in this way, the grant evidently extends to the public domain, the military and post-roads, and the navigable waters of the United States." For Waite, public domain included all lands not privately owned, not merely those lands the title to which lay with the federal government. Given that breadth, the exclusive rights Florida had given to the Pensacola company conflicted with the act of Congress and so could not prevent Western Union from operating in the same key counties.

It was on the point regarding the allowable reach of the federal statute that Justices Field and Hunt largely based their dissents. The commerce power of Congress, Field argued, "does not authorize any interference with the commerce which is carried on entirely within a state." The "doctrine that Congress can authorize foreign corporations to enter within its limits and participate in this commerce without the state's consent," Field continued, "is utterly subversive of our system of local state government. State control in local matters would thus be impossible." How Field would adjust national power in relation to in-state and interstate messages transmitted over the same in-state line was not explained. His values in preserving state autonomy, in this instance, trumped his usual hostility to state-granted monopolies.

The chief justice also spoke for the Court again in another case that recognized the sweep of congressional commerce clause powers. In 1869 Congress approved construction of a bridge by a group of entrepreneurs over the Ohio River between Cincinnati, Ohio, and Newport, Kentucky. However, the statute reserved the right of Congress to withdraw approval if the bridge obstructed "the free navigation of said river" and to direct "the necessary modifications and alterations of said bridge." After construction began, Army inspectors concluded that, even though the bridge adhered to approved specifications, the bridge as designed would still pose a risk to free navigation. In 1871 Congress declared the bridge unlawful, but allowed construction to continue subject to certain modifications. Those were major modifications, converting the bridge from a low bridge with a draw, to a high bridge without a draw. The same act also allowed the company to sue the government to determine (1) whether the bridge in its first manifestation had in fact adhered to the 1869 specifications and (2) whether the government owed damages to the company. Against dissents on differing grounds (Fifth Amendment, states-rights, and statutory) respectively by Bradley, Field, and Miller, the Court dismissed the bridge owners' suit on the ground that the act of 1871 had been within the authority Congress had claimed for itself in the act of 1869. What was significant in Waite's opinion was the assumption that Congress, not the Court, was the ultimate judge of what constituted an impediment to commerce on the river. Both "the Ohio and Kentucky divisional companies were . . . subjected to this paramount controlling power. . . . Congress . . . is the constitutional protector of foreign and interstate commerce. Its supervision of this subject is continuing in its nature. . . ." The power of Congress, he acknowledged, "may be abused, but it is one Congress saw fit to reserve. For protection against unjust or unwise legislation," the chief justice wrote in familiar words, "the people must look to the polls and not to the courts" (*Newport and Cincinnati Bridge Co. v. United States*, 1882).

The *Newport Bridge Case* on the powers of Congress under the commerce clause was thus a parallel statement to the Waite Court's view of the state police power as against the due process clause of the Fourteenth Amendment. Within the commerce clause lay a vast reservoir of congressional authority and discretion waiting to be tapped; the police power was an equally impressive and energetic source of authority for local regulations. For the most part, the Waite Court had an abiding faith in democracy—a broad deference to popular participation in the direction of public policy, including toleration of the improvident idiosyncrasies that government by the people invariably produced. Investors and other adventurers took their chances. They were indeed risk takers who had earned no unique protection from the courts.

References

Corwin, Edward S. 1987. "The Doctrine of Due Process of Law before the Civil War." In *Corwin on the Constitution: Volume Two: The Judiciary*, ed. Richard Loss. Ithaca, NY: Cornell University Press. Originally published in 1911 under the same title in *Harvard Law Review* 24: 366–385, 460–479.

Cummings, Homer S., and Carl McFarland. 1937. *Federal Justice: Chapters in the History of Justice and the Federal Executive.* New York: Macmillan.

Currie, David P. 1985. *The Constitution in the Supreme Court: The First Hundred Years, 1789–1888.* Chicago: University of Chicago Press.

Curtis, Michael Kent. 2000. *Free Speech, "The People's Darling Privilege:" Struggles for Freedom of Expression in American History.* Durham, NC: Duke University Press.

Davis, Bob. 2002. "Past Crisis Offers Hope for Economy, Warnings to Watch." *Wall Street Journal*, September 26, A1, A8.

Fairman, Charles. 1939. *Mr. Justice Miller and the Supreme Court: 1862–1890.* Cambridge, MA: Harvard University Press.

———. 1987. *Reconstruction and Reunion 1864–88, Part Two. History of the Supreme Court of the United States*, vol. 7. New York: Macmillan.

Frankfurter, Felix. 1937. *The Commerce Clause under Marshall, Taney and Waite.* Chapel Hill: University of North Carolina Press.

Frankfurter, Felix, and James M. Landis. 1928. *The Business of the Supreme Court.* New York: Macmillan.

Gillette, William. 1965. *The Right to Vote: Politics and the Passage of the Fifteenth Amendment.* Baltimore, MD: Johns Hopkins University Press.

Harlan, Malvina Shanklin. 1999. "Some Memories of a Long Life, 1854–1911." *Journal of Supreme Court History* 26: 109–211.

Harring, Sidney L., and Kathryn Swedlow. 2000. "'The Defendant Has Seemed to Live a Charmed Life': *Hopt* v. *Utah:* Territorial Justice, The Supreme Court of the United States, and Late Nineteenth-Century Death Penalty Jurisprudence." *Journal of Supreme Court History* 25: 40–71.

Keyssar, Alexander. 2000. *The Right to Vote: The Contested History of Democracy in the United States.* New York: Basic Books.

Magrath, C. Peter. 1963. *Morrison R. Waite: The Triumph of Character.* New York: Macmillan.

———. 1987. "The Case of the Unscrupulous Warehouseman." In *Quarrels That Have Shaped the Constitution,* rev. ed., ed. John A. Garraty. New York: Harper and Row.

Maine, Sir Henry Sumner. 1886. *Popular Government.* New York: Henry Holt.

Maltz, Earl M. 1996. "The Waite Court and Federal Power to Enforce the Reconstruction Amendments." In *The Supreme Court and the Civil War,* ed. Jennifer M. Lowe. Washington, DC: Supreme Court Historical Society.

Marshall, Charles C. 1890. "A New Constitutional Amendment." *American Law Review* 24: 908–931.

Mason, Alpheus Thomas, and Donald Grier Stephenson, Jr. 2002. *American Constitutional Law: Introductory Essays and Selected Cases.* Upper Saddle River, NJ: Prentice Hall.

Palmer, Robert R. 1960. *A History of the Modern World,* 2nd ed. New York: Knopf.

"The Right to Confiscate." 1874. *The Nation,* September 24, 199–201.

Stephenson, D. Grier, Jr. 1988. "The Supreme Court, the Franchise, and the Fifteenth Amendment: The First Sixty Years." *UMKC Law Review* 57: 47–65.

———. 1999. *Campaigns and the Court: The United States Supreme Court in Presidential Elections.* New York: Columbia University Press.

Swinney, Everette. 1962. "Enforcing the Fifteenth Amendment, 1870–1877." *Journal of Southern History* 1962: 202–218.

Urofsky, Melvin I. 2002. *Religious Freedom: Rights and Liberties under the Law.* Santa Barbara, CA: ABC-CLIO.

Warren, Charles. 1926. *The Supreme Court in United States History.* 2 vols., rev. ed. Boston: Little, Brown.

Yarbrough, Tinsley E. 1995. *Judicial Enigma: The First Justice Harlan.* New York: Oxford University Press.

4

Legacy and Impact

"I have at last finished the opinion," Chief Justice Waite wrote to Bancroft Davis, the Court's Reporter of Decisions, on March 5, 1888 (Magrath 1960, 309). One suspects that Waite audibly exhaled as he penned that sentence. His reference was to the *Telephone Cases*, the most significant patent litigation in the late nineteenth century in terms of effect on the development of the U.S. telecommunications industry. Waite had been at work on his opinion for months, and understandably so. Arguments in the cases had been heard over twelve days in January and February 1887. The bench had split 4–3 over these eight challenges in circuit courts to Alexander Graham Bell's 1876 patent for the telephone. A description of each of the patent disputes, Waite's opinion sustaining the patent, and Justice Bradley's much shorter dissent consumed more than 500 pages—all of volume 126 of the *U.S. Reports*. Waite's effort had been a burden even for a chief justice accustomed to being overworked.

The decision was scheduled to come down on Monday, March 19. On Sunday the 18th, the chief justice became ill. He insisted nonetheless on going to the Capitol the following day to read his opinion, despite an apparent diagnosis of pneumonia. He was concerned that his wife Amelia, then traveling in California, would be alarmed if she read newspaper accounts of his absence from Court. She knew that he had never fully regained his stamina following an 1885 breakdown that caused his brief absence from the bench. After Waite arrived in the courtroom on the 19th, however, it was immediately clear that he was too weak to carry on. Justice Blatchford instead announced the judgment in the *Telephone Cases*. Attorney General Augustus Garland later recalled the image of the enfeebled chief: "It was evident to the observer that death had almost placed its hand upon him" (Garland 1898, 35–36). At about 6:10 on the morning of Friday, March 23, in his seventy-second year, Morrison Remick Waite died at home, fourteen years and nineteen days after being sworn in by Justice Nathan Clifford.

Predecessors John Marshall, Roger Brooke Taney, and Salmon Portland Chase had also died as active chief justices, as later would Melville Weston Fuller, Edward Douglass White, Harlan Fiske Stone, and Fred Vinson. Among his six predecessors, Waite served longer than all but John Marshall and Taney, whose combined tenures practically encompassed the first two-thirds of the nineteenth century. Among the sixteen chiefs to date, as shown in Table 4.1, Waite's tenure ranks sixth. Fuller, whom President Grover Cleveland picked as his successor, would serve eight years longer than Waite, but after Fuller no chief justice would exceed the length of Waite's service until Eisenhower appointee Earl Warren, who retired in 1969. Moreover, Waite's fourteen years were hardly quiescent ones. Indeed, institutionally, politically, and legally they may fairly be described as eventful, and in some ways even tumultuous, years.

The fifteen justices who made up the Waite bench were by and large an impressive team both professionally and intellectually. The list included some individuals—Justices Miller, Field, Bradley, and Harlan come immediately to mind—who in sports vernacular would have been considered "starters" or even "all-stars" in any period of Supreme Court history; the Waite bench also had both strength and depth in the second tier. There was the chief justice himself, plus colleagues Blatchford, Davis, Gray, Matthews, Lamar (at the very end), Strong, and perhaps Woods. These justices could have more than qualified as members of any Court before or since. For twelve of the fifteen justices to have performed at a level ranging from able and workmanlike to outstanding is remarkable. That some members of the Waite Court have not been more acclaimed is probably due to the routine nature of much of their judicial business—"routine," that is, by late twentieth and early twenty-first century standards—and/or to their relatively brief tenures. It was not due to any unusual deficiencies on their parts.

However, talented people are frequently strong-willed people. That was true of Waite's colleagues. Moreover, several of them thought they, not Waite, should have become chief justice in 1874, and some continued to believe that they could have done a better job in the center chair. The Waite Court may not have been "nine scorpions in a bottle," as Justice O. W. Holmes was supposed to have described a later Court on which he sat (Lerner 1994), but by no means was Waite's a friction-free bench. These realities, combined with some peculiar difficulties caused by the weaker members of Waite's roster, posed special challenges for the chief's leadership skills. Furthermore, politics outside the Court also entangled Waite's colleagues. In the constitutional crisis of 1876–1877, several became the first members of the Supreme Court to help resolve a disputed presidential election.

Data presented in Chapter 1 demonstrated that the Waite justices were a hard-working lot. They had to be. No Court in history has encountered so heavy a mandatory caseload for so long a time. Indeed, the experience of the Waite years demonstrated the unfeasibility and inadequacy of the federal judicial system as it was then organized. The result was a major structural and jurisdictional reorganization soon after the chief's death.

In addition, Chapter 3 illustrated the variety of important questions that occupied the Court's time. Some of these had been fixtures in the *Reports* for decades, but others were just beginning to crowd their way onto the docket as Waite became chief. Waite was probably too close to his work to appreciate fully the changes that were

Table 4.1 Tenures of the Chief Justices of the United States

Chief Justice	*Appointing President*	*Tenure as Chief Justice*	*Rank order in Years of Service¶*
Jay	Washington	1789–1795	12th (6 yrs.)
Rutledge*#	Washington	1795	15th (1/3 yr.)
Ellsworth	Washington	1796–1800	14th (4 yrs.)
Marshall	Adams	1801–1835	1st (35 yrs.)
Taney	Jackson	1836–1864	2nd (28 yrs.)
Chase, S. P.	Lincoln	1864–1873	10th (8 yrs.)
Waite	Grant	1874–1888	6th (14 yrs.)
Fuller	Cleveland	1888–1910	3rd (22 yrs.)
White, E.+	Taft	1910–1921	8th (10 yrs.)
Taft	Harding	1921–1930	9th (9 yrs.)
Hughes#	Hoover	1930–1941	7th (11 yrs.)
Stone +	Roosevelt, F.	1941–1946	13th (5 yrs.)
Vinson	Truman	1946–1953	11th (7 yrs.)
Warren	Eisenhower	1953–1969	5th (16 yrs.)
Burger	Nixon	1969–1986	4th (tie) (17 yrs.)
Rehnquist** +	Reagan	1986–	4th (tie) (17 yrs.)

*Served on a recess appointment; nomination rejected by the Senate.
**To date, as of 2003.
¶Rounded off to nearest year, from date of judicial oath.
+Sworn in as chief justice while serving as associate justice. Years shown exclude service as associate justice.
#Previous service as associate justice terminated before appointment as chief justice. Years shown exclude service as associate justice.

underway. Yet, had he been conferred the perspective afforded by more than a century's hindsight, he would have recognized the situation for what it was: The U.S. Supreme Court on his watch was an institution truly in transition.

Part Classical, Part Modern: The Waite Bench as a Transition Court

As the Preface suggested, the Waite Court can usefully be viewed as a transition court, straddling a period during which the Supreme Court underwent an unprecedented metamorphosis from what might be called the "classical Court" to the "modern

Court." This is different terminology from what one usually sees in literature about the Supreme Court. Yet a classical/modern distinction may better highlight the place of the Waite era in Supreme Court history, making it easier to grasp the ways in which the Waite Court was both similar to, and different from, the courts that preceded and followed it.

Standard Supreme Court nomenclature draws a contrast between the "old Court" and the "new Court" (or, sometimes, the "modern Court"). By most accounts, the dividing line between the two falls during the years 1937–1940, when the nation witnessed a judicial revolution. The proverbial irresistible force (in the form of President Franklin Roosevelt's New Deal program to cope with the Great Depression) met the immovable object (in the form of the Supreme Court, under the leadership of Chief Justice Charles Evans Hughes, which stymied many of the president's initiatives). The result was Roosevelt's audacious plan of court packing and the hasty change of mind by Hughes and Justice Owen J. Roberts that gave Roosevelt the five sure votes he needed so that his agenda could receive constitutional approval. This flip-flop was promptly followed by the Court's adoption of a new agenda for itself.

From this perspective, the old Court in its constitutional decisions was property-oriented, with an emphasis on minimizing the restrictive role of government in commercial affairs. With commercial interests enjoying heightened protection, legislation regulating property was constitutional only if the Court was satisfied that the policy was reasonable. The agenda of the new Court, by contrast, turned that order of things on its head, guarding mainly the nonproprietary rights and liberties of individuals. Ever since, property matters have been deemed less important than, say, free speech or criminal justice issues, and so have been far less deserving of judicial protection than rights in the preferred category. Accordingly, since the late 1930s, regulations of property has been left to the discretion (and protection) of legislatures and are only rarely struck down, while restrictions on speech and other such liberties are nearly always viewed as constitutionally suspect.

The categories of old Court and new Court, as they are usually understood, are helpful in understanding a prominent watershed in Supreme Court history. Yet they may obscure as much as they reveal in depicting both fundamental changes in the Court's development across more than two centuries and the Waite Court's position in that development. For this task, different nomenclature seems particularly appropriate: hence the categories of classical Court and modern Court (albeit with the "new" or post-1937 Court being a subset of the latter). Compared to the relatively sudden transformation after 1937, the shift from classical to modern Court moved more slowly, spanning approximately the last third of the nineteenth century. Waite's chief justiceship, therefore, fell roughly in the middle of this period.

The era of the classical Court was marked by (1) an exceedingly limited federal jurisdiction, (2) a structure that made the bench mainly a court of errors, not a court of legal policy, and (3) onerous circuit-riding duties. Recall from Chapter 1 that the great bulk of litigation in the federal courts until after the Civil War consisted of admiralty and diversity cases. The latter generally posed questions that would have been heard by state courts except for the fact that the parties were citizens of more than one state and because the dollar amount at issue met a threshold set by Congress. Cases in the Supreme Court that raised federal constitutional questions usually came from the highest court of a state; these qualified for Supreme Court review only if the court below had ruled against the federal claim.

Moreover, except for admiralty and a handful of other cases, the Supreme Court was the sole tribunal to hear appeals within the federal judicial system (circuit courts were principally trial, not appellate, bodies). There was no intermediate appellate bench between the circuit courts and the Supreme Court. Thus, much of the justices' energy was expended reviewing circuit court decisions, regardless of their importance. It seemed every case in federal court had an equal claim on the Supreme Court's time, unless it was a criminal case. Congress did not extend a right of appeal to the Supreme Court in federal criminal cases until the 1890s. Thus, unless a criminal case managed to reach the Supreme Court through some extraordinary route such as habeas corpus or by certification, the federal trial (district or circuit) court had the final word.

The burden of review by right of an ever-expanding number of circuit court rulings was compounded by the system of judicial staffing that Congress had decreed in 1789. There were three types of federal courts (district, circuit, and Supreme Court), but only two types of federal judges (district judges and Supreme Court justices). Every state contained at least one federal judicial district, such as the District of Maryland. Some states contained more than one district, such as the Eastern, Middle, and Western districts of Pennsylvania. Districts in two or more states were in turn combined to form a circuit. The local district judge and the Supreme Court justice assigned to that circuit staffed a circuit court for a federal district. Thus, for example, the Circuit Court for the District of New Hampshire at the time Waite became chief justice was staffed by the district judge in that state plus Nathan Clifford, who was the designated justice for the First Circuit, which included all of New England except Vermont and Connecticut. If the circuit justice was unable to be present, and this was sometimes the case, the district judge held circuit court by himself. Therefore, the circuit court was, practically speaking, often a replica of the district court. For a brief period in 1801 Congress created separate circuit judgeships, but a new Congress repealed that measure in 1802. In 1855 Congress authorized a geography-driven creation of a circuit judgeship for California and then one for Oregon. Otherwise, there were no distinct circuit judges until 1869 when Congress also reduced the circuit-riding duties of the justices. Thereafter, justices were expected to sit on the circuit court bench in each district only once every two years.

The era of the modern Court has been marked by (1) a vastly expanded federal jurisdiction, (2) an increase in cases involving individual rights, and (3) a structure that has allowed the Court to become an arbiter of policy for the nation. The three Reconstruction amendments to the Constitution (the Thirteenth in 1865, the Fourteenth in 1868, and the Fifteenth in 1870), combined with congressional statutes intended to enforce those amendments, imposed new restrictions on state authority as a means of protecting individual rights.

Moreover, the "convenient vagueness" in the language of the all-important section one of the Fourteenth Amendment presented the Supreme Court with unprecedented opportunities to determine just how broad or narrow those protections for individual rights would be (Hough 1919, 218). The inclusion of the equal protection clause was itself a noteworthy event, because it handed the Supreme Court a far-reaching and entirely new mission: to have the final word on matters of racial justice. To be sure, the other guaranties of section one regarding privileges and immunities and due process of law initially were litigated more in the context of restrictions on occupational freedom and uses of property than they were in the context of attacks on racial discrimination. But in the nineteenth century, property interests were critical issues of civil liberties and civil rights. Property was then, as now, an indispensable basis of freedom.

The addition of the Thirteenth, Fourteenth, and Fifteenth Amendments proved even more significant for the federal judiciary because of the major jurisdictional leap Congress directed in 1875. Congress granted the circuit courts full Article III jurisdiction: the authority to entertain suits involving a statute, the Constitution, or a treaty of the United States, as well as a right of removal of such cases from state to federal court. Simultaneously, as Chapter 3 described, the number of cases raising issues under the Bill of Rights, while small by contemporary standards, became a discernible part of the Supreme Court's docket for the first time. Ratification of the Fourteenth Amendment also reopened the federalism-rattling question of the applicability of the Bill of Rights to the states.

Despite a docket invigorated by the arrival of novel issues, the organization of the federal courts during the 1870s and 1880s remained as it had in 1800. The only exceptions were the addition of separate circuit judges and the reduction (but not elimination) of the justices' circuit-riding duties. The Waite Court remained the sole court of appeal for most cases from the federal courts. This was distressing because the number of such cases was surging.

The first steps toward relief came in 1891, three years after Waite's death. (If any chief justice can be said to have died from overwork, it was Waite.) For all but the most stubborn congressional holdouts, the Waite Court had demonstrated how anachronistic the classical organization of the federal courts had become. The system was breaking down under the strain. Too many cases qualified for the Supreme

Court's attention and taxed the collective abilities of nine justices to do their work well and in a timely fashion. "The plan of providing some intermediate courts having final appellate jurisdiction of certain classes of questions and cases has, I think, received a more general approval from the bench and bar of the country than any other," declared President Benjamin Harrison in his first annual message to Congress in 1889. "Without attempting to discuss details, I recommend that provision be made for the establishment of such courts" (Richardson 1917, vol. 9, 42–43).

Congress responded in 1891 with the Circuit Court of Appeals Act. In at least three ways, the statute—passed 101 years after the Supreme Court's first session—radically broke with the classical tradition. First, it created a layer of intermediate appellate courts—the circuit courts of appeals. For the first time, for most cases in federal court, the first point of appeal would not be to the U.S. Supreme Court. The old circuit courts were soon merged with the district courts, and the latter became the primary federal trial court. Second, for certain categories of cases, the circuit courts of appeals would ordinarily be the court of last resort. Third, the Supreme Court was granted limited certiorari jurisdiction, under which the High Court's review of some cases would be discretionary, not mandatory. The effects of the 1891 legislation were nearly instantaneous. In Waite's last term, 482 new cases had been docketed, a number that grew to 623 new cases in 1890 after Melville Fuller had become chief justice. In 1891, with the new law in effect only a few months, new cases dropped to 379, and then to 275 in 1892 (Frankfurter and Landis 1928, 97, 102). The statute also eliminated circuit riding by the justices, although each justice retained certain circuit oversight responsibilities. Some of these circuit-related duties remain today, as happens in emergency appeals in death penalty cases.

The 1891 act was only a beginning toward the contemporary federal judicial system, but it was a crucially important first step. The Supreme Court began to move toward a time when, for the most part, it decided only those questions that the justices considered worthy of their time. That new day dawned with passage of the Judiciary Act of 1925 (popularly known as the Judges' Bill), which was the product of the prodigious efforts of Chief Justice (and former president) William Howard Taft. (Taft has not been ranked as the greatest chief justice, but no chief justice to date has equaled him in girth and weight.) Among other things, the legislation greatly expanded the discretionary side of the Court's docket. For the great mass of federal judicial business, review by right disappeared. Not only would there be fewer cases for the Supreme Court to decide, but the Court would have an even greater say in selecting them. In 1988, Congress conferred discretionary status on virtually all the Supreme Court's docket. The mandatory appeal category (or review by right) nearly disappeared, surviving only for decisions by three-judge district court panels (required by Congress in a few instances, such as in voting rights disputes, in place of a hearing before a single judge). These go directly to the Supreme Court, bypassing the court of appeals. Aside from that exception, the Court today has total control over its docket.

Viewed alongside these developments, the Waite Court was truly part classical and part modern. Organizationally, the Waite Court had far more in common with the Marshall Court (1801–1835) than with the Fuller Court (1888–1910) that succeeded it. Granted, Waite era justices had to do less circuit riding than did most of their predecessors, but the country was also larger. At least Waite and his colleagues could travel by rail from state to state, in Pullman palace cars no less, instead of on horseback or by stage coach and canal boat. But the fact remained that the Supreme Court possessed virtually no control over its docket. The notion of meriting Supreme Court review was under discussion, but its realization lay in the future.

Jurisdictionally in other respects, the Waite Court had more in common with the Fuller and later twentieth-century Courts than with any Court that preceded it. Looming over everything were the Reconstruction amendments that, with their implementing statutes, vastly expanded the kinds of cases the Supreme Court might hear. Not one of the subsequent twelve amendments to the Constitution, from the Sixteenth through the Twenty-seventh, has so affected the business of federal courts. Additionally, given the nature of those amendments, cases arising under them invariably involved a claim by an individual, an organization, or a business enterprise that constitutional rights had been violated. For Waite's Court, as compared to earlier Courts, there were not only more people but more laws that affected them. Indeed, Waite was chief justice at the same time that the volume of government regulations, particularly at the state level, was increasing dramatically (Hurst 1950, 16; Friedman 2002, 39). True, the claim was frequently a claim associated with property, but that was no less a claim than one based on another individual right. Moreover, the Waite docket had its share of juror and voting rights cases that went to the heart of the fundamental constitutional right of participation in the political community—the right to be counted among "We the People. . . ." Thus in the Waite Court one finds the earliest signs of a rights culture developing, in which Americans would routinely look to the judiciary to both vindicate and sustain their liberties.

The Justices and the Electoral Commission of 1877

Between the end of the Civil War in 1865 and the extended and fiercely contested presidential election of 2000, the United States confronted three constitutional crises: (1) the disputed presidential election of 1876; (2) the 1937 controversy over court packing; and (3) the Watergate affair of 1972–1974. In each one, justices of the Supreme Court were key participants.

In 1974 the Supreme Court virtually dictated President Richard M. Nixon's departure from office, the only instance in U.S. history when a president has stepped down during his term. Its decision in *United States v. Nixon* ordered the president, against a claim of executive privilege, to hand over certain documents and sound recordings to a court in the District of Columbia for use as evidence. The documents and recordings in turn amounted to the proverbial smoking gun that revealed the president's complicity in a two-year long illegal cover-up. The president thus had a choice between vacating the White House voluntarily or facing certain impeachment by the House of Representatives and near-certain conviction, and therefore removal from office, by the Senate.

In 1937, by contrast, the judiciary was on the defensive. It was the Court's own unprecedented obstinacy during 1935 and 1936 in reaction to President Franklin D. Roosevelt's major economic reforms of the Great Depression that prompted the president's equally unprecedented assault on the structure and composition of the Supreme Court. Roosevelt lost his bid to expand the Court with sympathetic justices (court packing) but, because he secured an administration-friendly bench, he won the war.

Waite Court justices were also involved in resolving the disputed election of 1876. The difference was that, in this crisis, the Court institutionally was not a participant. No decision rendered by the highest court in the land decided that election. Instead, the Court was indirectly entangled because five of its nine justices accepted appointment as members of a fifteen-person commission established by Congress to resolve contested returns. Indeed, one of the five justices sat in place of another who had been expected to serve. Thus, six members of the first Waite Court were connected in one way or another with the commission. Furthermore, one former justice, two future members of the Waite Court, and the older brother of a sitting justice had roles in the drama that unfolded as the United States, barely twelve years removed from the Civil War, found itself again on the brink of civil strife. Ironically, the Court itself had only recently managed to shed the partisan reputation acquired in 1857 as a result of the *Dred Scott Case.* Now the justices' service on the electoral commission cast them yet again as partisan actors, contributing "to that bitter and unscrupulous spirit of faction with which the politics of our day threatens to taint the judiciary" ("The Week" 1881, 62).

The election of 1876 was the third in the country's relatively short history in which the routine presidential electoral procedures failed to produce a winner. The first two arose when no candidate received a majority of electoral votes, as Article II of the Constitution requires. Not anticipating the formation of national political parties, the framers of the Constitution required presidential electors to cast two votes for president. The one who received the most votes would be president, and the runner-up would be vice president. The election of 1800 yielded a tie between top electoral vote recipients Thomas Jefferson and Aaron Burr, both of them

Democratic-Republicans. There were more Democratic-Republican than Federalist electors, and all seventy-three of the former uniformly, if unwisely, cast their votes for Jefferson and Burr. Pursuant to the Constitution, the House of Representatives then performed its backup function and, with each state's delegation casting one vote as the Constitution mandated, elected Jefferson as the third president. To greatly reduce the possibility of another tie vote for president and to take account of the rise of the political parties, Jefferson promptly secured ratification of the Twelfth Amendment (1804) that required electors to cast separate votes for president and vice president.

Again in the election of 1824 no candidate received a majority of the electoral vote. If the failure of the 1800 election occurred because of the advent of the party system, the election of 1824 yielded no winner because of its virtual collapse. Jefferson's party had so thoroughly eliminated the Federalists as a national political force that they had not fielded a presidential candidate since 1816. Without competition between two parties, factions emerged within the only party that remained. The electoral vote was badly split: ninety-nine for Andrew Jackson, eighty-four for John Quincy Adams, forty-one for William Crawford, and thirty-seven for Henry Clay. Again acting in its backup mode because no one had an electoral vote majority, the House elected Adams as the sixth president. The outcome was doubly difficult for Jackson and his followers to swallow. Not only had he enjoyed a plurality of electoral votes but a plurality (41.3 percent) of popular votes too. However, it was the vote in the House, not the vote in the precincts, that mattered.

The election of 1876 posed an altogether different predicament, one for which the elections of 1800 and 1824 offered no obvious solution. "I think the result of the election is more uncertain than I have felt it to be for twelve years," Justice Miller wrote to William Ballinger, his brother-in-law, in July of the election year. "There is enough of opposition to the *Administration*, perhaps enough to the Republican party, to defeat the latter if it could be combined. But the folly of the opposition has saved us before and will probably do it again" (Fairman 1939, 282). When the votes were counted months later, Miller's prediction was as right as it was wrong.

In the race against Ohio Republican Rutherford B. Hayes, Democrat Samuel J. Tilden of New York comfortably won the popular vote, with an edge of about 250,000, out of over 8 million votes cast. That statistic surely pleased Democrats: It was the first presidential election since 1856 in which they outpolled the Republicans and the first since 1852 in which the party received at least 50 percent of the vote. Their euphoria, however, was tempered by one sobering fact. Although Tilden seemed certain of 184 electoral votes, to Hayes's 165, twenty electoral votes remained in play because of disputed returns from Florida, Louisiana, Oregon, and South Carolina. From that pool of twenty, Tilden needed only one to reach the minimum majority of 185, and thus the White House. To reach the same magic number, Hayes required all twenty. Democrats were acutely aware of the fact that in three of those states Hayes's hopes rested on the legitimacy of actions taken by local canvassing officials who were themselves part of the Reconstruction governments that Republican congressional majorities had imposed on a vanquished South.

Of the four state controversies, South Carolina's seemed most encouraging for Hayes. Although Hayes electors had received a majority of the popular vote, Democrats claimed that the election results were tainted in part because of failure to comply with a state constitutional requirement for voter registration and because of the intimidating presence of federal troops (Fairman 1988, 117). By their reasoning, the state had not legitimately appointed electors because the federal troops made it impossible to know the will of the people with accuracy.

Oregon's situation was problematic for both Hayes and Tilden. As in South Carolina, Oregon's three Republican electors garnered more votes than Tilden's, but one of the three was a postmaster at the time of the election and was therefore constitutionally ineligible to be an elector. After he resigned his postal job, the state secretary of state, a Republican, officially certified him and the other two Republican electors and authorized them to cast Oregon's electoral votes. The state's Democratic governor then declared two Republicans and one Democrat as the duly chosen electors on the theory that the postmaster's resignation could not make valid what had been invalid on election day. Complicating matters further was a state law that allowed a vacancy among electors to be filled by the remaining electors. The result was a pair of competing returns. One set awarded three votes to Hayes; this number included the vote cast by the now ex-postmaster. The other awarded two votes to Hayes and one to Tilden.

The situations in Louisiana and Florida were considerably more convoluted. There were allegations of voter fraud in Louisiana, and white Democrats in both states had frightened off unknown numbers of black Republicans from the polls. With the voter canvassing boards in both states in Republican hands, returns from selected precincts were excluded and the election was certified for the Hayes electors. Believing that victory had been snatched from their hands, Democrats insisted that the Louisiana and Florida electoral votes belonged instead to Tilden.

The Twelfth Amendment specified that electors were to meet in their respective states to cast votes for president and vice president, and then to transmit those votes to the president of the Senate (otherwise known as the vice president, who was then a Republican). In the presence of both the Senate and the House of Representatives, the president of the Senate was to open the certificates of election "and the votes shall then be counted." However, the Constitution did not address what was to be done when rival sets of returns claimed to be "the votes." Nor was it clear whether the president of the Senate was the one who actually counted and thus, presumably, the one who separated valid from invalid votes.

Had one or the other party been in full control of Congress, the disputed returns would probably not have generated a crisis. A Democrat majority in the House and Senate would no doubt have accepted some returns for Tilden; after all, only one electoral vote stood between him and the White House. A Republican majority in the House and Senate would no doubt have uniformly accepted votes for Hayes, thus handing the White House to him. But control of Congress was split: Democrats held a majority in the House, and Republicans held a majority in the Senate. It was therefore highly improbable that a majority of both houses would vote to accept the same set of returns.

With no obvious solution to this conundrum apparent, each house of Congress created a special committee to investigate the controversies and to make recommendations. In January, the committees agreed that a special commission be established to weigh the conflicting claims and to report to a joint session of Congress. The majority position of the tribunal in turn would determine the fate of the twenty electoral votes unless (1) at least five senators and five representatives objected, and (2) each house, meeting separately, agreed to reject the findings of the tribunal.

President Grant signed into law a bill creating an electoral commission on January 29, 1877. Five of its members, or commissioners (three Democrats and two Republicans), would come from the House of Representatives, and five (three Republicans and two Democrats) from the Senate. The remaining five would consist of justices of the Supreme Court, including two Democrats (Clifford and Field—the Court's only professed members of the party) and two Republicans (Justices Miller and Strong). These four justices in turn would select a fifth, the expectation being that they would agree on Justice David Davis, who had once been a staunch Republican (and Lincoln's campaign manager in 1860) but whose recent vacillations left all unsure about his party loyalties. This arrangement thus provided for seven Democrats, seven Republicans, and one presumed independent. All seemed to be counting on Davis to "maintain the tribunal's equipoise," as the secretary to the House's special committee later recorded. "In the ponderous Illinois jurist was centered the hopes of Democracy, the apprehensions of Republicanism" (Northrup 1901, 926, 933). As senior justice, Clifford would chair the commission. The bill signed by Grant thus reflected both the widespread conviction that a way out of the morass had to be found quickly and the confidence of each party that the chosen device of the commission would work to its advantage. Moreover, inclusion of members of the Supreme Court suggested a belief that the justices would not be swayed by the partisanship that was expected to dictate the votes of the congressional membership; yet the struggle within Congress about the composition of the judicial component suggested that they would.

Expectations about Davis promptly went awry. Practically on the eve of the congressional vote establishing the commission, William P. Pelton, Tilden's nephew, colluded with Democrats in the Illinois legislature to engineer Davis's election to the

U.S. Senate. The thinking was that Davis, out of gratitude to Democrats, would then be obliged to favor Tilden over Hayes. However, neither Tilden nor congressional Democrats seem to have had any forewarning of this scheme. "Thunder out of a clear sky could not more thoroughly have startled the Democratic leaders in Washington" (Northrup 1901, 933). The intrigue backfired. Davis announced his resignation from the Court to take effect on March 4, 1877, whereupon he would be sworn in as senator. In the meanwhile, as senator-elect, Davis could hardly sit as a judicial member of the electoral tribunal. The four judicial members of the commission then named Justice Bradley to take Davis's place. Long a Republican, Bradley nonetheless was not an outspoken partisan. His political involvement over the years had been minimal, consisting of a single (and unsuccessful) campaign for a congressional seat in 1862. Ironically, the expectation that Davis would be the fifth judicial member had helped convince congressional Democrats to accept the commission plan. Now the timing of Davis's exit, coming as it did at such a late date, meant that the process had gone too far and gained too much momentum for Democrats to back out.

The commission meet between January 31 and March 2, hearing arguments and testimony in the Old Senate Chamber, now quarters for the Supreme Court. Able counsel did battle for both sides. Among those the Democrats enlisted were former justice John A. Campbell, who had represented the butchers in the *Slaughterhouse Cases;* former attorney general Jeremiah Black, whose nomination to the Court late in the Buchanan administration had died in the Senate; and, David Dudley Field, brother of Justice Field. The Republican team included future justice Stanley Matthews. Another future justice, L. Q. C. Lamar, was the member of the House of Representatives who officially nominated the five House members who had been chosen by their respective caucuses. Lamar shortly would have much to do with achieving the Democrats' acquiescence in, if hardly joyful acceptance of, Hayes's election. He also was instrumental in negotiations with the new administration that led to the withdrawal of the last federal troops from the South and the formal end of Reconstruction.

In resolving the disputes from Louisiana and Florida especially, the commission's initial task was to decide whether it would look behind the officially certified election returns. Democrats argued that the official tallying of electoral votes in the presence of Congress made no sense if Congress could not be assured of the integrity of the votes. The question was critical and had not been answered by the law setting up the commission. If the tribunal made its own independent assessment of the validity of the returns, it would then have to consider ample evidence of voter intimidation and fraud as well as the discounting of Democratic ballots. Under that broader mission, some of the electoral votes might be awarded to Tilden. This step would have been devastating for Republicans because of the obvious reality that Hayes needed all contested votes to win. On the other hand, if the commission decided it could not look behind the returns, then its role would encompass little more than assuring that the certifications had been presented in the proper form. Republicans argued that going behind the election returns would place Congress in the unprecedented position of second-guessing state canvassing officials. They raised the specter of Congress routinely making and unmaking election results from the states. So circumscribed a role would probably validate the Hayes electors. On this and all other substantively important questions, members of the commission, including Justice Bradley, voted by party affiliation, accepting the Hayes electors from Louisiana and Florida by a vote of 8–7.

Democrats hoped to prevail in the Oregon dispute based on the commission's decisions about the Louisiana and Florida returns. If so, they would pick up the necessary and sufficient single electoral vote for Tilden. Oregon's governor (a Democrat) had certified one Democratic and two Republican electors. The argument that reaped electors for Hayes in Florida and Louisiana favored Tilden in Oregon. If the commission was not to look behind the official returns, Hayes seemed to face certain defeat. Stanley Matthews and lead Republican counsel William Evarts, however, managed to turn facts to the Republican's advantage. State law made the secretary of state (a Republican) the official canvassing authority. Refusal by the governor to sign that certificate of election did not undercut the validity of the conclusion of the canvassing authority. Members of the commission, again voting by party, decided 8–7 that the secretary of state, not the governor, spoke for the people of Oregon. By the same margin the commissioners accepted the Hayes electors from South Carolina, the last of the four cases they considered.

With Oregon perhaps excepted, each side amazingly had effectively switched doctrinal position, reversing entrenched political views that had defined the parties since 1856. Democrats professed high nationalism, insisting on intervention by a federal authority into elections conducted by the states. Republicans argued for the sanctity of states' rights and congressional deference to state officials. As Justice Miller remarked eleven years later at a dinner at the University of Pennsylvania Law School, "To permit Congress to determine the vote would have resulted in the destruction of the Government. That body never acts judicially. It would be like their determination upon the rights to seats which are invariably decided in favor of those in sympathy with the majority" (Pennypacker 1918, 132).

The commission's rulings that favored Republican electors in each state made it virtually certain that Hayes, not Tilden, would be the nineteenth president. The Republican Senate accepted the verdicts, and the Democratic House rejected them. Under the terms of the law that created the commission, the commission's judgments were to stand unless a majority in both houses voted to discard them.

March 4, the usual inauguration day, fell on a Sunday in 1877. Therefore, Hayes privately took the oath of office on March 3, and the public inauguration occurred on

Monday, March 5. "I am just returned from the . . . ceremonies," Justice Miller wrote his brother-in-law Ballinger in Texas, "and the cannon are peacefully playing the last part in that drama. It is to me a great relief. . . ." In Miller's mind, the "peaceful inauguration of Hayes . . . is due largely, very largely, to the discretion, forbearance, good sense and patriotism of the southern leaders of the democratic party" (Fairman 1939, 291). Miller specifically cited the contributions of L. Q. C. Lamar, among three others.

If Miller was relieved, Bradley was anguished. More than any of the five justices on the commission, he incurred the greatest personal cost. As he wrote a year later, he had endured "immense gratuitous and unfounded abuse" (Fairman 1988, 123). Although all fifteen members had taken the same oath "impartially [to] examine and consider . . . and a true judgment give," no one seemed surprised (although many were decidedly unhappy) that fourteen voted by party. Bradley, the fifteenth member, was therefore in a unique and impossible position: Both sides expected him to act impartially on their behalf. But if unhappy Democrats aimed most of their invective at Bradley, they saved some for Miller and Strong. When the three were hung in effigy in Monticello, New York, Bradley's likeness was positioned in the center and bore this inscription: "I am crucified between two thieves" (Swisher 1930, 278).

The outcome was costly to the Court as well. Reflecting the consensus that Democrats had been duped into accepting the commission as a way out of the election dispute, Field and Clifford conspicuously absented themselves from the inauguration. One newspaper with Democratic leanings praised them for having a sense of propriety, but added that they would have served their country better had they refused appointment to the electoral commission. A Republican paper decried their absence as "an act of discourtesy as discreditable and unworthy as it was uncalled for and undignified. The only explanation . . . is that, not being able to forget that they were Democrats, they were unable to remember that they were justices" (Swisher 1930, 281–282). Never one to keep opinions to himself, Field was believed to have started a rumor that Bradley changed his mind at the last minute on critical issues after being visited by influential Republican leaders and railroad magnates. Bradley demanded that Field prove the accusation or retract it. Field insisted that he had been misquoted and misunderstood, but hard feelings between the two persisted. His commission experience steeled Clifford to remain on the bench, incapacitated or not, until a Democrat again occupied the White House. Although Garfield's election in 1880 made that hope impossible to realize, Clifford's mental deterioration soon posed a serious problem for Chief Justice Waite. With other members of the bench suffering various infirmities, a smaller number of justices were left to shoulder an increasingly burdensome caseload.

Yet Field and Clifford had performed a valuable public service, as distasteful as each man must have found the final resolution of the election of 1876. As the only two true Democrats on the Court, it seems improbable that there would have been an electoral commission had one or both refused to serve. How the disputed election would then have been resolved remains anyone's guess.

Nonetheless, participation by a majority of the bench in resolving the dispute over electoral votes meant that they (perhaps Bradley alone) were effectively determining the next president. Since 1877, this has happened only twice: in 1974, when the judicially driven ouster of Nixon made Vice President Gerald Ford the thirty-eighth president; and in 2000, when *Bush v. Gore* cut short a hastily arranged recount in Florida and handed the White House to George W. Bush.

Moreover, the Waite Court's part in the electoral debacle of 1876 shaped the Supreme Court. Had the commission not awarded the election to Hayes, it is highly improbable that either John Marshall Harlan or William Woods would ever have been appointed to the Court. Hayes owed a political debt to Harlan, and Tilden assuredly did not. As Chapter 1 explained, Woods was the right Republican in the right place at the right time for a Republican president who wanted to ease sectional tensions by elevating a southerner—albeit a recently relocated former Union Army officer—to the Court for the first time since the Civil War. Had the electoral controversy gone Tilden's way, the withdrawal of federal troops would probably have proceeded, as it did under Hayes. But there also would surely have been the nomination of a real southerner to the Court, well prior to Grover Cleveland's selection of L. Q. C. Lamar in the twilight of the Waite years.

Waite as Court Leader

Morrison Waite was the last person sworn in as "Chief Justice of the Supreme Court of the United States." Beginning with Melville Fuller, all successive commissions for the occupant of the Court's center chair have read "Chief Justice of the United States." That change in wording in 1888 was symbolic of the national stature that the office had acquired, but it was also prophetic. Beginning in 1922 every chief justice, working through the Judicial Conference of the United States, has been the administrative head of the entire federal court system (Fish 1973, 32–33). Given the caseload that swamped his Court, it is just as well that Waite was not saddled with that larger oversight responsibility. Instead, his responsibilities were similar to those shouldered by the six chiefs who preceded him: He was administrative head of the Supreme Court and its presiding officer. Any influence over other federal courts, outside of the Fourth Circuit (to which chiefs have traditionally been assigned), was informal at most and occasional at best.

In a formal sense, all chief justices, Waite included, have been primus inter pares—first among equals (Mason 1968, 21). With the post's supervisory duties has always come a modest differential in salary, but the chief justice is officially in charge with respect to the associate justices in a very limited sense. Although the chief traditionally is the one who controls the assignment of opinions, even that power applies only when he is in the majority. Furthermore, his vote in deciding cases is worth no more than the vote of any associate justice. Similarly, the associate justices are not accountable to the chief justice. They do not work for him. There is no chain of command on the bench. The relationship between chief justice and associate justice is not the relationship that exists between the president and a member of the cabinet. Associate justices do not serve at the pleasure of their chief. Thus, the lines of authority that might otherwise assure a smoothly functioning military unit, business, or other organization are absent at the Supreme Court. The Court is no well-oiled machine, but rather it seems to consist of nine little law firms where each justice "is his own sovereign" (Frankfurter 1953, 901). A right to preside does not carry with it a right to prevail. Nor does it entitle a chief to influence over the Court. A chief justice may reign without also ruling. "Being Chief Justice," laconically commented Justice Harlan F. Stone after observing Taft at work for five years, "is a good deal like being Dean of the law school—he has to do the things the janitor will not do" (Mason 1956, 218).

Nonetheless, even without the usual accoutrements of power, some chief justices have been known as Court leaders. John Marshall immediately stands out. For a variety of reasons, some of which were unique to his day, Marshall dominated the Court like no other chief justice. It was indisputably his Court in fact as well as in name. To what degree was the Supreme Court between 1874 and 1888 truly the *Waite* Court? Is the name suggestive of real impact and influence, or does it remain a mere linguistic convenience?

A pathbreaking paper written over four decades ago (and since reprinted in several anthologies on judicial behavior) applied the concept of small group leadership functions, specifically "task" and "social" leadership, to the chief justice. From this perspective, a task leader is one who presents his views with force and clarity, defends them successfully in discussion with colleagues, provides guidance for handling perplexing situations, and assumes responsibility for orienting conference deliberations and writing opinions. Someone who excels in social leadership relieves tensions, encourages solidarity and agreement, attends to the emotional needs of colleagues, and is often the best-liked member of the bench (Danelski 2002, 663). This concept of leadership confirms "the common sense observation that a man who wishes to exert influence over his fellows can do so most effectually if he is both intellectually disciplined and tactful in interpersonal relations" (Murphy 1962, 642). (Of course the same common sense observation would apply to a woman as well.)

Inherent in task leadership, however, are two distinct, if interrelated, functions: managerial and intellectual leadership. Considering these separately may offer a clearer window into judicial leadership, especially when a chief justice is stronger in one than the other (Stephenson 1973, 900; Seddig 1991, 64). A chief justice as managerial leader keeps the Court abreast of its docket, maintains a maximum degree of Court unity, provides expeditious direction of the judicial conference, and assigns opinions thoughtfully and purposefully. A chief justice as intellectual leader presents his views persuasively, is a principal source of ideas and doctrine, and provides tactical and strategic guidance in political dilemmas. This division thus allows a probing of three measures of leadership: social, managerial, and intellectual, a trichotomy that seems especially appropriate in assessing Waite. So judged, Waite excelled at social leadership, performed adequately as Court manager, and ordinarily looked to others for intellectual leadership.

From the beginning Waite attempted to fashion the camaraderie that would be necessary for the Court to function effectively. Given the mountain of work the Waite Court faced, the importance of this objective should not be minimized. His careful handling of some of the "problem brethren," particularly Field, Clifford, and Swayne, demonstrated that the chief was sensitive to the benefits that could be derived from relieving interpersonal tension and supporting fallen egos. He did so without the "judicial handshake" that his successor Melville Fuller introduced as a device to maintain harmony. To this day, upon entering the conference room, each justice shakes the hand of every other justice. It remains "a symbol that harmony of aims if not of views is the Court's guiding principle" (Brennan 1972, 42). The following examples elucidate Waite's style.

Soon after becoming chief justice, the Court held in *United States v. Union Pacific R.R. Co.* (1875) that the acts of Congress chartering the newly constructed western railroads did not require a railroad to pay semiannual interest prior to maturity of the government's second-mortgage bonds. Because the decision was in favor of the company, Waite assigned the opinion to Davis, then perceived as the member of the bench least friendly to corporate privilege. In fact, at the conference where the case was decided, the chief remarked that it would be best that the opinion not be written by anyone closely identified with the industry. Bradley had come to the Court as an experienced railroad attorney, but it was no doubt Field whom Waite identified with the industry because the Californian was a close friend of Leland Stanford, head of the Central Pacific. Field—always strong-willed, often tempestuous, and quick to take offense—vented his feelings in a note to the chief justice. "I had no idea that you specially desired it," Waite gingerly replied, "and when the announcement was made, supposed you would not fail to see its propriety." Unmoved, Field scratched off a second note, and Waite made a second attempt to mollify his colleague:

> I have just received and read your note of yesterday. I think you must be mistaken in your understanding of the words I used after the consultation. If those you give were the words I did use, certainly they were not used in the offensive sense you appear to have received them.

> We cannot conceal from ourselves the fact, that in the excited state of feeling which exists, or has existed, with the public in respect to the connexion of the government with the Union Pacific there may be some feeling of disappointment at the result of this case. It seems to me, therefore, to be specially important that the opinion should come from one who had not only been understood to be watchful of the government purse, but who would not be known as the personal friend of the parties representing these rail road interests. . . .
>
> No one appreciates your vigorous style more than I do, and, but for these considerations I should have been glad to have had its use in this case. . . . As for opinions in important cases, I don't know, but I think you fared better than the Judge [Davis,] who has the case[,] did at the last term. Certainly at the present term he has had no advantage over you. I certainly intend to treat all my brethren fairly in this most delicate and at the same time important part of my work. If I do not, it is the fault of the head and not of the heart. (Stephenson 1973, 909)

His second note may not have calmed Field entirely, but there is no evidence in Waite's papers or in other sources that Field ever again challenged his chief on an opinion assignment.

Nathan Clifford posed a different problem for Waite. A carryover from the Buchanan administration and the oldest member of the Court, his mental abilities weakened noticeably soon after Waite became chief justice. However, Clifford was alert enough to sense what others were thinking. Waite tried on several occasions to alleviate the situation. On one occasion, for example, Clifford voted with the majority in a case, was assigned to write the opinion, but later returned it to Waite, declining to write it because he was unprepared. Waite wrote the opinion himself. In a similar instance, Clifford had been upset by something and notified Waite: "I am not willing to write an opinion in No. 93 and therefore return it to you. If you want No. 99 for any of your friends you may have that also." Waite replied carefully and cautiously: "I regret that my assignment of cases to you last evening was not satisfactory. I gave you 93 because you were familiar with the law of copyright, and although the case was a simple one, I thought it might be made the foundation of one of your useful opinions. . . . If you still think you do not want 93, I will keep it. . . . I wanted to give you the two important land cases which Judge Miller has, but you said expressly in the conference that you did not want them" (Stephenson 1973, 910–911).

A misunderstanding between Swayne and Miller in conference in November 1879 led to a delicate note from the chief justice to Swayne in an attempt to quell the conflict. Not only did Miller consider Swayne unworthy of the judicial robe, but he was willing to say so. "As I said in the consultation room," Waite explained to Swayne, "I am entirely satisfied with your opinion." He continued:

> I think, however, Miller had the right to believe from what occurred when the case was decided, that the point which he suggested yesterday was not to go into the

> opinion. While no formal vote was taken he had good reason to believe his objection was assented to.
>
> I submit to you, therefore, whether, under all the circumstances, that part of the opinion had better not be left out. You know how important it is to avoid, as far as possible, all occasion for unpleasant criticism in our consultations, and if one judge is allowed to write an opinion on a different ground from that on which the decision was placed, it is easy to see how difficult it may sometimes be to enforce the rule as to others.
>
> I hope you will receive this suggestion in the same spirit it is made. . . . I leave the matter entirely to your own judgment. (Stephenson 1973, 999, n. 47)

Four years earlier, when Swayne complained about the amount of work he had to do, Waite had tried to accommodate him, even at a sacrifice to himself. "It was an imposition to ask you to take the French . . . case. Send it back to me and I will write it. I shall have plenty of time this week" (Trimble 1938, 265.)

As these incidents illustrate, opinion assignment is one of a chief justice's most important functions but can be fraught with controversy. How those assignments are administered thus speaks not only to social leadership but managerial leadership as well. Waite understood that the choice of the author of an opinion played a part in maintaining Court cohesion and in achieving public acceptance of the ruling.

In 1881, the chief justice compiled for historian George Bancroft a list of those cases decided since 1874 that Waite thought were of greatest constitutional significance. Of the seventy-two cases on the list, Waite was in the majority in all but six. Of those sixty-six, he had assigned the bulk to some of the most intellectually capable members of the bench: Waite had written fourteen, Field and Miller eleven each, Strong ten, Bradley seven, and Harlan, the newest member, five. Swayne and Davis wrote four and two, respectively, and Clifford and Hunt each had only one. By authoring a plurality of the important cases, Waite seemed to be suggesting both to his colleagues and to the public that a chief justice ought to write the greater number of opinions. This he routinely did across most categories of cases. As Chapter 1 showed, many of Waite's opinions may have amounted to little more than brief statements of fact and law, followed by an order of the Court, but they represented a clear commitment of time just the same.

Moreover, Waite made a conscious effort to vote with the majority, especially in important cases, in order to retain the opinion assignment power. His personal docket books indicate that he sometimes switched his vote after conference so that he would be able to choose the author of the opinion. Indeed, data presented in Chapter 1 showed that Waite was one of the Court's least frequent dissenters, especially during the first and second Waite Courts. This pattern of behavior also supported what Chapter 1 described as the norm of consensus, whereby published (that is, public) dissenting votes were discouraged. Waite took pride in unanimity, once writing his wife in 1878 about an unnamed case in which he had managed to persuade Field and Clifford not to dissent.

Waite also believed that the chief justice, at least up to a point, should move with his Court if his Court could not be persuaded to move with him. For instance, in *Stone v. Farmers' Loan and Trust Co.* (1886), the Court considered a challenge to the operation of a Mississippi regulatory commission based on a presumed contract in the state-granted charter to the Mobile and Ohio Railroad. In the first draft of his opinion upholding the state's position, Waite barely mentioned the issue of due process of law. Miller, Bradley, Matthews, and Gray had voted with Waite in conference, with Blatchford not taking part. Field, Woods, and Harlan dissented, mainly on contracts clause grounds. When the chief justice circulated the draft opinion, Matthews added several paragraphs indicating that state regulation of rates was limited by considerations of due process and just compensation if the regulation was deemed confiscatory and by the equal protection clause if it was discriminatory. Waite accepted Matthews's suggestion, apparently realizing how essential his vote was: A change of mind by Matthews would have resulted in an evenly split bench and an affirmation of the circuit court's holding for the railroad.

Managerial leadership also encompasses efficient handling of the Court's docket. That was an exceedingly difficult goal during the Waite Court. Recall that the bench was understaffed during part of Waite's tenure. Justice Hunt suffered a stroke in 1878 and thereafter did not participate in the Court's work during the three years that he waited for Congress to grant him a pension. Then there were the mental declines of Clifford and Swayne. That left more work to be done by the able-bodied (and able-minded). "I am hard at work, but still very well," Waite wrote in 1881. "The experience this fall has satisfied me entirely that six or seven is less than nine" (Trimble 1938, 273). It was during this period that Waite appointed a committee consisting of Miller, Swayne, and himself to make the workload more manageable by reducing the length of opinions. But as Miller complained in an 1879 letter, "we have not been able to suggest any satisfactory remedy. The truth," he continued, "is that the one man of our court who ought to take the lead and without whose firmness and courage nothing can be done is sadly wanting in both those qualities. He is much more anxious to be popular as an amiable, kind hearted man (which he is) than as the dignified and capable head of the greatest court the world ever knew" (Fairman 1939, 409). Miller's disparaging reference was to the chief justice.

But the situation would have been difficult for any chief with or without the infirmities that plagued the Waite bench. As noted, the Court would neither be entirely relieved of circuit-riding duty nor enjoy even modest control over its docket until after 1891. Instead, the justices were expected to spend part of each year on circuit and were obliged to decide all qualifying cases. With an expanded federal jurisdiction in the decade after the Civil War, that meant a docket increasingly in arrears.

A backlog of about 600 cases in May of 1876 ballooned to about 1500 at the time of Waite's death in March of 1888 (Trimble 1938, 250, n. 43). Such numbers pointed to what Waite himself called an "oppressive wrong." The chief justice spoke before a bar association meeting at the Academy of Music in Philadelphia in September 1887. There, he spelled out the grim reality: "Business is now more than three years and a half behind; that is to say, that cases entered now, when the term of 1887 is about to begin, are not likely to be reached in their regular order for hearing until late in the term of 1890" (Waite 1887, 318).

Waite made clear that responsibility for relief lay with Congress, although neither Waite nor any of his associate justices shared an enthusiasm for lobbying in which Chief Justice Taft would so handily engage for the Court's benefit in the 1920s. Even so, Waite went out of his way to issue what amounted to an advisory opinion that acceptable relief did not include the easy option of dividing the Court into panels so that it presumably would be able to move ahead at three times its usual pace. He reminded his audience that the Constitution precluded that alternative: "I beg you to note this language: *One* Supreme Court," he quoted from Article III. "Not a Supreme Court or Supreme Courts, but one—and only one."

As for intellectual leadership, there is little evidence that Waite led his Court doctrinally with consistency. One reason had nothing to do with Waite at all. The reality was that a few bright, articulate, and doctrinally aware justices were already in place when he arrived. It would have been difficult for any new chief to have led a Field, a Miller, a Bradley, or, later, a Harlan. It is, after all, far easier to lead colleagues who are in need of leadership. Felix Frankfurter much later pointed to what was perhaps a second reason: "The stuff of the artist was not him." The future Supreme Court justice opined that Waite's opinions were "not delectable reading. That is a defect for which he properly suffers." But the limited appeal of his opinions, in contrast to those of predecessors Marshall and Taney, "is due in part to something else—to fulfillment of one of the greatest duties of a judge, the duty not to enlarge his authority" (Frankfurter 1937, 79–80). Instead, Waite's important intellectual accomplishment as chief was that he tended to reinforce the dominant doctrinal views. For instance, he embraced the limited understanding of the *Slaughterhouse Cases* articulated by Miller regarding the intent and scope of the Fourteenth Amendment. The Court largely adhered to that construction throughout Waite's tenure in both economic and race discrimination cases. Yet the significance of Waite's support of that view should not be minimized. Salmon Chase, chief justice at the time of the *Slaughterhouse Cases*, cast a dissenting vote in that 5–4 decision. Waite's subsequent endorsement of Miller's position thus made the 1873 ruling far more enduring.

Also to be considered in the arena of intellectual leadership is the all-important ruling in *Munn v. Illinois* (1877), in which Waite wrote for a seven-justice majority. *Munn* affirmed the authority of states to set rates that could be charged by grain warehouses, and presumably by all other enterprises where property was "affected with a public interest." Bradley was of great help to Waite with the *Munn* opinion. In conference the Court had agreed that the Fourteenth Amendment's due process clause was no barrier to rate regulation in such instances. Bradley's contribution lay in supplying his chief with ample foundation, by way of an English treatise and English court decisions, for the Court's groundbreaking contribution to U.S. constitutional law. Waite's imprint on *Munn* lay in his insistence (1) that the Court give legislators wide latitude in selecting the property affected with a public interest, and (2) that, once the right to regulate was established, the reasonableness of the rate or other regulation was a legislative, not a judicial, question.

As Chapter 3 relates, *Munn* was one of the *Granger Cases*. The other cases involved state regulation of railroad rates. Those cases presented not only the due process issue that *Munn* resolved but a commerce clause problem as well. Waite steadfastly clung to his view in those cases that state regulation of railroads was acceptable under the commerce clause even when it impacted interstate travel and shipments. It was on this critical point that his 7–2 majority in the *Granger Cases* became a 6–3 majority against his position nine years later in *Wabash, St. Louis and Pacific Railway v. Illinois* (1886). Miller, who had been in the majority in the *Granger Cases*, led the new majority, with Bradley, Gray, and Waite in dissent. The chief not only failed to command his Court on this vital question but refused to adjust his own views to accommodate the new majority.

Perhaps Waite's singular contribution to the Court derived from his *character*, in the broadest sense of that word. It seemed to imbue all that he did as chief. The Court under Chief Justice Taney was badly sullied by *Dred Scott* in 1857. It took a group of Lincoln appointees before the Court again appeared reasonably trustworthy in the wake of secession and the Civil War. Even then, an occasional antiwar or anti-Reconstruction opinion such as Davis's in *Ex parte Milligan* (1866) or Field's in the *Test Oath Cases* (*Ex parte Garland* and *Cummings v. Missouri*, 1867) was enough to awaken doubts about the institution's devotion to the Union. Chief Justice Chase, Taney's successor, generated his own liabilities for the Court. A gifted but vain man—it was said that there were four persons in his conception of the Trinity—he was afflicted, as one colleague said, with "presidency on the brain." It was the White House, not the chief justiceship, that Chase coveted as the crowning jewel on an already impressive list of lifetime achievements. He had sought the Republican nomination in 1856, 1860, and 1864, and in 1868, while chief justice, courted the affections of both parties. His opinion for a 4–3 bench in *Hepburn v. Griswold* (1870), the decision that invalidated the greenback financing scheme enacted while he was secretary of the treasury, reinforced the view that he was trying to ingratiate himself to the Democratic party in hopes of a presidential nomination in 1872.

By contrast, Waite strove to be neither Taney nor Chase. He tried to avoid

Taney's mistake in *Dred Scott* by embracing a modest view of the federal judicial power. His most memorable phrase, perhaps his only, from fourteen years of service was: "For protection against abuses by legislatures, the people must resort to the polls, not to the courts" (*Munn v. Illinois*, 1877). Waite shunned the political aspirations that Chase pursued. When rumors circulated in 1876, in the last year of President Grant's second term, that Waite might be a prospect for the Republican nomination for the White House, the chief justice quickly squelched the idea. "The Court is now looked upon as the sheet anchor," the chief justice replied unequivocally to his nephew, John Turner Waite, who represented Connecticut in the U.S. House of Representatives.

> Will it be if its Chief Justice is placed in the political whirlpool? The office has come down to me covered with honor. When I accepted it, my duty was not to make it as stepping-stone to something else, but to preserve its purity and make my own name as honorable, if possible, as that of my predecessors. . . . The other field is altogether untried. If I should fail there, it would to a certain extent drag my office down with me. No man ought to accept this place unless he takes a vow to leave it as honorable as he found it. (Trimble 1938, 142)

Waite did. Even Miller, who never seemed hesitant to point to what he regarded as his chief's failings, developed increased respect for the man. As senior associate justice, he presided over the Court in 1885 because of Waite's illness. This experience with the full demands of the office led Miller, in a letter to his brother-in-law, to pay his chief a backhanded compliment. "I always knew that he did a great deal more work than I" (Fairman 1939, 391).

The Waite Court at the Bar of History

"That he should develop any great strength as a judge was not to be expected of him, and the public expectation was not disappointed," remarked the *American Law Review* soon after Waite's death. "Certain it is that he left no great memorials of his strength as a judge," the influential journal continued. "[A]nd it is saying much in favor of the character of Chief Justice Waite to say that he was able to avoid the display of any great deficiencies as a lawyer while occupying the seat of Chief Justice" ("Notes" 1888, 303). Because Waite was so closely identified with the decisions of his Court, the faint praise of this "it-could-have-been-worse" obituary would seem to be as much a commentary on the Court as a whole as it was on its late presiding judge. If so, and with that assessment as a baseline, one may fairly conclude that the stature of the Waite Court has waxed rather than waned in the intervening nearly twelve decades.

In at least one key respect, the Waite Court stands in partial contrast to the Chase Court (1864–1873) that preceded it and in sharp contrast to the Fuller Court (1888–1910) that followed: The Waite Court affirmed the power to govern. The corollary to that affirmation was equally important: Reasserted was the principle that the primary check on government was electoral, not judicial. The Waite Court's overall deference to the elected branches of both the national and state governments may place it in a class by itself in Supreme Court history. Rarely did one hear cries of "judicial usurpation" or "government by judiciary." Waite's insistence in *Munn* that, for protection against legislative abuses, the people were "to resort to the polls, not to the courts," echoed an idea that was nearly as old as the Republic. "We must be content to limit power, where we can," argued Justice James Iredell in 1798, "and where we cannot, . . . we must be content to repose a salutary confidence" (*Calder v. Bull*). Chief Justice Marshall was even more forceful: "The wisdom and the discretion of congress, their identity with the people, and the influence which their constituents possess at elections, are, in this, as in many other instances . . . the sole restraints on which they have relied, to secure them from its abuse" (*Gibbons v. Ogden*, 1824).

In less than a decade the Chase Court on eight occasions held unconstitutional all or part of an act of Congress. This does not include *Ex parte Milligan*, which in 1866 held unconstitutional an executive order of the Lincoln administration. The statistic was remarkable, because it was at sharp variance with the Marshall and Taney Courts (1801–1864), which combined struck down only two acts of Congress. Despite the Taney Court's debacle in *Dred Scott v. Sandford* (1857), the Chase Court invigorated judicial power as a major counterweight to congressional power.

At first glance the record of the Waite Court seemed nearly identical to the Chase Court. Seven decisions invalidated all or part of an act of Congress, and an eighth did so soon after Waite's death but before Fuller arrived (Epstein, Segal, Spaeth, and Walker 1994, 96). But it must be remembered that the Waite Court sat more than four years longer than the Chase Court. Moreover, it is important to note the kind of legislation in those two Court periods that suffered the judicial veto. Plainly, there is nothing comparable during the Waite years to the Chase Court's legal tender decision in *Hepburn v. Griswold* (1870). Whatever else might be said about that case, it is undeniable that it declared unconstitutional one of the essential means Congress had chosen to finance the Civil War. What would apply to a war among the states would apply to a war with a world power. From this perspective the Chase Court complicated the task of those charged with preserving the nation.

The exception to the Waite Court's general support for national power lay in its hostility to federal civil rights legislation. Four of the seven invalidations of federal law while Waite was chief fell into that category. Three involved predations against African Americans (*United States v. Reese*, 1876; *United States v. Harris*, 1883; and the *Civil Rights Cases*, 1883) and one involved acts against Chinese (*Baldwin v.*

Franks, 1887). Of the remaining three, one concerned trademarks (*Trade-Mark Cases*, 1879), one struck down a criminal statute associated with bankruptcy (*United States v. Fox*, 1878), and the other invalidated a customs law on Fourth and Fifth Amendment grounds (*Boyd v. United States*, 1886). In fairness to Chase, it should be noted that, based on his circuit court opinions, he was much more favorably disposed than Waite to a broad reading of the Reconstruction amendments and civil rights legislation (Hyman 1997, 129). Yet, as questionable as some Waite Court civil rights rulings might be, none of them threatened paralysis of the national government or blocked achievement of national goals on a grand scale. Even some civil rights defeats in the Waite Court were not constitutionally insurmountable, had Congress persevered. Otherwise, anything the national government wanted to do, the Waite Court was prepared to accept as constitutionally permissible. One thinks especially of Waite's vision of the commerce power in *Pensacola Telegraph Co. v. Western Union Telegraph Co.* (1878) that rivaled Marshall's nationalism in *Gibbons v. Ogden*.

Still, hostility to federal civil rights legislation merits close attention in any appraisal of the Waite Court. Recall from Chapter 3 the Waite Court's pattern in civil rights cases. The bench was far more hospitable to claims brought by private citizens against state laws and policies that arguably infringed the Fourteenth Amendment directly by fostering invidious discrimination. Alongside such civil rights defeats for the government in *Reese* and the *Civil Rights Cases* were civil rights victories for individuals in *Strauder v. West Virginia* (1880), *Neal v. Delaware* (1881), and *Yick Wo v. Hopkins* (1886). The key to proving a violation of the Fourteenth Amendment's equal protection clause lay in the adjective "invidious"; as Justice Strong stated in *Strauder*, the Fourteenth Amendment was violated by "unfriendly legislation against them distinctively as colored." When legislation was racially discriminatory but superficially treated blacks and whites equally, the Waite Court ordinarily let it pass (although *Yick Wo* was an obvious exception to that pattern). That perspective lay at the heart of *Pace v. Alabama* (1883) and was a precursor to the Fuller Court's formal adoption of the separate-but-equal rule in *Plessy v. Ferguson* (1896).

The Waite Court's stance obscured an important dynamic in the protection of civil rights. Prosecutions under any of the Reconstruction-era civil rights laws would be brought by a U.S. attorney in the appropriate judicial district. The U.S. attorney occupied the same place with respect to a federal criminal law as a local district attorney or county prosecutor occupied with respect to a state criminal law. Upon observance of a crime or on complaint by a victim, the U.S. attorney could bring to bear the full prosecutorial resources of the Department of Justice. An offense against one person became an offense against all Americans: hence the case name *United States v. Reese*. To the degree that the Waite Court narrowed or otherwise invalidated federal civil rights laws, the role of the U.S. attorney was severely marginalized.

Law suits brought to challenge state laws or policies that arguably conflicted with the Fourteenth Amendment were exactly that: actions instituted by individuals, not by the U.S. government. In the Waite Court era, these typically sprang from criminal prosecutions, as in challenges to racially based juror selection. Such challenges would be developed by counsel that defendants were able to employ or, in capital cases, that might be provided to them. It would not be a challenge backed by the full weight of the federal government. Outside the context of race discrimination in criminal prosecutions, the hostility of local community opinion might effectively censor challenges to other discriminatory practices. There might be a heavy price in terms of intimidation that any plaintiff would pay. That prospect alone might incline someone to accept second-class citizenship instead of challenging it. Without such challenges through litigation, a court could not act.

Therefore, the Waite Court's myopia on civil rights lay in believing that a person would vindicate rights properly through the ordinary workings of the judicial process, relying on the Reconstruction amendments alone, without help from Congress. There was a latent suspicion of an enlarged federal presence. Whatever benefit Congress might bring seemed not to be worth the destruction of a widely shared, pre-Civil War vision of the Union. The irony was that individuals would feel free to vindicate their rights only in the absence of the very intimidation that the federal statutes had been designed to prevent, and these statutes in some instances were gutted by the Waite Court.

A second part of this dynamic involved the results of litigation. Successful prosecutions by the government against persons violating the legal rights of another would mean fines and/or jail sentences for the individuals found guilty. Not only would these perpetrators be punished, but the punishments might deter others from committing similar offenses. In contrast, an individual's success in convincing the Supreme Court that a particular state law or policy violated constitutionally protected rights often had far more limited effects. No one was fined or imprisoned. True, the courtroom victory became a precedent henceforth to govern litigation in similar cases. But if a trial judge failed to heed the precedent, there was little an individual could do beyond an appeal to a higher court on the hope that the law would be applied correctly. The difference was between vindication of individual rights by government and vindication of those rights by individuals.

Still a third part of this dynamic involved power. Especially with respect to voting rights under the Fifteenth Amendment, energetic enforcement backed by a generous interpretation of federal civil rights statutes would have translated into a franchise generally free of racial discrimination and open to all otherwise eligible males. Then as now, voting is empowerment. Denial of the right to vote condemns a person to the collective mercies of those who may vote. This was Justice Hunt's point in his *Reese* dissent: "Just so far as the ballot to . . . the freedmen is abridged, in the same degree is their importance and their security diminished. . . . Punishment is the means, protection is the end." The truth of that comment became especially evident soon after the last federal troops withdrew from the South in 1877. By the end of the century, disfranchisement of blacks had become the rule in southern states. Additionally and not coincidentally, after the Fuller Court approved "separate but equal" facilities based on race in *Plessy v. Ferguson* (1896), a harsh system of racial segregation entrenched itself in southern legal systems and was mimicked by private discrimination elsewhere in the nation. Soon, little effort was made any longer to ensure that separate facilities were equal. Only after the Supreme Court's decision in *Brown v. Board of Education* (1954), holding that separate facilities were inherently unequal, and passage of the Civil Rights Act of 1964 and the Voting Rights Act of 1965 were significant inroads made on such marks of third-class citizenship.

With the exception of this negativity toward federal civil rights legislation, the Waite Court in affirming national power contrasts not only to the Chase Court but to the Fuller Court as well. During its twenty-two years, Chief Justice Fuller's bench handed down fourteen decisions that invalidated all or part of a congressional statute (Epstein, Segal, Spaeth, and Walker 1994, 96). That number was somewhat higher per term than Waite's seven, but the real difference lies in the significance of some of those fourteen. Among them was *Pollock v. Farmers' Loan and Trust Co.* (1895) that disallowed the income tax that Congress had enacted in 1894. In at least one respect *Pollock* was on a par with the Chase Court's ruling in *Hepburn.* At least Justice Harlan seemed to think so in terms of the risk *Pollock* posed for the nation: it "strikes at the very foundations of national authority, in that it denies to the general government a power which is, or may become, vital to the very existence and preservation of the Union in a national emergency. . . ."

Also among the Fuller Court's fourteen negations was *Adair v. United States* (1908), which struck down the Erdman Act of 1898. That law was the federal government's first significant attempt to use its commerce power on a broad scale in support of the rights of labor. It prohibited yellow dog contracts (by which workers as a condition of employment agreed not to join unions) as well as the firing or blacklisting of employees for union activity. Not counted among the fourteen, because it only emasculated but did not invalidate a statute, was *United States v. E. C. Knight Co.* (1895), sometimes called the *Sugar Trust Case.* Relying on an exceedingly narrow interpretation of the commerce power, a majority of five confined the constitutionally acceptable application of the Sherman Anti-Trust Act of 1890 to monopolies involving commerce, as distinct from manufacturing. The Court placed the refining of sugar in the latter category and so pushed the sugar business and all comparable enterprises beyond the statute's reach.

Arguably, of course, the Waite Court–Fuller Court comparison is unfair because Congress flexed its muscles during the Fuller years in ways it did not while Waite was chief justice. So, the argument goes, one does not know what the Waite-era justices would have done had they been faced with a similarly activist congressional agenda. Perhaps, but the same contrasting pattern concerning the power to govern emerges in the reactions of the Waite and Fuller courts to state legislation.

Outside the contexts of the contracts and commerce clauses, the legislative authority of the states did not surface in U.S. constitutional law as a major issue until the very end of the Chase Court. This was why the decision in the *Slaughterhouse Cases*, which denied a Fourteenth Amendment challenge to a state law restricting occupational rights, was so significant. *Munn v. Illinois*, easily among the most far-reaching decisions on that amendment in the nineteenth century, exemplified the Waite Court's jurisprudence respecting the state police power. On no occasion did the Waite Court strike down a statute as a violation of the due process clause of the Fourteenth Amendment. Practically to the end, the Waite bench was prepared to allow states a free hand with respect to rate regulation, even when those rates had an impact on interstate commerce.

Near the close of the Waite era there certainly were signs of judicial impatience with the near carte blanche handed state legislatures in *Munn*. Just as oral argument was about to begin in *Santa Clara County v. Southern Pacific Railroad Co.* (1886), a case challenging taxation of certain railroad property, Waite informed counsel that the bench was not interested in the question whether the word "person" in the Fourteenth Amendment included corporations. "We are all of the opinion that it does," the chief justice said, thus making explicit for the first time, and appearing to emphasize, an understanding that had been implicit in the Court's decisions at least since the *Granger Cases* (Corwin 1948, 194). *Mugler v. Kansas* (1887) then signaled that the Court would henceforth look for a connection between legislative means and ends, even as it upheld the statute in question in that case. But it was the Fuller Court that closed the era of judicial self-denial. In an opinion by Blatchford (joined by Fuller and Brewer plus Waite-era holdovers Field and Harlan, and with Miller concurring separately), *Chicago, Milwaukee and St. Paul Railroad Co. v. Minnesota* (1890) held that the state legislature could not allow the reasonableness of rates to be determined by a state commission. Reasonableness had to be subject to judicial review. That decision completed a judicial revolution, because Waite had insisted in *Munn* that reasonableness was a legislative, not a judicial, question. The Court was well on its way to becoming what Miller himself had feared in the *Slaughterhouse Cases*—a "perpetual censor" of state legislation.

The Fuller Court built on the Minnesota rate case in *Smyth v. Ames* (1898). Writing for a unanimous bench, Harlan invalidated a set of rates promulgated by Nebraska. In the process of holding that regulated industries were entitled to a fair return, Harlan also laid out a formula by which to determine that return. In the same year, in *Allgeyer v. Louisiana*, the Fuller Court found in the Fourteenth Amendment a right not previously recognized by the Court: liberty of contract. Employee and employer now enjoyed a constitutionally protected right to bargain individually over the terms of labor, free of undue interference by the government. The vast implications of this new right were soon realized in *Lochner v. New York* (1905), in which Fuller and four other members of his Court struck down a New York statute limiting the hours of labor in bakeries. Justice Rufus Peckham's opinion for the majority asserted that it would be the Court's task to ascertain which restrictions on liberty of contract were reasonable and which ones were not. For many years the ruling cast doubt over the constitutionality of any governmental regulation of the workplace.

It took several decades for the legislative-friendly posture of the Waite Court again to prevail. *Smyth v. Ames* was expressly overruled in *Federal Power Commission v. Hope Natural Gas Co.* (1944). *Munn* was restored to a prominent place in U.S. constitutional law by *Nebbia v. New York* (1934). *Lochner v. New York*, along with decisions that it spawned such as *Adkins v. Children's Hospital* (1923), was overruled by *West Coast Hotel Co. v. Parrish* (1937). In *United States v. Carolene Products Co.* (1938), Justice Stone revealed the breadth and depth of the deference the Court was prepared to extend to legislators: "Regulatory legislation affecting ordinary commercial transactions," Stone wrote in a most Waite-like sentence, "is not to be pronounced unconstitutional unless in the light of the facts made known or generally assumed it is of such a character as to preclude the assumption that it rests upon some rational basis within the knowledge and experience of the legislators."

Attached to that sentence was footnote number four, probably the most famous footnote in all the *U.S. Reports*. Instead of a focus on property interests, the Court would now take seriously infringements on the nonproprietarian liberties of the Bill of Rights, as well as laws that adversely affected "discrete and insular minorities." That latter reference heralded the civil rights revolution of the 1950s and 1960s. Lest there be any doubt remaining about the shift of direction in the nation's fundamental law, *Ferguson v. Skrupa* (1963) reiterated the proposition that states enjoy nearly a free hand under their police power, unless regulations infringed on those preferred provisions of the Bill of Rights or on other liberties the Court deemed to be fundamental.

So the Waite Court was transitional, but not merely in terms of its chronological place in the development of the federal judicial system and the questions that it confronted. It was a transition Court as well in terms of its rulings. On matters of civil rights, it was reluctant to admit that the Reconstruction amendments had radically altered the constitutional structure of the Union. It acknowledged some change, but not much. Today it is commonplace to find references in the literature to the Reconstruction amendments as the second Constitution. Most of Waite's bench did not read them that way. To the degree that the outcome of the Civil War had launched a second revolution in U.S. government, that revolution had ground to a halt by the 1880s. It would fall to later congresses and courts to recognize broader protections within those amendments. In view of the depth and breadth of Jim Crow legislation in the years that followed, and the pervasive and ingenious devices deployed until well after the middle of the twentieth century to deny African Americans the vote, the Waite Court could have saved the nation much anguish by accelerating, not retarding, congressional protection of individual rights.

Still, it may be unfair to criticize Waite's Court for an absence of omniscience. After all, the trend of the Court's civil rights decisions after 1875 conformed to dominant white opinion in both North and South. If blacks gained their freedom as a result of a war among whites, they were, for a very long time, denied the full realization of that freedom because of reconciliation among whites. Sectional harmony took priority over fulfillment of the promises of Reconstruction. Thus, the fact that Waite's bench did not behave like a late twentieth-century bench is only to recognize the fallibility that pervades all human undertakings. His Court was a collection of jurists whose worldviews had been shaped by a pre–Civil War, mainly Jacksonian, United States. It was that United States, minus slavery, that most of them seemed to want to preserve.

If so, that goal—outside the context of civil rights—generally served the nation well. On questions of the scope of the state police power, the Waite Court's understanding of the Fourteenth Amendment was very close to the interpretation that controls today. On commerce clause issues, viewed in the light of the change of course in the *Wabash* case, its holdings were not that far from those of later courts. On Bill of Rights questions that have so defined the Court since 1937, the Waite Court deserves credit at least for engaging a few of them seriously. On balance and in terms of its legacy for a nation more than a century later, the Waite Court performed admirably overall. If Waite and his Court did not achieve true greatness, they at least touched the hems of greatness.

On March 13, 1874, just nine days after his swearing-in as chief justice, Waite wrote a letter to Amelia, who was still in Toledo at the time. "What does all this mean? I suppose I shall realize it all bye and by. But it seems strange now" (Stephenson 1973, 899). Little did he realize what lay in store. It was an exciting time in U.S. constitutional law. Americans can be glad that Waite was at the helm.

References

Brennan, William J., Jr. 1972. "Inside View of the High Court." In Leonard W. Levy, ed., *The Supreme Court under Earl Warren.* New York: Quadrangle Books, pp. 38–47.

Corwin, Edward S. 1948. *Liberty against Government.* Baton Rouge: Louisiana State University Press.

Danelski, David. 2002. "The Influence of the Chief Justice in the Decisional Process of the Supreme Court." In *Courts, Judges, and Politics: An Introduction to the Judicial Process*, 5th ed., edited by Walter F. Murphy, C. Herman Pritchett, and Lee Epstein. Boston: McGraw Hill.

Epstein, Lee, Jeffrey A. Segal, Harold J. Spaeth, and Thomas G. Walker. 1994. *The Supreme Court Compendium.* Washington, DC: Congressional Quarterly Press.

Fairman, Charles. 1939. *Mr. Justice Miller and the Supreme Court: 1862–1890.* Cambridge, MA: Harvard University Press.

———. 1988. *Five Justices and the Electoral Commission of 1877. History of the Supreme Court of the United States.* Supp. to vol. 7. New York: Macmillan.

Fish, Peter Graham. 1973. *The Politics of Federal Judicial Administration.* Princeton, NJ: Princeton University Press.

Frankfurter, Felix. 1937. *The Commerce Clause under Marshall, Taney, and Waite.* Chapel Hill: University of North Carolina Press.

———. 1953. "Chief Justices I Have Known." *Virginia Law Review* 39: 883–905.

Frankfurter, Felix, and James M. Landis. 1928. *The Business of the Supreme Court.* New York: Macmillan.

Friedman, Lawrence M. 2002. *Law in America.* New York: Modern Library.

Garland, Augustus H. 1898. *Experience in the Supreme Court of the United States.* Washington, DC: J. Byrne.

Hough, Charles M. 1919. "Due Process of Law—Today." *Harvard Law Review* 32: 218–233.

Hurst, James Willard. 1950. *The Growth of American Law.* Boston: Little, Brown.

Hyman, Harold M. 1997. *The Reconstruction Justice of Salmon P. Chase.* Lawrence: University Press of Kansas.

Magrath, C. Peter. 1963. *Morrison R. Waite: The Triumph of Character.* New York: Macmillan.

Mason, Alpheus Thomas. 1956. *Harlan Fiske Stone: Pillar of the Law.* New York: Viking.

———. 1968. "The Chief Justice of the United States: *Primus Inter Pares.*" *Journal of Public Law* 17:20–60.

Murphy, Walter F. 1962. "Marshaling the Court: Leadership, Bargaining, and the Judicial Process." *University of Chicago Law Review* 29: 640–672.

Northrup, Milton Harlow. 1901. "A Grave Crisis in American History." *Century Magazine* 62: 923–934.

"Notes: Death of Chief Justice Waite." 1888. *American Law Review* 22: 301–303.

Pennypacker, S. W. 1918. *The Autobiography of a Pennsylvanian.* Philadelphia: Winston.

Richardson, James D. 1917. *A Compilation of Messages and Papers of the Presidents, 1789–1902.* 20 vols. New York: Bureau of National Literature.

Seddig, Robert G. 1991. "John Marshall and the Origins of Supreme Court Leadership." *Journal of Supreme Court History* 1991: 63–85.

Stephenson, D. Grier, Jr. 1973. "The Chief Justice as Leader: The Case of Morrison Remick Waite." *William and Mary Law Review* 14: 899–927.

Swisher, Carl Brent. 1930. *Stephen J. Field: Craftsman of the Law.* Chicago: University of Chicago Press.

Trimble, Bruce R. 1938. *Chief Justice Waite: Defender of the Public Interest.* Princeton, NJ: Princeton University Press.

Waite, Morrison R. 1887. "Remarks of Chief Justice Waite." *Albany Law Journal* 36: 318.

"The Week." 1881. *The Nation*, July 23.

PART TWO

Reference Materials

Key People, Laws, and Events

Arthur, Chester A. (1830–1886)

The twenty-first American president (1881–1885), Chester Alan Arthur was born in Vermont, was educated at Union College, and practiced law in New York City. Thanks to Senator Roscoe Conkling, President Grant made Arthur collector of customs for the port of New York, a patronage-rich position. Favoring reform, President Hayes removed Arthur from office in 1878. The act widened the split within the Republican Party between those who favored the spoils system and those who thought government employment ought to be tied to merit, not party loyalty. Arthur's nomination in 1880 as vice presidential candidate was an effort by the party to bridge that gap, in that James Garfield, the presidential candidate, was perceived generally as favoring civil service reform.

Arthur became president on September 19, 1881, after Garfield was assassinated on July 2. A dignified chief executive (he was known as "Elegant Arthur"), he strove to curtail congressional pork-barrel spending and, bowing to pressures from the West Coast, signed into law a measure that curbed all Chinese immigration for ten years. Ironically, he backed passage of the Pendleton Act in 1883, which laid the foundations for the civil service system in operation today. That support cost him renomination for a second term. Conkling stalwarts viewed him as a traitor, and reform elements within the party were still unsure where his true loyalties lay. The nomination went instead to Secretary of State James G. Blaine of Maine, whose earlier nomination to head the Department of State had been blocked by Conkling.

Barron v. Baltimore (1833)

This decision in the twilight of the Marshall Court posed the question whether the first eight amendments to the Constitution (the Bill of Rights) limited state governments and their municipalities as well as the national government. To Chief Justice Marshall this was a question "of great importance, but not of much difficulty." The case arose after the city of Baltimore diverted the flow of several streams. As a result, silt was deposited around Barron's wharf, making it unfit for shipping. Barron claimed the action deprived him of property without just compensation. Holding that the Supreme Court had no jurisdiction in the case, Marshall observed, "We are of the opinion, that the provision in the Fifth Amendment to the Constitution, declaring that private property shall not be taken for public use without just compensation is intended solely as a limitation of the power of the United States, and is not applicable to the legislation of the states." A contrary ruling would have had immense consequences for the jurisdiction of the Court. As it was, most legal disputes between a state government and one of its citizens remained outside the federal judicial system, unless the commerce or contracts clause was involved. This is important because, until recent decades, government action and policy largely meant the action and policy of state and local governments. Not until after ratification of the Fourteenth Amendment in 1868 was there a serious effort to convince the Supreme Court that the Bill of Rights also applied to the states. Even so, incorporation of the Bill of Rights into the Fourteenth Amendment made little progress until well into the twentieth century.

Brown v. Board of Education (1954)

This landmark case in the Warren Court considered the question whether legally mandated racially segregated public schools were consistent with the equal protection clause of the Fourteenth Amendment. Racial segregation in schools and other pubic facilities had long been acceptable under the separate-but-equal doctrine of *Plessy v. Ferguson* (1896). The answer the Court gave in *Brown* would have far-reaching ramifications because a total of seventeen states and the District of Columbia required segregated schools and another four states permitted it as an option in local communities. "We come . . . to the question presented," wrote Chief Justice Earl Warren for a unanimous bench: "Does segregation of children in public schools solely on the basis of race, even though the physical facilities and other 'tangible' factors may be equal, deprive the children of the minority group of equal educational opportunities? We believe that it does. . . . [I]n the field of public education the doctrine of 'separate but equal' has no place. Separate educational facilities are inherently unequal." *Brown* thus not only turned away from *Plessy* and marked the beginning of the end of legally enforced segregated schooling but by implication spelled doom for any other racially segregated public enterprise or policy. *Brown* also inspired much of the civil rights movement that culminated in passage of the Civil Rights Act of 1964.

Brown v. Maryland (1827)

This case represented one of the Marshall Court's attempts to mark the boundary of state power with respect to the Constitution's grant to Congress of control over foreign and interstate commerce. Maryland had imposed a license fee on persons who sold goods imported from another country. Chief Justice Marshall's opinion held that the license was in effect a tax on imported goods, in violation of section ten of Article I and an interference with commerce with other nations in violation of the commerce clause in section eight of the same article. A state's authority to regulate in this area, Marshall said, began only when the goods were no longer in their "original package" and but had mixed with the general property of a state. Marshall suggested that this "original package doctrine" would also apply to goods from another state, but the Chase Court later held in *Woodruff v. Parham* (1869) that the rule did not apply to interstate commerce. The Waite Court held similarly in the important commerce clause case of *Brown v. Houston* (1885).

Buchanan, James (1791–1868)

The fifteenth president (1857–1861), Buchanan reached the White House prepared as well or better than any other American chief executive. Yet probably no president has fallen so short of his potential or so failed to rise to the challenge posed by crisis. Born and reared in Pennsylvania, Buchanan was educated at Dickinson College and was elected to the state legislature after admission to the bar. As a member of the U.S. House of Representatives (1821–1831) he became an ardent supporter of Andrew Jackson who named him minister to Russia in 1832. Service as a U.S. senator (1835–1845) was interrupted when President James K. Polk appointed him secretary of state (1845–1849), a position that involved him in the annexation of Texas, the Mexican War (1846–1848), and settlement of the Oregon boundary dispute with Great Britain. His public service resumed when President Franklin Pierce appointed him minister to Great Britain (1853–1856). Simultaneously Buchanan became the first president of the Board of Trustees of Franklin and Marshall College, a position he held until 1865.

For the Democratic Party, Buchanan's background made him an ideal nominee for the presidency in 1856 because his experience in foreign affairs meant that he had no firm public record on the most troubling issue of the day: the future of slavery in the western territories. With strong southern support, he handily defeated Republican John C. Fremont and American or Know-Nothing (and ex-president) Millard Fillmore. As president, however, Buchanan had difficulty managing the tensions within his own party over slavery that had secured his nomination. Near the end of his term he had become identified with the party's pro-southern (and proslavery) wing, to the dismay of northern Democrats such as Senator (and 1860 presidential candidate) Stephen Douglas, who sought a middle ground. Such turmoil would have made Buchanan's renomination in 1860 unlikely even had he wanted a second term. In December 1860, when Abraham Lincoln's election was a certainty, South Carolina, followed by other southern states, seceded from the Union. Buchanan seemed unprepared or unwilling to cope with this unprecedented development. He believed that secession was illegal but also believed that, as president, he lacked authority to compel the departing states to return. Ironically, this protégé of Andrew Jackson lacked both his mentor's nationalistic vision as well as Jackson's view of the presidency as an office to employ in the service of grand objectives.

Campbell, John A. (1811–1889)

Associate justice of the Supreme Court (1853–1861), John Archibald Campbell was born in Georgia and educated at Franklin College (now the University of Georgia). He attended the U.S. Military Academy but resigned before commissioning. Returning home, he studied law and was admitted to the bar at the age of eighteen by a special act of the legislature. He soon established a successful practice in Alabama, turned down two offers of appointment to the Alabama Supreme Court, and in 1851 argued six cases before the U.S. Supreme Court. When President Franklin Pierce inherited a Supreme Court vacancy in 1853 from the Fillmore administration, Chief Justice Taney and the other members of the bench took the unprecedented step of urging the inept president to name Campbell.

Campbell's tenure on the Court generally reflected the values of Jacksonian Democracy but was cut short by secession and Civil War. Opposed to both, Campbell intervened at the eleventh hour, pleading unsuccessfully with Secretary of State William Seward to meet with commissioners from the Confederacy. Campbell resigned from the Court on April 26 after fighting broke out. Denounced in the North for quitting, he was nearly lynched upon his return to Alabama because of his efforts for peace, whereupon he prudently moved his law practice to New Orleans. Accepting appointment as assistant secretary of war for the Confederacy, Campbell continued his efforts for a negotiated peace. After the surrender he was temporarily barred from practice in any federal court because of a test oath imposed by Congress. After the Supreme Court invalidated the oath in *Ex parte Garland* (1867), Campbell became the most renowned attorney of his day in Louisiana. Among other high profile appearances, he argued for an expansive interpretation of the new Fourteenth Amendment in the *Slaughterhouse Cases* (1873) and on behalf of Democrats before the electoral commission of 1877. Until he retired from full-time practice in 1884, Campbell appeared before the Supreme Court in some six cases on average each year.

Charles River Bridge v. Warren Bridge (1837)

This important contracts clause case was among the first decided by the Supreme Court after Roger B. Taney succeeded John Marshall as chief justice. In 1785 the

Massachusetts legislature granted to the Charles River Bridge Company the right to construct a bridge between Charlestown and Boston, with a right to collect tolls for forty years that was later extended to seventy years. In 1828, some Charlestown merchants received a legislative charter for construction of the Warren Bridge, with the power to collect tolls until they had recovered their investment. At that point title to the Warren Bridge would pass to the state and passage would become free. Proprietors of the Charles River Bridge Company, who would be deprived of most of their anticipated tolls because the new bridge was to be built close to the old one, claimed that the chartering of the second bridge impaired the obligation of their contract in violation of section ten of Article I of the Constitution. Although accepting Marshall's conclusion in the *Dartmouth College Case* (1819) that corporate charters were contracts within the meaning of the Constitution, the Taney Court held that no impairment had occurred. Ambiguities in a contract were to be resolved in favor of the public, not the investors. Contracts were to be construed strictly. By rejecting the concept of implied contractual rights, the Court made the contracts clause a far less formidable restraint on the state police power. This was especially so in light of the fact that most states soon insisted on reservation clauses within charters, whereby the state retained the right to alter or amend a previous corporate agreement.

Chase, Salmon P. (1808–1873)

The sixth chief justice of the United States, Salmon Portland Chase was born in New Hampshire and was graduated from Dartmouth College in 1826. He moved to Washington and studied law with William Wirt, John Quincy Adams's attorney general. Detesting the newly elected President Andrew Jackson, Chase moved to Cincinnati, Ohio, after his admission to the District of Columbia bar in 1829. There he established a prosperous practice—his fourth and most enduring partnership, between 1838 and 1858, being with a man with the improbable name of Flamen Ball. Chase pioneered the use of the courtroom as a forum and litigation as a force for change on the most pressing issue of the day—slavery—earning the epithet "attorney general for runaway slaves." He formulated and articulated a theory for antislavery activists that was a respectable alternative to extreme abolitionism, a view he held until war broke out in 1861. According to Chase, the law of a state was final regarding someone's status as slave or free. The national government was as powerless to interfere with the status of slavery within a state that prohibited or recognized it as a state's recognition of slavery was to determine a person's status outside its borders. Thus, slaves arriving by whatever means on free soil were free. Chase was convinced that this doctrine, which the Supreme Court rejected in *Jones v. Van Zandt* (1847), would lead to the eventual abandonment of slavery everywhere.

Chase's activism on the slavery issue led him on a political pilgrimage, first from the Whig to the Liberty parties and then to the Free Soil and Democratic parties that sent him to the U.S. Senate in 1849. In 1855 he won the Ohio governorship as a Republican and was reelected in 1857. As much as any politician before or since, Chase craved the presidency, unsuccessfully courting the Republican nomination in 1856, 1860, and 1864, and the Democratic nomination in 1868. Had his health not deteriorated, he would have accepted the nomination of either major party in 1872. Throughout Chase remained ideologically closest to the Democrats on most issues, including that of sound money, except their opposition to central banking, their prewar acceptance of slavery, and their postwar resistance to Reconstruction. President Lincoln brought Chase into his cabinet as secretary of the treasury, soon after the Ohio legislature had again elected him to the Senate. His finance policies equipped an army of 1 million and a navy that, briefly, was second only to Great Britain's. He mildly opposed, but acquiesced in, Lincoln's decision to help pay for the war by issuing paper money.

Upon Chief Justice Taney's death in 1864, Lincoln picked Chase, by now having resigned from the cabinet, for the Court's center chair. Lincoln firmly believed that Chase would stand by the constitutionality of the many extraordinary measures, including legal tender, that the federal government had taken to prosecute the war. On the Court, Chase became the first of only two chief justices to date to preside over the Senate in an impeachment trial of a president. His meticulous regard for fair procedure probably accounted for the Senate's narrow acquittal of President Andrew Johnson in 1868 and most certainly eliminated Chase as a contender for the Republican nomination in that year's presidential election. Chase's contributions to American constitutional law are reflected in his opinions for the Court in three cases and a separate opinion in a fourth. He joined Justice Davis's opinion for the Court in *Ex parte Milligan* (1866), holding that the president lacked authority to order the trial of civilians by military tribunals in areas where civil courts were functioning, but wrote separately to insist that in certain circumstances Congress might authorize such proceedings. *Mississippi v. Johnson* (1867) denied the authority of a court to enjoin the president from enforcing an arguably unconstitutional statute, in this instance the Reconstruction laws. *Texas v. White* (1869) espoused Lincoln's theory of the war: (1) that secession was illegal, (2) that the Union was perpetual, (3) that the rebellion had temporarily suspented the states' rights as members of the Union, and (4) acknowledged Congress's authority to maintain provisional governments in the southern states. The short-lived *Hepburn v. Griswold* (1870) confounded Lincoln's judgment about Chase by denying the authority of Congress to make paper currency legal tender for existing debts.

Circuit Court of Appeals Act

This landmark legislation passed by Congress in 1891 instituted the first major permanent organizational change for the federal judiciary since the Judiciary Act of 1789 established the federal judicial system. Some of its key features are still in place today. With the exception of a very limited appellate jurisdiction exercised by circuit courts over district courts in a small category of cases, the Supreme Court until 1891 was the only appellate body in the federal judicial system. The 1891 act created the circuit courts of appeals, a bench of three judges for each circuit. (In 1948, the name of these courts was changed to the court of appeals.) For diversity jurisdiction cases as well as admiralty, patent, and revenue cases, the new circuit courts of appeals would ordinarily be the exclusive appellate court. No longer would such cases enjoy an appeal by right to the Supreme Court. Instead, such cases could be heard only if the Supreme Court wanted to accept them for decision on certiorari. Thus, for the first time, the justices enjoyed some discretion over cases that they would decide. Moreover, circuit-riding responsibilities by Supreme Court justices that had been reduced by the Judiciary Act of 1869 were now eliminated entirely. Nonetheless, the existing circuit courts, dating from the Judiciary Act of 1869, remained. These were not abolished until 1911 when their trial jurisdiction was blended with that of the district courts. The Judiciary Act of 1925, also called the Judges' Bill, greatly enlarged the discretionary part of the Court's docket. With passage of legislation in 1988 the Court's appellate jurisdiction became almost entirely discretionary.

Civil Rights Act of 1866

This statute was the first of several civil rights laws that Congress enacted during Reconstruction. Passed over President Andrew Johnson's veto, the 1866 statute attempted to assure some measure of equality for the newly freed slaves and other African Americans. Section one declared that "all persons born in the United States, and not subject to any foreign power, excluding Indians not taxed," were "citizens of the United States; and such citizens, of every race and color, without regard to any previous condition of slavery or involuntary servitude shall have the same right, in every State and Territory . . . , to make and enforce contracts, to sue, be parties, and give evidence, to inherit, purchase, lease, sell, hold, and convey real and personal property, and to full and equal benefit of all laws and proceedings for the security of person and property, as is enjoyed by white citizens, and shall be subject to like punishment, pains and penalties, and to none other, any law, statute, ordinance, regulation, or custom to the contrary not withstanding." Section one of the Fourteenth Amendment (1868), in its declaration of national and state citizenship and guarantee of equal protection of the laws, was intended in part to shore up the constitutionality of the 1866 act. Significantly neither the 1866 law nor the Fourteenth Amendment protected the right to vote. That would not be affirmatively addressed until ratification of the Fifteenth Amendment in 1870.

Civil Rights Acts of 1870 and 1871

These statutes were usually referred to as the "Enforcement Acts" (or the "Force Acts" by their opponents) because they were intended to enforce the terms of the Fourteenth and Fifteenth Amendments. The first one restated some provisions from the Civil Rights Act of 1866 and added voting protections, making it a federal offense to interfere with the right to vote. The 1871 statute, also called the "Ku Klux Act," was aimed at vigilante-style intimidation. It criminalized actions by anyone to deny another person any federally protected right as well as interference with federal law enforcement agents in carrying out the terms of the act. Parts of the 1870 law were invalidated or narrowly construed by the Supreme Court in *United States v. Reese* (1876) and *United States v. Cruikshank* (1876), making it far less effective than Congress had intended.

Civil Rights Act of 1875

This statute was the last civil rights legislation that Congress passed until 1957. Section one of the 1875 law guaranteed "the full and equal enjoyment of the accommodations, advantages, facilities, and privileges of inns, public conveyances on land or water, theatres, and other places of public amusement; subject only to the conditions and limitations established by law, and applicable alike to citizens of every race and color, regardless of any previous condition of servitude." The legislation was grounded on both the Thirteenth and Fourteenth Amendments. However, in the *Civil Rights Cases* (1883), the Supreme Court struck down the provision. The Thirteenth Amendment was inadequate authority because, in the Court's view, it only abolished slavery. The Fourteenth Amendment was equally inadequate as a base because its various prohibitions were directed at state discrimination, not at discrimination maintained by private persons or businesses. Only Justice Harlan dissented. For him, the Thirteenth Amendment entitled Congress to redress the inequalities stemming from slavery, and the national and state citizenship that the Fourteenth Amendment conferred on all persons born in the United States encompassed the rights of equal access protected by the statute. The 1875 legislation was significant in that it attempted to legislate a measure of social equality, as distinct from the civic equality mandated in the Civil Rights Act of 1866. A broad guarantee of racially neutral access to places of public accommodation did not reappear in federal law until the Civil Rights Act of 1964, which offered an alternate constitutional basis for its prohibitions.

Civil Rights Act of 1964

This statute remains the most sweeping and comprehensive civil rights legislation ever passed by Congress. Title II of the act covered discrimination in places of public accommodation, as had the Civil Rights Act of 1875: "All persons shall be entitled to the full and equal enjoyment of the goods, services, facilities, privileges, advantages, and accommodations of any place of public accommodation, as defined in this section, without discrimination or segregation on the ground of race, color, religion, or national origin." An enterprise was a covered place of public accommodation "if its operations affect commerce, or if discrimination or segregation by it is supported by State action." Thus Congress expressly based the 1964 ban on discrimination partly on its commerce power and partly on the Fourteenth Amendment. To have relied on the Fourteenth Amendment entirely would have challenged the Supreme Court to overturn its decision in the *Civil Rights Cases* (1883) that held that the Fourteenth Amendment reached only state action, not discrimination by private individuals or businesses. By contrast, at least since 1937, the Court in a series of cases had broadly construed Congress's powers with respect to commerce among the states, suggesting that the deleterious effects of racial discrimination on travel and business could be addressed by Congress as a matter of regulating interstate commerce.

The Supreme Court upheld Title II of the 1964 act in *Heart of Atlanta Motel v. United States* (1964). Moreover, in a series of cases, the Court gave an exceedingly generous reading to the terms "affect commerce," allowing application of the law to a local family restaurant (*Katzenbach v. McClung*, 1964), a 232-acre recreational facility (*Daniel v. Paul*, 1969), and a community swimming pool (*Tillman v. Wheaton-Haven Recreational Association*, 1973). Such interpretations mean that no facility, otherwise open to the public, may any longer discriminate on the basis of race or any of the other protected classifications.

Cleveland, Grover (1837–1908)

As the twenty-second and twenty-fourth presidents, Grover Cleveland is the only American chief executive to have served bifurcated terms (1885–1889, 1893–1897). Because of stubborn opposition to high tariffs and vigorous championing of civil service reform, some presidential scholars regard Cleveland as the most effective president (or presidents) between Lincoln and Theodore Roosevelt (1901–1909).

Born in New Jersey and the son of a Presbyterian pastor, Cleveland read law, entered politics in New York, and was elected mayor of Buffalo. (He also fathered an illegitimate child, allowing political opponents years later to heckle him with "Ma, Ma, where's my Pa? He's gone to the White House, ha, ha, ha!") As governor of New York, he quickly established a reputation for clean government by opposing patronage and fighting corruption. (His party's Tammany organization in New York City offered ample examples of both.) In 1884 he narrowly defeated Republican James G. Blaine and claimed the White House. Opposed to an ever-larger government as well as to government largesse, he vetoed more bills than all his predecessors combined.

He managed to secure repeal of a constitutionally dubious statute dating from the days of the radical Republicans in 1867 that required Senate approval of appointed officials whom the president chose to dismiss. It was Cleveland who signed the groundbreaking Interstate Commerce Act into law in 1887 following the Supreme Court's decision in *Wabash, St. Louis and Pacific Ry. Co. v. Illinois* (1886). Cleveland lost a close race to Republican Benjamin Harrison in 1888, but reclaimed his old office from Harrison in 1892. During his second term he confronted an economic depression, probably made worse by his opposition to the soft money policies favored by the newly formed Populist Party and some Democrats.

Compromise of 1877

The term collectively encompasses acquiescence by Democrats, southern members of Congress in particular, in the decision by the electoral commission of 1877. The compromise awarded all disputed electoral votes to Rutherford B. Hayes, thus handing the key to the White House door to the Republican nominee, instead of to the Democratic nominee Samuel Tilden, who had received the most popular votes. Democrats in return received promises of (1) federal subsidies to rebuild devastated southern infrastructure (largely left unfulfilled) and (2) prompt withdrawal of federal troops that had occupied most of the former states of the Confederacy since 1865 (fulfilled).

Conkling, Roscoe (1829–1888)

Born into a politically well-connected family, Roscoe Conkling was appointed district attorney of Albany, New York, immediately following his admission to the bar in 1850. His law practice was interspersed with service as a Republican in Congress, first in the House of Representatives (1859–1863, 1865–1867) and then in the Senate (1867–1881). During the Grant administration, he became the undisputed leader of the Republican Party in New York and wielded vast amounts of patronage. He understood the crucial link between government jobs as rewards and a strong party organization and so both understandably and strenuously opposed civil service reform. A dispute with President Garfield over Conkling's authority to dictate federal appointments led to the latter's resignation from the Senate in 1881. Twice Conkling had a chance to take a seat on the Supreme Court. He turned down Grant's offer of the chief justiceship following Salmon Chase's death. When Justice Ward Hunt left the bench in 1882, President Arthur nominated his mentor and benefactor and the Senate confirmed. Faced with a broad-based public outcry over the appointment, however, Conkling declined the appointment.

Court Packing

Generically, court packing is a pejorative term that refers to any attempt by a president (or by a governor of a state with an appointed judiciary) to change the course of judicial decisions by placing friendly justices or judges on the bench. Thus, following the Supreme Court's decision in the first round of the *Legal Tender Cases*, President Grant was accused of court packing after newly arrived appointees Strong and Bradley joined a new majority in the second round of legal tender litigation to reverse the earlier decision that had been adverse to the administration's position.

More specifically, court packing refers to President Franklin D. Roosevelt's assault on the Supreme Court in 1937 following the Court's earlier rejection of much of Roosevelt's New Deal legislation. Roosevelt's difficulty was compounded by the fact that he had earned the distinction of being only the second president in American history to have served an entire first term of office (1933–1937) without having a single opportunity to make an appointment to the Supreme Court. The proposed legislation, among other things, would have allowed the president to name an additional justice for each justice who continued to serve after reaching the age of seventy, up to a maximum bench size of fifteen. Given the ages of the justices in 1937, this would have permitted Roosevelt to name as many as six new justices at once. Roosevelt never persuaded Congress to approve the plan, but as events unfolded, he did not need to. Within weeks after the plan became public, two justices, in the famous "switch in time that saved nine," changed their minds and now looked favorably on the New Deal agenda. Moreover, justices who had been hostile to the president's program soon began to retire, thus giving Roosevelt an opportunity to appoint administration-friendly justices.

Cummings v. Missouri (1867)

See *Test Oath Cases.*

Curtis, Benjamin R. (1809–1874)

Associate justice of the Supreme Court (1851–1857), Benjamin Robbins Curtis was born in Massachusetts and received degrees from Harvard College (1829) and Harvard Law School (1832). A Whig in politics, Curtis quickly established a reputation as a skilled attorney, specializing in patent law. When he was only thirty-six, he was named a fellow of the Harvard Corporation, replacing U.S. Supreme Court Justice Joseph Story. In 1851 President Millard Fillmore, hoping to lend Whig influence to a bench populated by Jacksonian Democrats, picked Curtis for Justice Levi Woodbury's seat on the U.S. Supreme Court. Fillmore made it known that he wanted someone of "vigorous constitution with a high moral and intellectual qualifications, a good judicial mind, and such age as gives a prospect of long service." The president got at least half of what he wanted: without doubt Curtis was intellectually and professionally gifted.

Curtis's Supreme Court career was noteworthy in at least two respects. With respect to commerce clause issues, he promptly led his colleagues out of a theoretical quagmire. Heretofore, the Court had split badly over the authority states retained with respect to interstate commerce. Was the commerce power exclusively Congress's? If so, were states still permitted to enact local regulations that arguably affected commerce but were not themselves regulations of commerce? Or, was the commerce power concurrent—that is, was a power shared with the states? *Cooley v. Board of Wardens* (1852) involved a pilotage regulation of the port of Philadelphia. Cooley challenged it as an unconstitutional intrusion upon Congress's authority to regulate commerce. Although it hardly eliminated further litigation about the role of states under the commerce clause, Curtis's solution was to say that some aspects of interstate commerce were local in character and could be locally regulated unless Congress intervened. Yet aspects of commerce national in scope that practically called for uniform regulation lay exclusively under the control of Congress. This doctrine of selective exclusiveness has shaped commerce clause cases ever since. Curtis's second most notable opinion was his dissent in *Scott v. Sandford* (1857), which challenged Chief Justice Taney's principal conclusions that African Americans had never been constitutionally intended to be citizens of the United States and that the Constitution gave Congress no authority to ban slavery in the territories. A rift soon developed between Taney and Curtis, and the latter chose to resign. As a practicing attorney, Curtis presented the first argument to the Senate in 1868 against President Andrew Johnson's removal from office, and he argued the losing side in *Hepburn v. Griswold* (1870). This was the first of the legal tender cases; Curtis's arguments prevailed on reversal a year later.

Dartmouth College v. Woodward (1819)

In terms of restrictions that the Constitution imposed on the states, this landmark case from the Marshall era was probably the high-water mark of the Supreme Court's interpretation of the contracts clause in section ten of Article I. It involved competing claims to control of Dartmouth College. College trustees, mainly Federalists who had been displaced by a rival group, based their claim to governance on the charter granted by King George III in 1769. They sought to regain control from a mainly Democratic-Republican group whose authority had been created by three New Hampshire statutes in 1816. These amended the original charter by increasing the number of trustees and vesting the future power of appointment of trustees in the governor and his council. The highest court of the state upheld the new control group. With one dissenting vote, the U.S. Supreme Court reversed. Admitting that, after 1776 and prior to ratification of the Constitution in 1788, New Hampshire would have been free to alter the charter in any way or even to abolish the college, Chief Justice Marshall's opinion of the Court stated that the contracts clause imposed an entirely new restriction on state authority. The old guard trustees were the true governing body of the College because the royal charter was a contract within the meaning of the Constitution that New Hampshire was forbidden to impair. Moreover, any ambiguity in a charter was to be construed in favor of the adventurers or investors and against the state. The charter was thus placed beyond the reach of the legislature. The significance of the ruling extended far beyond higher education, however, because the charters of profit-seeking corporations, with their grants of privileges, were now likewise beyond the control of legislative majorities.

Dred Scott Case (1857)

See *Scott v. Sandford.*

Emancipation Proclamation

Promulgated by President Abraham Lincoln on January 1, 1863, this order declared that slaves in states or parts of states then "in rebellion against the United States . . . henceforward shall be free." So worded, the proclamation did not apply to slaves in states such as Missouri and Maryland that had remained in the Union; nor did it apply to regions in the southern states under the control of federal troops. Limited in this way, the order accomplished several objectives. Slave-holding border states would be less likely to secede and join the Confederacy, particularly in light of the Union Army's partial, albeit costly, victory at Antietam in September 1862. Second, the Lincoln administration avoided a near certain and potentially embarrassing constitutional challenge to the president's unilateral authority to end slavery. Third, the proclamation—justified on grounds of military necessity—was consistent with Lincoln's theory of the conflict: that the southern states had never left the Union but were in rebellion against it. Fourth, by encouraging slaves in areas controlled by the Confederacy to flee, Lincoln's declaration might well cut into the South's labor supply and thus hamper its war effort. Fifth, it helped to doom southern hopes for recognition of the Confederacy by foreign governments. Finally, and most important, the order linked the abolition of slavery, and with it an eventual economic and social revolution in the South, to the North's success on the battlefields, making explicit that the war was not only about preservation of the Union but about the end of slavery itself. The version of the proclamation issued on January 1 lacked one important element that a preliminary draft, dated September 22, 1862 (five days after Antietam), had contained: a promise of colonization—the resettlement of the freed slaves to Africa. Repatriation would have appeased loyal southerners and those in the North who feared the economic consequences for the workplace were blacks to join the labor force in large numbers. Eliminating this commitment indicated that Lincoln had become emboldened by the end of December 1862. Indeed the document of January 1st advised the freed slaves "that in all cases when allowed they labor faithfully for reasonable wages."

Ex parte Garland (1867)

See *Test Oath Cases.*

Footnote Four

See *United States v. Carolene Products Co.*

Fuller, Melville W. (1833–1910)

The eighth chief justice of the United States (1888–1910), Melville Weston Fuller was born in Augusta, Maine, was graduated from Bowdoin College in 1853 (where he developed his talent for writing poetry), read law in Bangor, and attended six months of lectures at Harvard Law School. That experience would make him the first chief justice to have attended, even if briefly, a professional law school. After a brief time in Augusta where he was city solicitor, Fuller moved his practice to Chicago. He became active in Democratic politics, serving a term in the Illinois legislature in 1863, and prospered professionally. By the mid-1880s, his legal fees and real estate investments were earning him $30,000 a year. Fuller was a delegate to four Democratic national conventions. After Grover Cleveland was elected in 1884, he sought Fuller's advice and offered him the chair of the newly created Civil Service Commission, which Fuller declined. Upon Chief Justice Waite's death in 1888, Cleveland tendered an offer to Fuller that he could not refuse. The relationship between chief justice and president remained sound: When Cleveland began his nonconsecutive second term in 1893, he offered Fuller the job as secretary of state. This time it was an offer Fuller could refuse.

Like his predecessor, Fuller came to the Court with almost no national stature and presided over a bench containing several strong-willed and capable jurists. It was Fuller who instituted the custom of handshaking among the justices prior to conferences and to going on the bench. His strengths were more social than intellectual, tending to leave some, although hardly all, of the most important opinions to colleagues while focusing his energies on conciliation. Jurisprudentially, he cast his lot with justices concerned about preserving states' rights and suspicious of an enlarged national police power. To his credit, Fuller was instrumental in passage of the Circuit

Court of Appeals Act of 1891, which marked the first major reorganization of the federal judicial system since 1789.

Garfield, James (1831–1881)

The twentieth U.S. president (1881) and the second to have been assassinated, James Abram Garfield was born in Ohio, was educated at Williams College, was admitted to the bar in 1859, and was a lay minister in the Disciples of Christ church. He resigned his commission as a major general in 1863 to serve in the U.S. House of Representatives from Ohio (1863–1880). In 1877 he was one of two House Republicans to serve on the commission that resolved the electoral vote dispute between Rutherford Hayes and Samuel Tilden. Garfield became a compromise candidate for the presidency in 1880, winning the Republican nomination on the thirty-sixth ballot. He was perceived generally to favor civil service reform, and to help heal the sharp division over that issue, the party nominated Chester Arthur of New York, protégé of patronage-wielder Roscoe Conkling, for vice president. The plan worked: Garfield beat Democratic nominee General Winfield Scott Hancock. On July 2, 1881, a bitter and probably mentally disturbed office seeker named Charles J. Guiteau shot the president at Washington's railroad station. Garfield lingered until September 19 when he died. Ironically, much of his short time in office had been consumed by the need to distribute federal jobs to deserving Republicans. Nonetheless, his assassination helped to galvanize public opinion over the issue of reform, resulting in establishment of a civil service system two years later.

Grange

Officially known as the Patrons of Husbandry, the Grange was founded in Washington, D.C., in 1867 by government clerk and ex-farmer Oliver Hudson Kelly. The country's first mass-membership association of farmers and their spouses, Kelly envisioned it as mainly a social organization to break the monotony of isolated farm life. The Grange soon acquired an educational dimension as members focused on local schools and land-grant colleges and debated issues of the day. Soon the Grange added an economic role as well through the formation of cooperatives and farmer-owned enterprises. As farmers began to feel increasingly at the mercy of markets and railroads, especially in the Midwest, it became politically active, too. The Grange was largely responsible for passage of the so-called Granger laws in Illinois, Wisconsin, Minnesota, and Iowa that the U.S. Supreme Court sustained in its landmark decision in *Munn v. Illinois* (1877). This litigation also coincided with the Grange's peak national membership, with some 775,000 members divided among some 20,000 local organizations. By the end of the nineteenth century, other agrarian movements had supplanted the Grange, and it survived mainly as a social organization in northeastern states.

Grant, Ulysses S. (1822–1885)

The eighteenth president (1869–1877), Ulysses Simpson Grant was reared in Ohio and was educated and commissioned at the U.S. Military Academy. Service in the Mexican War was followed by an assignment to California in 1852. He resigned from the army in 1854 for personal reasons, although rumors persisted for the rest of his life that his departure had been prompted by heavy drinking. Unsuccessful as a farmer in Missouri, Grant was working at his father's leather goods store in Illinois when the Civil War started in 1861. The Illinois governor placed him in charge of a regiment, he was shortly promoted to brigadier general, and he quickly demonstrated his skill as a battlefield commander. Strategic victories at Vicksburg, Mississippi, on July 4, 1863, and then at Chattanooga, Tennessee, on November 25, 1863, moved President Lincoln to hand Grant the supreme command of the Union armies in March 1864. After General Robert E. Lee surrendered to Grant at Appomattox Courthouse, Virginia, on April 9, 1865, Grant continued to head the army during Reconstruction.

As a military hero he was a natural choice for the Republican presidential nomination in 1868. A reluctant candidate, he nonetheless defeated the Democratic nominee, New York Governor Horatio Seymour. He became the first president responsible for enforcement of the full panoply of measures enacted by Congress to protect the civil rights of the newly freed slaves, but his administration is probably better remembered for the graft and scandal that plagued it. Even so, Grant won reelection in 1872 against newspaper publisher Horace Greeley, the Democratic and Liberal Republican nominee.

Resolute, direct, and decisive as general, Grant as president vacillated, seemed naive, and lacked sound judgment, particularly in terms of those he named to key positions of trust in the executive branch. Alongside a few persons of talent and integrity like Hamilton Fish and Benjamin Bristow were others who lacked both characteristics. During the Grant years, twenty-five people rotated through the eight existing cabinet offices.

Hayes, Rutherford B. (1822–1893)

The nineteenth president (1877–1881), Rutherford Birchard Hayes was the third Civil War veteran (and third Civil War general) elected to the White House. Born in Ohio, he was educated at Kenyon College and Harvard Law School. After the war he served a single term as a Republican in the U.S. House of Representatives (1865–1867), followed by three terms as Ohio governor (1868–1872, 1876–1877) where his sound money policies and personal integrity led Republicans to nominate him for the White House in

1876. His Democratic opponent Samuel Tilden won the popular vote, but Republicans contested electoral votes from Oregon and three southern states. A special commission created by Congress eventually resolved the imbroglio, delivering the presidency to Hayes by a margin of one electoral vote. Hayes's overall effectiveness as president was doubtless impaired because many Democrats clung to the claim that he was a usurper, a view shared even by some Republicans. Hayes also alienated many in both parties, including Roscoe Conkling in his own, because he resolutely favored civil service reform in place of the spoils system as a way to modernize the federal government and to make it more responsive to the needs of the day.

Hayes restored integrity to the White House after the ethically embarrassing Grant years. Moreover, by insisting on presidential prerogatives with respect to a Congress that had been too eager to curtail them after Lincoln's death, the office that he bequeathed to his successor was stronger than the one Grant had handed to him. He may be best remembered by one of the first acts of his administration: the withdrawal of federal troops from the South, which signaled the end of Reconstruction and was designed to reconcile North and South. This part of the Compromise of 1877 (the other being Democratic acquiescence in the electoral commission's decision) restored white (and soon entirely Democratic) rule to the states of the former Confederacy. It also led to a steady contraction of the rights of African Americans in those states. Hayes chose not to seek a second term, and, given his difficulties with leaders of his own party, even his renomination would have been in doubt.

Ironclad Test Oath

In 1862, during the Civil War, Congress enacted the so-called Ironclad Test Oath. Added to the traditional oath of office, it required civil servants and military officers to swear not only to future loyalty but also to affirm that they had never previously been disloyal to the United States. In 1864, the Senate changed its rules to make the oath mandatory for senators; many members of the House and others took it voluntarily as a symbolic act of patriotism and loyalty. Because the oath would exclude any future duly elected and pardoned senator who had supported the Confederacy, Congress in 1868 exempted southerners from the ironclad oath by creating an alternate version that was less demanding and burdensome. Ironically, that meant that loyal northerners were required to take the more stringent version, while ex-Confederates were not. In 1884, lawmakers quietly repealed the old wartime oath.

Jackson, Andrew (1767–1845)

The seventh president (1829–1837), Jackson remolded American government by founding the Democratic Party, the prototype of modern mass-based political organizations. Without question, he was the dominant White House figure between Thomas Jefferson (1801–1809) and Abraham Lincoln (1861–1865). Born in up-country South Carolina, Jackson was barely more than a child when he saw service in the Revolutionary War. Taken prisoner, he was struck across the face with the flat of a sword after he refused to polish a British officer's boots. Some years later Jackson got revenge (and a hero's persona) when he led the American army at the battle of New Orleans in 1815, where some 2,000 British regulars fell alongside only thirteen American soldiers. Between those events, he was admitted to the bar in North Carolina and moved to Tennessee in 1788 where he served in a series of offices: prosecutor, judge, U.S. representative, and U.S. senator. He sparked an international incident when he led troops in an incursion against the Seminoles in Spanish-held Florida in 1818. He was appointed its military governor in 1821 after the region's sale to the United States, and was again elected to the Senate in 1823. After an unsuccessful race for the presidency in 1824 that had to be decided by the House of Representatives, Jackson beat incumbent John Quincy Adams in 1828 and easily won a second term in 1832 against a challenge by Henry Clay. Jackson was not only the first trans-Appalachian president but also the first self-made person to grace that office.

Jackson was an energetic nationalist in terms of expansion of American influence and in resistance to the nullification movement in South Carolina in 1833. Yet, as an advocate of an unobtrusive national government and a defender of states' rights, he vigorously opposed the Second Bank of the United States and vetoed internal improvement legislation. As a party-strengthening device, he perfected the spoils system, whereby loyal party members were rewarded with government jobs. Most of all, he opposed privilege and, in an era when nearly every state had adopted universal adult male suffrage, relished (and benefited from) his reputation as champion of the common man. Jackson electrified the electorate, a phenomenon that persisted for a time and infected the opposition as well. According to some estimates, voter turnout among eligible males in some elections during the thirty-two years prior to the Civil War exceeded 80 percent. Indeed, Jackson's belief in government as the people's servant dominated American politics for three decades, leading historians to refer to that period before the Civil War as the age of Jackson.

Judiciary Act of 1866

With the creation of the seat to which Justice Field was appointed in 1863, the Supreme Court's roster was increased from nine to ten. In 1866 Congress reset the roster at seven, with the reduction to take place through resignations or deaths. The change virtually eliminated any chance that President Andrew Johnson might have to make any appointments to the Court, a consequence Republican leaders in Congress surely did not fail to notice. Chief Justice Chase had supported the measure in the hope that Congress would then see fit to raise judicial salaries. It did not.

Judiciary Act of 1869

This legislation made four important changes in the federal judiciary. First, with President Andrew Johnson gone from the White House, the Supreme Court's roster was increased by two seats to nine, where it had been fixed from 1837 until 1863, and where it has remained ever since. Second, Congress created a separate circuit court judiciary consisting of nine judges, one for each circuit. With the exception of a distance-driven circuit judgeship allowed for California in 1855 and later in Oregon, and a fleeting circuit judiciary in 1801 that was promptly eliminated in 1802, these circuit judgeships were the first new category of federal judges authorized by Congress since the federal judicial system was established in 1789. Heretofore, a circuit court had been presided over by the district judge in that circuit and the Supreme Court justice assigned to that circuit. Third, circuit-riding by Supreme Court justices was significantly reduced. A justice was to sit on the circuit court in each district within his circuit only once every two years. Fourth, as an inducement for ailing jurists to leave the bench, pensions at full pay were authorized for judges who had ten years of service and who were seventy years old.

Judiciary Act of 1875

Also called the Removal Act, this legislation conferred on federal courts the full panoply of jurisdiction authorized by Article III of the Constitution, encompassing "all Cases, in Law and Equity, arising under this Constitution, the Laws of the United States, and Treaties." In other words, the lower federal courts could now be the courts of first instance to hear cases involving a federal question, that is, any case the resolution of which turned on the meaning of the Constitution, an act of Congress, or a treaty. Previously much of such federal business had been heard initially in state courts. The federal courts would now be the preferred forum for those seeking protection of U.S. constitutional rights. The legislation also made it much easier to remove, or to transfer, a case from state court to federal court in which a federal question was involved.

Judiciary Act of 1891

See *Circuit Court of Appeals Act.*

Legal Tender Cases (1870, 1871)

In 1870 and 1871 the Supreme Court decided three cases that involved the power of Congress over money and the rights of creditors. In Supreme Court literature, the collective name *Legal Tender Cases* technically refers to the second two, although legal tender lay at the heart of all three.

To finance the Civil War the Lincoln administration, through Treasury Secretary Salmon Chase, convinced Congress in 1862 to issue paper money ("greenbacks") not redeemable in gold. To bolster their acceptance Congress mandated that this new currency be legal tender for payment of private debts and taxes. Because the greenbacks soon deteriorated in value, creditors objected that debts were being repaid with cheaper dollars. Legal tender became a party-defining issue: Republicans stood by the legislation, and Democrats condemned it. In *Hepburn v. Griswold* (1870), the first of the legal tender cases, Chase (now chief justice) declared for a 4–3 bench that the 1862 legislation was unconstitutional with respect to contracts made before its passage. Congress had violated the Fifth Amendment by taking property without due process of law and had impaired the obligation of contracts. Admittedly the latter limitation applied only to the states, but Congress had nonetheless violated the "spirit of the Constitution." With Chase in the majority were Democrats Nelson, Clifford, and Field; in dissent were Republicans Swayne, Davis, and Miller. Soon after President Grant appointed Justices Strong and Bradley to the bench, the Court decided *Knox v. Lee* (1871) and *Parker v. Davis* (1871), which upheld the legislation not only with respect to debts contracted after passage of the law but existing debts as well. Joining Justice Strong's opinion of the Court were the three *Hepburn* dissenters plus Bradley. The four justices from the *Hepburn* majority dissented. Although the 1871 decisions were a broad affirmation of Congress's authority over the nation's currency, the quick reversal cost the Court the appearance of consistency and led to unfounded charges of court packing. Writing a half-century later, future Chief Justice Charles Evans Hughes labeled the *Legal Tender Cases* one of the Court's "self-inflicted wounds."

Lincoln, Abraham (1809–1865)

The sixteenth American chief executive (1861–1865), Abraham Lincoln bore witness to the proposition that presidential greatness is in large measure a product of character and force of circumstance. If Lincoln had not been part of the political scene in 1861, the decade might well have unfolded altogether differently. Had the Civil War not happened on Lincoln's watch, he might today be no better remembered or more highly regarded than a dozen or more fairly mediocre nineteenth-century occupants of the White House.

Born in a Kentucky log cabin, Lincoln's father moved the family to Indiana in 1818 and to Illinois in 1830. Largely self-taught, the future president fought in the Black Hawk War (1832), gained admission to the bar in 1836, and moved to Springfield in 1837 where he established a successful practice with several partners. A Whig in politics, Lincoln served in the state legislature (1834–1841) and in the U.S. House of Representatives (1847–1849). There he proposed a measure providing for a gradual and compensated emancipation of slaves and took issue with the Mexican War, the latter position costing him a second term. An unsuccessful try for the U.S. Senate in 1855 was followed by another attempt in 1858. Illinois Republicans picked Lincoln to oppose Senator Stephen A. Douglas, whose national stature ranked him among the most prominent Democratic figures of the decade. Douglas was reelected, but the seven debates of the campaign, in which Lincoln opposed slavery's westward extension in contrast to Douglas's plea for local sovereignty, gave Lincoln national visibility. That fame led to his third ballot nomination for the presidency in 1860 as the Republican candidate and, in a four-way contest for White House, a victory over Douglas and a badly fractured Democratic Party.

Lincoln's election precipitated southern secession. The attack on Fort Sumter in Charleston harbor on April 12, 1816, barely a month after his inauguration, furnished the event he needed to galvanize the North behind his resolve to preserve the Union. Lincoln called for 75,000 volunteers (after which four more southern states seceded), instituted a naval blockade of southern ports, suspended the writ of habeas corpus in certain areas, and then supported his commanders in defying Chief Justice Taney's ruling on circuit in *Ex parte Merryman* (1861), which stated that the president had no authority to unilaterally suspend the writ. Never had a president made such use of executive powers. His eventual success in finding generals who were a match for the South's allowed the North's overwhelming advantages in manpower and materiel finally to begin to prevail. Their success assured his reelection on a Union ticket in 1864 against a Democratic challenge by General George McClellan.

Conclusion of the war came quickly. General Ulysses Grant accepted General Robert E. Lee's surrender at Appomattox Courthouse in Virginia on April 9, 1865, and General Joseph E. Johnston surrendered his army to General William T. Sherman at Durham Station, North Carolina, on April 26. Yet Lincoln's plans for a postwar America characterized by magnanimity toward a defeated South came to naught when he was shot by an assassin on April 14, 1865 and died the next day. His successor, Vice President and Tennessee war Democrat Andrew Johnson, lacked the slain president's stature, magnetic oratorical skills, political astuteness, and leadership abilities. The center of power in Washington consequently shifted to the radical wing of the Republican Party in Congress that pursued a more extreme Reconstruction.

Marshall, John (1755–1835)

The fourth and, to date, longest serving chief justice of the United States (1801–1835), John Marshall was born into a frontier Virginia family of some stature. Largely educated at home and self-taught in the law, his entire formal education consisted of several weeks of law lectures in 1780 at the College of William and Mary. Marshall was an early example of the versatile lawyer moving in and out of government service. An officer in Washington's army during the Revolution, he was a member of the Virginia legislature, the Governor's Council, and the Virginia convention for ratification of the federal Constitution. He concluded his pre-Court career with a diplomatic mission to France that was followed by election to the U.S. House of Representatives (1799–1800) and appointment as secretary of state in President John Adams's administration (1800–1801). Upon the resignation of Chief Justice Oliver Ellsworth, Adams named him to the Supreme Court.

As chief justice, Marshall transformed the Court into an effective legal and political institution. More than any other chief, he deserves credit for making the Supreme Court a coequal branch of government. Through his opinion in *Marbury v. Madison* (1803), he fathered the doctrine of judicial review in American constitutional law that has enabled the Court to sit in judgment on the validity of acts of Congress and state legislatures. He made permanent the practice of the opinion of the Court—still followed today—whereby the justices speak through a single opinion rather than adhering to the earlier pattern of individual, or seriatim, opinions. Against claims of states rights asserted by Thomas Jefferson and his disciples, Marshall consistently championed a strong nationalistic interpretation of the Constitution that included a generous reading of the powers of Congress. Indeed, President Andrew Jackson's veto of the renewal of the charter of the Second Bank of the United States in 1832 was in large measure an attack on Marshall's opinion in *McCulloch v. Maryland* (1819) that had upheld the authority of Congress to create the bank. Widely acclaimed as "the great chief justice," he dominated the Court like no one before or since, writing more than half of the opinions in the approximately 1,000 decisions handed down during his tenure. Thus, to study the Supreme Court in the first third of the nineteenth century is nearly the same as studying Marshall himself. Tradition has it that the Liberty Bell at Philadelphia's Independence Hall acquired its famous crack while tolling his passing.

Plessy v. Ferguson (1896)

This decision by the Fuller Court is usually cited as the origin of the separate-but-equal doctrine that provided a constitutional rationale for legally enforced segregation of blacks from whites. Yet the Waite Court in *Pace v. Alabama* (1882) had already implicitly accepted the controlling principle of *Plessy* when it upheld a state law punishing interracial adultery and fornication more severely than the same offenses when committed by persons of the same race. The 1896 decision involved a Louisiana statute passed in 1890 that required railroad companies carrying passengers within the state to provide equal but separate accommodations for whites and blacks. With only Justice Harlan dissenting, Justice Henry Billings Brown explained for the majority that the law was a reasonable regulation designed to promote "public peace and good order." The Waite Court had held in *Strauder v. West Virginia* (1880) that the equal protection clause of the Fourteenth Amendment conferred on blacks "the right to exemption from unfriendly legislation against them distinctively as colored; exemption from legal discriminations, implying inferiority in civil society, and discriminations which are steps towards reducing them to the condition of a subject race." But that was not the situation here, insisted Brown. "We consider the underlying fallacy of the plaintiff's argument to consist in the assumption that the enforced separation of the two races stamps the colored race with a badge of inferiority. If this be so, it is not by reason of anything found in the act, but solely because the colored race chooses to put that construction upon it." Coupled with a broad disfranchisement of black voters in southern states in the decade after *Plessy*, it soon became clear that, in practice, segregated facilities and services for blacks and whites were merely that: separate but hardly equal. The separate-but-equal doctrine remained a valid part of American constitutional law until it was overturned by *Brown v. Board of Education* (1954).

Reconstruction

Reconstruction was both an era and a national policy objective. As a period of time, Reconstruction included at least the twelve years after the end of the Civil War when U.S. Army troops occupied most of the states of the defeated Confederacy. As policy, Reconstruction encompassed an amalgam of statutes that were enacted and constitutional amendments that were adopted between 1865 and 1875. Statutorily, Reconstruction began with creation of the Freedman's Bureau in 1865 and passage of the Civil Rights Act of 1866 and ended with passage of the Civil Rights Act of 1875. Constitutionally, Reconstruction was symbolized by ratification of the Thirteenth (1865), Fourteenth (1868), and Fifteenth (1870) Amendments. Overall, their aim was an outright political, economic, and social transformation of the conquered territory and, secondarily, a reshaping of race relations in the rest of the nation.

Surrender of southern armies in the spring of 1865 was followed by ratification of the Thirteenth Amendment in December that abolished slavery. Yet the newly freed slave population remained in a legally undefined, unprotected, and therefore precarious position. Legislatures in states of the former Confederacy promptly adopted Black Codes that denied the vote and other basic civil and legal rights to blacks and relegated them to a subservient status—barely a notch above slavery itself. Pushed through Congress by Republicans and largely opposed by Democrats, including Lincoln's successor President Andrew Johnson, Reconstruction measures, now backed by federal troops, overrode the Black Codes and required the southern states to rewrite their laws and constitutions to reflect the new order by enfranchising black males. These men in turn were as reliably Republican at the polls as most southern whites were reliably Democratic. Moreover, reseating of a southern state's congressional delegation was made dependent upon that state's ratification of the Fourteenth Amendment, which sought to federalize protection of basic rights. Such demands, coupled with ratification of the Fifteenth Amendment in 1870, which removed race everywhere as a criterion for voting, made Republicans the dominant party in much of the South until after federal troops were withdrawn following Democratic acquiescence in Rutherford Hayes's controversial ascension to the presidency in 1877. The close identification between Reconstruction and the Republican Party, combined with a near-total disfranchisement of blacks after the end of the century, helped to assure white Democratic dominance of the politics of the region until well after the middle of the twentieth century.

Scott v. Sandford (1857)

The *Dred Scott Case* is nearly universally regarded as the Supreme Court's most disastrous decision. By denying Congress's authority to ban slavery in the territories, the ruling inflamed public opinion on both sides, forced candidates for national office to take a position on one side or the other, split the Democratic Party, and thus helped to precipitate Abraham Lincoln's election as president in 1860. By placing itself on the wrong side of history, the Court badly tarnished its reputation.

The origins of the case date to 1834 when Dr. John Emerson, an army surgeon, took his slave named Dred Scott from the slave state of Missouri to the free state of Illinois. In 1836 Emerson took Scott to Fort Snelling in present-day Minnesota, well north of 36° 30' in the old Louisiana territory, where slavery had been banned by the Missouri Compromise of 1820. In 1838 Emerson returned to Missouri with Scott. After Emerson died, a suit was brought in the Missouri courts against his widow, claiming that Scott's residence in free territory had made him a free person. The trial court held for Scott, but the state supreme court reversed in 1852. Whatever Scott's legal status outside Missouri, it concluded, he remained a slave under Missouri law. By this time Mrs. Emerson had married Dr. C. C. Chaffee, an abolitionist from Massachusetts. To reopen the case, and to shield both his reputation and the friendly nature of the litigation, he transferred ownership of Scott to Mrs. Chaffee's brother, John Sanford, of New York. In 1853 Chaffee arranged for Roswell Field, an abolitionist attorney in St. Louis, to file suit on Scott's behalf against Sanford in the U.S. Circuit Court in Missouri. (The court reporter incorrectly spelled "Sanford" as "Sandford.") After an adverse judgment, Scott appealed to the Supreme Court. The justices twice heard arguments in the case, in February and December of 1856. The case came down on March 6, 1857, just two days after President James Buchanan's inauguration. Strong pressures from all sides pushed the justices to try to accomplish judicially what the elected branches had been unable to resolve.

The case involved three questions that could be, but did not necessarily all have to be, answered. First, was Scott's status settled by Missouri law, under which he had already been declared to be a slave? Second, was Scott a citizen of the United States, for the purpose of maintaining a suit in federal court against a citizen of another state? Third, what was the effect on his status as a slave of his sojourn in territory declared free by the Missouri Compromise? If the Court decided one or the other, or both, of the first two questions against Scott, there would be no need to answer the third. After reargument, the Court seemed to have agreed to focus on the first question alone, with Justice Nelson assigned the task of writing the opinion. As first cast, then, *Dred Scott* would have avoided the most sensitive issues and, had the case come down that way, would hardly have been a bombshell. Several justices, however, wanted the decision to do more, "to quiet all agitation on the question of slavery in the Territories," Justice Curtis explained later. As a result, nine justices filed nine opinions, seven holding for Sanford and two (McLean and Curtis) for Scott. Traditionally viewed as the majority opinion, Chief Justice Taney's addressed all three questions. First, while a state might grant citizenship to blacks, they were not citizens of the United States within the meaning of the Constitution and so could not press a suit in federal court. The circuit court therefore had no jurisdiction in Scott's suit. Second, Scott was a slave because he had never been free. The provision of the Missouri Compromise of 1820 banning slavery in certain areas was unconstitutional because of the absence of language in the Constitution granting Congress authority to prohibit slavery in the territories and because the law interfered with rights of property the Constitution protected through the Fifth Amendment. Furthermore, Taney reasoned, "if Congress itself cannot do this—if it is beyond the powers conferred on the Federal Government— . . . it could not authorize a Territorial Government to exercise them. It could confer no power on any local Government, established by its authority, to violate the provisions of the Constitution." Last, and almost as an afterthought, whatever the status of slaves in a free state or territory, once they returned to a slave state, their status depended on the law of that state. And Missouri had decided that Scott was a slave. Thus, of all the possible policies Congress might adopt with respect to slavery in the territories, the only constitutionally acceptable one was the protection of slavery.

Taney, Roger B. (1777–1864)

The fifth chief justice of the United States, Roger Brooke Taney sat from the last full year of Andrew Jackson's presidency (1836) until the last full year of the Civil War (1864). Born in southern Maryland into a wealthy Roman Catholic plantation family and graduated from Dickinson College (1795), Taney was admitted to the Maryland bar (1799), served several years as a Federalist in the state legislature, and was elected state attorney general in 1827. By this time he had become an ardent Jacksonian Democrat. His efforts on behalf of Jackson in 1828 were rewarded by appointment as U.S. attorney general in 1831. When Jackson decided to make war on the Second Bank of the United States, Taney drafted Jackson's veto message after Congress tried to renew the bank's charter in 1832. Jackson then directed Secretary of the Treasury William Duane to withdraw all federal deposits from the bank. Duane refused and was replaced by Taney, who carried out the president's directive. The Senate's rejection of his nomination as treasury secretary in July 1834 gave Taney the distinction of being the first cabinet nominee to suffer such a fate. In 1835 Jackson again sent Taney's name to the Senate, this time to fill the seat on the Supreme Court vacated by Justice Gabriel Duval. That nomination also failed after the Senate postponed consideration indefinitely. Jackson and Taney ultimately prevailed, however, when the Senate confirmed Taney in March 1836 to fill the chief justiceship, after John Marshall's death in July 1835.

Taney's twenty-eight years in the Court's center chair were marked by several jurisprudential themes. Almost immediately, he outraged Whigs by his opinion in the *Charles River Bridge Case* (1837), which moderated Marshall's theory of the contracts clause by rejecting a claim of implied privilege in a corporate charter. He enlarged the power of the federal judiciary in *Propeller Genesee Chief v. Fitzhugh* (1851) by extending its admiralty jurisdiction to navigable inland waters. A similar elevation of the federal judiciary followed from Taney's theory of federalism. In contrast to Marshall's theory of national supremacy that subordinated state to national power and saw the Supreme Court as a defender of the latter, Taney advocated a theory of federal equilibrium that carved out a larger role for the states. Within the powers reserved to the states by the Tenth Amendment, states were sovereign, but final authority to determine the scope of state powers rested with the Supreme Court that sat as an arbitrator standing aloof from the pretensions of both national and state governments (*Ableman v. Booth*, 1859). On balance, Taney was a worthy successor to Marshall. But Taney's reputation has never recovered from his opinion for the Court in *Scott v. Sandford* (1857), which firmly placed the Supreme Court on the wrong side of history and confirmed the suspicions of those who viewed the Court as a handmaiden of slavery. Taney not only declared that African Americans, slave or free, were never intended to be citizens of the United States but he foreclosed any option for Congress respecting extension of slavery in the territories—the overriding moral and political issue of the day—except that of defending slavery. Viewed by President Lincoln as a nemesis, feelings among Republicans regarding Taney were so negative at the time of his death that Congress refused to appropriate funds for a bust in his honor.

Test Oath Cases

This is the collective name given to two cases the Supreme Court decided on the same day in 1867: *Cummings v. Missouri* and *Ex parte Garland.* Both involved retrospective Civil War loyalty oaths that required an affirmation by those taking the oath that they had not supported the Confederacy. In *Cummings*, Missouri mandated the oath for persons in various occupations; in *Garland,* Congress mandated the oath for attorneys practicing in federal court. The effect of each was economically punitive and exclusionary. In both cases the Supreme Court invalidated the statutes by votes of 5–4, with Justice Field writing for the majority that the oaths were bills of attainder and ex post facto laws, both prohibited by the Constitution. Justice Miller argued in dissent that the laws did no more than set qualifications, including that of good moral character, for those at work in certain professions.

United States v. Carolene Products Co. (1938)

This decision was one of several in the late 1930s that heralded the Court's return to an attitude of judicial restraint with respect to laws regulating property and other aspects of the economy. "Regulatory legislation affecting ordinary commercial transactions," wrote Justice Harlan Fiske Stone, "is not to be pronounced unconstitutional unless in the light of the facts made known or generally assumed it is of such a character as to preclude the assumption that it rests upon some rational basis within the knowledge and experience of the legislators." That attitude had largely permeated the Waite Court, as illustrated by Chief Justice Waite's opinion in *Munn v. Illinois* (1877). After Waite's death in 1888 the Supreme Court increasingly involved itself in determining the reasonableness of such laws, in effect second-guessing legislators. Yet the *Carolene Products Case* was important in a second way too. Attached to the sentence quoted above was footnote number four—probably the most famous footnote in all of American constitutional law—in which Stone suggested that the Court would now concern itself more directly with laws that infringed upon nonproprietarian constitutional rights and those that mistreated "discrete and insular minorities." *Brown v. Board of Education* (1954), which heralded an end to legally enforced racial segregation, was an example of the ideas in that footnote at work.

Chronology

1857 March 4 James Buchanan is inaugurated as fifteenth U.S. president.

March 6 *Scott v. Sandford* holds that Congress has no authority to ban slavery in the territories. The decision inflames the slavery issue.

September 30 Justice Benjamin R. Curtis resigns from the Supreme Court.

1858 January 21 Nathan Clifford replaces Justice Curtis on the Supreme Court.

1860 May 31 Justice Peter Daniel dies.

December 20 News of Abraham Lincoln's election as president prompts South Carolina to secede from the Union. By the spring of 1861, ten additional southern states have followed its lead.

1861 February 21 Senate rejects Buchanan's nomination of Jeremiah Black to fill Justice Daniel's seat.

March 4 Abraham Lincoln is inaugurated as sixteenth U.S. president.

April 12 South Carolina troops commence bombardment of Fort Sumter in Charleston harbor. Civil War begins.

April 14 Justice John McLean dies.

April 30 Justice John Campbell resigns from Supreme Court to return to Alabama.

1862 January 27 Noah Swayne replaces Justice McLean on the Supreme Court.

1862, cont. July 21 Samuel Miller replaces Justice Daniel on the Supreme Court.

December 10 David Davis replaces Justice Campbell on the Supreme Court.

1863 January 1 President Lincoln formally issues the Emancipation Proclamation freeing slaves in areas under the control of the Confederacy.

March 3 Concerned about the views of some Supreme Court justices regarding the Lincoln administration's war policies, and understanding the need to join California firmly to the Union, Congress reorganizes the judicial circuit on the Pacific Coast and authorizes the appointment of a tenth justice to the Supreme Court.

March 10 The *Prize Cases* uphold, 5–4, the legality of Lincoln's blockade of southern ports and adhere to the administration's insistence that the Confederacy is not an independent state.

May 20 Stephen Field of California occupies the new tenth seat on the Supreme Court.

1864 October 12 Chief Justice Taney dies.

December 15 Salmon P. Chase becomes the sixth chief justice.

1865 March 3 Congress passes the first Freedmen's Bureau Act to begin to cope with the postwar situation in the South.

March 4 Lincoln begins his second term as president.

April 9 Confederate General Robert E. Lee surrenders his army to General Ulysses S. Grant at Appomattox Courthouse, Virginia.

April 14 Lincoln is mortally wounded by assassin John Wilkes Booth.

April 15 Lincoln dies. Vice President Andrew Johnson becomes president.

April 26 Confederate General Joseph E. Johnston surrenders his army to General William T. Sherman at Durham Station, North Carolina, thus ending the Civil War.

May 30 Justice John Catron dies.

December 18 The Thirteenth Amendment, abolishing slavery, is ratified.

1866 April 3 *Ex parte Milligan* holds that military tribunals established by Lincoln during the Civil War lacked jurisdiction to try civilians in areas in which the civilian courts were functioning.

April 9 A civil rights law confers on the newly freed slaves and other African Americans a measure of civic equality, with rights enforceable in federal courts.

April 16 Johnson nominates Attorney General Henry Stanberry to fill the vacancy occasioned by Justice Catron's death, but legislation three months later dissolves the vacancy.

July 23 Congress trims the roster of the Supreme Court from ten to seven justices, with the districts reorganized into nine circuits.

1867 January 14 In the *Test Oath Cases* (*Ex parte Garland* and *Cummings v. Missouri*), the Supreme Court, 5–4, invalidates federal and state laws, respectively, that imposed retrospective loyalty oaths on former Confederates and their supporters that barred them from certain occupations.

March 2 Congress passes the first Reconstruction statute.

1868 May 28 In the impeachment trial of Andrew Johnson, over which Chief Justice Chase presided, the Senate fails to secure the required two-thirds vote to remove the president from office.

July 28 The Fourteenth Amendment, imposing broad but undefined restrictions on the states, is ratified.

1869 March 4 Ulysses S. Grant is inaugurated as the eighteenth U.S. president.

April 10 Congress increases the membership of the Supreme Court from seven to nine and authorizes a separate circuit judge for each circuit.

1870 January 31 Justice Robert C. Grier retires from the Supreme Court.

1870, cont. February 7 *Hepburn v. Griswold,* the first round of the legal tender litigation, holds unconstitutional, 4–3, the Legal Tender Act of 1862 as applied to debts contracted before its passage.

March 14 William Strong replaces Justice Grier on the Supreme Court.

March 23 Joseph Bradley fills the new (or restored) seat on the Supreme Court authorized by Congress in 1869.

March 30 The Fifteenth Amendment, prohibiting race as a criterion for voting, is ratified.

May 31 The Enforcement Act to protect rights under the new Fifteenth Amendment becomes law.

1871 April 20 The second Enforcement Act provides broad protection against infringement of any federal right.

May 1 *Knox v. Lee* and *Parker v. Davis,* the second round of the legal tender litigation, uphold, 5–4, the constitutionality of the Legal Tender Act of 1862, as applied to debts contracted before and after its passage. *Hepburn v. Griswold* (1870) is reversed.

1872 November 28 Justice Samuel Nelson retires from the Supreme Court.

1873 January 9 Ward Hunt takes Justice Nelson's place on the Supreme Court.

March 4 Grant begins his second term as president.

April 14 In the *Slaughterhouse Cases,* the Supreme Court gives the Fourteenth Amendment its first interpretation and, 5–4, construes its protections very narrowly.

May 7 Chief Justice Chase dies.

1874 March 4 Morrison R. Waite becomes the seventh chief justice.

1875 March 1 A supplement to the Civil Rights Act of 1866 bars discrimination based on race in public conveyances and places of public accommodation and thus is aimed at discrimination perpetrated by private individuals and businesses.

March 3 Congress gives the federal courts jurisdiction over all federal questions—those involving the Constitution, a statute, or treaty of the United States.

1876 March 27 *United States v. Reese* invalidates, 8–1, part of the Enforcement Act of 1870 and makes it more difficult to protect voting rights, especially in state and local elections. *Cruikshank v. United States* renders, 9–0, a narrow construction of another part of the Enforcement Act, invalidating indictments because the defendants were not charged with violating rights actually protected by the Constitution.

November 7 The presidential election between Democrat Samuel Tilden and Republican Rutherford Hayes yields inconclusive results because of disputed election returns in four states.

1877 January 29 President Grant signs the bill creating a special electoral commission to resolve the disputed returns. It consists of five members of the House of Representatives, five members of the Senate, and five justices of the Supreme Court.

March 1 *Munn v. Illinois* holds, 7–2, that states may set the rates charged by enterprises such as grain warehouses and railroads affected with a public interest and that the reasonableness of a rate is a legislative, not a judicial, question.

March 2 The electoral commission resolves all disputed returns in favor of Hayes, who wins the White House by a margin of one electoral vote.

March 4 Justice Davis resigns from the Court after his election to the Senate from Illinois.

March 5 Hayes is formally inaugurated as the nineteenth president of the United States, after having taken the oath of office privately on Saturday, March 3.

December 10 John Marshall Harlan takes Justice Davis's place on the Supreme Court.

1878 January 14 *Hall v. De Cuir* invalidates, 9–0, on commerce clause grounds a state statute banning racial discrimination on public conveyances.

1879 May 5 *Reynolds v. United States* provides the first interpretation of the First Amendment's guarantee of free exercise of religion, holding, 9–0, that it does not excuse a man who practices polygamy because of sincerely held religious beliefs.

1880 March 1 *Strauder v. West Virginia* invalidates, 7–2, a state law barring blacks from serving on juries as a violation of the Fourteenth Amendment's equal protection clause.

December 14 Justice Strong retires.

1881 January 5 William Woods takes Justice Strong's seat on the Supreme Court.

January 24 Justice Swayne retires.

March 4 James A. Garfield becomes the twentieth U.S. president.
May 17 Stanley Matthews is appointed to fill the seat vacated by Justice Swayne. This was the result of Matthews's second nomination for the Swayne seat; the first, by President Hayes, had been allowed to die in early March when the Senate adjourned.

July 2 President Garfield is shot by an assassin.

July 25 Justice Clifford dies.

September 19 President Garfield dies; Vice President Chester A. Arthur becomes president.

1882 January 9 Horace Gray takes Justice Clifford's seat on the Supreme Court.

January 27 Justice Hunt retires.

April 3 Samuel Blatchford takes Justice Hunt's seat on the Supreme Court.

1883 October 15 The *Civil Rights Cases* invalidate, 8–1, the section of the Civil Rights Act of 1875 that bans racial discrimination in public conveyances and in places of public accommodation. The majority concludes that the Fourteenth Amendment is directed only against state action, while the statute banned discrimination by private individuals and businesses.

1884 March 3 *Hurtado v. California* rejects, 8–1, the claim that the Fourteenth Amendment's due process clause makes the Fifth Amendment applicable to the states. This is the most important case in the second half of the nineteenth century on the applicability of the Bill of Rights to the states.

1885 March 4 Grover Cleveland becomes the twenty-first U.S. president.

1886 May 10 *Yick Wo v. Hopkins* invalidates, 9–0, a San Francisco ordinance vesting laundry licensing authority with city officials. Of those businesses that were licensed, only one was owned by a Chinese. In the Court's view, the Fourteenth Amendment's equal protection clause was violated if a statute in practice fosters racial discrimination, even though in its words it was racially neutral.

October 25 *Wabash, St. Louis and Pacific Railway Co. v. Illinois* reverses, 6–3, that part of *Munn v. Illinois* (1877) that allowed states to set railroad rates even when those rates affected interstate transportation and shipments.

1887 May 14 Justice Woods dies.

1888 January 18 L. Q. C. Lamar takes Justice Woods's seat on the Supreme Court.

March 23 Chief Justice Waite dies.

October 8 Melville Weston Fuller becomes the eighth chief justice of the United States.

1890 March 24 *Chicago, Milwaukee and St. Paul Railway Co. v. Minnesota* holds, 6–3, that railroad rates set by a commission must be judicially reviewable.

1891 March 3 Congress creates the circuit courts of appeals, the first authentic appellate courts in the federal judicial system below the Supreme Court. Circuit-riding duties for the justices are eliminated. The Supreme Court is given some discretionary control over its docket in certain classes of cases.

Table of Cases

Ableman v. Booth, 62 U.S. (21 Howard) 506 (1859)
Adair v. United States, 208 U.S. 161 (1908)
Ah Kow v. Nunan (The Queue Case), 12 Fed. Cas. 252 (C.C.D. Calif. 1879)
Alaska Mining Co. v. Whelan, 168 U.S. 86 (1897)
Allgeyer v. Louisiana, 165 U.S. 578 (1897)
Ames v. Kansas, 111 U.S. 449 (1884)
Anderson v. Dunn, 19 U.S. (6 Wheaton) 204 (1821)
Antoni v. Greenhow, 107 U.S. 769 (1883)
Baldwin v. Franks, 120 U.S. 678 (1887)
Bank of Augusta v. Earle, 38 U.S. (13 Peters) 519 (1839)
Barron v. Baltimore, 32 U.S. (7 Peters) 243 (1833)
Bartemeyer v. Iowa, 85 U.S. 129 (1874)
Blyew v. United States, 80 U.S. (13 Wallace) 581 (1872)
Boyd v. United States, 116 U.S. 616 (1886)
Bradwell v. Illinois, 83 U.S. (16 Wallace) 130 (1873)
Brown v. Houston, 114 U.S. 622 (1885)
Brown v. Maryland, 25 U.S. (12 Wheaton) 419 (1827)
Buck v. Bell, 274 U.S. 200 (1927)
Budd v. New York, 142 U.S. 517 (1892)
Burlington Township v. Beasley, 94 U.S. 310 (1877)
Bush v. Gore, 531 U.S. 98 (2000)
Butchers' Benevolent Assoc. v. Crescent City Co. See Slaughterhouse Cases
Butchers' Union Co. v. Crescent City Co., 111 U.S. 746 (1884)
Calder v. Bull, 3 U.S. (3 Dallas) 386 (1798)
Cannon v. United States, 116 U.S. 55 (1885)
Cantwell v. Connecticut, 310 U.S. 296 (1940)
Champion v. Ames, 188 U.S. 321 (1903)
Charles River Bridge v. Warren Bridge, 36 U.S. (11 Peters) 420 (1837)
Chicago, B. and Q. Railroad Co. v. Chicago, 166 U.S. 226 (1897)
Chicago, B. and Q. Railroad Co. v. Cutts, 94 U.S. 161 (1877)

Chicago, B. and Q. Railroad Co. v. Iowa, 94 U.S. 155 (1877)
Chicago, Milwaukee, and St. Paul Railroad Co. v. Minnesota, 134 U.S. 418 (1890)
Chy Lung v. Freeman, 92 U.S. 275 (1876)
Cincinnati Bridge Case. See Newport and Cincinnati Bridge Co. v. United States
Civil Rights Cases, 109 U.S. 3 (1883)
Clawson v. United States, 114 U.S. 477 (1885)
Clinton Bridge Case, 1 Woolworth 150, Fed. Case No. 2900 (1867), 77 U.S. (10 Wallace) 454 (1870)
Collector v. Day, 78 U.S. (11 Wallace) 113 (1871)
Commissioners v. Thayer, 94 U.S. 631 (1877)
Cooley v. Board of Wardens, 53 U.S. (12 Howard) 299 (1851)
Counselman v. Hitchcock, 142 U.S. 547 (1892)
Cummings v. Missouri, 71 U.S. (4 Wallace) 277 (1867)
Daniel v. Paul, 395 U.S. 298 (1969)
Dartmouth College v. Woodward, 17 U.S. (4 Wheaton) 518 (1819)
Davidson v. New Orleans, 96 U.S. 97 (1878)
Davis v. Beason, 133 U.S. 333 (1890)
Dobson v. Dornan. 118 U.S. 10 (1886)
Dobson v. Hartford Carpet Co., 114 U.S. 439 (1885)
Doyle v. Continental Insurance Co., 94 U.S. 535 (1877)
Dred Scott Case. See Scott v. Sandford
Elk v. Watkins, 112 U.S. 94 (1884)
Employment Division v. Smith, 494 U.S. 872 (1990)
Entick v. Carrington, 19 Howell State Trials 1029 (1765)
Erie Railroad v. Tompkins, 304 U.S. 64 (1938)
Ex parte Boyer, 109 U.S. 629 (1884)
Ex parte Curtis, 106 U.S. 371 (1882)
Ex parte Garland, 71 U.S. (4 Wallace) 333 (1867)
Ex parte Jackson, 96 U.S. 727 (1878)
Ex parte McCardle, 74 U.S. (7 Wallace) 506 (1869)
Ex parte Merryman, 17 Fed. Cas. 144 (D. Md. 1861)
Ex parte Milligan, 71 U.S. (4 Wallace) 2 (1866)
Ex parte Siebold, 100 U.S. 371 (1880)
Ex parte Vallandigham, 68 U.S. (1 Wallace) 243 (1864)
Ex parte Virginia, 100 U.S. 339 (1880)
Ex parte Yarbrough, 110 U.S. 651 (1884)
Fletcher v. Peck, 10 U.S. (6 Cranch) 87 (1810)
Fong Yue Ting v. United States, 149 U.S. 698 (1893)
Gelpcke v. Dubuque, 68 (1 Wallace) U.S. 175 (1864)
Georgia v. Stanton, 73 U.S. (6 Wallace) 50 (1867)

Gibbons v. Ogden, 22 U.S. (9 Wheaton) 1 (1824)

Granger Cases. See Munn v. Illinois

Hall v. DeCuir, 95 U.S. 485 (1877)

Hannibal and St. Joseph Rail-Road Co. v. Husen, 95 U.S. 465 (1878)

Head v. Amoskeag Manufacturing, 113 U.S. 9 (1885)

Heart of Atlanta Motel v. United States, 379 U.S. 241 (1964)

Henderson v. Mayor of New York, 92 U.S. 259 (1876)

Hepburn v. Griswold, 75 U.S. (8 Wallace) 603 (1870)

Hilton v. Guyot, 159 U.S. 113 (1895)

Hoffman v. Hancock Mutual Life Insurance Co., 92 U.S. 161 (1876)

Home Insurance Co. v. Morse, 87 U.S. (20 Wallace) 445 (1874)

Hood v. Du Mond, 363 U.S. 525 (1949)

Hopt v. Utah, 110 U.S. 574 (1884)

Hopt v. Utah, 120 U.S. 430 (1887)

Hot Springs Cases, 92 U.S. 698 (1876)

Hurtado v. California, 110 U.S. 516 (1884)

Hylton v. United States, 3 U.S. (3 Dallas) 171 (1796)

In re Neagle, 135 U.S. 1 (1890)

Jones v. Van Zandt, 46 U.S. (5 Howard) 215 (1847)

Juilliard v. Greenman, 110 U.S. 421 (1884)

Kastigar v. United States, 406 U.S. 441 (1972)

Katzenbach v. McClung, 379 U.S. 294 (1964)

Kidd v. Pearson, 128 U.S. 1 (1888)

Kilbourn v. Thompson, 103 U.S. 168 (1881)

Knox v. Lee, 79 U.S. (12 Wallace) 457 (1871)

Kohl v. United States, 91 U.S. 367 (1876)

Kring v. Missouri, 107 U.S. 221 (1883)

Late Corporation of the Church of Jesus Christ of Latter-Day Saints v. United States, 136 U.S. 1 (1890)

Legal Tender Cases (*Knox v. Lee, Parker v. Davis*), 79 U.S. (12 Wallace) 457 (1871)

License Cases, 46 U.S. (5 Howard) 504 (1847)

Liverpool and Great Western Steam v. Phoenix Insurance, 129 U.S. 397 (1889)

Lochner v. New York, 198 U.S. 45 (1905)

Logan v. United States, 144 U.S. 263 (1892)

Louisville, N. O. and T. Railway v. Mississippi, 133 U.S. 587 (1890)

Mapp v. Ohio, 367 U.S. 643 (1961)

Marbury v. Madison, 5 U.S. (1 Cranch) 137 (1803)

Maxwell v. Dow, 176 U.S. 581 (1900)

McCall v. California, 136 U.S. 104 (1892)

McCulloch v. Maryland, 17 U.S. (4 Wheaton) 316 (1819)

McGrain v. Daugherty, 274 U.S. 135 (1927)
Minnesota Rate Case. See Chicago, Milwaukee, and St. Paul Railroad Co. v. Minnesota
Minor v. Board of Education, 23 Ohio 211 (1873)
Minor v. Happersett, 88 U.S. 162 (1875)
Mississippi v. Johnson, 71 U.S. (4 Wallace) 475 (1867)
Missouri Pacific Railway v. Humes, 115 U.S. 512 (1885)
Mobile v. Watson, 116 U.S. 289 (1886)
Mugler v. Kansas, 123 U.S. 623 (1887)
Muhiker v. N.Y. and Harlem R.R. Co., 197 U.S. 544 (1905)
Munn v. Illinois, 94 U.S. 113 (1877)
Murdock v. Memphis, 87 U.S. (20 Wallace) 590 (1875)
Murphy v. Ramsey, 114 U.S. 15 (1885)
Murray's Lessee v. Hoboken Land and Improvement Co., 59 U.S. (18 Howard) 272 (1856)
Neal v. Delaware, 103 U.S. 370 (1881)
Newport and Cincinnati Bridge Co. v. United States, 105 U.S. 70 (1882)
New York Central v. Lockwood, 84 U.S. (17 Wallace) 357 (1873)
New York v. Miln, 36 U.S. (11 Peters) 102 (1837)
Nix v. Hedden, 149 U.S. 304 (1893)
Northern Securities Co. v. United States, 193 U.S. 197 (1904)
Northwestern Fertilizing Co. v. Hyde Park, 97 U.S. 659 (1878)
Olmstead v. United States, 277 U.S. 438 (1928)
O'Neil v. Vermont, 144 U.S. 323 (1892)
Pace v. Alabama, 106 U.S. 583 (1883)
Parker v. Davis, 79 U.S. (12 Wallace) 457 (1871)
Passenger Cases, 48 U.S. (7 Howard) 283 (1849)
Patterson v. Colorado, 205 U.S. 454 (1907)
Paul v. Virginia, 75 U.S. (8 Wallace) 168 (1869)
Peik v. Chicago and Northwestern Railway, 94 U.S. 164 (1877)
Pensacola Telegraph Co. v. Western Union Telegraph Co., 96 U.S. 1 (1878)
Philadelphia and Reading Railroad Co. v. Pennsylvania, 82 U.S. (15 Wallace) 232 (1873a)
Philadelphia and Reading Railroad Co. v. Pennsylvania, 82 U.S. (15 Wallace) 284 (1873b)
Pickard v. Pullman Southern Car Co., 117 U.S. 34 (1886)
Plessy v. Ferguson, 163 U.S. 537 (1896)
Poindexter v. Greenhow, 114 U.S. 270 (1885)
Pollock v. Farmers' Loan and Trust Co., 158 U.S. 601 (1895)
Presser v. Illinois, 116 U.S. 252 (1886)

Prize Cases, 67 U.S. (2 Black) 635 (1863)
Propeller Genesee Chief v. Fitzhugh, 53 U.S. (12 Howard) 443 (1852)
Randolph v. Post County, 93 U.S. 502 (1877)
Reynolds v. United States, 98 U.S. 145 (1879)
R. F. and P. Railroad Co. v. City of Richmond, 96 U.S. 521 (1878)
Santa Clara County v. Southern Pacific R.R., 118 U.S. 394 (1886)
Savings and Loan Association v. Topeka City, 87 U.S. (20 Wallace) 655 (1875)
Schooner Sarah Watson v. Steamer Sea Gull, 90 U.S. (23 Wallace) 165 (1875)
Scott v. Sandford, 60 U.S. (19 Howard) 393 (1857)
Sewing Machine Companies Case, 85 U.S. (18 Wallace) 553 (1874)
Sherbert v. Verner, 374 U.S. 398 (1963)
Shollenberger v. Brinton, 52 Pa. 9 (1866)
Sinking Fund Cases, 99 U.S. 700 (1879)
Slaughterhouse Cases, 83 U.S. (16 Wallace) 36 (1873)
Smith v. Alabama, 124 U.S. 465 (1888)
Smyth v. Ames, 171 U.S. 361 (1898)
Soon Hing v. Crowley, 113 U.S. 703 (1885)
Springer v. United States, 102 U.S. 586 (1881)
Stone v. Farmers' Loan and Trust Co., 116 U.S. 307 (1886)
Stone v. Mississippi, 101 U.S. 814 (1880)
Strauder v. West Virginia, 100 U.S. 303 (1880)
Swift v. Tyson, 41 U.S. (16 Peters) 1 (1842)
Telephone Cases, 126 U.S. 1 (1888)
Texas v. White, 74 U.S. (7 Wallace) 700 (1869)
Tillman v. Wheaton-Haven Recreational Association, 410 U.S. 431 (1973)
Trade-Mark Cases, 100 U.S. 82 (1879)
Turner v. Maryland, 107 U.S. 38 (1883)
Twining v. New Jersey, 211 U.S. 78 (1908)
United States v. Anthony, Fed. Cas. No. 14,459 (C.C.D.N.Y., 1873)
United States v. Ashfield, 91 U.S. 317 (1876)
United States v. Baltimore and Ohio Railroad Co., 84 U.S. (17 Wallace) 322 (1873)
United States v. Carolene Products Co., 304 U.S. 144 (1938)
United States v. Cruikshank, 92 U.S. 542 (1876)
United States v. E. C. Knight Co., 156 U.S. 1 (1895)
United States v. Fox, 94 U.S. 315 (1877)
United States v. Hall, 26 Fed. Cases 79 (C.C.S.D. Ala., 1871)
United States v. Harris, 106 U.S. 629 (1883)
United States v. Home Insurance Co., 89 U.S. (22 Wallace) 99 (1875)
United States v. Lee, 106 U.S. 196 (1882)
United States v. Lopez, 514 U.S. 549 (1995)

United States v. Nixon, 418 U.S. 683 (1974)
United States v. Reese, 92 U.S. 214 (1876)
United States v. Stanley. See Civil Rights Cases
United States v. Teller, 107 U.S. 64 (1883)
United States v. Union Pacific Railroad Co., 91 U.S. 72 (1875)
United States v. Wong Kim Ark, 169 U.S. 649 (1898)
Vannever v. Bryant, 88 U.S. 41 (1874)
Virginia v. Rives, 100 U.S. 313 (1880)
Wabash, St. Louis and Pacific Ry. Co. v. Illinois, 118 U.S. 557 (1886)
Walker v. Sauvinet, 92 U.S. 90 (1876)
Watkins v. United States, 354 U.S. 178 (1957)
Weeks v. United States, 232 U.S. 383 (1914)
Welton v. Missouri, 91 U.S. 275 (1876)
Wilkerson v. Utah, 99 U.S. 130 (1879)
Williams v. Mississippi, 170 U.S. 213 (1898)
Willson v. Black Bird Creek Marsh Co., 27 U.S. (2 Peters) 245 (1829)
Woodruff v. Parham, 75 U.S. (8 Wallace) 123 (1869)
Wynehamer v. People, 13 N.Y. 378 (1856)
Yick Wo v. Hopkins, 118 U.S. 356 (1886)

Glossary

amicus curiae Literally "friend of the court"; the term (the plural form is "amici") refers to a person, organization, or governmental entity that files a brief with a court in a case to which it is not a party but in which it has an interest as to the outcome. Amici briefs filed by the solicitor general of the United States are among the most influential of such legal papers.

appeal The process by which the losing party in a case requests a higher court to review the decision of the lower court.

appellate jurisdiction As distinguished from original jurisdiction, the authority of a court to review and revise the decisions of a lower court. Most cases that the Supreme Court decides fall into its appellate jurisdiction, which is defined by Congress.

associate justices Except for the chief justice, the judges on the Supreme Court (and many state supreme courts) are called associate justices.

bill of attainder A law that punishes an individual and bypasses the procedural safeguards of the legal process; prohibited by the Constitution.

Bill of Rights Added to the Constitution in 1791, it consists of the first ten amendments and includes protections for the most basic civil liberties. Some commentators limit the Bill of Rights to the first eight amendments. Most state constitutions also contain a bill of rights.

Bloody shirt Rhetorically "waved" by Republicans for nearly three decades after the Civil War, it recalled the bloodshed of the conflict and attempted to link Democrats to the Confederacy and warmongering.

briefs Documents filed with a court containing the arguments of the opposing parties to a case.

capital case A criminal proceeding in which the defendant may be on trial for his or her life.

case A controversy to be decided by a court.

certification A process by which some cases reached the Supreme Court, especially in the nineteenth century. If judges in a lower court divided over a legal issue, they could certify that question to the higher court.

certiorari, writ of Literally "to be informed" or "to make sure"; notification by an appellate court to a lower court to forward the record in a case so that the appellate court can determine whether certain alleged mistakes were committed below. Use of a writ of certiorari indicates that the reviewing court has discretion whether to accept the case. It is not a review by right. The U.S. Supreme Court acquired its first such discretionary jurisdiction as part of the Circuit Court of Appeals Act of 1891; that discretionary jurisdiction was substantially enlarged in 1925. Today nearly all cases that the Supreme Court decides arrive on the docket by way of a writ of certiorari.

chief justice The presiding officer of a court. Since 1888 all presiding officers of the Supreme Court have been commissioned as "chief justice of the United States."

circuit In the federal court system, a judicial division of the United States; so named because judges would travel from place to place within the area to hold court.

circuit court Until 1911, the more important of two trial courts (the other being the district court) in the federal court system; circuit courts also had a very limited appellate jurisdiction over district courts, even though the same judge sat on both district and circuit courts. In 1911 the jurisdiction of the circuit courts was merged into that of the district courts.

circuit courts of appeals A series of nine intermediate appellate courts—organizationally situated between the district and circuit courts, below, and the Supreme Court, above—established by Congress in 1891; since 1948 they have been called the courts of appeals; today there are thirteen such courts of appeals.

civil case A noncriminal legal action, such as a proceeding in divorce or in an attempt to recover damages after an accident.

civil liberty A legally protected freedom to act or not to act, or to be free from unwarranted governmental intrusion in one's life.

civil right A legal protection to participate in society and in the political system on an equal footing with others.

civil service Distinguished from the spoils system, a system of public employment in which hiring, promotion, and firing are done on the basis of an objective assessment of qualifications and performance on the job rather than on the basis of party loyalty.

Cold War The period of tension, distrust, and proxy wars between the Soviet Union and the United States that followed World War II and persisted until about 1991.

commerce clause Provision in section eight of Article I of the Constitution granting Congress authority to "regulate Commerce with foreign Nations, and among the several States, and with the Indian Tribes." In its passive or dormant mode, the commerce clause also limits interference with commerce by the states, even in the absence of congressional legislation.

concurrent jurisdiction Authority that is shared by different courts that may be asserted or exercised at the same time and place.

concurrent power A power that may be exercised by two governments in the same place at the same time, such as the power of taxation.

concurring opinion A statement issued separately in a case by a judge voting with the majority, indicating a different basis for the judge's decision in the case or providing additional perspective on the case.

confederacy A loose association of states in which dominant political power lies with the member states, not with the central government. Used as a proper noun, it is a reference to the Confederate States of America (1861–1865), the temporary nation formed when eleven southern states seceded from the Union in 1860 and 1861.

conference The closed meetings of the justices of the Supreme Court at which they conduct all business relating to the deciding of cases.

court below From the perspective of a higher appellate court, the most recent court to have rendered a decision in a case. For the U.S. Supreme Court in Waite's day, the court below would have been a state supreme court, a U.S. circuit court, or the Court of Claims.

Court of Claims Established by Congress in 1855 to hear cases against the United States involving demands for monetary compensation. In 1982 it was renamed the United States Claims Court, and in 1992 the Court of Claims.

court of last resort Highest court within a judicial system to which a litigant may appeal a case.

court packing An attempt to affect the decisions of a court by appointing judges known to be predisposed to a certain outcome.

crime A public wrong; an offense, such as murder, against society at large even though it may have been committed against only a single individual.

criminal case A legal proceeding that the government initiates against someone following the commission of a crime.

criminal procedure Rules that guide law enforcement agents, prosecutors, and judges in the investigation, arrest, and trial of persons accused of crimes.

defendant The person or other party against whom legal action has been initiated.

delegated powers Legal authority that the people in the states, through ratification of the Constitution, granted to the national government for certain purposes. Delegated powers can be either express or implied.

democracy System of government based on majority rule, protection of minority and individual rights, and the equality of all citizens before the law.

Democratic Party The older of America's two major political parties, it traces its roots to remnants of the Democratic-Republican Party that coalesced around Andrew Jackson in the mid-1820s.

dissenting opinion A statement by a judge explaining his or her disagreement with the majority position in a case.

district court Until 1911, the less important in terms of its business of two trial courts (the other being the circuit court) in the federal court system. Since 1911, it has been the basic federal trial court.

diversity jurisdiction Conferred by the Constitution, it allows cases that would ordinarily be heard in state court to be tried in federal court where the parties are citizens of different states and the dollar amount at issue meets a threshold set by Congress.

due process of law The Fifth (applying to the national government) and Fourteenth (applying to state governments) Amendments to the Constitution prohibit the taking of "life, liberty, or property without due process of law." These words command government to follow established procedures and to adhere to fundamental fairness in its interactions with persons and organizations. The due process clause of the Fourteenth Amendment has also been the vehicle by which most provisions of the Bill of Rights have been applied to the states. *See also substantive due process.*

Eighth Amendment That part of the Bill of Rights in the Constitution that, among other things, prohibits cruel and unusual punishments.

electoral college Institution established by the Constitution for electing the president and vice president. Electors chosen by the voters cast their ballots for president and vice president. Each state has a number of electors (and hence that number of electoral votes) equal to its total representation in Congress. A candidate for president or vice president needs a majority of electoral votes to win.

equal protection clause Part of the Fourteenth Amendment that is a mainstay of civil rights and declares that no state shall deny to any person the equal protection of the laws.

error, writ of Notification by an appellate court to a lower court to forward the record in a case so that the appellate court can determine whether certain alleged mistakes were committed. Almost all cases reached the Supreme Court in the nineteenth century by a writ of error. It was a review by right.

establishment clause Provision of the First Amendment barring government support for religion.

exclusionary rule Judge-made rule in criminal procedure that bars the use of illegally obtained evidence at a suspect's trial.

exclusive power A power that belongs in its entirety to one government or to a part of that government. The power to declare war, for example, is an exclusive power of the U.S. Congress and may not be exercised by a state government.

ex parte Literally "on one side only," or "by or for one party"; a way of entitling a legal proceeding that is initiated by and for the benefit of one party, without notice to, or argument by, any other party that might be adversely interested.

ex post facto law Prohibited by the Constitution, a law that makes an act a crime after it was committed or that increases the punishment for a crime already committed. All ex post facto laws are retrospective, but not all retrospective laws are ex post facto laws.

express powers Powers specifically enumerated in the Constitution as belonging to the national government.

federal courts The courts of the United States, as distinguished from the courts of the states.

federal question An issue that involves the interpretation of the Constitution or a statute or a treaty of the United States.

federalism A system of government with a division of political authority between a central government and subordinate units such as states, in which each possesses its own constitutional authority to act and each operates in the same territory.

felony A serious criminal offense, usually punishable by more than one year in prison.

female suffrage The right of women to vote, bestowed nationally by the Nineteenth Amendment in 1920.

Fifteenth Amendment Adopted in 1870, it barred the use of race as a criterion for voting in state and federal elections.

First Amendment Part of the Bill of Rights containing protections for political and religious expression.

Fourteenth Amendment Adopted in 1868, it altered the nature of the Union by placing new, if undefined, limitations on state authority.

Fourth Amendment Part of the Bill of Rights that prohibits unreasonable searches and seizures of persons and their property.

franchise The right to vote.

free exercise clause Provision of the First Amendment guaranteeing religious freedom.

government The political and administrative organization of a state, nation, or locality.

grand jury A panel of citizens, ranging in number from twelve to twenty-three, used by federal courts and the courts of most states to review evidence against those suspected of a crime. If the evidence presented to the grand jury by the prosecutor seems sufficient, the grand jury issues an indictment, and the case moves to trial.

habeas corpus Literally "you have the body"; a procedure by which a judge inquires into the legality of a person's imprisonment.

implied powers Powers of the national government not specifically cited in the Constitution but implicit in powers that are specifically cited; authorized by the necessary and proper clause of section eight of Article I.

incorporation The process, mainly in the twentieth century, by which the Supreme Court applied most of the provisions of the Bill of Rights to the states via the due process clause of the Fourteenth Amendment.

indictment The written accusation issued by a grand jury to a trial court, charging someone with commission of a criminal offense.

in re Literally "in the matter of"; a way of entitling a proceeding where formally there are no adversary parties but rather the existence of a legal matter requiring resolution by a court.

Jim Crow System of laws and arrangements by which blacks were kept in political and social subjugation in the post–Civil War South, and in other parts of the United States as well.

judgment of the court The holding or decision in a case, as distinguished from the opinion, which provides the reasoning for the decision.

judicial activism In contrast to judicial restraint, an approach to judicial decisionmaking by which judges are inclined to attempt to achieve desirable policy objectives through their decisions, even if that means declaring unconstitutional actions taken by other branches of the government. Judicial activism may result in either politically liberal or conservative decisions.

judicial restraint In contrast to judicial activism, an approach to judicial decisionmaking by which judges defer to actions taken by the elected and politically accountable branches of government. Thus, proponents of judicial restraint would be less disposed than proponents of judicial activism to invalidate an act of Congress or of a state legislature.

judicial review The authority of courts to set aside a legislative act as being in violation of the Constitution; first applied and defended by the Supreme Court in *Marbury v. Madison* (1803).

jurisdiction Authority of a court to hear a particular case.

legal right *See civil liberty; civil right; right.*

majority opinion *See opinion of the court.*

misdemeanor Less serious criminal offense, usually punishable by not more than one year in jail.

New Deal Legislative program of the first two terms of President Franklin D. Roosevelt (1933–1945) to respond to the Great Depression of the 1930s; its revolutionary policy initiatives established a pervasive and active role for the national government.

opinion of the court Statement representing the views of a majority of the judges of a court in deciding a case.

original jurisdiction As distinguished from appellate jurisdiction, the authority a court possesses over cases that are first heard—that is, originate—in that court. The Supreme Court's original jurisdiction is small and is defined by Article III of the Constitution.

party One by whom or against whom a legal action is brought. A party could be a person, a government, a business, or other organization.

peculiar institution The term given to the system of slavery in the United States. Slavery was peculiar because it existed only in positive, not natural, law. On the assumption that all persons were free and equal in the eyes of the law (the central idea of the Declaration of Independence), slavery could exist only in situations where exceptions were made to that basic premise.

Pendleton Act Legislation passed by Congress in 1883 that created a civil service commission and a system that used merit, rather than partisan political connections, as a condition of government employment.

plaintiff The person or other party initiating legal action against another.

police power Within the American political system, that mass of comprehensive governmental regulatory authority—to protect public health, safety, welfare, and morals—not delegated to the national government under the Constitution but retained by the states. In exercising their police powers states must do so in conformity with the Constitution. In theory the national government does not possess a general police power. However, Congress has used its powers to tax and to regulate interstate commerce to accomplish similar objectives. The term "police power" appears in *Brown v. Maryland* (1827), in which Chief Justice Marshall spoke of it as residual, comprising what was left over of the state's powers beyond those other great prerogatives of eminent domain and taxation.

political party Organization that seeks to influence public policy by placing its members in positions of governmental authority, such as Congress and the presidency.

precedent Prior decision of a court, cited as authority by that court or by another.

removal jurisdiction Authority that allows a case to be transferred, prior to hearing or conclusion, from one court to another on petition of one of the parties, for example, from state to federal court.

reporter of decisions The person designated by a court to collect and to disseminate the decisions of that court. Prior to 1875, decisions by the U.S. Supreme Court were cited by the name of the reporter who had them published: for example, *Wallace's Reports* (for John William Wallace) between 1863 and 1874, or *Black's Reports* (for Jeremiah Black) in 1861 and 1862.

Republican Party The younger of the two major American political parties, it emerged in the mid-1850s as the Whig Party collapsed.

reserved powers Powers not delegated to the national government by express grant or implication; these remain with the respective state governments, subject to state laws and constitutions.

resulting powers National powers derived from the mass of delegated powers or from a group of them; examples include the taking of property by eminent domain for a purpose not spelled out in the Constitution, carrying into effect treaties to which the United States is a party, and making paper money legal tender in payment of public and private debts.

right A legally protected interest to which one is entitled, or a legally enforceable claim of one person against another to act, or not to act, in a certain way. It may derive from the Constitution, a statute, a judicial decision, or even an administrative rule. *See also civil liberty* and *civil right.*

separate-but-equal doctrine Standard announced by the Supreme Court in *Plessy v. Ferguson* (1896) that allowed racially separate facilities on trains (and by implication in public services such as education) as long as the separate facilities were equal. Rejected by *Brown v. Board of Education* (1954).

separation of powers A principle of American government implicit in the organization of the first three articles of the Constitution, providing for a Congress with legislative power, a president with executive power, and a Supreme Court with judicial power. Abuse of power would be less likely to occur, the framers believed, if the powers of government were divided. From this separation is derived the doctrine that certain functions, because of their essential nature, may properly be exercised by only a particular branch of the government; that such functions cannot be delegated to any other branch; and that one department may not usurp the powers of another or supervise their exercise. Yet to a degree the term is a misnomer. Although the Constitution separates organs of government, it fuses some functions and powers, thus putting in place a system of checks and balances as an additional restraint on power.

solicitor general The chief lawyer for the executive branch in the Supreme Court. Congress created the position in 1870 when it established the Department of Justice; the solicitor general serves under the attorney general. Under current policy, the solicitor general decides whether to appeal a government defeat in a court of appeals to the Supreme Court. The solicitor general and assistants present the government's side in all cases heard by the Court to which the government is a party and may be heard as amicus curiae in other cases in which the executive branch has an interest.

spoils system A view of government employment that jobs belong to supporters of the victorious party. The phrase apparently originated with Senator William Marcy of New York who declared in 1832, "to the victor belong the spoils." Probably perfected in the administration of Andrew Jackson, the spoils system became pervasive after the Whig Party won the presidency in 1841. Contraction of the spoils system in federal employment began after President Garfield's assassination in 1881 with passage of the Pendleton Act in 1883, which created the civil service system.

state action Action taken by an official or agency of government, not that taken by private individuals or organizations. For example, the Fourteenth Amendment restrains the former, but according to the *Civil Rights Cases* (1883), not the latter. In its broadest sense, it refers to action by any level of government, not merely action by state governments.

substantive due process A view of due process of law that developed in the second half of the nineteenth century and that the Supreme Court gradually adopted after 1888. Rather than viewing due process solely as a restraint on the manner in which government carried out a policy, courts began to look at the fairness or reasonableness, that is, the substance, of the policy itself. *See also due process of law.*

supremacy clause A provision of Article VI of the Constitution and the keystone of the federal system; it states that if the legitimate powers of state and national government collide, the powers of the latter prevail.

trial court A court of limited or general jurisdiction in which the disputed facts of a case are heard and decided. A trial court ordinarily has jurisdiction over both civil and criminal cases.

United States Reports The officially published decisions of the U.S. Supreme Court. In a citation to a Supreme Court case, "U.S." signifies the *United States Reports. See also reporter of decisions.*

v. (or vs.) Versus, or against. It is present in the title of most cases, separating the identities of the parties that oppose each other. The petitioner, prosecuting authority, or appellant (the party bringing the case) is listed first; the respondent, defendant, or appellee (the party against whom the case is brought) is listed second.

warrant Official authorization for government action; for example, the Fourth Amendment requires that a judge issue a warrant before police may conduct many searches.

Whig Party The major American political party of business and entrepreneurship between about 1830 and 1856; displaced by the Republican Party.

writ A written judicial order to perform a certain act or providing authority for that act to be done.

Annotated Bibliography

Books and Articles

Abraham, Henry J. 1992. *Justices and Presidents: A Political History of Appointments to the Supreme Court.* 3rd ed. New York: Oxford University Press.

A concise study of the circumstances surrounding appointment of each justice to the Supreme Court, through that of Justice David Souter in 1990. Includes evaluations of each appointee's performance on the bench, especially in terms of presidential expectations, and accounts of failed nominations as well. An updated version by the same author, current through the appointment of Justice Stephen Breyer in 1994 is also available under a different title: *Justices, Presidents, and Senators* (Lanham, MD: Rowman and Littlefield, 1999).

Atkinson, David N. 1999. *Leaving the Bench: Supreme Court Justices at the End.* Lawrence: University Press of Kansas.

Comprehensive account of the circumstances surrounding the departures of Supreme Court justices from the Court, whether by death, resignation, or retirement. Attention is paid as well to various disabilities that handicapped some justices while still on the bench.

Bardolph, Richard, ed. 1970. *The Civil Rights Record: Black Americans and the Law, 1849–1870.* New York: Crowell.

A comprehensive collection of state and federal statutes, court decisions, and other documents relating to racial equality and supported by narrative and analysis, covering the years 1849–1970.

Basler, Roy P. 1953–1955. *The Collected Works of Abraham Lincoln.* Vol. 5. New Brunswick, NJ: Rutgers University Press.

One of several sources for anyone interested in Lincoln's speeches and other public papers, both before and after his election to the presidency.

Baynes, Thomas E. 1978. "Yankee from Georgia." *Supreme Court Historical Society Yearbook* 31–42.

An account of the life of Justice (and General) William B. Woods, including his contributions as a circuit judge in the South after the Civil War and the circumstances of his appointment to the Supreme Court.

Beth, Loren P. 1971. *Development of the American Constitution, 1877–1917.* New York: Harper and Row.

A volume in the New American Nation Series that explores constitutional development in the United States on a variety of fronts during the years of the Waite and Fuller Courts, and during most of the White Court.

———. 1992. *John Marshall Harlan: The Last Whig Justice.* Lexington: University Press of Kentucky.

The first of three modern biographies of Harlan (the two more recent ones were authored by Yarbrough and Przbyszewski); stresses the contrasts between Harlan and his colleagues on the Court as well as the contrasts between Harlan as a justice and his background and upbringing.

Bradley, Joseph P. 1901. *Miscellaneous Writings of the Late Hon. Joseph P. Bradley.* C. Bradley, ed. Newark, NJ: Hardham.

Collection of many of Justice Bradley's addresses and other public papers.

Brennan, William J., Jr. 1972. "Inside View of the High Court." In *The Supreme Court under Earl Warren*, ed. Leonard W. Levy. New York: Quadrangle Books, pp. 38–47.

Perspectives on the business and decision-making procedures of the Supreme Court by a sitting justice; originally published under the same title in the *New York Times Magazine*, October 6, 1963.

Clifford, Philip G. 1922. *Nathan Clifford, Democrat.* New York: G. P. Putnam's Sons.

Admiring biography by a grandson of the justice who was President Buchanan's only appointee to the Supreme Court. Includes excerpts from the justice's letters and other papers.

Clinton, Robert Lowry, and Kevin Walsh. 1999. "Judicial Sobriety: Nathan P. Clifford." In *Sober as a Judge: The Supreme Court and Republican Liberty*, ed. Richard G. Stevens and Matthew J. Franck. Lanham, MD: Lexington, pp. 25–49.

One of the few recent separate treatments of Nathan Clifford as justice; the authors find evidence in Clifford's opinions and votes that he favored a restrained role for the federal judiciary.

Conkling, Alfred R. 1889. *The Life and Letters of Roscoe Conkling.* New York: C. L. Webster.

An account of the political career of the powerful Republican leader and New York senator who was given two opportunities to go on the Supreme Court. Written in the customary uncritical style of nineteenth-century biography, the volume is useful as a source of basic information and letters.

Corwin, Edward S. 1938. *Court over Constitution.* Princeton, NJ: Princeton University Press (reissued by Peter Smith in 1957).

Analysis of the Supreme Court's evolution as a major maker of public policy, especially after 1890, by one of the preeminent constitutional scholars of the twentieth century. Includes useful documents from the founding era of American government in the appendix.

———. 1987. "The Doctrine of Due Process of Law before the Civil War." In *Corwin on the Constitution: Volume Two: The Judiciary*, ed. Richard Loss. Ithaca, NY: Cornell University Press.

Essential article for understanding the development of due process as a potent judicial tool in American constitutional law; originally published in the *Harvard Law Review* 24: 366–385, 460–479 (1911).

———. 1948. *Liberty against Government.* Baton Rouge: Louisiana State University Press.

Analysis of the use of the due process clause as a check on governmental power, especially prior to 1937.

Cummings, Homer S., and Carl McFarland. 1937. *Federal Justice: Chapters in the History of Justice and the Federal Executive.* New York: Macmillan.

Helpful volume, authored by two key New Deal figures, in understanding the role of the U.S. Department of Justice, especially during Reconstruction.

Currie, David P. 1985. *The Constitution in the Supreme Court: The First Hundred Years, 1789–1888.* Chicago: University of Chicago Press.

The first of a two-volume study of American constitutional history, with a heavy emphasis on the Supreme Court. The second volume, subtitled *The Second Century 1888–1986*, was published by the same press in 1990.

Curtis, Benjamin Robbins. 1879. *A Memoir of Benjamin Robbins Curtis, LL.D.*, 2 vols. George Tichnor Curtis, ed. Boston: Little, Brown.

Contains biographical material of Justice Curtis written by George Tichnor Curtis, plus letters and professional writings.

Curtis, Michael Kent. 2000. *Free Speech, "The People's Darling Privilege:" Struggles for Freedom of Expression in American History.* Durham, NC: Duke University Press.

The most thorough account of the development of ideas concerning free speech; the emphasis is on the years between 1798 and 1866. Useful in trying to grasp the intentions of the framers of the Fourteenth Amendment.

Danelski, David. 2002. "The Influence of the Chief Justice in the Decisional Process of the Supreme Court." In *Courts, Judges, and Politics: An Introduction to the Judicial Process*, 5th ed. Walter F. Murphy, C. Herman Pritchett, and Lee Epstein, eds. Boston: McGraw Hill, pp. 662–670.

Definitive article, first delivered as a conference paper more than four decades ago, on the chief justice's leadership role at the Supreme Court.

Davis, Bob. 2002. "Past Crisis Offers Hope for Economy, Warnings to Watch." *Wall Street Journal*, September 26, pp. A1, A8.

Contains data on major late nineteenth-century economic crises.

Epstein, Lee, Jeffrey A. Segal, and Harold J. Spaeth. 2001."The Norm of Consensus on the U.S. Supreme Court." *American Journal of Political Science* 45: 362–377.

Important statistical study on voting patters in the Waite Court that compares voting in conference with voting records as they appear in the *U.S. Reports.* The conclusion is that there was an usually high percentage of unanimous decisions, not because most of the cases were easy, but because of a norm of consensus at work.

Epstein, Lee, Jeffrey A. Segal, Harold J. Spaeth, and Thomas G. Walker. 1996. *The Supreme Court Compendium.* Washington, DC: Congressional Quarterly Press.

Highly useful collection of various statistics about the Supreme Court over the years, its justices, and its decisions.

Fairman, Charles. 1988. *Five Justices and the Electoral Commission of 1877. History of the Supreme Court of the United States*, supp. to vol. 7. New York: Macmillan.

The electoral crisis of 1876–1877, with an emphasis on the roles played by the five justices of the Supreme Court who served on the Electoral Commission of 1877. The volume is a supplement to Fairman's volume 7 on the Waite Court, in the Oliver Wendell Holmes devised *History of the Supreme Court of the United States.*

———. 1964. "Mr. Justice Bradley." In *Mr. Justice*, rev. and enl. ed., ed. Allison Dunham and Philip B. Kurland. Chicago: University of Chicago Press, pp. 64–91.

An essay that draws upon Fairman's earlier writings about Justice Bradley (see below); a useful summation of his life and judicial career.

———. 1941. "Mr. Justice Bradley's Appointment to the Supreme Court and the Legal Tender Cases." *Harvard Law Review* 54: 977–1034, 1128–1155.

Comprehensive study by Justice Miller's biographer of the Legal Tender Cases and the circumstances surrounding Justice Joseph Bradley's appointment by President Grant to the Supreme Court, after which the Court reversed its earlier holding on the legal tender question. Generally debunks the claim that President Grant packed the Supreme Court in order to obtain a reversal.

———. 1939. *Mr. Justice Miller and the Supreme Court: 1862–1890.* Cambridge, MA: Harvard University Press.

The definitive study of Justice Miller's life and judicial career, written by an eminent constitutional scholar who specialized in American constitutional development during the last third of the nineteenth century.

———. 1971. *Reconstruction and Reunion 1864–88, Part One. History of the Supreme Court of the United States.* Vol. 6. New York: Macmillan.

An exceedingly detailed account of the personalities, politics, and decisions of the Chase Court. The volume is an installment in the Oliver Wendell Holmes devised *History of the Supreme Court of the United States.* Part Two (volume 7) provides a similarly detailed account of the Waite Court.

———. 1987. *Reconstruction and Reunion 1864–1888, Part Two. History of the Supreme Court of the United States.* Vol. 7. New York: Macmillan.

An exceedingly detailed account of the personalities, politics, and decisions of the Waite Court. The volume is an installment in the Oliver Wendell Holmes devised *History of the Supreme Court of the United States.* Part One (volume 6) provides a similarly detailed account of the Chase Court.

———. 1950. "What Makes a Great Justice? Mr. Justice Bradley and the Supreme Court, 1870–1892." *Boston University Law Review* 30: 49–102.

Analysis of Bradley in terms of his preparation for the bench and his contributions to American jurisprudence.

Field, Stephen J. 1893. *Personal Reminiscences of Early Days in California.* Washington, DC: privately published.

Earlier editions were probably intended by Field as a campaign biography to promote his candidacy for president. The 1877 edition was reissued by Da Capo in 1968. According to Field biographer Carl Brent Swisher, the manuscript version of *Personal Reminiscences* contains some material not included in the published editions. The former is filed in the Sutro Branch of the California State Library in San Francisco.

Filler, Louis. 1969. "Horace Gray." In *The Justices of the United States Supreme Court 1789–1969: Their Lives and Major Opinions*, vol. 2, ed. Leon Friedman and Fred L. Israel. New York: Chelsea House, pp. 1379–1389.

An essay stressing Justice Gray's upbringing and his service on the Supreme Judicial Court of Massachusetts, as well as on the U.S. Supreme Court. Ponders the question why Gray, who possessed an excellent legal mind and who was highly regarded in his day, has today largely dropped from sight as a subject of interest.

———. 1969. "John M. Harlan." In *The Justices of the United States Supreme Court 1789–1969: Their Lives and Major Opinions*, vol. 2, ed. Leon Friedman and Fred L. Israel. New York: Chelsea House, pp. 1281–1295.

An essay stressing Justice Harlan's variegated and colorful pre-Court career as well as his jurisprudential contributions while a justice.

Fish, Peter Graham. 1973. *The Politics of Federal Judicial Administration.* Princeton, NJ: Princeton University Press.

The role of the chief justice in a unified federal judicial system since the 1920s, with an emphasis on the workings of the Judicial Conference of the United States.

Frank, John P. 1964. *Justice Daniel Dissenting.* Cambridge, MA: Harvard University Press.

A biography of the Van Buren appointee whose seat lay vacant for more than two years after his death in 1860, until it was filled by Justice Miller.

Frankfurter, Felix. 1953. "Chief Justices I Have Known." *Virginia Law Review* 39: 883–905.

The title of the article is self-explanatory. A lecture to law students and law faculty by a sitting justice of the Supreme Court, who, prior to his appointment to the Court in 1939, was an outspoken faculty member at the Harvard Law School and an adviser to President Franklin D. Roosevelt.

———. 1937. *The Commerce Clause under Marshall, Taney and Waite.* Chapel Hill: University of North Carolina Press.

Concise analysis of the commerce clause in the Constitution, as it was the subject of decisions in the Marshall, Taney, and Waite courts. Originally delivered as a series of lectures shortly before the author was appointed to the Supreme Court by President Franklin Roosevelt.

Frankfurter, Felix, and James M. Landis. 1928. *The Business of the Supreme Court.* New York: Macmillan.

A study of the organization and jurisdiction of the Supreme Court and other federal courts from passage of the Judiciary Act of 1789 until passage of the Judges' Bill of 1925.

Fridlington, Robert. 1987. *The Reconstruction Court 1864–1888.* Millwood, NY: Associated Faculty Press.

A collection of short biographical essays about justices who served during the Chase and Waite eras; the book is volume four in a series entitled *The Supreme Court in American Life.*

Friedman, Lawrence M. 2002. *Law in America: A Brief History.* New York: Modern Library.

Sweeping and concise study in the grand style of the development of law and legal institutions in the United States.

Friedman, Leon. 1969. "Joseph P. Bradley." In *The Justices of the United States Supreme Court 1789–1969: Their Lives and Major Opinions*, vol. 2, ed. Leon Friedman and Fred L. Israel. New York: Chelsea House, pp. 1181–1200.

Useful essay detailing Justice Bradley's life both before and after his appointment to the Supreme Court; the emphasis throughout is on Bradley's jurisprudential contributions to the High Court.

Garland, Augustus H. 1898. *Experience in the Supreme Court of the United States.* Washington, DC: J. Byrne.

A memoir by the person who was attorney general of the United States in the first administration of President Grover Cleveland (1885–1889).

Gillette, William. 1969. "John A. Campbell." In *The Justices of the United States Supreme Court 1789–1969: Their Lives and Major Opinions*, vol. 2, ed. Leon Friedman and Fred L. Israel. New York: Chelsea House, pp. 927–939.

Because Justice Campbell's tenure on the Supreme Court was relatively short, this essay stresses not only his judicial work, but the personally and professionally painful circumstances of his 1861 departure from the bench and his career after the Civil War as the preeminent Louisiana attorney of his day.

———. 1969. "Noah H. Swayne." In *The Justices of the United States Supreme Court 1789–1969: Their Lives and Major Opinions*, vol. 2, ed. Leon Friedman and Fred L. Israel. New York: Chelsea House, pp. 989–999.

Because Justice Swayne has not been the subject of a modern judicial biography, this essay is a helpful overview of the person who proved to be the weakest of Lincoln's appointees to the Supreme Court.

———. 1965. *The Right to Vote: Politics and the Passage of the Fifteenth Amendment.* Baltimore, MD: Johns Hopkins University Press.

Contains background on the origin and purposes of the Fifteenth Amendment that attempted to remove race as a criterion for voting. Sees the amendment as much as an effort to shore up the Republican Party as a civically motivated movement to broaden the franchise.

Harlan, Malvina Shanklin. 1999. "Some Memories of a Long Life, 1854–1911." *Journal of Supreme Court History* 26: 109–211.

A remarkable account of the marriage of Malvina and John Marshall Harlan. Contains reflections on her reactions to the slaves that the Harlan family owned before the Civil War as well as insights on the life of a justice and his family in Washington in the last quarter of the nineteenth century and the first decade of the twentieth. The memoir was published in book form by Modern Library in 2002.

Harring, Sidney L., and Kathryn Swedlow. 2000. "'The Defendant Has Seemed to Live a Charmed Life': *Hopt* v. *Utah:* Territorial Justice, The Supreme Court of the United States, and Late Nineteenth-Century Death Penalty Jurisprudence." *Journal of Supreme Court History* 25: 40–71.

Unusually detailed article about a major capital case heard several times by the Waite Court; contains comparative data with the Fuller Court.

Holzer, Harold, ed. 1993. *The Lincoln-Douglas Debates.* New York: Harper Collins.

Useful collection of the debates between Senator Stephen Douglas and challenger Abraham Lincoln in Illinois in 1858. Douglas won reelection to the Senate, but Lincoln's performance gave him a national visibility that made credible his candidacy for the Republican presidential nomination in 1860. He went on to defeat Douglas for the presidency in 1860.

Hough, Charles M. 1919. "Due Process of Law—Today." *Harvard Law Review* 32: 218–233.

An account of the rise and status of due process of law as a significant judicial check on legislative power, as seen through the eyes of a prominent early twentieth-century jurist.

Howard, John R. 1999. *The Shifting Wind: The Supreme Court and Civil Rights from Reconstruction to* Brown. Albany: State University of New York Press.

A concise review of Supreme Court decisions affecting civil rights from the last years of the Chase Court into the Warren Court in the twentieth century. Includes commentary on all major Waite Court civil rights decisions.

Hughes, David. F. 1965. "Salmon P. Chase: Chief Justice." *Vanderbilt Law Review* 18: 569–614.

Helpful article on Chase's tenure as chief justice, including a review of his jurisprudence and his persistent presidential ambitions.

Hurst, James Willard. 1950. *The Growth of American Law.* Boston: Little, Brown.

Study of the development of law and legal institutions in America, including the role of legislatures and administrative agencies at the state and federal levels.

Hyman, Harold M. 1997. *The Reconstruction Justice of Salmon P. Chase.* Lawrence: University Press of Kansas.

The views of Chief Justice Chase in cases relating to Reconstruction, in the Supreme Court and on circuit.

Kammen, Michael. 1986. *A Machine That Would Go of Itself: The Constitution in American Culture.* New York: Knopf.

A study of the role of the Constitution as symbol in the American mind and culture.

Kennedy, John F. 1956. *Profiles in Courage.* New York: Harper.

Chapter seven focuses on the congressional role of L. Q. C. Lamar in sectional reconciliation, especially concerning his eulogy of Charles Sumner.

Kens, Paul. 1997. *Justice Stephen Field: Shaping Liberty from the Gold Rush to the Gilded Age.* Lawrence: University Press of Kansas.

One of two excellent biographies of the justice who, until William O. Douglas, held the record for length of service on the Supreme Court. Field and Waite often expressed very different views on the scope of the Fourteenth Amendment.

Keyssar, Alexander. 2000. *The Right to Vote: The Contested History of Democracy in the United States.* New York: Basic Books.

Emphasis on expansion of the franchise in the nineteenth and early twentieth centuries, and its connection with a changing conception of democratic government.

King, Willard L. 1960. *Lincoln's Manager: David Davis.* Cambridge, MA: Harvard University Press.

Engaging biography of the talented Illinois lawyer and trial judge who devised Lincoln's strategy to obtain the presidential nomination in 1860. Lincoln rewarded Davis's service and loyalty with an appointment to the Supreme Court; fourteen years later Davis left the Court to serve in the Senate.

———. 1950. *Melville Weston Fuller.* Chicago: University of Chicago Press.

The only modern book-length biographical study of the eighth chief justice.

Kutler, Stanley I. 1969. "David Davis." In *The Justices of the United States Supreme Court 1789–1969: Their Lives and Major Opinions*, vol. 2, ed. Leon Friedman and Fred L. Israel. New York: Chelsea House, pp. 1045–1053.

An essay on Justice Davis's remarkable judicial and political career in Illinois and Washington, and his relationship with Abraham Lincoln.

———. 1968. *Judicial Power and Reconstruction Politics.* Chicago: University of Chicago Press.

Emphasis on the place of the Supreme Court during the Chase era; the author's thesis is that the Court played a more activist role than is commonly thought, especially given the loss of prestige suffered in the *Dred Scott* decision of 1857.

———. 1969. "Ward Hunt." In *The Justices of the United States Supreme Court 1789–1969: Their Lives and Major Opinions*, vol. 2, ed. Leon Friedman and Fred L. Israel. New York: Chelsea House, pp. 1221–1229.

Reviews the life of Grant's third appointee to the Supreme Court as a New York attorney and judge, his critical connection with Senator Roscoe Conkling, as well as his Court years.

———. 1969. "William Strong." In *The Justices of the United States Supreme Court 1789–1969: Their Lives and Major Opinions*, vol. 2, ed. Leon Friedman and Fred L. Israel. New York: Chelsea House, pp. 1153–1161.

Strangely one of the most understudied justices of the Supreme Court, the essay depicts Strong as a capable Pennsylvania judge who later relinquished his career on the Supreme Court as an example to colleagues whom he believed had stayed too long.

Lerner, Max. 1994. *Nine Scorpions in a Bottle: Great Judges and Cases of the Supreme Court.* Ed. Richard Cummings. New York: Arcade.

A collection of essays, written over a period of a half century, by a well-known commentator on the Supreme Court. The title derives from Justice O. W. Holmes's supposed description of the Court on which he sat from 1902 until 1932 as "nine scorpions in a bottle."

Magrath, C. Peter. 1987. "The Case of the Unscrupulous Warehouseman." In *Quarrels That Have Shaped the Constitution*, rev. ed., ed. John A. Garraty. New York: Harper and Row, pp. 119–138.

Written by a biographer of Chief Justice Waite, the essay is a detailed examination of the landmark case of *Munn v. Illinois* (1877).

———. 1963. *Morrison R. Waite: The Triumph of Character.* New York: Macmillan.

One of two excellent biographies of the seventh chief justice. Both make ample use of Waite's letters and other papers, as well as the papers of other justices with whom he sat, in an effort not only to understand the internal workings of the Waite Court but to grasp Waite as a person.

Maine, Sir Henry Sumner. 1886. *Popular Government.* New York: Henry Holt.

Essays by an English legal historian, largely on democratic government in general, and on U.S. political institutions in particular, in comparison to British political institutions.

Maltese, John Anthony. 1995. *The Selling of Supreme Court Nominees.* Baltimore: Johns Hopkins University Press.

One of several books written in the past fifteen years on the politics of judicial appointments, this one is distinctive in its focus on the efforts, or lack thereof, by the White House to secure Senate confirmation of nominees, especially those that have aroused significant controversy. The volume opens with an account of the unusual circumstances surrounding Justice Matthews's appointment.

Maltz, Earl M. 1996. "The Waite Court and Federal Power to Enforce the Reconstruction Amendments." In *The Supreme Court and the Civil War,* ed. Jennifer M. Lowe. Washington, D.C.: Supreme Court Historical Society, pp. 75–88.

An analysis of Waite Court cases on civil rights; concludes that, despite some lapses, the record shows a stronger protection of civil rights than is sometimes believed.

Marshall, Charles C. 1890. "A New Constitutional Amendment." *American Law Review* 24: 908–931.

Article by a prominent attorney defending *Munn v. Illinois* (1877) as a correct construction of the Constitution, but calling for a constitutional amendment to change it.

Mason, Alpheus Thomas. 1968. "The Chief Justice of the United States: *Primus Inter Pares.*" *Journal of Public Law* 17:20–60.

Analysis of the origins and changing roles of the presiding justice of the Supreme Court.

———. 1956. *Harlan Fiske Stone: Pillar of the Law.* New York: Viking.

Groundbreaking biography of an important twentieth-century justice and chief justice who helped lead the Supreme Court through an abandonment of its post-Waite role as a censor of economic legislation and into a role that stressed the protection of nonproprietarian civil liberties and civil rights.

Mason, Alpheus Thomas, and Donald Grier Stephenson, Jr. 2002. *American Constitutional Law: Introductory Essays and Selected Cases.* 13th ed. Upper Saddle River, NJ: Prentice Hall.

One of several textbooks on most topics of American constitutional law and interpretation; essays on each topic are followed by excerpts from leading cases, including some from, and related to, the Waite era.

McCloskey, Robert G. 1960. *The American Supreme Court.* Chicago: University of Chicago Press.

Concise, broad-stroke history of the Court from its founding into the first years of the Warren Court that emphasizes the growth of the power of judicial review and finds the seeds of the activism of the Fuller and later courts within some Waite Court decisions. An updated third edition of this classic work adds a review of Supreme Court decisions during the four decades after 1960. It was prepared by Sanford Levinson and issued under the same title by the same publisher in 2000.

———. 1969. "Stephen J. Field." In *The Justices of the United States Supreme Court 1789–1969: Their Lives and Major Opinions*, vol. 2, ed. Leon Friedman and Fred L. Israel. New York: Chelsea House, pp. 1069–1089.

Written by one of the most accomplished students of the Supreme Court in the mid-twentieth century, the essay depicts Justice Field as an agent of laissez-faire economic theory on the Supreme Court. McCloskey's introduction to the 1968 edition of Swisher's 1930 biography of Field maintains a similar theme. Both McCloskey's and Swisher's treatments of Field should be considered alongside that of Kens's.

Meador, Daniel J. 1986. "Lamar to the Court: Last Step to National Reunion." *Supreme Court Historical Society Yearbook:* 27–47.

Depicts the controversial nomination and appointment of L.Q.C. Lamar by President Grover Cleveland to the Supreme Court in 1888, and the role of that event in sectional reconciliation.

Miller, George H. 1971. *Railroads and the Granger Laws.* Madison: University of Wisconsin Press.

The origin of the Granger laws and reactions to them by the courts of the late nineteenth century; contains important background information for understanding *Munn v. Illinois* (1877).

Morris, Roy, Jr. 2002. *Fraud of the Century: Rutherford B. Hayes, Samuel Tilden, and the Stolen Election of 1876.* New York: Simon and Schuster.

As the title indicates, this volume on the election controversy of 1876–1877 concludes that Tilden's defeat was the product of voting frauds perpetrated by Republican election officials.

Murphy, James B. 1973. *L. Q. C. Lamar: Pragmatic Patriot.* Baton Rouge: Louisiana State University Press.

One of several biographies of someone who might be described as the late nineteenth- century comeback kid. Lamar held posts in the Confederate government and in all three branches of the national government. His service in Washington after the Civil War contributed substantially to sectional reconciliation.

Murphy, Walter F. 1962. "Marshaling the Court: Leadership, Bargaining, and the Judicial Process." *University of Chicago Law Review* 29: 640–672.

One of the earlier studies of leadership on the Supreme Court; makes particular use of the private papers of justices in reaching conclusions about how justices attempted to influence their colleagues.

Nash, A. E. Keir. 1994. "Horace Gray." In *The Supreme Court Justices: A Biographical Dictionary*, ed. Melvin I. Urofsky. New York: Garland, pp. 197–201.

More than most essays about Justice Gray, Keir's stresses the jurisprudential contributions made by this most well-born member of the Waite Court's roster.

Niehoff, Leonard M. 1993. "David Davis." In *The Supreme Court Justices: Illustrated Biographies, 1789–1993*, ed. Clare Cushman. Washington, DC: Congressional Quarterly Press, pp. 181–185.

An excellent source of information about Judge Davis's career before and after his years of service on the Supreme Court.

Northrup, Milton Harlow. 1901. "A Grave Crisis in American History." *Century Magazine* 62: 923–934.

Recollections of the electoral crisis of 1876–1877 by the secretary to the special committee formed by the House of Representatives in December 1876 to propose a resolution to the controversy.

"Notes: Death of Chief Justice Waite." 1888. *American Law Review* 22: 301–303.

Commentary on Waite at the time of his death by an influential legal periodical of the day.

Palmer, Robert R. 1960. *A History of the Modern World*, 2nd ed. New York: Knopf.

Broad-stroke world history, with an emphasis on the Western world.

Pennypacker, S. W. 1918. *The Autobiography of a Pennsylvanian.* Philadelphia: Winston.

Political memoir of a governor of Pennsylvania (1903–1907) published after his death.

Przbyszewski, Linda. 1999. *The Republic According to John Marshall Harlan.* Chapel Hill: University of North Carolina Press.

The most recent of three modern biographies of the first Justice Harlan (the other two have been written by Loren Beth and Tinsley Yarbrough). A strength of the Przbyszewski volume is the emphasis on Harlan's political ideas and his considerable service to the Presbyterian Church.

Richardson, James D. 1917. *A Compilation of Messages and Papers of the Presidents, 1789–1902.* 20 vols. New York: Bureau of National Literature.

Essential source for mainly nineteenth-century presidential pronouncements and other official papers.

"The Right to Confiscate." 1874. *The Nation*, September 24, pp. 199–201.

Editorial in a prominent periodical concerning the railroad litigation in the *Granger Cases.*

Roper, Donald. 1993. "Stanley Matthews." In *The Supreme Court Justices: Illustrated*

Biographies, 1789–1993, ed. Clare Cushman. Washington, DC: Congressional Quarterly Press, pp. 226–230.

Contains helpful biographical information about an important figure on the Waite Court, many of whose most important contributions were nonjudicial.

Scaturro, Frank J. 2000. *The Supreme Court's Retreat from Reconstruction: A Distortion of Constitutional Jurisprudence.* Westport, CT: Greenwood.

The scope of the volume extends beyond the Waite Court, but considerable attention is paid to the major civil rights decisions by that Court. A principal thesis of the book is that the Court of late nineteenth century contributed in a significant way to the demise of Reconstruction policies and the declining mainstream interest in the protection of the civil rights of African Americans.

Seddig, Robert G. 1991. "John Marshall and the Origins of Supreme Court Leadership." *Journal of Supreme Court History:* 63–85.

A study of Supreme Court leadership that uses Chief Justice Marshall as a case study; originally published in the *University of Pittsburgh Law Review* 36: 785–833 (1975).

Silver, David M. 1998. *Lincoln's Supreme Court.* Urbana: University of Illinois Press (reissue of 1956 edition).

An essential volume for anyone interested in the unfriendly confines of the Supreme Court during the Lincoln administration, especially its early years. Reviews key decisions and judicial appointments and how each related to Lincoln's goals.

Spitzer, Robert J. 2001. *The Right to Bear Arms.* Santa Barbara, CA: ABC-CLIO.

Thorough analysis of this issue in American constitutional law. Helpful in understanding the legal and cultural context of the Waite Court's decision in *Presser v. Illinois* (1886) relating to the Second Amendment.

Stephenson, Donald Grier, Jr. 1999. *Campaigns and the Court: The United States Supreme Court in Presidential Elections.* New York: Columbia University Press.

Studies the effect of presidential elections on the Supreme Court and the effect of the Court on presidential elections.

———. 1973. "The Chief Justice as Leader: The Case of Morrison Remick Waite." *William and Mary Law Review* 14: 899–927.

Proposes a framework to measure leadership on the Supreme Court, and applies that to Waite's chief justiceship. Draws heavily on the collection of Waite Papers at the Library of Congress.

———. 1988. "The Supreme Court, the Franchise, and the Fifteenth Amendment: The First Sixty Years." *University of Missouri at Kansas City Law Review* 57: 47–65.

Analysis of Supreme Court decisions construing the Fifteenth Amendment from 1870 through the 1930s.

Stevens, Richard G. 1999. "Due Process of Law: Stanley Matthews." In *Sober as a*

Judge: The Supreme Court and Republican Liberty, ed. Richard G. Stevens and Matthew J. Franck. Lanham, MD: Lexington, pp. 53–93.

Emphasizes aspects of Justice Matthews's years on the Supreme Court that bore witness to the value of a restrained judicial role in American government, particularly in the context of Matthews's opinion in *Hurtado v. California* (1884).

Strong, William. 1890. "Relief for the Supreme Court." *North American Review* 151: 567–575.

Important statement by the former justice on the need for organizational and jurisdictional changes in the federal courts.

———. 1875. *Two Lectures upon the Relation of Civil Law to Church Polity, Discipline, and Property.* New York: Dodd and Mead.

Discusses allowable government control of church affairs.

"Supreme Court Proceedings in Memoriam of Morrison R. Waite." 1888. 126 U.S. 585.

The official eulogies and comments on Waite as presented at the bar of the Supreme Court on March 26, following his death.

Swinney, Everette. 1962. "Enforcing the Fifteenth Amendment, 1870–1877." *Journal of Southern History:* 202–218.

Analysis of voting rights cases during the seven-year period after ratification of the Fifteenth Amendment.

Swisher, Carl Brent. 1935. *Roger B. Taney.* Washington, DC: Brookings Institution.

One of the first serious biographical treatments of the fifth chief justice that sought to look beyond (but not to overlook) Taney's (and his Court's) serious misjudgment in the *Dred Scott* case toward his many positive contributions to American constitutional law. The volume concludes with an account of the tensions between Taney and President Lincoln.

———. 1930. *Stephen J. Field: Craftsman of the Law.* Chicago: University of Chicago Press.

The first modern biography of Justice Field, and still an essential source to be consulted about this important late nineteenth-century jurist.

Trimble, Bruce R. 1938. *Chief Justice Waite: Defender of the Public Interest.* Princeton, NJ: Princeton University Press (reissued by Russell and Russell in 1970).

The older of two modern biographies of the seventh chief justice. The author's perspective is that of one writing about Waite during the years of the Great Depression, when the Supreme Court challenged national power to an unprecedented extent.

Urofsky, Melvin I. 2002. *Religious Freedom: Rights and Liberties under the Law.* Santa Barbara, CA: ABC-CLIO.

Broad and helpful survey of the constitutional rights relating both to the establishment and free exercise clauses of the First Amendment, from the founding era to the present. Contains an excellent review of the Waite Court's decisions affecting the Mormons.

Vile, John R., ed. 2003. *Great American Judges: An Encyclopedia.* 2 vols. Santa Barbara, CA: ABC-CLIO.

A collection of essays about some 100 state and federal judges, including Waite Court justices Field (by James W. Ely, Jr.), Gray (by Slyde Willis), and Harlan (by Linda Przybyszewski). Also included is Thomas Drummond (by Kevin Collins), who was a contender for the Supreme Court seat Lincoldn handed to David Davis.

Waite, Morrison R. 1887. "Remarks of Chief Justice Waite." *Albany Law Journal* 36: 318.

Reprints comments made by Chief Justice Waite, mainly concerning judicial reform and reorganization, at a bar association meeting in Philadelphia a year before his death.

Ward, Artemus. 2003. *Deciding to Leave: The Politics of Retirment from the United States Supreme Court.* Albany: State University of New York Press.

Similar in content and organization to David Atkinson's *Leaving the Bench*, the volume emphasizes factors contributing to a justice's decision to retire. Concludes that more fenerous retirement benefits have been most influential during most decades.

Warren, Charles. 1926. *The Supreme Court in U.S. History.* 2 vols., rev. ed. Boston: Little, Brown.

A classic study in Supreme Court history that draws heavily from contemporary sources, including newspapers and congressional comment. The first volume is devoted entirely to the years through John Marshall's chief justiceship. Volume two begins with the Taney Court and provides a detailed look at the evolution of the Court through Waite's chief justiceship. The Fuller and White Courts, through 1918, are briefly treated at the end.

"The Week." 1881. *The Nation*, July 23, p. 62.

Commentary in an influential periodical about partisanship on the Supreme Court; written on the occasion of Justice Clifford's death.

Yarbrough, Tinsley E. 1995. *Judicial Enigma: The First Justice Harlan.* New York: Oxford University Press.

One of three recent biographies of the first justice named to the Supreme Court after Waite became chief justice. In most respects Harlan was very much a part of the Waite Court, but in a few ways he was noticeably different. Reference to the first Justice Harlan relates to the fact that his grandson, also named John Marshall Harlan, sat on a later Supreme Court (1955–1971).

Supreme Court Decisions and Related Legal Sources

Decisions by the U.S. Supreme Court are available in printed form in several editions and are widely available on the Internet.

United States Reports

This is the official edition, now published by the Government Printing Office. Until 1875, the reports were cited according to the name of the reporter of decisions, with the reporter's name sometimes abbreviated. Beginning with volume 91 in 1875, the reports have been cited with only the designation "U.S." For example, a case cited as 444 U.S. 130 is located in volume 444 of the U.S. Reports, beginning on page 130.

1789–1800 Dallas (1–4 Dallas = 1–4 U.S.)
1801–1815 Cranch (1–9 Cranch = 5–13 U.S.)
1816–1827 Wheaton (1–12 Wheaton = 14–25 U.S.)
1828–1842 Peters (1–16 Peters = 26–41 U.S.)
1843–1860 Howard (1–24 Howard = 42–65 U.S.)
1861–1862 Black (1–2 Black = 66–67 U.S.)
1863–1874 Wallace (1–23 Wallace = 68–90 U.S.)
1875–present (91– U.S.)

U.S. Supreme Court Reports, Lawyers' Edition

Until 1996 published by Lawyers' Cooperative Publishing Company; now published by Lexis-Nexis. The advantage of this complete edition lies in the inclusion of summaries of briefs of counsel plus notes and annotations on various topics of constitutional law. Lawyers' Edition is cited as L.Ed. (e.g., 96 L.Ed. 954). Decisions since 1956 appear in a second series (e.g., 118 L.Ed. 2d 293).

Supreme Court Reporter

Until 1996 published by West Publishing Company; now published by West Group. This is similar in concept to Lawyers' Edition but only includes decisions since 1882. Thus for cases in volumes 1–105 U.S., one must consult U.S. Supreme Court Reports, Lawyers' Edition or U.S. Reports. It is cited as S.Ct. (e.g., 58 S.Ct. 166).

Decisions of Lower Federal Courts

Until 1879, many opinions issued by U.S. district and circuit courts were published in Federal Cases (abbreviated Fed. Cas.). Beginning in 1880, opinions issued by the circuit courts (and after 1891 the courts of appeals) appeared in the Federal Reporter, as did opinions issued by district courts until 1932. Since 1932 the latter have been published in the Federal Supplement.

Internet Resources

Supreme Court decisions are accessible through Westlaw and Lexis-Nexis (both available through many college and university libraries or by subscription), on CD-ROM, and at various locations on the World Wide Web. As of this writing, the sites listed below are available at no charge. Be advised that any Web address (or Universal Resource Locator, abbreviated URL) is subject to change.

(a) The LII and Hermes: The Legal Information Institute and Project Hermes provide decisions since May 1990 through Cornell University. Decisions are ordinarily accessible within hours of their announcement by the Supreme Court. Several hundred selected decisions prior to 1990 are available from LII at the second address.
http://supct.law.cornell.edu/supct/html
http://supct.law.cornell.edu/supct/cases/historic.htm

(b) FindLaw: FindLaw Internet Legal Resources includes decisions since 1791.
http://www.findlaw.com/casecode/supreme.html

(c) The Supreme Court's web site: This official site features the High Court's current docket, calendar, court rules, decisions, orders, and press releases.
http://www.supremecourtus.gov/index.html

(d) Federal Judicial Center: In addition to helpful links, this site connects to the "History of the Federal Judiciary," which contains biographical data about all federal judges since 1789 as well as other documents and information.
http://www.fjc.gov/

(e) Yahoo Law: Primarily a search engine, this site contains a listing of other law-related sites on the Internet.
http://dir.yahoo.com/government/law/

(f) Emory University School of Law: A virtual reference library, this site is a helpful starting place for state and federal statutes and many other legal topics. The second URL listed below provides links to Supreme Court decisions and to recent decisions of all United States Courts of Appeals.

http://www.law.emory.edu/law/refdesk/toc.html
http://www.law.emory.edu/FEDCTS

Manuscript Sources

Aside from judicial decisions, other public records, and contemporary accounts, much that is known about the individual justices and the internal workings of the Waite Court derives from the justices' papers—letters, memoranda, draft opinions, and the like—that survive in manuscript form. In an age when even the telephone was still a novelty, much communication occurred through exchange of handwritten documents. Such collections, however, do not exist for all justices. Some of the works cited above by Fairman, Kens, Magrath, Stephenson, Swisher, Trimble, and Yarbrough, among others, draw heavily on such papers. Not intended to be exhaustive, major sites of the Waite-era justices' papers are listed below.

Joseph P. Bradley

Bradley Papers, Manuscript Division, Library of Congress, Washington, D.C.; some Bradley correspondence can also be found in the Arthur Wallace Dunn Papers.

Bradley Papers, New Jersey Historical Society, Newark; some correspondence with Bradley can also be found in the Philemon Dickerson Papers.

John A. Campbell

Campbell Papers, Southern Historical Collection, University of North Carolina at Chapel Hill.

Robert E. Lee Papers, Virginia Historical Society, Richmond.

Salmon P. Chase

David Davis Papers, Chicago Historical Society.

Chase Papers, Historical and Philosophical Society of Ohio, Cincinnati.

Chase Papers, Historical Society of Pennsylvania, Philadelphia.

Chase Papers, Manuscript Division, Library of Congress, Washington, D.C.

Nathan Clifford

Clifford Papers, Maine Historical Society, Portland.

Albert Hatch Papers, New Hampshire Historical Society, Concord.

Benjamin R. Curtis

Curtis Papers, Manuscript Division, Library of Congress, Washington, D.C.

David Davis

Davis Papers, Chicago Historical Society.
Davis Papers, Illinois State Historical Society, Springfield.
Davis Papers, Illinois State University, Normal.

Stephen J. Field

Field Papers, Bancroft Library, University of California at Berkeley.
Field Papers, Oregon Historical Society, Portland; also some Field items in the Matthew P. Deady Papers.
Theodore Hittell Papers, Sutro Library, San Francisco.

Melville W. Fuller

Fuller Papers, Chicago Historical Society.
Fuller Papers, Manuscript Division, Library of Congress, Washington, D.C.
Henry Wade Rogers Papers, University of Michigan Historical Collections, Ann Arbor.

Horace Gray

Gray Papers, Manuscript Division, Library of Congress, Washington, D.C.

Robert C. Grier

John Kame Papers, American Philosophical Society, Philadelphia.

John M. Harlan

Harlan Papers, Filson Club, Louisville, Ky.
Harlan Papers, Manuscript Division, Library of Congress, Washington, D.C.
Jacob McGavock Papers, Tennessee State Archives, Nashville.
Harlan Papers, University of Louisville (Ky.) Law School Library.

L. Q. C. Lamar

Thomas F. Bayard Papers, Manuscript Division, Library of Congress, Washington, D.C.
Lamar Papers, Mississippi Department of Archives and History, Jackson.

Stanley Matthews

Matthews Papers, Cincinnati Historical Society.
Matthews Papers, Rutherford B. Hayes Library, Fremont, Ohio.

Samuel F. Miller

Miller Papers, Manuscript Division, Library of Congress, Washington, D.C.
Nathan Clifford Papers, Maine Historical Society, Portland.

Noah H. Swayne

Thomas Ewing Papers, Manuscript Division, Library of Congress, Washington, D.C.
Swayne Papers, Ohio Historical Society, Columbus.

Morrison R. Waite

Waite Papers, Manuscript Division, Library of Congress, Washington, D.C.
Edwards Pierrepont Papers, University of Iowa Library, Iowa City.

Index

About the Author

Donald Grier Stephenson, Jr., is Charles A. Dana Professor of Government at Franklin and Marshall College. He is general editor of ABC-CLIO's America's Freedoms series, author of *Campaigns and the Court: The U.S. Supreme Court in Presidential Elections* (Columbia University Press, 1999), and coauthor with Alpheus Thomas Mason of *American Constitutional Law: Introductory Essays and Selected Cases*, 13th ed. (Prentice Hall, 2002).